D1320926

THE
LEGACY OF EGYPT

THE
LEGACY OF EGYPT

Edited by

S. R. K. GLANVILLE

OXFORD
AT THE CLARENDON PRESS

OXFORD UNIVERSITY PRESS
AMEN HOUSE, E.C. 4
London Edinburgh Glasgow New York
Toronto Melbourne Cape Town Bombay
Calcutta Madras
GEOFFREY CUMBERLEGE
PUBLISHER TO THE UNIVERSITY

FIRST PUBLISHED AUGUST 1942
REPRINTED DECEMBER 1942,
1943, 1947

PRINTED IN GREAT BRITAIN

NOTE

A WORD of apology is due for the delay in the publication of *The Legacy of Egypt*. Most of the chapters had been received by September 1939, but the difficulties of communication under war conditions and the preoccupation of those contributors, whose chapters were outstanding, with national service in one form or another resulted in prolonged interruptions to the progress of the book. In this respect the Editor, though he could not help himself, was the chief sinner.

We also regretfully record the sad dispersion which has overtaken the group of colleagues whose original undertaking to co-operate in the writing of the *Legacy* made its appearance possible. Three have since died: Professor Hocart early in 1939, Canon Creed in the Spring of 1940, and Brigadier-General Sewell in August 1941. The last-named had already seen and passed his chapter in print; to Mrs. Creed and Mrs. Hocart the editor is indebted for their help in correcting the proofs of chapters twelve and fifteen respectively. Professor Capart has not been heard of since Belgium was overrun; Professor Seidl is for the time being, unhappily, without the Law. Neither therefore has seen proofs of his contribution to *The Legacy of Egypt*, but both had warmly approved the English translations of their respective texts, and in checking over these had made some small revisions. Our thanks are due to Mr. H. St. L. B. Moss for the care he bestowed on Professor Capart's chapter, and to Professor N. H. Baynes, Dr. H. I. Bell, and Professor H. M. Last for help in rendering many of the technical phrases in that of Professor Seidl.

It has not been possible to secure complete consistency in the spelling of Ancient Egyptian proper names, though this has been the broad aim. Since, however, Egyptologists themselves are not willing to be entirely consistent, it is perhaps as well that the reading public should be familiarized with certain ineradicable discrepancies, and it is hoped that the index will solve any confusions. Egyptian dynastic chronology throughout the book has been harmonized with that proposed by General Sewell. It will be noted that he uses the astronomical reckoning of years B.C. (but without the prefixed –) and that consequently precise dates appear to be one year later than they would by normal historical reckoning. Professor Sidney Smith's new dating discussed in his *Alalakh and Chronology* (London, 1940) has been followed for Hammurabi's reign and, tentatively, for the Eighteenth dynasty in Egypt.

Mr. Engelbach writes, with reference to his chapter: 'I owe my warmest thanks to my colleague Mr. Alfred Lucas for permission to quote freely from his *Ancient Materials and Industries*. I also want to thank Isma'il Effendi Shehâb, Photographer to the Antiquities Department, for his trouble in taking especially for *The Legacy of Egypt* the photographs shown in Figs. 1, 2, 5, 8–12, 20, 33, and 34. The remainder of the figures are all from *Ancient Egyptian Masonry*, Figs. 13, 14, 21, and 25 being also the work of Isma'il Effendi Shehâb.' The Editor also wishes to record his grateful appreciation of Miss M. A. Chubb's painstaking and constructive reading of the book in proof.

S. R. K. G.

LONDON
December 1941

CONTENTS

viii Contents

LIST OF ILLUSTRATIONS

WRITING AND LITERATURE

INTRODUCTION

BROADLY speaking we recover human history backwards. It is logical, therefore, that Egypt should have had to wait her turn for admission to the *Legacy* series, which is an attempt to assess our debt to phases of civilization earlier than our own. Now that turn has come Egypt can show, in her own way, as good a claim to it as her predecessors—a claim conceded alike by classical tradition and present-day opinion.

It may be that Egypt's contributions to our way of life are not alone sufficient to entitle her to an equal place with Greece and Rome, Israel and Islam, Medieval Europe and India, in an estimate of our indebtedness to past generations. It is probably true that, with the possible exception of our alphabet, nothing that can be traced directly to Egypt in our Western civilization is so obviously or so integrally a part of it as, for instance, Roman Law or Greek Philosophy or the Bible, and that nothing so practically concerns it as the Arabic language or Indian racial traditions; though in all but the last of these Egypt has had some part as contributor or transmitter. Yet Egypt has a unique quality which enables her to present to our judgement the best possible case for herself, a quality exhibited equally by the land itself and by the people who inhabited it, namely, a capacity for conservation exceeding that of any other country in the world.

This capacity is a matter of geography, and although in its immediate application it is by now almost a commonplace, its implications are not easily appreciated except at first hand. A soil which is sand except for the Delta and the river-banks, heated by a sub-tropical sun, with its surface continually shifted by wind, provides a perfect self-sealing medium. As rocks and ice have preserved for us the whole forms or vestigial evidence of vegetable and animal life from geological time, so the sterilizing sand of Egypt's desert fringe has conserved, for our admiration and interpretation, the perfect specimens and scattered fragments of all those material possessions which are the tangible witness of some thousands of years of human history.

True the sand was handicapped in its race with time: it had to contend with deliberate demolition, casual vandalism, robbery, and the melting pot. Much thus escaped it; much it sealed successfully once but had to cover up a second time after thieves had broken in; and borne on the wind the sand itself frequently wore away the surfaces of monuments it could not wholly protect. But in spite of all these setbacks such a work of conservation was done here that objects which are immediately affected by an indoor atmosphere of normal humidity in our climate have retained their original forms for centuries. In this way not only massive temples and colossal stone statues, extravagant funerary furniture in rock-hewn chambers, and its humbler counterpart at the bottom of deep shafts, have been recovered in our time; but also the sun-dried mud-brick walls of houses, and within them household trinkets, where they were dropped, and charcoal still on the hearth; as well as papyri in the pots where they were stored for safety, and middens rich with the contents of dust-bin and waste-paper basket.

Another aspect of Egypt's capacity for conservation was the ease and consistency with which she maintained her traditional frontiers, except for rare intervals, from the time a united kingdom first was formed. During the three thousand years of her independent history before the Christian Era, the contemporary civilized world lay to the north, east, and south, and on these three sides she was protected by the sea, the desert, and the narrow gorge of the Nile respectively. Thus, except from the direction of the Libyan desert, whence came continuous infiltration and sporadic attacks, which, however, only rarely constituted a serious challenge and were never supported by a powerful state in the hinterland, Egypt proper was a compara-

tively easy country to defend; and her natural defences remained
her natural boundaries, though her 'empire' over subject peoples
extended beyond them at different times. Moreover, within
these boundaries she was self-sufficient except for lumber and
a few luxury products, thanks to her amazingly fertile soil and
the mineral wealth of her eastern mountains.

These advantages were no doubt contributory agents to that
third side of Egyptian conservatism which is manifested in the
people themselves. It is a quality essential to them to-day, and
though it may well have been inherent in the original Hamitic
stocks which gave us the earliest known predynastic population
of Upper Egypt, it is clearly an attitude of mind which was
fostered by climatic and topographical conditions: the depen-
dability of the weather and of the annual Nile flood, and the
homogeneity of the natural surroundings at any point on the
river from Kôm Ombo to Memphis. The climate, too, encouraged a slothful temper, as did probably the ease with which a
bare living could be obtained, though this cannot have been as
simple a process as it is to-day. For such a temper innovations
have no attraction. It was in fact a land in which Nature,
once tamed, ceased to change except within the cycle of her
seasons, the recurrence of which reiterated both their monotony
and their inevitability. Why then should men change their
habits of mind or body, except under strong pressure from
without? From time to time the Egyptians received such
violent impressions from their neighbours, but the effect even
of these tended to be erased after a return to normal conditions. For the rest their abiding frontiers presented high walls
which turned their vision back on themselves and on the Nile
valley.

We may suppose that some such explanation accounts for a
tendency to conservatism in the Egyptian which may be traced
in every phase of his life that we can watch. In agriculture and
craftsmanship the simplest tools, once evolved, were retained

with barely any modification; in his art, designs and forms which took shape under the pyramid-builders are recognizable on the temple walls of the Ptolemaic and Roman periods; the most primitive formulae and practices continued to be the bases of religious ceremonies, which took no account of a slow but definite spiritual development; the fundamental attitude to Kingship, by virtue of which Egypt was first united, out-lasted all political changes and external assaults, and after the disappearance of the native pharaohs was sustained by the Macedonian conquerors to further their control of the country; and it was not until the advent of these last, three centuries after the invention of coinage, that Egypt was persuaded to accept stamped money as a medium of exchange in the markets.

It is thus in two main fields that, thanks to her capacity for conservation, Egypt displays herself as our benefactor. Firstly, there is the extraordinary mass of her material remains, which, including her standing monuments, surpass in bulk, as it is beginning to be recognized they rival in quality, the similar contributions of any other single ancient people. These present, with their artistic, literary, and documentary content, an appeal to our senses and to our minds which will become more impor-tant as it is more universally appreciated, and which may already be regarded as a significant element in the make-up of our civilization. Secondly, Egypt's changelessness has preserved for our examination her undoubted right to be considered as a pioneer in the fields of religion and craftsmanship, art, letters, and politics. How far we are directly indebted to these first steps of hers for integral elements in our Western civilization the chapters of this book will show. But even where no connexion is evident—as must be the case more often than not—the revelation of these beginnings is in itself a factor in any attempt to assess our own way of life.

The logical implication of the last paragraph is that the real legacy of Egypt to our times may be defined by a single word—Egyptology. Whatever we have acquired from Egypt by the natural process of historical development, and unconsciously made our own, is as yet of little consequence beside the opportunity, made available by the work of scholars during the last 150 years, to enlarge our experience by the deliberate study of every side of Egyptian life from its earliest stages. Nor is this conclusion so paradoxical as it might appear; for though professional Egyptologists in any single European country to-day may be counted on the fingers of two hands, and their labours are in general looked upon as something exotic, this is due only to the comparative youth of their science. As that science ages, and its outlines at any rate are given a place in the curriculum of every liberal education, so Egypt's legacy will become not only more universally shared but also an automatic part of everyman's inheritance. When the art of Egypt has been assimilated by the art-loving public, so that it forms part of the background against which the average individual's aesthetic appreciation is set; when her literature is part of the stock-in-trade of literary criticism; when Egyptian history is recognized by all as one of the tributaries of that continuous stream of human development on which we are borne to-day—then only shall we have entered into full possession of the Legacy of Egypt.

It is in this spirit that the contributors to the present volume, representing the exiguous minority who at present enjoy the heritage, have approached their task. But like all ideals, the enrichment of experience which is available in Egyptology has to be met half-way. These chapters indicate the wealth that has come down to us and the approach to their store-house; final access has to be sought by a long road, and satisfaction is as much in the search as in the discovery.

The reader will by now have asked himself how it is that in spite of the very early tradition of Egypt's cultural importance, any adequate attempt to recover a knowledge of the culture has been so long delayed. There are traces of two separate lines of descent for the tradition; a more superficial, which until the beginning of the last century was the more effective, and a more penetrating which though often hopelessly astray in its search for the real Egypt eventually found the clue and made possible the science of Egyptology. The clue was the decipherment of hieroglyphic writing, and it is clear that already in Herodotus' time the two lines were separate and that the former claimed by far the greater attention from the civilized world. Egypt's history was already a mystery to her admirers. She was known almost entirely by her outward forms, and even the major periods of her artistic development, then more amply witnessed by standing monuments and by statues *in situ* than to-day, were confused in the minds of the contemporary Greeks.

Through succeeding ages we catch glimpses of Ancient Egypt still courted by the world for her material remains, which soon became mere curios. Julian emperors removed to Rome pharaonic obelisks the names of whose original dedicators they must still have been able to discover. Flavians, content with the Egyptian form and material, had shafts quarried at Aswân and caused them to be inscribed in Latin when they reached the imperial capital. Most of these monuments survived to be re-erected 'To the glory of Christ and the Cross' in the sixteenth, seventeenth, and even eighteenth centuries, by which time their hieroglyphic inscriptions were of course unintelligible. Under the early Empire temples were built in Rome to serve Greekish mystery-cults in honour of Egyptian deities; and down to the Muslim conquest of Egypt the workshops of Alexandria continued to advertise Egyptian craftsmanship to the world with bronzes of hybrid design, whose recovery in the eighteenth century from the ruins of Herculaneum and Pompeii revived Egyptian motifs and gave them a facile popularity with European taste. This process has continued. The French clock supported with female sphinxes and model bronze pylons followed Napoleon's expedition; and European political rivalry in the next decades produced the export of eighteenth- and nineteenth-dynasty obelisks to London and Paris—and also to New York. In our own time the discovery of Tutankhamen's tomb flooded the shops with bastard imitations of Egyptian jewellery which equally displayed the admiration of the curious and the ignorance of the admirers. But there are now signs that the rapid strides in our knowledge and in its dissemination are producing a more instructed taste, just as the Edwardian novelists' romantic presentation of life in Ancient Egypt can never again satisfy any but the simplest.

These adventitious impetuses to popular interest in Egyptian forms might well have been followed by real understanding, but for the failure of the legitimate line of descent to bear fruit. When in the eighteenth century the Dilettanti gave the inspiration which led to the glories of classical archaeology they had behind them the whole array of Greek and Latin authors, recovered at the Renaissance and already reaching mature interpretation. But the knowledge of hieroglyphic writing had passed even from the Egyptians by the sixth century A.D. The phonetic nature of the script had been entirely obscured by the crude symbolism attributed to it by late Greek and Roman writers, and even as late as the seventeenth century, at the time when Pope Sixtus V was excavating and re-erecting many of the obelisks set up in Rome by the early emperors, the Jesuit Kircher's serious attempt, based on a considerable knowledge of Coptic, to decipher the hieroglyphs, was completely wide of the mark. It was not till the chance find by one of Napoleon's soldiers of a stone engraved with a Ptolemaic decree in Greek, Hieroglyphic, and Demotic presented modern students with the first bilingual text that decipherment came within sight. At that moment Egyptology may be said to have been born. And though it took some years before sufficient information was derived from the texts, which now began to yield meaning, to enable students to catch up with the guess-work that had done duty for Egyptology while only buildings and an entirely haphazard assortment of antiquities were available, the true perspective was assured from then on.

If our knowledge of Ancient Egypt had to wait in the first instance on the recovery of the ability to read her contemporary written documents, it depended by no means on that alone. On the contrary, the whole history of that study since Champollion announced his decipherment of the hieroglyphs in 1823, and indeed from the time of Napoleon's expedition with its attendant body of savants at the end of the previous century, has been the gradual synthesizing of its three different aspects; the philological, archaeological, and aesthetic. It has taken over a century for the specialist students of these different aspects to discipline themselves to the necessary co-operation, and in the interval one or another party has ruled the field. This may well have been inevitable, for obsessional types were required to overcome the inertia of governments, inadequate finance, and other forms of obstruction, and some of the greatest names in nineteenth-century Egyptology were those of men willing to see one or another branch of their subject neglected for the sake of their own vision. It is only recently that general assent has been given to the proposition that the critical appreciation of art forms and of style, the interpretive reconstruction of life from material remains, and the translation and evaluation of contemporary writing are interdependent as means to the recovery of the whole Egyptian scene.

S. R. K. GLANVILLE

CHAPTER 1

THE CALENDARS AND CHRONOLOGY

THE chronology of Egypt is an inexact science; and must so remain, in the absence of far more data than are at present available. The primary evidence lies in records, scattered over many centuries, from which must be inferred the use of several calendars and of a seasonal year with a special definition. These records prior, at any rate, to the period of the Eighteenth Dynasty are open to more than one interpretation. The solution of the chronological problem therefore lies in finding that interpretation in each case which will produce concordance; so that the resulting inferences will afford a conclusion which is logical, acceptable, and consistent with all the evidence at present known, such as old chronological records partially preserved, monumental records, and the conclusions drawn from other archaeological remains. To aid in this study, it is necessary to invoke the assistance of astronomers, numismatists, historians of other peoples, and other experts.

The question may be asked, indeed has been asked, whether it is credible that a people whose writing was in its infancy at the opening of dynastic history should be capable of astronomical observations and computations. The primary answer is that there is ample evidence that they actually did make surprisingly accurate observations. It is unnecessary to offer conjectures as to the method adopted for observation of an equinox, since the only reasonable inference from the evidence is that they knew the length of a year measured from autumn equinox to autumn equinox within one or two minutes. Such accuracy could be attained only by the use of records which showed the interval which had elapsed between autumn equinoxes, for example, 100 years apart. It was perhaps the very fact that the science of writing was in its infancy which accounts for the use of a peculiar calendar for the purpose of official records.

This calendar contained 365 days in a calendar year; no intercalary day was inserted in any year. It resulted that the opening day of this calendar worked back through the solar year, until a whole cycle of that year had been completed in a period of 1,456 to 1,506 years, according to the definition employed of 'a solar year'. It is beyond reasonable doubt that this official calendar, often called the sliding calendar, was in use from the protodynastic period until the Roman period.

It was the fundamental postulate of the chronology, which may now be regarded as the orthodox chronology of Egypt [1] (subject, however, to some reservations),[1] that there was no break in the continuity of this calendar during the whole of the above-mentioned period. Closer examination of all the chronological evidence has supported the validity of this postulate to the extent that it may now reasonably be regarded as axiomatic.

The organization of this calendar is in itself instructive; for it throws light on the mathematical science of the early period of the Old Kingdom. It consisted of 3 seasons each of 4 months, each of 30 days, with 5 extra days which are now known as the epagomenal days. These 5 days were the birthday festivals of 5 principal deities. The result was to give a 'temple' year of 360 days, with 5 *dies-non*. The 'temple' year was readily fractionalized; whilst the *dies-non* were days of grace for business purposes.[2]

[1] The chronology given by Meyer in *Aegyptische Chronologie*, in 1904, is generally regarded as substantially correct, inasmuch as it has withstood the results of subsequent research. A few amendments are required, with the result of reducing his date for the opening of dynastic history by about 130 years, and of placing his astronomical key dates about 7 years later. Space will not permit the inclusion here of the proofs of these amendments. It is hoped, however, that these proofs, with those also of the incidence of a third calendar, will be published in a subsequent work.

[2] In some records of a late period reference is made to days of the months

With the evidence before us that the ancient Egyptians appreciated fully the fact that the seasonal year was about $365\frac{1}{4}$ days in length, it is impossible to accept the view that the 365 days calendar, whose sanctity was so fully preserved down to the Roman period, was introduced as a rough representation of the length of the year. We are impelled to regard it as having some scientific significance.

The importance of this calendar lay in its use as an automatic record of the passage of years in an era. Suppose that at some date which defines the beginning of an era, such as A.U.C., two calendars are set in operation conjointly, with their opening days (I. I)[1] coincident; one a calendar of 365 days (the sliding calendar), the other a calendar which has a 366th day every fourth year (such as the Julian calendar). At some subsequent date, it results from the operation of these two calendars that I. I Julian is coincident with I. IV Sliding. It is clear that the opening days have separated by 90 days since A.U.C. I. The era date must therefore be A.U.C. 361. Such is the only conceivable scientific reason for the sliding calendar.

The other calendars, against which this sliding calendar moved, must now be considered. These were organized to keep their opening days near the annual celestial events which defined the beginning of the solar year. The solar year which is known to have been used officially from at least as early as the Twelfth Dynasty (1990–1777) period was defined as beginning at the heliacal rising of Sirius. This means the first day in the year on which Sirius is seen, about 42 minutes before sunrise, for a minute or so, after the star rises, and before its light is damped out by the advent of dawn.[2] The nature of

as fractions. Thus the 27th day, which in official records always appears as 'day 27', may in business matters be referred to as 'the half, and the third, and the fifteenth'.   [1] This notation is used to express 'day I of month I'.

[2] At the present epoch Sirius is first visible at dawn on August 3 (Gregorian) from Cairo. At the epoch −2769, first visibility (heliacal rising) occurred

the astronomical computations and other premisses necessary to determine the precise day in the Egyptian sliding calendar on which this event occurred in any named year cannot be given here. One important record is that the event fell on 16. VIII of the sliding calendar in a year (Year 7 Sesostris III) which from monumental records can be determined as Year 120 of the Twelfth Dynasty.

With the postulate assumed and a further minor postulate that the observation of the heliacal rising was made always at Heliopolis before the Ptolemaic period, the year has been determined astronomically as either 1871[1] or 1,456 years earlier [2]. The latter alternative is historically impossible. Therefore the commencement of the Twelfth Dynasty is placed in 1990. The record of 1871 is the earliest recorded date of the heliacal rising. Projecting backward, however, the astronomical computations show that the heliacal rising occurred on 1. I of the sliding calendar in 2769. Further it can be shown that this day was then July 17 (Julian) and that the summer solstice of 2769 occurred (by Heliopolis time) at 11 p.m. on July 16. Since 1. I began at sunset on July 16, and the solstice occurred about 6 hours later in each of the next 3 years, it follows that the day of the heliacal rising and the day of the solstice were in effect coincident at this epoch. For this, and other reasons, it is concluded that this curious sidereal year was introduced in 2769, not 1,458 years earlier. Further, there is reason to associate this invention with Imhôtep, who was in a late period deified as the Father of Egyptian Science. Imhôtep is known to have been the Minister of King Zoser of the Third Dynasty, the 19th King of the line of Menes [3].

at the dawn following the summer solstice, as observed from Heliopolis. In A.D. 138 the event as observed from Alexandria occurred on July 20 Julian, i.e. July 19 Gregorian.

[1] The dates are given in the astronomical notation: 1871 must be read as —1871, i.e. 1872 B.C.

When the heliacal rising of Sirius was constituted the event which marked the beginning of the seasonal year, the reform was accompanied by the introduction of a calendar (the 'Sothic' calendar) whose opening day (1. I Sothic) always coincided with the heliacal rising: a 6th epagomenal day was intercalated as required, normally every 4th year, in order to maintain the relation [4]. It was necessary to maintain a calendar which (more or less) kept step with the seasons for the purpose of fixing festival days (other than those of the New Moon and Full Mocn festivals); for festivals were the occasions of the payment of tithes in kind to the temples.

Before considering the scientific significance of the Sothic year and its calendar, it is desirable to go farther back in order to ascertain the calendric system and the 'year' which were superseded, officially at least, by the Sothic arrangement. The evidence is scanty, and consists mainly of the records of festivals shown as held at cyclic intervals of years on the Palermo Stone and the Cairo fragment;[1] supplemented by an inscription from the Edfu temple of about 200 B.C. which associates Imhôtep with a revolt of the Set worshippers in Year 363 of an 'era of Horakhti' [5]. In consequence the conclusions drawn from this evidence must be regarded as conjectural.

In the records down as far as the reign of Rameses II (1289–1229) glimpses are obtained of a third calendar, in which 1. X was coincident with 1. I Sothic or on occasion with 2. I Sothic. Clearly then this calendar started each year with a day which was soon after the autumn equinox, and moving so as to keep about the same distance from it as 1. I Sothic was from the summer solstice.

Computation shows that such a calendar would result from

[1] These are two fragments representing probably less than one-tenth of a tablet, possibly of three panels, of black diorite inscribed apparently during the period of the Fifth Dynasty with records which purport to show the principal events of each regnal year since the accession of Menes.

putting the 3rd epagomenal day, which was the festival of Set, on the day of the autumn equinox, 372 years before 2769 (i.e. in 3141) and thereafter maintaining a Julian calendar of $365\frac{1}{4}$ days; so that the calendar or conventional autumn equinox would move forward in the solar year at the rate of a day in about 135 years.

Again the Palermo Stone divides the last year of Menes, which was also the first year of his successor, into two portions which aggregate to 320 days only. It seems clear that at this period the opening day of the seasonal year was moved back 45 days in the seasons. Since then we find a calendar which opened at the autumn equinox, we may reasonably infer that prior to this change the opening day was about November 6 of our present calendar.

Further, the apparent movement of this conventional autumn equinox in the seasons indicates that the New Year day was subsequently determined not by the celestial event, but by the New Year day of a calendar of $365\frac{1}{4}$ days.

The picture so far presented of the origins of the calendars of Egypt is admittedly conjectural as regards the first four centuries of dynastic history, inasmuch as the scanty and indeed ambiguous evidence available is insufficient to prove the theory. On the other hand, it is claimed that the picture now to be presented is logical and consistent both with permissible interpretations of the evidence and with the general view of this period held by Egyptologists.

We see then the kings of Upper Egypt extending their sovereignty northwards until, about the epoch of the accession of Menes, they conquered the peoples of Lower Egypt and absorbed the Delta in their realm. The people of Lower Egypt already at this period had trading contacts with Knossos and Syria, exchanging the surplus produce of the Delta perhaps for the metals collected by the fleets of Knossos and for the timber of Lebanon. It seems to be a reasonable assumption that they would have shared with the Mediterranean and Syrian peoples a common scientific lore. It may well be that their Southern conquerors were at the epoch of the conquest considerably behind their new subjects in science. In this connexion it has to be observed that our knowledge of the culture of Egypt at this period is derived mainly from the remains of the Southern Kingdom. The calendric inferences then indicate that at the epoch of the conquest a seasonal year was observed in Lower Egypt which began 45 days after the autumn equinox. This day represents clearly the day of the Baal festival of Samhain, whose traces still linger in Britain. It is practically certain that this New Year festival was imported into Britain by the Mediterranean colonists of Cornwall. Thus we have some evidence of that scientific link between Egypt and the Mediterranean peoples which we should expect to result from the trade contact.

Next, in the year of the death of Menes, the first recognized monarch of the 'Two Lands' of Upper and Lower Egypt, we find the institution of a revised calendric system, possibly a compromise resulting from the union of the two races. From the evidence quoted above, this year may be dated as 3141. The revision adopted the festival of Set, the Lower Egypt equivalent of Baal, as the New Year day, but removed it from the day of Samhain to that of the autumn equinox. On the assumption that two calendars were then deliberately instituted, one of 365 days, the other of $365\frac{1}{4}$ days, this system, combined with the internal organization of the calendar itself, was in fact the most scientific organization of calendars which has yet been used by man. From the $365\frac{1}{4}$ days calendar derive the calendars which have been used by the peoples of Europe throughout the Christian era.[1]

[1] The Julian calendar introduced by Julius Caesar, on the advice of the Alexandrian scientist, Sosigenes, was the old $365\frac{1}{4}$ days calendar of Egypt. In the form in which it was in use in England down to 1752 it was a correction

At the epoch 2769, 372 years later, in the early years of the Third Dynasty, and within a century of the construction of

by Augustus of the original Julian calendar of 45 B.C. which had been mis-applied in operation. From the internal evidence it appears that Sosigenes originally intended it to begin at the winter solstice with 5 epagomenal days so that Jan. 1 should have been 5 days after the solstice. The proleptic result of the revision by Augustus was to place Jan. 1, 45 B.C., 7 days after the solstice, and to scatter, or to leave scattered, the 5 epagomenal days through-out the year. The Saints' days calendar of the Christian Churches preserves more clearly the traces of the old Egyptian calendar. Examination shows an organization with the solstice as the first epagomenal day, Christmas day as the 4th epagomenal day (preserving here the calendric position of the Isis festival) and Boxing day (St. Stephen's day) as the 5th epagomenal day.

The arrangement of the principal Saints' days may be expressed in terms of a hypothetical Egyptian calendar, commencing at the winter solstice as follows:

Date in Gregorian Calendar	Feast	Hypothetic Egyptian Calendar date
Dec. 22	[winter solstice]	1st epagomena
,, 25	Christmas	4th epagomena
,, 26	St. Stephen	5th epagomena
,, 27	St. John	1. I
Jan. 25	St. Paul	30. I
Feb. 24	St. Matthias	30. II
Mar. 25	Annunciation	29. III
Apr. 25	St. Mark	30. IV
June 24	St. John Baptist	30. VI
July 25	St. James	1. VIII
Aug. 24	St. Bartholomew	1. IX
Sept. 21	St. Matthew	29. IX
Oct. 17	St. Luke	26. X
Dec. 21	St. Thomas	30. XII

Even the divergences from the normal intervals are curiously reminiscent of some of the slight shifts in the date of the Egyptian festivals which occurred between 1541 B.C. and 200 B.C. They suggest that these saints' days were introduced by the Church of Alexandria in order to supplant the Egyptian festivals of the months.

the Pyramid of Khufu, a period has been reached when the picture passes from the conjectural to the factual. The astronomical science displayed by the reform of Imhôtep accords well with the astronomical, geometric, and engineering science exhibited in the construction of the Great Pyramid. Clearly the critic of the $365\frac{1}{4}$ days calendar year may have objected to the fact that the result was that the Set festival, i.e. the calendar New Year day, moved forward from the actual autumn equinox at the rate of about 3 days in 400 years. It was perhaps in order to meet that criticism that Imhôtep invented a seasonal year which no doubt he thought was precisely $365\frac{1}{4}$ days in length, that is, the same length as the calendar year. Actually the mean Sothic year at this epoch was nearly a minute longer than $365\frac{1}{4}$ days; but the 372 years of records which alone can have been available to him would hardly exhibit the error. Nevertheless there was this small error.

The reform of Imhôtep must therefore be recognized as the first retrogression from the scientific calendars of 3141.[1]

For the next 2,800 years the sliding and the Sothic calendars remained the principal calendars of Egypt, although, as stated above, we find traces of the Set calendar still in use in some temples as late as the reign of Rameses II. At the Roman period the confusion of calendars had become so involved that it is impossible to sort them clearly. Records exist which show 5 or 6 New Year days. In addition to 1. I of the sliding calendar and 1. I Sothic are the present 'Night of the Drop' (June 18–19 Gregorian), a New Year of Horus, which was possibly a relic of the Samhain festival, and another New Year day in the

[1] An interesting illustration of the dictum of Solomon is afforded by the last step in this scientific retrogression, namely the introduction of our present calendar by Pope Gregory IX in 1582. The same objection to the $365\frac{1}{4}$ days calendar was then raised as in the days of Imhôtep. Whereas, however, Imhôtep met it by fitting a year to the calendar, the method adopted by the Vatican was that of attempting to fit a calendar to the tropical year. It represented the final degradation of the calendar of 3141.

spring; besides these was the New Year day (Aug. 29 Julian) of the Alexandrine calendar of 365¼ days.

Throughout their history it is clearly evidenced that the Egyptians measured long periods of time in terms of cycles defined by the periods in which a celestial event passed through a calendric period. Thus the Sothic cycle was the period in which the observed heliacal rising of Sirius passed through the whole gamut of the 365 days calendar; 1,456 years in the first cycle from 2769; 1,455 years in the next cycle. At the beginning of the cycle in 1313 and again in A.D. 138 this cycle is referred to as a 'period of eternity'. Tacitus refers to it as a Phoenix cycle. That concept is also borne out by the inscription of *AIΩN* with a phoenix on the coins of Pius from his second year. Similarly the eras of Horakhti appear to have been defined at first by the passage of the actual equinox through the sliding calendar. The autumn equinox would then pass through 9 days of the calendar in 37 years, 30 days in 123 years, and the full calendar in about 1,506 years. Now on the Palermo Stone and the Cairo fragment is found evidence of a festival of Desher recurring at intervals of 37 years, and also of a festival 'of eternity' which appears to recur at intervals of 123 years. It is then possible that the 500-years Phoenix cycle of Herodotus refers to the passage of the equinox through one season of 4 × 30 days. On the other hand, the Set stele of Rameses II is dated in Year 400 of an era of Nubti, an attribute of Set. Since this stele was erected probably before 1236, it must be inferred that the Set cycle was defined by the passage of 1. I of the Set calendar through the sliding calendar, in which case a full cycle would clearly be accomplished in 1,460 years. This would date this stele in 1282, which is distinctly plausible.

As already stated, the beginning of the Twelfth Dynasty is fixed in 1990, as a result of a record of the date of a heliacal rising of Sirius. A similar record determines the 9th year of

Amenhotep I, the second king of the Eighteenth Dynasty, as 1540. Further, the proof adduced by Sethe following Struwe [6] that Year 1 of Seti I coincided with the first year of a Sothic cycle fixes the date of the accession of Seti I as 1313. In consequence the Nineteenth Dynasty began in 1314.[1]

For the period of the first eleven dynasties the Turin papyrus determines a limit. Damaged as it is, two chronological summaries remain: the skilful piecing together of the fragments leaves it beyond reasonable doubt that these two summaries added together cover the whole period of the eleven dynasties. The first indicates a period of 949 years 'from Menes' followed by an interregnum of 6 years. From the position of the fragment in the King list, this appears to summarize the period of the first eight dynasties. The second summary (on fragment 64) appears to summarize the duration of 24 reigns after the Eighth Dynasty, and ends at the death of the last king of the Eleventh Dynasty. It states a period of 243 years [7].

The date of the accession of Menes is thus determined as 3188, which assigns him a reign of 47 years, as compared with the 62 years propounded by Africanus. A series of key dates has now been given, upon which the chronology may be hung.

To fill in the detail is a task of more complexity, involving the careful comparison and piecing together of evidence derived from many sources. If, however, the key dates are accepted, dynastic periods at least can be fitted in with a reasonable assurance that the dates proposed cannot be materially in error.

The result is given in the following table:

Menes	.	.	.	.	.	.	.	.	3188–3141
End of Dynasty II	.	.	.	.	.	.	.	.	2815
Dynasty III (Bebti–Snofru)		.	.	.	.	.	.	.	2815–2690
Dynasties IV and V	.	.	.	.	.	.	.	.	2690–2420
Dynasty VI	.	.	.	.	.	.	.	.	2420–2294

[1] This results in the identification of Theon's Menophres with either Seti I or Rameses I, who reigned 16 months according to Manetho, and died in 1313.

Dynasty VII	.	.	.	.	.	.	.	.	2294–2248
Dynasty VIII (an overlapping dynasty) ends	.	.	.	.		2239
Interregnum	.	.	.	.	.	.	.	.	2239–2233
Dynasties IX, X, XI (overlapping)		.	.	.	.	.	2233–1990
Dynasty XII	.	.	.	.	.	.	.	.	1990–1777
Dynasty XVIII	.	.	.	.	.	.	.	.	1573–1314
Dynasty XIX	.	.	.	.	.	.	.	.	1314–1194

Controversy has revolved mainly on the durations of the two periods when United Egypt broke up into petty kingdoms; the first from the end of the Sixth Dynasty to the time when the Theban princes of the Eleventh Dynasty (Mentuhotep I–V) assumed the rule of the Two Lands. Putting this date at about 95 years before the beginning of the Twelfth Dynasty, the 'first intermediate period' then lasted about 209 years, which agrees well with the cultural evidence. The second intermediate period lasted from 1777 to 1573. This also agrees with the inferences drawn from the cultural evidence.

An assured chronology of Egypt is important for the synchronisms established with periods in the history of other races. Thus the epoch of Menes was contemporary with the Jemdt Nasr period of Sumer, and also with the first cultural period (Early Minoan I) of Crete. The date of Menes thus provides an important key date in the history of Mesopotamia and in that of Knossos. The destruction of Knossos is similarly determined by the cultural synchronisms as having occurred about 1400. The closing years of the Nineteenth Dynasty again determine the date of the Siege of Troy as occurring between 1200 and 1195.

Finally, new light is thrown on the chronology of the second intermediate period, and of the Eighteenth Dynasty by Mr. Sidney Smith's work, *Alalakh and Chronology*.[1] He proves that the First Dynasty of Babylon must be dated as lasting from

[1] At the moment of writing, Mr. Sidney Smith's work is in the press. I am much indebted to him for kind permission to make use of his conclusions.

1893 to 1594;[1] thus dating the reign of Hammurabi as 1791–1749. He then showed that, on the evidence obtained from recent researches in Syria, a domination of Syria by Hammurabi followed immediately upon a period of Egyptian influence, which must be ascribed to the great kings of the Twelfth Dynasty. The importance of this synchronism can hardly be over-estimated; one immediate result is that it offers the best proof yet adduced of the validity of Meyer's hypothesis of the continuity of the 365-days calendar; and thus establishes the limitation of the second intermediate period to about two centuries.

Subsequent to the close of the Nineteenth Dynasty Egypt entered the period of her decline. The chronology is reasonably assured. In any case from that date the chronological detail of the Near East can be followed more closely in the records of Assyria and Babylon; synchronisms are plentiful. In the domain of science, the legacy of Egypt must be regarded as having passed then to her heirs in the domination of the Near East.

A discussion of the chronology of Egypt cannot be complete without reference to the history written by Manetho. The recapitulation of the chronology given in that history by Africanus undoubtedly involves some manipulation of Manetho's figures.

Assuming that the book summaries were quoted correctly by Africanus, it may be inferred that Book III began with the reign of Rameses I and carried the history down to Manetho's own epoch, about 270 B.C. In that case the fundamental

[1] Students of Hebrew chronology may be interested in this new date for the foundation of the First Dynasty of Babylon. The shortest of the Hebrew chronologies dates the migration of Abraham as occurring 910 years before year 4 Solomon. The accession of Solomon is placed by *Cambridge Ancient History* as having occurred in 970 B.C. It will then be observed that Mr. Sidney Smith's chronology confirms the chronology of Babylon, which may be derived from the tradition preserved in the Talmud that Abraham was a contemporary of the founder of the Babylonian dynasty.

theory of his chronology of the first eighteen dynasties appears to have been that a whole Sothic cycle (of about 1,460 years) intervened between the Twelfth and Nineteenth Dynasties extra to the period assigned above; and further that the cycle which began at the death of Menes was not a Set cycle but a Sothic cycle. In consequence his chronology would put the death of Menes some 2,548 years[1] earlier than 3141. The chronology given here allots a period of 1,874 years to the first eighteen dynasties. The first two books of Manetho assigned 4,421 years apparently to the same period, a difference of 2,547 years. His chronology, or rather that of Africanus, is of interest inasmuch as it indicates the probable source of the chronology of the Septuagint, and of the date assigned by the Church of Alexandria for the Creation, namely 5498 (5499).

The aim of this chapter has been to provide a few chronological pegs upon which the history of ancient Egypt may be hung. In the endeavour to fulfil that aim it has seemed desirable to enter a somewhat conjectural realm in search of the origins of the calendars of Egypt. The conclusions here suggested cannot be regarded as established until they can be substantiated by far more assured evidence than is at present available. It was, however, necessary to show that the chronological inferences drawn from the Turin papyrus are at least not inconsistent with the calendric evidence as it now stands.

The question of the sceptic remains without a direct answer: but it pales to insignificance beside the more profound problem of the Near East, namely, 'What was the science which enabled the master mariners of Knossos, *without the aid of a compass*, to navigate their ships to the shores of Britain and Norway, and whence came that science?'[2]

---

[1] i.e. 1460+ (1460−372).

[2] The answer supplied by the historian of the Victorian era was as naïve as it was dogmatic. Apart from the elementary fact that at the epoch 3000 B.C. there was no 'North Star' in the accepted sense of that term, the historian

That Egypt and the peoples of the Mediterranean islands shared a common knowledge of astronomy has been established. Equally it can be shown that they shared to some extent a common metrology. That science should follow the trade routes was only natural; but we cannot tell in which direction science flowed along these routes. Much information on that matter may well lie buried beneath the Nile silt accumulated in the Delta during the passage of the last fifty centuries. Even, however, if that is unearthed, it is improbable that it will enable scholars to determine the origin of this science which admittedly appears to accord little with the picture, as we see it, of the cultural development of the peoples of the epoch of Menes.

It may be, as some indeed suspect, that the science which we see at the dawn of recorded history was not science at its dawn but represents the remnants of the science of some great and as yet untraced civilization. Where, however, is the seat of that civilization to be located? The Assyriologist traces the culture of Sumer back towards Central Asia, properly preferring the tangible evidence to the legends of Sumer. Central Asia, however, is not a happy source for navigational science. We must look elsewhere for that. Some students of the ancient civilizations of America, coupling the evidence found in that continent with the mythologies of Greece and of Egypt, place it beneath the waves of the Atlantic Ocean: there the problem may appropriately be left.

J. W. S. SEWELL

failed to show how the stars were used to give a bearing during 18 hours of the 24 in the latitudes of Britain in summer.

BIBLIOGRAPHICAL REFERENCES

1. E. MEYER, *Aegyptische Chronologie*, Berlin, 1904.
2. P. V. NEUGEBAUER, *Astronomische Chronologie*, Berlin & Leipzig, 1929.
3. A. SCHARFF, *Grundzüge der ägyptischen Vorgeschichte, Morgenland*, Heft 12, Leipzig, 1927.
4. R. WEILL, *Bases, Méthodes, et Résultats de la Chronologie Égyptienne*, Paris, 1925.
5. P. E. NEWBERRY, in *Ancient Egypt*, 1922, ii, London.
6. *Zeitschrift für Aegyptische Sprache*, vols. lxiii (1928), 45–50 and lxvi (1931), 1–7, Leipzig.
7. L. BORCHARDT, *Die Annalen und die zeitliche Festlegung von Punkten der ägyptischen Geschichte*, 1917.

CHAPTER 2

THE POLITICAL APPROACH TO THE CLASSICAL WORLD

In 450 B.C. Babylon was falling into decay and dynastic Egypt was nearing the end of its long history. Their palaces, tombs, and temples stood as witnesses to a great past; their priests told tales of the mighty kings of long ago. The Greek visitor, coming from a homeland still in the vigour of youth, still eagerly experimenting with new ideas and developing new methods of expression, was awed by the vast antiquity of the lands of the Near East, their reverence for tradition, their preoccupation with past greatness. Herodotus of Halicarnassus was one of those who saw and marvelled. He felt something of the debt which his own civilization owed to these countries which had been old when the first Greeks sighted the Aegean Sea, and in his history of the struggle between East and West he set down what he knew of their past. He had been told of Semiramis and Nitocris, of Sesostris and Rhampsinitus; eleven thousand years, said the Egyptians, had passed since the reign of the first Pharaoh. It is probable that his history, distorted and exaggerated though it is, represents the sum of knowledge current among his hosts. Even Manetho, who later had access to the official records, was far from presenting a satisfactory outline of his country's past.

To-day we are more fortunate. Excavation and research have told us more of the ancient civilizations of the East than they could know who saw them in the last stages of their decline. We do not yet possess the whole drama; some acts are still imperfect, some scenes wholly veiled from our sight. But the main lines of development are now clear, and the unfolding of the plot in detail, which goes on year after year, itself gives an added fascination to the study of the past. A stroke of the pick, a turn of the spade may reveal some document of historic value, some vital clue to a problem hitherto unsolved.

In these countries of the ancient East we can trace the first attempts of man to chronicle for posterity his experiences and his achievements, the first beginnings of history. These beginnings are crude and tentative—we may even hesitate to call them history in the modern sense. The kings whose inscriptions vaunted their achievements, the nobles who perpetuated their moral virtues in stone, had little sense of proportion and seldom a strict regard for truth; but with the invention of writing came the desire to record, and by maintaining record offices, compiling annals, and copying king-lists the scribes of antiquity were laying the foundations of a great science which found its first full expression in the historians of Greece and Rome. The historical experience of the ancient Near East is expressed in language which for the most part cannot claim a place among the world's great literature. Here the Old Testament stands alone. The kings and rulers of the Hebrew people have had but a small part to play in the story of empires; their poets and their prophets have brought them glory for all time. But the records of Egypt and Babylonia are as a rule dry reading; the Assyrians, whose annals form the most complete body of historical texts from the pre-classical world, related their campaigns in language for the most part monotonous in its repetition of phrase and repellent in the brutality of its expression. Yet in spite of the strangeness of the setting, these recitals of unembellished fact often need little imagination to give them colour and life. Numerous examples could be quoted; let the reader turn to such passages of Egyptian historical literature as the exploits of the general Amenemhab, who saved the life of King Tuthmosis III when he was charged by an angry elephant, or the description of the arrival in Egypt of the Hittite princess, walking proudly at the head of her soldiers. Vivid similes are a characteristic of the Assyrian chroniclers; an advancing army is said to come on 'like swarms of locusts in the springtime'. Further, the history of the first great civilizations is pictorially illustrated for us in stone. The great temple reliefs of Egypt, the palace reliefs of Assyria and Persia, are themselves history books; we are shown the Babylonian Naram-Sin campaigning with his archers in the mountains of the Zagros, we see the Pharaoh charging in his chariot, and the plight of Egypt's enemies in the battle of Kadesh, when they must escape by swimming the River Orontes, while the 'wretched ruler of Aleppo' is held upside down on the farther bank to rid him of the water he has swallowed in his ducking. Similar lively reliefs from Assyria picture the army of Ashurnasirpal swimming a river on inflated skins, or the siege engines of Sennacherib operating against the walls of the city of Lachish. Classical history was not thus illustrated for us until Trajan erected his column in the Forum at Rome.

It is from such sources as these that we are to-day in a position to examine the political legacy which has come down to us from the ancient world. We shall find that this legacy is a limited one. The history of the ancient Near East is more concerned with international relations than with internal politics. In this respect it stands in marked contrast to that of the Greek states, whose individual development was the main care of their historians and political theorists. But such a limitation does not lessen its importance to the student. The classical world must be approached from the East. The Greeks and the Romans were new-comers in a world already old in time and experience, and they received and transmitted their inheritance. Their parts were played on a stage already set by the ancient monarchies, and our task in this chapter must be to sketch in brief outline the political development of the Near East through some three millennia, as we can at present reconstruct it, in order to understand how the civilized world came to have that shape in which Herodotus and the Greeks of his age knew it, and to gain some knowledge of the long chain of political experience to which the classical world was heir.

Our especial concern must be with Egypt. Her semi-isolated position, shut in on either side by the desert, together with the wealth of her natural resources, made her far more self-contained than other countries. Movements of world-wide significance touched her but indirectly; within her confines she could develop her own highly characteristic civilization. But no nation can remain isolated that lacks any one essential raw material, none can withdraw from the outside world that produces any sought-after commodity. Egypt's need for copper led her early to Sinai, her lack of timber brought her to the Syrian ports of the Lebanon. In return, she exported gold, and such manufactures as linen and faience which were in universal demand. And thus she was brought more and more into touch with the surrounding world, and played her part in the making and unmaking of nations.

In the long period of prehistory, when no written records can help us, and our only sources of information are archaeological, we are still groping dimly among suppositions. Some facts stand out clearly against a background of doubt. We can distinguish, by their different weapons and utensils, their ornaments, their modes of life, various peoples in the Near East and various movements of peoples, and it is thereby possible to attempt a reconstruction, if a tentative one, of the main story of this distant past.

Which was the oldest of the Near Eastern civilizations? It is a question still disputed among archaeologists, each of whom is apt to claim the honour for his own field of study. The answer must be that we do not know, that perhaps we shall never know. It cannot have been Sumer, for that country was not yet in existence when the people of Cilicia and Syria were producing their earliest pottery. It may have been Egypt. But a scheme of comparative chronology cannot yet be established for so early a period, and the beginnings of civilization hardly concern us here.

The introduction of writing in the Near East seems to have coincided more or less with the introduction of the technique of metal-working on a large scale. Before this, that is to say in that stage of man's development sometimes called the 'Chalcolithic' period, when copper was still a rare and precious commodity, and the working of stone was therefore a laborious and costly process, fine pottery was the chief output of the artistic workshops. And so the age before bronze is marked almost universally by the fine painted pottery which it produced. In Persia, in Mesopotamia, in Syria, in Egypt such pottery is found, differing widely in its shapes, its designs, and its technique, but having in common that careful workmanship which makes it the finest artistic product of its time. How long this prehistoric age lasted we do not know. The Persian Gulf, gradually receding, left in its wake marshes and salty lagoons. As these dried up, patches of dry land appeared; the Tigris and the Euphrates brought down fertile mud and deposited it at their mouths, and the land of Sumer rose from the sea. Into this now habitable land came down people from the Iranian highlands, who settled in the valley, building their villages of 'wattle and daub' on reed platforms in the marshy ground, tilling the patches of dry land and moving about the lagoons in reed boats, just as the Marsh Arabs of Southern Iraq do to this day. To the north and west another group of peoples occupied Subartu in the apex of the Fertile Crescent, an area stretching from Syria on the west by way of the valleys of the Euphrates and Khabur rivers to the upper waters of the Tigris. These, the owners of the most handsome pottery of the age, followed a mode of life very different from that of the marsh dwellers of Sumer. Their houses were already of brick and stone, their villages walled, with cobbled streets. The pre-dynastic peoples of Egypt needed less protection from the weather; their rude huts were often mere wind-shelters. In the reeds of the Nile swamps they hunted the hippopotamus, and on the edge of the valley they cultivated grain and flax.

As time went on, villages grew into towns and life became more complicated. In Mesopotamia men learnt to scratch symbols and numerals on clay tablets, accounts for so many sheep and so much barley, which are the beginnings of writing. They built temples for their gods, ornamented with elaborate mosaic designs, and they began to import stone from the hills to carve into vases and to lay firm foundations for their shrines. The Egyptians were already familiar with the use of stone. It had always lain ready to their hand—flint in the high desert, limestone and harder materials in the cliffs and wadies bordering the valley. But as the pre-dynastic people developed their skill, the objects they produced improved in technique; their slate-palettes, with scenes of the chase and mythological subjects, surpass anything that the Near East could produce at the time. They too, by carving symbols on stone and ivory, discovered a system of writing. They too built shrines to their gods.

The prosperity of the town communities increased. At Ur, the city of the moon-god, local rulers were interred in deep pits with great pomp and magnificence, adorned with their jewels and finery. They were accompanied in the grave by their entourage, the servants and ladies of the court, the musicians with their harps, and chariots with their charioteers and horses, all ritually slain to accompany their master to the next world. In Egypt, the king was also buried in a deep shaft, surrounded by the members of his household, but in separate tombs that they might occupy when they died—a survival, perhaps, of a less innocent custom, as the Sumerian burial-rite suggests. It was a custom which soon died out in the great countries of antiquity, but it lingered on on the fringes of the civilized world, among the savage tribes of further Nubia and the Scythians of the northern steppes.

By now, Egyptian writing was not only used to mark owner-ship, to make inventories and to send simple messages, but had developed to a point where historical facts, the names of kings, the number of years in their reigns, and any outstanding events of a given year could be recorded. So we enter the historical period. In Sumer the beginnings of history are not so clearly defined. No contemporary records of the earliest dynasties have yet been found; we are forced to rely on the compilations of later annalists who no doubt had access to early documents but whose king-lists are a mixture of fact and mythological fancy. The kings of the first Sumerian dynasties are credited with fabulous reigns of thousands of years, but later more reasonable figures appear and the data become acceptable to an historian.

The Egyptians came early into contact with the world around them. Even in the age before history, raw materials were exchanged between nations and travelling merchants introduced, with their wares, new techniques and new artistic motifs, new religious ideas and new gods. The Sumerians had already established contact with that great source of metal, Anatolia and the southern Caucasus region. They had access to the stone of the Elamite hills, the prized lapis-lazuli of Afghanistan. Egypt very early developed a sea-going fleet. In the Third Dynasty Egypt was already engaged in maritime commerce with the Syrian coast for the coniferous woods which she needed for shipbuilding and other purposes. Sinai was the chief source of her copper, Nubia of her gold. Contact between Egypt and Sumer in the pre-dynastic period, whether direct or indirect, is attested by various artistic motifs and by material evidence.

In the Mediterranean Crete was now entering upon that brilliant phase of her civilization which we have christened 'Minoan'. Here, too, after a long Neolithic period in which the inhabitants lived in caves and rude shelters, had come the age of painted pottery. The early Minoans already showed themselves a seafaring race, daring long voyages in the open Mediterranean and visiting the lands around its eastern shores, for stone vessels and other objects of Egyptian manufacture are found in the island. Minoan Crete has as yet no history. Her hieroglyphic writing remains undeciphered, and the chronology of her culture depends upon the evidence of contacts with her greater neighbours, and above all with Egypt.

It seems probable that Egypt was the first large stretch of territory in the ancient world to be unified under one ruler. In Syria, so far as we know, and in Mesopotamia the country was divided into a number of small city-states, each with its centre around the shrine of the local god, each governed by a ruler who was regarded as the earthly representative of that god. These states pursued a self-centred policy of aggrandizement, warring on each other and united only by the common culture which they shared alike. The plain of the Tigris and Euphrates is wide; there is no sharp borderline between it and the desert, and by an energetic system of irrigation any city-state could enlarge the area of its cultivated land and so its wealth. Egypt, on the other hand, is a very narrow country. It measures on an average only about fourteen miles across from cliff to cliff and is many hundreds of miles long. The prosperity of Egypt therefore depends on the proper regulation and control of the Nile, that great and vital artery without which Egypt would be one with the deserts which border it. And so it was that at some very early date, before we have written records, the whole land of Egypt from the Delta to Aswân was united under the rule of one king. Throughout the history of Egypt, periods marked by poverty of material culture, craftsmanship of poor quality, a low level of artistic achievement, were those periods in which the central authority had been overthrown and the country was split into petty princedoms or oppressed by foreign rule.

By about 2700 B.C. Egypt had reached the first peak of her prosperity. Her rise had been rapid. Internal unity, and a series of able rulers, had led to a remarkable advance in civilization. Only a few generations after the first tentative attempts at substituting stone slabs for wooden planks, King Zoser's famous architect Imhôtep built him the beautiful limestone temple of carved columns and fluted pilasters at Saqqâra. It was the age of Pyramid Builders. Zoser's tomb was out-topped by those of his successors of the Fourth Dynasty, Cheops, Chephren, and Mycerinus, who mustered the resources of the State for vast building enterprises, to ensure that their bodies should have a safe resting-place and so secure immortality.

Meanwhile the Sumerians maintained their local dynasties. In the south of Mesopotamia the ruler of a city-state occasionally managed to impose his rule for a time upon other individual cities; thus Eannatum of Lagash conquered Ur and Uruk, and Lugal-zaggisi of Umma even claimed to have carried his arms from the Mediterranean to the Persian Gulf. But such ephemeral successes seldom outlasted their authors; the first to take a lasting hold on the Valley of the Two Rivers were newcomers from the West.

It is probable that the Sumerians had already long been in contact with the nomads of the western deserts. These peoples of Semitic speech must have been constantly filtering into the fertile plains and settling there. Now, however, there was a wave of invasion, impelled by we know not what movements of populations farther west. Some made their way to the north of Mesopotamia, subduing the original Subarean inhabitants and putting an end to that flourishing Sumerian civilization in which Asshur had hitherto taken part. Others, known to us as the Akkadians, reached the central part of the valley and established a strong dynasty at Agade, near Kish, whence they set out to conquer Sumer. These two groups may or may not have been related. They spoke Semitic dialects akin but far from identical, and each must already have contained a considerable mixture of racial elements. The northern group, the first Assyrians, retained for a time their individuality. But the Sumerians of the south took their conquerors captive, and the new-comers wrote their own tongue in Sumerian cuneiform characters, clothed their gods in the guise of the Sumerian pantheon, worshipped them with Sumerian rites, adopted the laws and customs of the land, and became to a large extent merged in the ancient civilization of their adoption. The great kings of the Dynasty of Akkad, Sargon and Naram-Sin, extended the boundaries of their domains ever more widely. Assyria and eastern Subartu, the north as far as Diarbekr, the south to the Persian Gulf, the west to Syria, were subject to them. One legend tells how Sargon, the King of Battle, led his armies even as far west as Asia Minor; his inscriptions claim that he, like his successor, Naram-Sin, was master of the cedar forests of Amanus and the 'silver mountains' of Cilicia.

A traveller passing at this time along one of the great trade routes from Syria to the junction of the Khabur river and thence to Asshur on the Upper Tigris, or through Mari down the Euphrates to any of the cities of Sumer, would find in every city he visited the same essential features of civilization; art and architecture were common to all, and cuneiform was the universal script of business. But in spite of this commercial and cultural unity of Syria and Mesopotamia, no permanent political settlement was achieved by the Akkadian conquerors. As soon as they left the conquered territory, the inhabitants 'revolted' and the labour of years was undone. Sargon and Naram-Sin cannot therefore be said to have founded an empire, in spite of their spectacular campaigns. It is probable that they were masters of Elam and Assyria, at least intermittently. But they held even their own country precariously enough, for the cities of Sumer and Akkad were constantly rising to claim their freedom.

The first age of great rulers passed, in Mesopotamia as in Egypt. Hordes of mountaineers, perhaps ancestors of the modern Kurds, descended from the hills of Gutium, the region of the Zagros on the north-east of the Tigris plain, and the dynasty of Akkad came to a violent end. Under Gutian rule, the country split up once more into city units. Occasionally a local prince was able to bring prosperity and virtual independence to his state. Such a one was Gudea of Lagash, who embarked on extensive building projects, and for his temple procured cedar from Amanus and Taurus, stone from northern Syria, and wood and diorite from far down the Persian Gulf. The trade routes were evidently still open and the country not in a state of complete confusion. But records are few and it may be that in that dark period few city-states fared so well as Lagash.

In Egypt anarchy came a little later and more gradually, and it came from within rather than from without. The strong kings of the Fourth Dynasty at the height of their power had sown the seeds of future disintegration. Their too ambitious building schemes had exhausted the country financially, their injudicious marriages had created a split in the royal house. The Pharaohs of the Fifth Dynasty built smaller tombs, embarked on fewer enterprises; the Sixth Dynasty witnessed the increasing independence of the nomarchs, the district rulers; and the long reign of Pepy II, whose ninety years on the throne can seldom have been exceeded in the whole range of history, resulted in the enfeeblement and final collapse of the central authority. By about 2300 B.C. there was complete disorder. Local princes established their ephemeral dynasties up and down the country; the Delta, left unguarded, was overrun by tribes of marauding Bedawîn, and it was not until a line of more competent rulers arose at Heracleopolis that order was restored in this region and the invaders driven out. Finally a line of Theban nobles became strong enough to bring the whole country under their rule, and the latter Mentuhoteps of the Eleventh Dynasty achieved once again the unification of Egypt.

Under the centralized government of the Middle Kingdom, Egypt prospered exceedingly. Art revived in a number of vigorous local schools, trade and agriculture flourished. The kings of the Twelfth Dynasty moved their capital to the Faiyûm, where they set about the task of draining and cultivating stretches of that great lake, Nubia was conquered and settled as far as the Second Cataract, and peaceful trading relations established with the Sudanese tribes of the further south. As in the Old Kingdom, sailors made the long voyage to Somaliland for frankincense and the products of Inner Africa, and north to Syria for timber.

The Gutian invaders remained in Babylonia for more than a century. At last a liberator arose to drive out the foreigners, and a partly Sumerian dynasty was set up at Ur. All Sumer and Akkad, and even Assyria, were subject to the kings of the moon-city; the ships of the merchants of Ur sailed the Persian Gulf, their caravans traversed the network of routes of Western Asia. But this brilliant revival of an ancient people did not long survive the reign of its greatest king, Shulgi. His successors were threatened from either side. To the east, the men of Elam, always a menace to the fertile plains which they periodically raided, were again pressing in; and another branch of Semitic peoples, the Amorites, were advancing upon Sumer from the west. When the inevitable disaster came, Ibi-Sin could do nothing to save Ur, and he and his gods were borne off to captivity in Elam.

There followed a period of some confusion in Sumer and Akkad. Rival dynasties of rulers at Isin and Larsa were championed by the two external powers, who each hoped by such interference to gain a permanent footing in the country. Eventually it fell to the Amorite Hammurabi, of the First Dynasty of Babylon, to conquer the whole of the Southland and drive out the Elamites. The Assyrians in the meantime had developed into a powerful State round their capital, Asshur. Like the Akkadians they had absorbed a considerable amount of Sumerian culture, had adopted and modified the Sumerian pantheon, and wrote their Semitic language in the old cuneiform script. A vigorous race of fighters, they had continually to guard against the raids of envious hill peoples to the north and east. In order to do this effectively they needed to forge weapons, and already in the beginning of the second millennium we find colonies of Assyrian traders settled in Cappadocia, the chief source of metal, and sending caravans thence to the mother city. Assyria grew and prospered. King Shamshi-Adad, a contemporary of Hammurabi, ruled over a strong and united country; his younger son ruled as vice-regent over Mari on the Upper Euphrates, and the diplomatic correspondence which passed between father and son, and later when he died, between brother and brother, shows the extent of Assyrian domination at the time. But there is a layer of ash over this city of Mari and over Asshur. Hammurabi marched upstream and destroyed them one after the other, before turning west to march across Subartu to the Amanus mountains; proudly he claimed the title 'king of the four quarters of the world'.

Syria now came strongly under Babylonian influence; the Sumerian culture, which had become more and more localized and debased, was revived in its new Babylonian form in the Canaanite cities of the West. Ugarit, at the mouth of the Orontes, kept its place as one of the chief Mediterranean ports of Asiatic commerce, as well as a market of exchange between Minoan and Egyptian goods. Merchants from Mesopotamia, as well as Cretans and Egyptians, found hospitality in this great cosmopolitan city.

We have no evidence that the Egyptians ever at this time came into conflict with the Babylonians. Their spheres of influence just overlapped, but no more, on the Phoenician coast. The tombs of local princes at Byblus show how strong was the Egyptian interest in that city; as at Ugarit, the presence of an Egyptian colony is attested by numerous finds. In these maritime cities the Egyptians may have come into more direct contact with the Minoan Cretans, whose fine polychrome wares are found in Ugarit. Minoan traders were now ranging the eastern

Mediterranean in their ships. They certainly visited Egypt, for these same handsome wares are found on Twelfth-Dynasty sites in the Nile valley, while small Egyptian objects such as scarabs and statuettes in faience and stone, which they brought home in exchange, have been unearthed in Crete. Egypt and Babylonia may have traded indirectly through the Syrian ports. A recent discovery of an Asiatic treasure deposited in chests beneath a temple in Upper Egypt contained just such a miscellaneous hoard—lapis-lazuli seals of Mesopotamian type, gold bars, silver cups from the Aegean—as one might expect to form the gift or tribute of some Syrian prince whose city was a meeting-place of trade-routes.

The organization of Egyptian society was now very different from the authoritarian aristocracy of the Old Kingdom. The Middle Kingdom saw the rise of a new class in society, the craftsmen and artists, the scribes and government officials. Hitherto these had been virtually serfs, working for the noble masters; now, as order was restored after the civil wars, the 'small man' emerged as a being with a definite status in society, and it was a part of the policy of the Pharaohs to encourage this new middle class in order to counteract the almost feudal power of the nomarchs in their local spheres of jurisdiction. A similar development can be seen in the organization of Babylonian society; between the ruling caste and the slaves an intermediate class is now recognized, the 'poor men' who are free but have not the privileges of the nobles. In the elaborate legal code which is to us the chief glory of Hammurabi's reign a graded scale of punishments is prescribed for the three social classes. A crime committed against a member of the aristocracy is more serious than the same injury to a man of lesser rank; on the other hand, fines are lightened for those less able to pay. This code of laws must have been in force over a large area of the Near East, wherever the Babylonian civilization had taken root. It reflects a highly organized society in which the rights of the individual, and even those of women, were recognized, a society based on commerce and agriculture alike. Hammurabi's letters, of which we have a number, show that there was a well-regulated system of local government in the Sumerian cities, under the direct control of the king himself.

But Hammurabi's organization did not long outlast him. Under his successors Babylonia once more tended to disintegrate. A rival line of dynasts established themselves in the 'sea-land'—the salt marshes around the mouth of the Tigris and Euphrates, and the enfeebled Babylonian dynasty found itself threatened on either side, for the Cassites, mountain tribesmen of the Zagros to the north-east of Mesopotamia, were now an increasing menace to the plains. But the *coup de grâce* was delivered from a new and unexpected quarter. From distant Cappadocia a Hittite army marched down the Euphrates into Babylonia and sacked the capital, carrying off its god Marduk among the spoil.

The *Hatti* who thus made their first appearance on the stage of international politics were not the same as those inhabitants of Cappadocia, often called Proto-Hittites, among whom the traders from Asshur had their homes two centuries before. The immigration of new peoples from Europe may even then have been taking place. These new-comers, at first barbarians, gradually adopted much of the civilization that they found in the regions in which they settled. An amalgamation of their Indo-European speech with the Asianic of the earlier inhabitants of Anatolia resulted in a mixed language which we call Hittite. This they learned to write in cuneiform characters on tablets of clay, and they incorporated the local gods of their subjects in their pantheon. The 'thousand gods of Hatti' included those of every nation which the Hittites later added to their empire. At first divided into a number of small warring kingdoms, they were at length united under the leadership of the kings of Hattusas (the modern Boghaz-keui), on the river

Halys, which became the capital of the Hittite kingdom. The early history of this newly formed nation is little more than a list of names. Murshil I seems to have been one of the first kings to embark on campaigns of expansion; he subdued at least part of North Syria and captured Carchemish and Aleppo; Babylon marks the limit of his advance eastwards. He seems to have withdrawn almost at once, and the history of the Hittite kingdom lapses strangely into obscurity for another two hundred years or more. Babylonia, robbed by the Hittite raid of the last of her line of strong kings, fell an easy prey to the oncoming Cassites.

The Cassites ruled in Babylonia for over five centuries. During that period records are scarce, and we know sadly little about them or their rule. But one thing is clear. Like the Hittites, the dominant caste among them was of Indo-Aryan tongue, as the names of their kings and deities show. A third branch of this southward migration of Indo-European peoples found its way to Khurri, north of the Subarean plain. They found here a native population of hillsmen who had spread over a wide area of the plain. Their presence east of the Tigris is attested by a number of cuneiform tablets from Nuzi near Kirkuk. Here they clearly enjoyed peaceable commercial relations with the local inhabitants. But the fresh impetus of the arrival of a new and vigorous stock in the hills drove the Khurrians south as it had impelled the Hittites and the Cassites. In each case, with their own gods, they brought with them the knowledge of horse-breeding and the use of the chariot, and it was no doubt with the use of this new instrument of war, useless in the hills but formidable in the plains, that the Cassites with their Aryan leaders conquered the Babylonians, the Hittites made their first conquest of North Syria, and the Khurrians, descending upon the plain of the Khabur and the Middle Euphrates, finally established the political kingdom of Mitanni. The inhabitants of this State of Mitanni thus contained three main elements—the native Subarean population, the conquering Khurrians, and the ruling caste who introduced Indo-European words into the language and called their own gods to witness their treaties with foreign Powers.

This southward movement of peoples into Asia Minor, Subartu, and Mesopotamia naturally caused a displacement of the populations already settled in the Fertile Crescent, and it drove down into Syria and Palestine the dreaded Hyksos, the Shepherd Kings. Their identity is a matter of debate; perhaps it is safest to assume that they were a mixed race, speaking a Semitic language and worshipping the storm-god Sutekh. From the northern invaders they had learnt the use of the chariot; their fortresses were massive structures surrounded by a smooth sloping glacis which made approach difficult. Through Palestine they came, conquering and destroying, and into Egypt, where the Thirteenth Dynasty was maintaining a feeble hold and no leader was found strong enough to unite the country in resistance. Again Egypt split into local principalities, and now, for the first time in her history, she suffered the indignities of conquest by foreigners. At first destroyers, the later Hyksos kings did their best, it seems, to adapt themselves to Egyptian ways; they adopted hieroglyphic writing and identified their storm-god with the Egyptian Set, and they forbore to interfere with their subjects more than was necessary. But the Egyptians never forgot that they were foreigners, and centuries later their name was still anathema. At last a line of deliverers arose, again in the city of Thebes. The last princes of the Seventeenth Dynasty fought against the foreigners and gradually, step by step, drove them out of Egypt. Not content with the liberation of their country, the first kings of the Eighteenth Dynasty pressed on into Palestine, and so the Egyptians, carried northward by the impetus of their pursuit, found themselves embarking on a career of conquest in Asia such as they had never before attempted.

The first Tuthmosis set the boundary of this new empire as far as Naharain, the land between the two rivers Orontes and Euphrates. Governors were put in charge of the conquered territories in Syria and Palestine, and Egyptian influence soon spread over the Near East. This egyptianizing process continued even when a firm political control was not maintained. After the peaceful reign of Queen Hatshepsut, who being a woman could not, or would not, lead her forces to war, her energetic nephew Tuthmosis III set out to win back the empire of his grandfather. In the plain of Armageddon, one of the great battlegrounds of history, a coalition of Syrians lay in wait for him. Against the advice of the more prudent of his counsellors, he decided on a bold course that was justified by success. Defiling from a narrow pass through the hills, the Egyptian army surprised the enemy and defeated them. The city was taken after a short siege, dramatically described by the annalist. In a series of seventeen campaigns, Tuthmosis pushed his boundary up to the Taurus mountains and to the Euphrates. It is even possible that he conquered Assyria; at any rate, he received tribute, or diplomatic presents, from both Babylonia and Assyria; all Hither Asia seemed to wait upon Egypt's pleasure.

Foreigners now came in ever-increasing numbers to the cities of the Nile; foreign motives of design, foreign gods were the fashion. Ambassadors from Asia arrived with their caravans, to be entertained at the Egyptian court; merchants brought luxury articles, scents and embroideries, inlays and precious stones. The dockyards were kept busy. Boats sailed to the Phoenician coast to bring back timber for more boats. Through the port of Ugarit a flourishing trade was carried on with Crete. Cretan merchants even formed a colony there, as perhaps elsewhere along the coast. Some of the tribute-bearing 'Keftiu' who are depicted in Egyptian tombs may be Cretans from Crete, while others bringing objects of Syrian design may be Cretan colonists from the mainland of Phoenicia, who would come under the aegis of the Egyptian empire.

Under Amenophis III, called 'The Magnificent', Egypt reached the zenith of her wealth and power. The State treasuries overflowed with the tribute of Syria, the gold of Nubia, and the costly products of the land of Punt. The Pharaoh himself, who as a young man had prided himself on his prowess in the hunting field, grew stout and indolent with middle age, and was content to leave the management of his empire to his officials. Egypt may claim to have been the first Power in the Near East to possess an imperial organization. True, it was not a very elaborate one. It had no centralized system of officials and subordinates like the Assyrian, and still more, the Persian Empire. It was on a much smaller scale. But it was a system which under a strong and energetic Pharaoh worked well enough. Native governors were installed in most of the subject cities, and Egyptian garrisons were maintained in some. The sons of the rulers were sent to Egypt to be educated at court with the royal princes; here they would learn Egyptian methods and return to govern with an Egyptian outlook. A postal service was established between the capital and the cities of the empire; the reports and dispatches of the vassal rulers, written not in hieroglyphic but in the Akkadian cuneiform which was the lingua franca of the day, were filed in the Record Office.

But disintegrating influences were already at work. Assyria under her new ruler Ashuruballit had recovered some of her ancient prestige; Mitanni, profiting by the lapse of hostilities, was increasing in influence. At Hattusas, the Hittite capital, a king had arisen who was to dominate for a time the international stage, and build for his people an empire such as his predecessor Murshil had perhaps once dreamed of. Shubbiluliuma came to the Hittite throne towards the end of the long reign of Amenophis III, in about 1390 B.C., and having driven back the turbulent peoples who harried his northern and north-western borders, he at once set about encouraging the disintegrating tendencies of the Syrian possessions of Egypt.

Our knowledge of this interesting stage of Near Eastern politics, with which Egypt was so vitally concerned, is mainly derived from two sources, the Tell el-'Amarna letters and the royal tablets from Boghaz-keui. The former are what remains of the diplomatic correspondence which passed between the Pharaohs Amenophis III and Amenophis IV (Akhenaton), and their brother monarchs and subject princes of the Near East. The latter are a collection of similar documents from the Hittite court record office. Both series are written in Akkadian, the language of diplomacy, and from them the main sequence of events can be reconstructed.

The key-state in Hither Asia at that time was Mitanni. Lying as she did in an arena of constant dispute, surrounded by growing Powers all hungry for territory, she was bound to be the pivot round which events turned. For a century or more after the collapse of Babylonia and the retirement of the Hittites, she may for a time have been the most powerful State in the Near East, with an empire stretching from the North Syrian coast to the Tigris. Tuthmosis III in his campaigns limited the territory of Mitanni, but there remained a strong Khurrian element in the population of the cities of the west, and by the time of Amenophis III she seems again to have extended her domination over much of North Syria. Egypt, now unable to check her expansion, courted her friendship instead, by subsidies of Nubian gold and by a series of marriages between the Pharaohs and the princesses of Mitanni. But the Khurrians found themselves menaced on either side. While Shubbiluliuma and Ashuruballit wrote letters protesting friendship to Egypt, they were each plotting the annexation of Mitanni. At this stage Egypt would have done well to consider the danger of the situation and reinforce her Syrian possessions. But Amenophis did little, and he was followed by his son Akhenaton, whose preoccupation with religious problems led him to abandon the capital and withdraw to a new city, the modern Tell el-'Amarna. By his championship of the worship of the sun-disk Aten exclusively, he alienated a large and powerful section of his subjects, including the priests of the wealthy State god, Amon. Through their hands came much of the produce of the Nubian gold-mines, and Akhenaton, even if he had had time and inclination to interest himself in foreign affairs, would still have found it difficult to maintain enough agents in his pay and keep up the needful subsidies. A large military campaign might have saved the situation and driven the Hittites back, but Akhenaton was no warrior. So the unfortunate governors of the Egyptian possessions in the north wrote in vain for help. The crafty Shubbiluliuma employed indirect methods, encouraging the anti-Egyptian faction in the Syrian cities and no doubt subsidizing the Amorites to attack the cities of the Phoenician coast, until one by one Byblos, Simyra, Tyre, and Sidon fell or went over to the enemy. All Syria would have been lost to Egypt had not Shubbiluliuma been called home to fight wars in Asia Minor.

In the south, the Egyptian possessions were being threatened by different foes. The governor of Jerusalem writes complaining that he is being attacked by the Khabiru, bands of robber nomads who appear elsewhere, in texts of the period from Boghaz-keui, from Nuzi, and from Babylonia, as adventurers, mercenaries, and bandits. It has been suggested that this account of the raids of the Khabiru in Palestine is a version of the campaign of Joshua told from the Canaanite point of view. Even if the philological equation Khabiru = 'Aperu be not accepted, there is nothing improbable in the suggestion that the Hebrews were at this time entering Palestine over the Jordan, and that they were classed by the more civilized town-dwellers of Canaan with the nomadic plunderers of the desert familiar to all townsmen. On various computations the date for the entry into Palestine can be brought to this period.

The Amarna letters come to an abrupt stop and we do not hear from them whether Jerusalem was taken; the Old Testament tells us that it was not. It is probable that Egyptian influence swiftly declined in the south, and that the Canaanite cities of the plain declared their independence. When the Pharaohs of the Nineteenth Dynasty came north to win back an empire, they had to reconquer Palestine as well as Syria.

In the Mitannian capital, Hittite and Assyrian agents had been at work. A fatal split in the royal house drove Mattiwaza, the rightful heir, to appeal to Shubbiluliuma for help. He was rewarded by restoration to his throne and the hand of a Hittite princess, but with it went a more ominous gift, the 'protection' of the Hittite monarch. A treaty provided that on Mattiwaza's death the kingdom should pass to his Hittite relatives. Finally, Assyria stepped in and the State of Mitanni ceased to exist.

The Aton religion was already declining when Akhenaton its founder died. Shortly afterwards, the royal residence was moved back to Thebes, and Amon became more wealthy and powerful than ever before. The kings of the latter part of the Eighteenth Dynasty were more occupied with restoring order and prosperity at home than with external affairs. Among the archives of Boghaz-keui there is a very interesting document. It is a letter from a queen of Egypt, the widow, possibly, of Tutankhamen. Her husband, she says, is dead, and she has no son to succeed. If therefore the Hittite king will send one of his sons to Egypt, she will make him her husband. Now the kingship in Egypt descended in the female line, so that had this offer of marriage been at once accepted, two great empires would have been united. But Shubbiluliuma was suspicious and delayed his answer while he made further inquiries; the queen's plan was evidently discovered, and when a Hittite prince was at last sent, he was murdered on his way to Egypt. Shubbiluliuma had missed his great opportunity, and had to content himself with his policy of encroaching on Egyptian territory in Syria, down to the borders of Palestine. When he died, in about 1350 B.C., his successors carried on his work, and it was left for the vigorous Pharaohs of the next dynasty to re-establish Egypt's position in Asia.

Sethos I, in a series of brilliant campaigns, came into conflict with a Hittite confederation and defeated them more than once. His son Ramesses II advanced farther into Syria and met the coalition in the plain of Coele-Syria, between the mountains of Lebanon and Anti-Lebanon. Here at Kadesh on the Orontes was fought that great battle between the Egyptian army, with its auxiliaries from the still loyal Phoenician cities, and the Hittites with their host of allies from Asia Minor and Syria, which became an epic theme for the Egyptian court poets. Rashly advancing in divisions too widely spaced, Ramesses found himself ambushed near the city and cut off from the bulk of his army. But his bravery in charging the enemy, and the timely arrival of reinforcements from the coast, saved the situation. The battle was to neither side, though the Egyptians claimed to have routed their enemies, and the king caused long hymns of victory to be inscribed on the walls of his temples. Both nations were weary of the struggle and not long after, on the accession of a less bellicose king to the Hittite throne, hostilities came to an end. A treaty, of which we have both the Egyptian and the Hittite versions, was drawn up between Hattusil and Ramesses II, and cemented by vows of eternal friendship and the marriage of the Pharaoh to a Hittite princess. By the terms of the treaty the *status quo* was maintained—in writing at least. But there has been a tendency in recent years to underestimate the extent of Ramesses' achievement, and evidence has recently been accumulating that in reality much of Syria renewed its allegiance to Egypt not long after the battle of Kadesh. Centres of commercial activity, especially those on the Phoenician coast, were no doubt anxious to renew good terms with their old ally; the Hittites had never been powerful on sea as the Egyptians were, and so it may be no coincidence that in Ugarit, a short time afterwards, we find an Egyptian official of high rank making offering to the god Baal, and at the same time the Hittite king Hattusil admitting, in a letter to the king of Babylon, that he has no longer jurisdiction over Amurru and Ugarit.

The truth is that the Hittite sun was sinking. Assyria was gaining strength, and from the west a far greater peril was approaching. Vigorous northerners were entering Asia Minor from the European side and threatening the Hittite Empire on its most vulnerable flank. In 1400 or thereabouts the Cretan monarchies were overthrown. The great palace of Knossos was destroyed. Henceforward Mycenaean goods from the mainland of Greece replaced Minoan and were even more widely distributed through the Mediterranean lands. And at about the same time, a state Akhkhiyawa appears in the archives of Boghaz-keui. It seems to be situated in the extreme south-west of Asia Minor, and it is at least possible that this name is an attempt to render into the cuneiform script the word Ἀχαία. Various familiar Achaean names such as Atreus have also been identified by some scholars, and it seems that we have here a record of the relations which existed between a branch of the new-comers from Europe and the great Hittite Power which dominated the peninsula. That these relations were at first friendly is testified by the documents; it is even possible that Shubbiluliuma himself married an Achaean princess. But now the pressure from central Europe was becoming more insistent. The inhabitants of western Asia Minor were being driven out of their homes, some to seek a living by piracy round the Mediterranean. Their menace was felt in Egypt. Merenptah, the successor of Ramesses II, had to deal with an invading horde of 'peoples of the sea' who had joined forces with the marauding Libyan tribes of the Western Desert and were threatening to overrun the Delta. Among these were the Lycians and the Tyrsenoi, Tyrrhenians who may later have sailed to Italy and, settling on the coast of Tuscany, have become the great Etruscan nation.

These movements, however, were but a foreshadowing of disaster to come. In about 1200 B.C. a fresh wave of Sea-peoples rolled down upon Asia Minor. On the Ilian peninsula some of them met with opposition from the wealthy citizens of Troy, whose vain resistance gave us the great epic of the *Iliad*. The peoples of Asia Minor were swept eastward. The Hittite Empire crumbled before the flood; Hattusas was destroyed, the Hittites as a political entity cease to exist. Onward pushed the immigrants, some with their families and possessions in bullock-carts, others skirting the coast in ships. Down into Syria and through to Palestine they came; Ugarit and Byblos fell, and Egypt trembled at the news. Who could stay their advance? Useless to appeal to the Babylonians for aid, for they were weakened by internal strife. The last of the Cassite rulers was maintaining a feeble hold on a part of Babylonia, and Assyria itself was threatened by the eastward thrust of populations. Ramesses III saw that the Egyptians alone, with such small allies as they could muster, must stop the on-coming host. Preparations were rapidly made; a great force advanced into South Palestine, and there, in a double battle by sea and land, the invaders were turned from the gates of Egypt.

Some were dispersed and returned whence they had come. Some remained in Asia Minor, others in Syria. The Shekelesh and the Sherden may have sailed westwards, giving their names to the islands of Sicily and Sardinia. The Philistines, who appear among the combatants in the Egyptian battle-scenes wearing plumed crests on their helmets and sailing in beak-prowed ships, settled in the coastal plain of Southern Palestine and formed there a pentarchical State around their five main cities, Gaza, Askelon, Gath, Ashdod, and Ekron. The displacement of populations was extensive; the ethnographical and political map of Hither Asia was profoundly altered. The Gasgas, tribes who had long harassed the Hittite kingdom on its northern and western fronts, had been carried as far east as the borders of Assyria. Remnants of the Hittites themselves were to be found in Syria. The new-comers from Europe settled down to form prosperous States in Asia Minor; the Mushki of Phrygia appear later as powerful neighbours and opponents of the Assyrian Empire. The collapse of the Hittite power led to the establishment of the Aramaeans in the Fertile Crescent. For centuries past, semi-nomadic tribes had been filtering in from the desert oases. Now, finding the land disorganized and depopulated, they settled in greater numbers and began to form independent States, each ruled by a petty king. They quickly adopted the civilization which they found in their new homes—a civilization in which Hittite and Babylonian elements were blended—but they introduced their own language. Being able business men, they soon restored to the cities of Syria, Hamath and Aleppo, Carchemish, Damascus, and the rest, their old prosperity, so that these Semitic States achieved considerable importance within the limited sphere of their several interests. In the south of Palestine, the sheikhs of Edom and Moab set up independent kingdoms as neighbours of the Philistines. Only in the wealthy Phoenician cities of the coast, Ugarit and Byblus, Tyre and Sidon, there was little change. They recovered from the shock of the foreign invasions and continued in their role of middle-men for the trade of the civilized world.

For a time there was no great Power in the Near East. Egypt, exhausted by her efforts abroad and weakened by a line of ineffective Pharaohs, came under the rule of priest kings. Babylonia, emerging from the long obscurity of Cassite rule, was still troubled by Elamite raids and by an influx from the Western Desert of Semitic tribes, the Chaldeans. Under the leadership of a king of the old native stock, Nebuchadnezzar I, the country was for a brief period united and mistress of considerable territory, but he failed against Assyria, and with him perished the political ambitions of a people whose main interest was commercial gain. For a time it looked as if Assyria, little affected by the great *Völkerwanderung*, might step into the dominant position. One remarkable monarch, Tiglath-pileser I, did in fact take advantage of the general confusion, in 1100 or thereabouts, to march across to the west, defeating the Aramaean princelings, and after a very profitable campaign among the cities of North Syria, even reached the coast of Phoenicia, enjoying the novelty of a short sea-trip from Arvad to Simyra. In his career of conquest, as in his love of hunting, his interest in natural history, his building activities, and his care for the agricultural welfare of his country, he is the prototype of the typical Assyrian monarch of the future. But he was four hundred years too soon. His campaigns were little more than summer raids, not repeated by his successors, and Assyria shrank once more to her natural boundaries. Her hour was not yet come.

In the safety of their hills, the Hebrews had watched successive invasions of Palestine pass by, and they now began to descend upon the Canaanite cities of the western plain. Coming into conflict with the Philistines, they were at first defeated and for over fifty years enslaved, forbidden to forge themselves weapons, and oppressed by taxes. Then, under their kings Saul and David, they waged a war of liberation. Jerusalem, that Canaanite city on the rock that had withstood attacks in the days of Abdkhiba, yielded to David, the Philistines were driven back, and Israel and Judah joined in a united Hebrew monarchy which under Solomon reached the hey-day of its brief glory. For the only time in her history, Palestine was a political entity of some importance in world affairs. Moab and Edom were added to the kingdom, Ammon was annexed, and the conquest of Damascus brought the Hebrews into close proximity with the Aramaeans of North Syria. Solomon was careful to keep on good terms with them and with his valuable neighbours the cities of Phoenicia. With the aid of his ally King Hiram of Tyre he was able to finance trading expeditions to the ends of the known world. His Tyrian ships sailed to Arabia for frankincense and the luxuries of India, and to the kingdom of Tartessos in distant Spain for tin which came from the Cassiterides, the tin islands of the Atlantic. The description of the building of Solomon's temple, roofed and panelled with Lebanon cedar, adorned with gold and ivory, reveals the wealth and influence of its builder.

But the old religious and racial enmity between Israel and Judah soon burst out again. Egypt had a hand in the disruption; she could not afford to see Palestine become a formidable Power which might threaten her borders. The court which had sent a princess richly dowered to be Solomon's bride now received his son's enemy the rebel Jeroboam. The prestige of Egypt abroad had now dwindled to a shadow. The story of the wanderings and misfortunes of a certain Wen-Amun shows only too clearly the contempt in which Egypt was held by the independent cities of the Syrian coast. He was sent thither to buy timber for the Egyptian government, and in endeavouring to carry out his orders was everywhere shown such disrespect, was so hounded from place to place, so slighted and so mocked that at length he sat down on the sea-shore at Byblos and wept. Such treatment contrasts sadly with the deference which an Egyptian official on such an errand might have expected even a century before.

Now Assyria was at last coming into her own. Since her brief bid for ascendancy in the eleventh century she had been a minor Power, mainly occupied in securing her borders from the attacks of tribesmen from the north-eastern hills, and waging an economic warfare against the merchants of Babylonia. But in the ninth century the kings of Assyria set out on that career of conquest which gradually gained for them an empire greater

than any the world had hitherto seen. The national temper
was war-like, and the geographical situation of Assyria imparted
a tendency to expansion. An absence of natural frontiers necessitated the subjection of an ever-widening circle of rapacious
neighbours. Lack of a seaboard from which to dispatch her
merchants and her distance from the metal mines of Cappadocia, made it imperative that she should secure access to the
source of those materials which were vital to her existence.
Finally, like all empire builders, she was tempted by greed of
gain; lists of tribute from the wealthy Aramaean and Phoenician
cities on the western trade-routes bear witness to the prize that
was to be won by campaigns in that quarter.

The acquisition of this empire was not a matter of years but
of centuries. Its frontiers ebbed and flowed, expanded under
an energetic warrior king, contracted under a weakling, or when
dynastic strife, that fatal weakness of oriental monarchies,
threatened to destroy from within the whole structure of
government.

One of the most dangerous and persistent opponents of
Assyria was the kingdom of Urartu on her northern borders.
A war-like people of Asianic speech had settled around Lake
Van in the Armenian mountains, and by their skill in forging
iron weapons had established a powerful and aggressive State.
For centuries Assyria and Van disputed between them the hill-
lands to the west of Urartu. Van was repeatedly attacked by
the Assyrians, but the rocky fortress-capital proved impreg-
nable. When Assyria was weak, Van was at its strongest.
Sarduris III even held for a time the Aramaean cities of the
west, Carchemish and Aleppo. But Tiglath-pileser soon drove
the Urartians back into their mountains, and there they were
gradually hemmed in by other enemies, and ceased to trouble
Assyria.

These foes that encompassed Van were divided into two main
groups—the Scythians on the north-west, the Medes on the

north-east. The former group, gradually crossing the Caucasus from the region of the Danube basin, were gathering strength in the north Armenian plateau as the latter, Iranians from beyond the Caspian Sea, moved westwards to Lake Urmia and the Zagros area, and spread as far south as the borders of Elam. The Scythians at first came little into contact with Assyria; the eastern group of peoples was a continual menace to her, and necessitated constant campaigns in that direction.

The Aramaeans to the west of Assyria were never such formidable opponents. The petty kingdoms of the Euphrates and Khabur valleys proved incapable of combining against their common enemy. Assyria attacked them singly, and they were easily reduced to submission. Occasionally they allied with the Chaldaeans and Babylonians to the south, and then the Assyrians had to face a dangerous coalition. The Babylonians themselves were as a rule more interested in maintaining friendly relations with the Power which held the northern trade-routes than with any political ambitions. It was the Chaldaean tribes settled in the south of Mesopotamia, under their five paramount sheikhs, who managed occasionally to rouse national feeling and stir up a general revolt. Merodach-baladan, one of these tribal chieftains, was the source of considerable anxiety to successive kings of Assyria. Defeated by Tiglath-pileser III, and more than once by Sargon II, he still proved irrepressible, and when he tried to raise a coalition of Aramaeans, Elamites, and Arabs against Sennacherib, and even drew Hezekiah of Judah into the plot, the time had come to take firm action against Chaldaea. It was colonized by settlers from the west, and a native Babylonian governor was installed in Babylon, after which the country gave little trouble until its final successful bid for liberty.

The acquisition of Assyria's western possessions was her most vital and her most difficult task. Ashur-nasir-pal and his son Shalmaneser III already in the ninth century penetrated to the Aramaean cities of Syria; the Phoenicians were easily blackmailed into paying large tribute; the States which resisted, under the leadership of Damascus, among whom was Israel, were defeated at the battle of Karkar, and Shalmaneser was able to extract indemnities from almost all the rest. After these kings there was a period of comparative weakness in Assyria for over eighty years, until the advent of Tiglath-pileser III, who usurped the throne in 745 B.C. He and his successors spent much time in the west, effecting a more thorough conquest and settlement than had been attempted before. Palestine had broken up into small States; the Israelite kings of Samaria were pursuing a short-sighted policy of aggression against Judah and against Damascus, to whom they should have looked for leadership against the Assyrian peril. Damascus fell to Tiglath-pileser, North Syria was made into a province which included Hamath and Byblos, Palestine submitted, and Hoshea of Judah ceded half his territory. Under his successors, the Assyrian Empire was consolidated and its boundaries extended to their farthest limits. Periodic revolts in Palestine received harsh treatment. Israel suffered wholesale deportation at the hands of Sargon; in the place of the Israelites was put a mixed population from various parts of the empire whom we know later as the Samaritans. Hezekiah of Judah, organizing a western revolt against Sennacherib, was besieged in Jerusalem and forced to submit.

In nearly all these revolts Egypt had played a covert part. Against this invincible army of disciplined soldiers she could take no effective military action. Her prestige in Palestine and Syria was now practically non-existent. The line of priest kings had petered out; for a time Thebes shared supremacy with Tanis in the Delta in a dual kingship; then a vigorous family of native chieftains arose in Nubia, which had not long been independent of Egypt. They came down the Nile to Thebes and thence found the subjugation of the whole country a simple matter. Emboldened by the ease with which they had conquered a great nation they dared to challenge the authority of Assyria over

Egypt's erstwhile empire, not by force of arms, but by constant intrigues, by subsidies of Nubian gold, and by promises of help to those client States which could be induced to risk revolt from their overlords.

This could not go unpunished for ever. An Egyptian contingent sent to help Hezekiah was defeated by Sennacherib, and it was with the aim of securing, once and for all, the south-western boundaries of the Assyrian Empire against Egyptian interference, rather than with any desire to incorporate Egypt within these boundaries, that Esarhaddon at length undertook the conquest of the country. After persistent revolts, his successor Ashurbanipal was even forced to order the destruction of Thebes. For the first time, the helmets of a northern Power gleamed among the ruins of the city of Amun.

At the end of the eighth century a new danger threatened the west from the direction of the Caucasus. Fierce Cimmerian horsemen from eastern Europe entered Asia Minor and Sargon, campaigning in Anatolia, may even have been killed in battle against them. Soon afterwards, the Phrygian kingdom fell. As the conquerors retired, the kingdom of Lydia took its place in western Asia Minor. Esarhaddon fought with the Cimmerians in Cilicia to protect the borders of his empire, and Ashurbanipal sent help to Gyges of Lydia when they again turned west and threatened Sardis and Ephesus. But Gyges played his cards unwisely. By sending assistance to Psammetichus, the Egyptian vassal of Assyria, in his revolt against Ashurbanipal, he antagonized a valuable ally, and when the Cimmerians attacked Lydia again, Sardis fell and he met his fate. The northerners were now pressing south in increasing numbers. A motley horde of Scythians, Cimmerians, and others, the 'Umman-Manda' as they were collectively called, invaded Cilicia and North Syria, and Ashurbanipal in a critical battle only just managed to save his western empire from being overrun. But he was the last of the great Assyrians. They had been ill-advised to break the power of Elam, and now, by the collapse of Urartu, the last bulwark against the invaders was removed. Assyria was assailed from all sides at once. The Umman-Manda closed in from the north, and a united Babylonia under the Chaldaean Nabopolassar marched up the Euphrates. In 612 B.C. Scythians, Medes, and Babylonians joined in the final assault on the capital; the Assyrian Empire perished in the flames of Nineveh.

The victorious allies divided Hither Asia between them. Cyaxares the Mede kept Assyria and the northern possessions of the empire; the Halys was fixed as the boundary between his realm and the kingdom of Lydia. Nebuchadnezzar II established Babylonian control over Palestine, Syria, and the Euphrates valley, and his sphere of influence extended even into Asia Minor. The Egyptians, taking advantage of the fall of Assyria to seize Palestine, were defeated at Carchemish; years later they returned to stir up revolt in Jerusalem and among the cities of Phoenicia, but again they failed. Judah was heavily punished; the Jews were taken off into captivity to Babylon, and Jeremiah was left to chant his lamentations on the ruins of Jerusalem. Some of the Jews sought refuge in Egypt, that 'broken reed' that had failed to support them, and were granted permission to settle in the Delta towns. Others are found later as mercenaries in Upper Egypt, where they formed a colony at Elephantine.

After the final overthrow of the Elamites in the middle of the seventh century, a group of Iranian tribes had moved south and held the country as vassals of the Medes. Gradually the Persians gained the ascendancy; Cyrus of Anshan, about sixty years after the fall of Nineveh, managed to unite them, and his revolt against the Median Astyages was successful. Ecbatana was captured, and he proclaimed himself King of the Medes and Persians. The empire of Babylonia was threatened. Unfortunately for her, Nebuchadnezzar was now dead and an unpractical man of letters, the antiquarian king Nabonidus, took no steps to oppose the danger. Cyrus delayed his attack until he had secured the northern empire. In a spectacular series of campaigns he reconquered the whole Median Empire and beyond it. Croesus of Lydia, whose ambition had led him to cross the Halys into Cappadocia, provoked his special attention. The result we are told by Herodotus; Sardis fell before the Persian advance, Lydia and the Ionian cities of the Aegean coast became provinces of the empire. For the next five years Cyrus was employed in conquering the east, then in 539 he turned south to Babylonia. Meeting with little resistance, he entered the great gates of Babylon and took the hands of its god. Nabonidus' general Belshazzar perished; the writing on the wall had warned in vain.

With the conquest of Egypt by Cambyses, the Persian Empire was complete. From the Nile to the Black Sea and the Caspian, from the Aegean almost to the borders of India, stretched that amazing empire which Alexander still more astonishingly set himself to win. At the new capital Persepolis, Darius the Achaemenid perfected his organization of the known world. In the course of their long experience the Assyrians had made great progress in imperial administration. It was they who had first divided their territorial possessions into provinces under district governors, each with a staff of subordinate officials, and each with the duty of sending regular reports to the king. The Persian satrapies were organized after the model of these provinces, but more elaborately; each satrap was surrounded by a miniature court of officials and dignitaries. Each province had had to pay tribute to Assyria and tithes to the royal temples. Darius fixed a quota for each satrapy and an elaborate staff of officials to see that it was paid. The Assyrian system of royal roads was adopted and carried much farther by the Persians, whose empire was traversed by a network of highways, valuable for military purposes and used for swift communication by the well organized courier service.

The Greeks had been in close touch with the oriental world for centuries past. Since early times bands of adventurers from Ionia and Greece had hired themselves out as mercenaries to Lydians and Egyptians, Assyrians and Persians. We have discussed the probability of contact between the Hittites and the peoples of the Aegean coast. The Ionians lived alongside the civilizations of Asia Minor, and the Greeks of the south coast of the peninsula came into contact with the Assyrians when the latter extended their hegemony over Cilicia. The Phoenicians had acted as intermediaries of culture. Greek ships sailed continually across the Mediterranean. We know of a Greek trading centre at the mouth of the Orontes in the eighth century B.C., importing a wealth of pottery from Rhodes, Cyprus, Athens, and Corinth. In the Delta of Egypt, Naukratis was well established under the patronage of the Saite kings as the prosperous Greek emporium which travellers like Solon and Pythagoras visited. And so through this contact between East and West, before it had resolved into a struggle for supremacy, was transmitted the heritage of experience from the ancient world.

In the course of our brief historical survey we have seen the growth of successive political conceptions which formed part of this heritage. In the third millennium the village community had already developed into the city-state. In Hither Asia a number of small unit Powers were united not politically but culturally by a great civilization. Egypt had been the first to show the benefits of centralized government over a wide area. In the second millennium a new order arose—that of national States, limited by fixed boundaries. This was an age of cosmopolitanism, of wars on a large scale, and of the beginnings of diplomacy; letters were interchanged between the great Powers, treaties drawn up, marriages arranged to link the ruling lines. Finally, the first millennium saw the growth of great empires. Here again Egypt had pointed the way. The Assyrian Empire was a far bigger conception than the Egyptian had been, and the

Persian surpassed each in its vast range, but the Egyptians were the first nation, so far as we know, to follow up the triumphal progress of the conqueror with any lasting organization of the territory conquered.

M. S. DROWER

CHAPTER 3

WRITING AND LITERATURE

THE modern world has inherited from Ancient Egypt, as from Greece, in two different ways. In the first place there has been simple historical transmission, things of value having come down to us, to use the old Egyptian expression, 'son to son, heir to heir'. But secondly there has existed also a deferred mode of acquisition, in which Champollion and his successors have played for Egypt the same role as the scholars of the Renaissance played for Greece. Examination of the latter form of inheritance really resolves itself into the question: How far should we, judging by our own standards of value, be the poorer without the new knowledge and beauty accruing from Egyptological research? Obviously this is a very different question from that raised by the other kind of legacy, where the problem is of even greater interest, but unfortunately also of far greater difficulty. The task before us in this chapter is to treat the writing and literature of Pharaonic Egypt from both points of view, and it will be well to start with the more exacting of the two problems.

Elements of art, of law, and of religion may have passed straight from Egypt to Rome, there to join the broad stream of ancient culture that has descended to ourselves. As regards literature and writing, Rome has to be eliminated as an immediate point of contact, and in so far as there has been direct inheritance, the intermediaries will have been Palestine and Greece, in many cases doubtless both. The chances of an influence passing from Egypt to Greece via Crete do not seem particularly great. Classical scholars have not in the past taken very kindly to the idea of Hellenic dependence upon Egyptian civilization, but in one important case the debt is universally admitted, as will be seen from the following quotations from the Cambridge *Companion to Greek Studies* (p. 606):

'The vehicle by which Greek literature was preserved and transmitted from the earliest times until perhaps the second or third century after Christ was the papyrus roll. Alike in respect of form and of material, this was an import from Egypt, where it had been in use from a very remote time. A detailed account of the way in which the papyrus was treated in the Egyptian paper-factories is given by Pliny (*N.H.* xiii. 74 sqq.), but it is obscure in many points. Without going into the minute details of the process, it may be said here that the material used was the pith of the papyrus-reed (πάπυρος, βύβλος, βίβλος, botanically *Cyperus papyrus*) cut vertically into slices. In order to make a sheet of paper, these slices were laid some vertically and others transversely, pressed together, and dried in the sun: unevennesses were then smoothed or pressed away, and the sheets glued together into a roll.'

Needless to say, this material basis was not without effect upon the subject-matter inscribed thereon.

'It is at least clear that from a fairly early period authors were influenced by the size of the papyrus rolls ordinarily manufactured, and divided their works into such portions as could conveniently be contained in single rolls. . . . In Pliny's day the standard quantity of a roll was twenty sheets.'

One ancient trade-route was probably through Byblus on the Phoenician coast, though an oft-quoted statement from the story of Wenamûn (*circa* 1100 B.C.) that Smendes of Tanis sent five hundred rolls of papyrus to the prince of Byblus is a mistranslation. It is often confidently asserted that the actual Greek words for 'papyrus-reed' (βύβλος) and for 'book' (βιβλίον) are derived from the name of the said Phoenician city, *Gublu* in Babylonian, and *Kupni* in Egyptian. Perhaps a more plausible view is that the Greek form of that place-name was in part due to the assonance, and in part to the knowledge of the role played by Byblus in the diffusion of papyrus. That this writing-material was widely used at an early date throughout Palestine and Syria is wellnigh certain, but there is no indisputable evidence. In Babylonian and Assyrian reliefs of the eighth century and later two scribes are often depicted, the one writing on a clay tablet and the other upon some flexible material which Breasted took for papyrus, but which R. P. Dougherty has shown to be leather.[1] On the other hand, Breasted was able to point to a relief from Zenjirli where an Aramaean scribe carries under his arm an undoubted Egyptian palette.

More important even than the Egyptian origin of the principal writing-material used by the Greeks would be their debt in connexion with the alphabet, if it could be proved beyond a peradventure that Egypt was the source. Herodotus (v. 58) explicitly states that the Ionians derived their letters from the Phoenicians, and a comparison of the earliest forms places the relationship beyond a doubt. Which people of the two were the originators is indicated by the Greek letter-names, of which some, e.g. *alpha*, Hebr. *âleph* 'ox', *bêta*, Hebr. *bêth* 'house', *delta*, Hebr. *dâleth* 'door', are common Semitic words. However, the further question whence the Phoenicians themselves derived their script has been and still is a matter of endless controversy. The present writer is none too well placed to be an impartial judge in this matter, since he was the actual author of the hypothesis which counts the largest number of adherents. The issue is, however, so vital to the present chapter, that the *pros* and *cons* must necessarily be given a large place. To simplify exposition I find it easiest to drop the pronoun of the third person and to tell my story directly.

Some twenty-five years ago the Egypt Exploration Fund entrusted the late Professor Peet and myself with the publication of the inscriptions discovered and copied by Sir Flinders Petrie at Serâbît el-Khâdim in central Sinai. Most were written

[1] See *Am. J. Sem. Lang. Lit.*, xxxii. 230 ff. and *J. Am. Or. Soc.* xlviii. 2. 109 ff. I owe the latter reference to Mr. Gadd.

in Egyptian hieroglyphic and were votive stelae, statues, or the like dedicated by Egyptian officials in the local temple amidst the turquoise mines that explain the object of their quest. Included among the materials handed over to us were copies of ten rock tablets carved in characters of which some were clearly borrowed from the hieroglyphs, whilst others were equally clearly not so borrowed. Reluctantly we turned to the study of these enigmatic texts, for there seemed little hope of eliciting their nature. Almost the first sign to attract my attention was the ox-head at the beginning (top right) of the inscription reproduced in Plate I, fig. 1. This brought to mind the old contention of Gesenius that the prototypes of the Phoenician letters must originally have had the shapes indicated by the Hebrew letter-names, and accordingly I exclaimed to my companion 'Surely we must here have the origin of the Phoenician *âleph*'. His reply was not encouraging, so there the matter rested for several weeks. On taking up the problem afresh, my first step was to see what confirmation of my surmise could be found. To my astonishment, almost perfect equivalents were at once forthcoming for *bêth* 'house' ⬛, ⌂, *mêm* 'water' 𐤌— the Egyptians always depicted water as a zigzag line ∿—'*ayin* 'eye' ◁ and *rêsh* 'head' ⌐, besides others for one reason or another less convincing. The total number of different signs contained in these inscriptions did not exceed thirty-two and of these some might well be variants; the natural inference was that the writing was alphabetic. But if so, there would have to be some sequences of letters which would yield indi-

vidual words. It was easy to isolate one sequence of four letters that occurred no less than six times; a typical example is given in the adjoining cut. Applying my principle, I read the first sign as *b*, the second as '(*ayin*)—this is a peculiar guttural sound not heard in English—and the last as *t*—the Hebrew letter-name *tau* means 'a mark' and the Phoenician form is † or ✗ The third sign puzzled me, since it was not clear what it represented. Running my eye down the Phoenician alphabet in the first reference book that came to hand, I naturally stopped at *lâmedh* ∠, though here the hook was at the bottom, not at the top. Disregarding this trifling difficulty, I now read Ba'alat, the female Ba'al, familiar as the designation of a prominent Semitic goddess. Were then the enigmatic tablets votive offerings to Ba'alat? I had the strongest reasons for believing it, since (1) the regular Egyptian translation of the Semitic divine name Ba'alat was Hathor (so at Byblus) and (2) the goddess of the temple of Serâbît was well-known to be 'Hathor, lady of the Turquoise', her name occurring on a large majority of the hieroglyphic inscriptions there found.

Thus, without any forcing or *parti pris* on my part, by the mere combination of a few simple observations with a few established facts, the Sinai texts in the unknown script had yielded the precise name one might most have expected to find there. Could this be mere coincidence? I thought and still think not. But if not, obviously I had hit upon the origin of our alphabet, for the train of reasoning employed formed a rigid system, and if the conclusion were accepted, it would be wellnigh impossible to deny the premises. In other words, but for an almost unbelievable chance, the name Ba'alat is the true reading and demonstrates a genetic relationship between the Egyptian hieroglyphs, the Sinai characters, and the Phoenician letters with their traditional names. It was only some years later, after the conclusion of the War of 1914–18, that there came into my hands an article by the Göttingen scholar Kurt Sethe written about the same time as my own, in which by a number of brilliant *a priori* arguments he sought to prove that the Phoenician alphabet must have been derived, though with the employment of much originality and genius on the part of its Semitic inventor, from the Egyptian hieroglyphs. In particular Sethe elaborated Schäfer's argument that the absence of vowels common to Egyptian and the scripts akin to Phoenician could be due only to a causal nexus between latter and former. This conclusion is admitted in the recent monograph by the late Professor Bauer, one of the most strenuous opponents of the Sinai hypothesis. When at last my own article came to Sethe's knowledge, he espoused its conclusions with enthusiasm, and his second article proved the starting-point for nearly two hundred papers and books that have supported or disputed my contention from every angle. Three American expeditions organized by Professor Kirsopp Lake and a Finnish one led by Professor Hjelt have increased the number of proto-Sinaitic inscriptions found at Serâbît from ten to thirty-six, few of them, however, well preserved and some offering no more than two or three signs. In summing up the result of all these labours and discoveries it must be frankly admitted that the outcome has been disappointing. About half a dozen words or phrases appear to have been identified with probability, but for none except the name Ba'alat does convergent confirmatory evidence exist to prove the identification, nor can we point to such self-verification as would ensue if any of the inscriptions could be convincingly translated from beginning to end. Certain scholars like Butin and Grimme have, indeed, published translations, but the supposed import does not inspire confidence, and few experts would be ready to accept their versions as the true message of the Sinai texts.

Happily, however, this negative result has been offset by striking new testimony from Palestine itself. It was Albright who first observed the resemblance to the Sinai characters borne by a three-letter inscription found at Tell el-Hesi by Bliss in 1891. A similar fragment of pottery from Gezer shows as one of its signs a clear hand suggesting *yôdh* or *kâf*; this fragment has been assigned to a very early age, several scholars dating it to the first half of the second millennium. Much more disputed are the date and nature of a sherd inscribed in

PLATE I

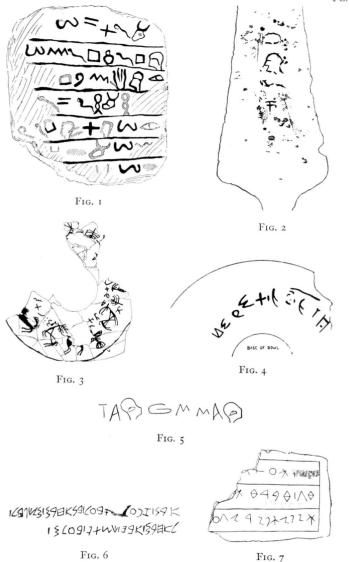

Fig. 1

Fig. 2

Fig. 3

Fig. 4

BASE OF BOWL

Fig. 5

Fig. 6

Fig. 7

EARLY SEMITIC ALPHABETIC WRITING

1. Serâbît el-Khâdim, no. 349. 2. The Tell el-Duweir dagger. 3. The Tell el-Duweir ewer. 4. The Tell el-Duweir bowl. 5. The Shechem plaque. 6. From the sarcophagus of Ahirâm. 7. Inscription from Byblus.

ink from Beth Shemesh, the characters upon which are certainly archaic but not pictorial. Of greater importance is the series of inscriptions discovered by the foully murdered excavator Starkey at Tell el-Duweir (Lachish). Of these the oldest is a dagger bearing four letters placed vertically (see Plate I, fig. 2), the second of them a clear head like that common at Serâbît, and the third possibly but not certainly a snake. The dagger is dated by Starkey 'perhaps before, but not later than 1600 B.C.' Next in order of development is a ewer bearing ten or eleven letters clearly less pictorial, which Starkey placed without hesitation at the beginning of the thirteenth century B.C. (Plate I, fig. 3). Several of the signs correspond pretty obviously to Serâbît characters on the one hand, and to Phoenician letters on the other. The zigzag for *m*, the cross for *t*, and the snake for *n* are confidently interpreted by many as the common Hebrew word *mattân* 'gift of . . .', and the probability of this interpretation is enhanced by the presence, after these letters, of three dots, obviously a word-divider as in certain early Greek inscriptions. Further along are a *lâmedh* with the crook at the bottom as in Phoenician and Latin, and an *âleph* that no longer much resembles an ox-head, but has affinities with the *âleph* of the Moabite Stone on the one hand, and with a Greek *alpha* on the other. A third text from Tell el-Duweir (Pl. I, fig. 4)[1] has a combination of five letters followed by a word-divider like that on the inscription of Ahirâm (see below), and Hebraists and Serâbîtists alike have joined hands in reading these letters as *beshelôsheth* 'for the third time'. Here we are nearer to Phoenician both in graphic development and in date; Starkey assigns the bowl to the third quarter of the thirteenth century, Yeivin to the fourth. If the first character on the bowl ⋃ be really *bêth*, then the divergency

---

[1] Doubts have been felt as to which way up this inscription should be placed. I have followed the opinion of J. Obermann, who places it in such a way that it reads from left to right.

between the Sinaitic form □ and the Phoenician 𐤁 is neatly bridged over. A last discovery to be mentioned is the most important of all, since it emanated from Shechem, nearly as far north as Samaria (Pl. I, fig. 5). On the Shechem plaque we again have the human head supposed to be *rêsh*, and the zigzag for *mêm*, reduced to a form uncommonly like a Greek *m*; if the sign twice seen to the left of the head is really *âleph*, it resembles the Greek and Latin forms more than it does the Phoenician. Archaeologists seem agreed in assigning the plaque to about the same time as the Lachish dagger.

Observe now what these discoveries in Philistia and Palestine have revealed. In the first place we find the Sinai script creeping up in the direction of Phoenicia, and obviously wide-spread in its use during the centuries preceding 1200 B.C. In the second place we can trace at Tell el-Duweir a gradual reduction of pictorial to non-pictorial letters, the latter bearing an ever closer resemblance to Phoenician. The difficulties of translation still remain a serious obstacle, but the Palestinian discoveries have very greatly enhanced the likelihood of the Serâbît theory.

Why then have scholars of the calibre of Bauer and Dussaud, not to mention others, so resolutely set their faces against that theory? The failure to produce satisfactory translations of the Sinai texts has undoubtedly been a powerful factor, and the wild speculations of some of my successors have not unnaturally created an anti-Serâbît prejudice. A more solid reason, however, was afforded by Montet's discovery of the sarcophagus of King Ahirâm at Byblus in 1923. Since fragments of two vases bearing the name of Ramesses II (1292–1223 B.C.) were found in the same tomb, the writings on this sarcophagus were at once hailed as the oldest Phoenician inscriptions extant; see Plate I, fig. 6. Not only were they translatable without any great difficulty, but also the forms of the letters closely resembled those of the other earliest Phoenician monuments, though none of the latter could be dated earlier than the end of the tenth century B.C.—to the statue of Abiba'al, bearing the names of Shoshenk I and published by Dussaud at the same time as the sarcophagus, was soon added another statue commemorating a third king of Byblus named Eliba'al, this showing the pre-nomen of Osorkon I. Still more remarkable was the apparently very slight change in the Phoenician writing right down to the fourth century before our era. Dussaud and Bauer are correct in stating that the letter-forms of Ahirâm are, if anything, still more unlike the objects signified by the Hebrew letter-names than the forms on the Moabite Stone (about 842 B.C.). Thus Ahirâm's *âleph* is 𝕂, where the supposed muzzle of the ox has completely vanished and the horns are a very doubtful quantity; the *mêm* 𝄢 is upright, and consequently ceases to show any similarity to the Egyptian sign for water 〰. The *bêth, dâleth,* '*ayin* and *rêsh* are no more like a house, a door, an eye, or a human head than they were five centuries later. In fact Gesenius' theory of the original conformity of letter-forms and letter-names appeared to vanish into smoke.

Impelled by these considerations, Dussaud emphatically re-asserted the claims of the Phoenicians to have been the real inventors of the alphabet. 'At the first attempt', he wrote, 'they attained perfection; the deformations which time has brought about in their system have not improved it.' Perhaps Bauer is the only other Semitist who has strongly defended this curious analogy to the theological doctrine of special creation, his recent monograph quoting several examples of native tribes that have similarly fabricated complete systems of writing of their own. The reasons which swayed Dussaud and Bauer were, however, sufficiently potent to turn many students against the Serâbît hypothesis, some reviving de Rougé's quite untenable theory of a derivation of the Phoenician alphabet from the Egyptian hieratic script, while others looked for an explanation to a new-comer into this controversial field, the cuneiform alphabet of Râs Shamra. That new alphabet from a coast-town a full hundred miles north of Byblus is a very notable discovery in the domain of early epigraphy, and the perspicacity with which its decipherers Bauer, Dhorme, and Virolleaud have unravelled the texts written by its means is worthy of the deepest respect. Still, it is difficult to see what importance this discovery can possess for the history of the Greek and Phoenician alphabets. The most plausible explanation of the Râs Shamra script is that it was invented by a community which had recognized the usefulness of purely alphabetic writing as employed by their southern neighbours, but felt itself too much tied by its clay writing-material and its centuries-old addiction to the wedge-shaped (cuneiform) characters of Babylonia to abandon these completely. The sole sidelight which on this view could be cast by the Râs Shamra tablets upon the problem of the Phoenician alphabet would be to suggest its existence as early as the fourteenth century, since it seems certain that the tablets go back to that date.

It is impossible here to do more than glance at the complications offered by the discovery, also at Byblus, of an inscription in a new, entirely unparalleled hieroglyphic script, and by the evidence to be found in the ancient alphabets of Arabia, namely the Thamûdic and the Sabaean. The latter, so far as they sway the balance in any direction at all, obviously do so on the side of the Serâbît hypothesis. For us it is more important to revert to the sarcophagus of Ahirâm. If the dating to the reign of Ramesses II be correct, then it would indeed present an obstacle, though perhaps not an insurmountable one, to the theory proposed by myself. Accordingly several Serâbîtists have cast doubt upon that date. If this should seem a rather arbitrary proceeding, at least it has in its favour the extraordinary similarity of Ahirâm's alphabet to that of the two statues of the Egyptian Twenty-second Dynasty mentioned above. As eminent an epigraphist as Lidzbarski took the view that Ahirâm must be later than the date attributed to him by Montet and Dussaud, and similar doubts have been expressed in more than one other competent quarter. Albright is inclined to place the tomb round about 1100 B.C. upon the basis of the potsherds found in it. However this may be, I myself must venture upon the remark that even if the Ramesside date be maintained, typologically the letter-forms of Ahirâm can hardly be early ones. As regards the letter *âleph*, the Moabite Stone and the earliest inscriptions of Zenjirli far away in the north of Syria agree in showing the muzzle of the ox, which moreover is very clearly presupposed by the oldest Greek forms, and in view of the great distances involved, the eccentric form used by Ahirâm cannot well be the common ancestor. The Moabite stone and early Greek inscriptions agree in showing a horizontal *mêm*, and the oldest Zenjirli form is at any rate not vertical. To add to the difficulties of Dussaud's theory, there has now emerged at Byblus a linear inscription of undetermined date which Dunand, its discoverer, considers to be Phoenician (Pl. I, fig. 7), and to this Ahirâm must apparently yield the priority. Thus we are forced to the conclusion that the demonstrative value of the sarcophagus has been considerably overrated. Furthermore, no serious attempt is made by either Bauer or Dussaud to account for the proto-Sinaitic inscriptions, which are merely pushed aside as tentative essays in the direction of alphabetic writing. Let it be admitted, accordingly, that the Serâbît hypothesis remains an hypothesis, and that barely one-half of the alphabet can as yet claim to have received well-grounded explanation, but the cumulative evidence in its favour completely outweighs that in favour of any alternative theory hitherto advanced.

The date of the Sinai inscriptions has been much disputed. I had thought it likely that they belonged to the close of the Twelfth Dynasty, but Sethe preferred attribution to the Hyksos period. Butin returned to my view, but the evidence is slight, and this point is best left in abeyance.

Assuming the Serâbît theory to be correct, exactly how much

does the modern world owe the Egyptians in connexion with the alphabet? It owes at least some of the letter-forms, but that is no great debt, since any shapes might serve equally well, and in our own alphabet hardly anything is left of the original pictorial appearance. The *idea* of alphabetic writing is, however, a very great achievement. Can it be said that we are indebted to the Egyptians for that? Hardly, I think, since the presence of alphabetic signs in the complex hieroglyphic system was accidental rather than designed. One principle underlying the hieroglyphs was that of the rebus or charade, little pictures being taken to signify, not the things which they represented, but the sounds of the words denoting those things. Thus ⊓, the picture of a house, received the value *p+r* because the Egyptian word for a house was *pôr*, whence—the vowels being felt as of little account—the hieroglyph ⊓ was adopted for the writing of a number of other words, e.g. *pîre* 'to go forth', which possessed the sounds *p+r* in that order, Now since some of the signs thus phonetically used were taken from uniconsonantal words like ⇔ *ro* 'mouth', alphabetic letters (in this case *r*) were automatically obtained without any deliberate intention, and these remained embedded in the hieroglyphic system side by side with biconsonantal, triconsonantal, and purely pictorial signs. In other terms, the Egyptians themselves never discerned the great advantages of an alphabet unmixed with other graphic elements. The recognition of those advantages was the achievement of a Semitic people, and is a glory that can never be taken from them. To the Egyptians we do owe, however—always granting the Serâbît hypothesis—the all-important discovery of the possibility of phonetic writing.

If Greece was thus indebted to Egypt both for her writing-material and for the very technique of writing, may she not also have had some similar obligation in respect of her literature? A case for such an obligation might possibly be based upon the insistence with which Greek authors point to Egypt as the source of their philosophy. Thales, Solon, Pythagoras, Democritus of Abdera, and Plato are all asserted to have visited Egypt and to have sat at the feet of the Egyptian priests. Of Pythagoras it is even related that he had been initiated into ancient Egyptian literature by the high-priest Sonchis. And where philosophy owed so great a debt, could *belles lettres* owe none at all? The answer to such an argument would begin by showing that the supposed dependence of Greek upon Egyptian philosophy proves on examination to be the merest moonshine. Thales may indeed have travelled in Egypt, but if he did so he could hardly have come into close relations with the priests, who, moreover, would have looked with extreme disfavour upon his purely physical speculations. As for the other sages above enumerated, it is significant that the reports of their voyages become frequent only as the distance from their historical lifetime widens. The explanation of the Greek tradition is twofold. On the one hand, it acquires intensity only at a time when the Ptolemies had made themselves the masters of Egypt and the priesthoods of Heliopolis, Memphis, and Thebes felt their authority seriously challenged. In such a situation their insistence upon the priority of their own civilization would become increasingly vocal. On the other hand, just at the same time the Greeks, weary of two centuries of purely intellectual discussion, were beginning to seek refuge in mysticism and the revival of religion, and thus were willing enough to give ear to the Egyptian claims, provided that the crudities of the old mythology might be mitigated by purely Hellenic allegorical interpretations. Again, if we examine the actual literature of the Greeks and Romans, little or no trace of Egyptian influence can be detected. Under the Ptolemies and Romans Alexandria was an entirely Greek city, deemed by its inhabitants to be adjacent to Egypt (*Alexandria ad Aegyptum*), but not in it. Callimachus and Theocritus are purely Greek in both feeling and expression. The quality of such pretensions as the Egyptians had to be the inspirers of Greek literature is indicated by the assertion of Heliodorus, in the third century of our era, that Homer was the son of the god Thoth by the wife of an Egyptian priest.

Nevertheless, in a vaguer and less direct way, it is barely deniable that the earlier literatures of Egypt and Babylonia supplied something of the stimulus which spurred on the Greeks to their sublime achievements in the fields of poetry and prose. Our own ignorance until comparatively recently prevented us from realizing how far those older civilizations formed for the Greeks themselves their conscious intellectual background. The Phoenicians must have carried tidings of the vast learning and ceaseless scribal activity of the Egyptians. Distorted versions of genuine Egyptian stories will have been wafted to the shores of Greece—who knows to what extent an imperceptible and undefinable literary pressure starting in the old Egyptian culture may not there have been exerted? It is useless, however, to dwell upon possibilities so intangible, and we pass on, therefore, to a more profitable topic, namely the question as to what influence Egypt may have had upon the Old Testament, and through this upon our own literary tradition.

Excavation has revealed ever more clearly the extent to which Palestinian culture was dependent upon the land of the Pharaohs. The most obvious evidence is of a material kind—scarabs, pottery, faience, ivories, and weapons. These must necessarily, however, have had an intellectual counterpart. There was opportunity enough for both the Israelites and their predecessors in Canaan to become acquainted with Egyptian literature. Whatever the reality behind the Exodus narratives, the fact of the invasion of the Delta by the Hyksos and their subsequent expulsion is sufficient guarantee that southern Palestine was largely inhabited by descendants of a people that had once dwelt in Egypt. From the Eighteenth Dynasty onward right down to Greek times the Egyptians were in constant contact with their north-easterly neighbours either as conquerors or as traders. In Ramesside times witness is borne to the intensive traffic between the two countries by the number of Semitic words which were adopted into the Egyptian tongue, and Hebrew similarly displays a considerable number of loan-words taken over from Egypt. An erudite, but none too judicious scholar recently wrote a large book to show that the language of the Pentateuch is absolutely permeated with Egyptian idioms. He has doubtless greatly exaggerated his thesis, but there may well have been more borrowing than is actually demonstrable. A celebrated satirical composition contained in the first Anastasi papyrus draws a vivid picture of the journeyings of Egyptian scribes in Philistia and Syria, and from such visitors the natives will have learnt something of the Egyptian classics. Nor did this intercourse slacken appreciably when, after the close of the Twentieth Dynasty, disruption and feebleness befell the land of Egypt. In the reign of Solomon, who ascended the throne about 970 B.C., the friendship between Israel and Egypt was particularly close, and it was just about this time that Hebrew literary activity began to bear its first-fruits.

Happily the dependence of the so-called Wisdom literature upon Egyptian models is no mere speculation, but can be demonstrated by cogent testimony. The best proof is afforded by one of the six collections of sayings which together constitute the canonical book known as The Proverbs of Solomon. Almost every verse in Prov. xxii. 17–xxiii. 11 finds its fellow in an Egyptian didactic work that came to our knowledge about fifteen years ago. The Teaching of Amenope is found in a papyrus purchased for the British Museum by the late Sir E. Wallis Budge, and first edited by him. The date of the actual manuscript is not quite certain, but Griffith, a judge of the highest qualifications, placed it somewhere between the Twenty-first Dynasty and the reign of Darius. The composition of the book may have been a good deal earlier, and competent authorities

date it to about 1000 B.C. A longish introduction describes
the purpose of the book and the personalities of the author and
of the young son to whom, in accordance with traditional
custom, its counsels were addressed. Then follow the counsels
themselves in thirty chapters or, as the Egyptians and the Arabs
after them were wont to say, 'houses'; cf. the Italian *stanza*.
Budge had been struck by the resemblance of two of the precepts to others found in the Hebrew Proverbs, but it was
Erman who first brought to light the full range of the parallelism. Since then many scholars have dealt with the subject, and
complete unanimity exists as to the dependence of the one book
upon the other. Perhaps the most tempting observation of all
is concerned with a verse near the beginning of the section of
Proverbs here in question. The first words of that section are
strikingly similar to the Egyptian:

> (Prov. xxii. 17)[1] Incline thine ear and hear my words,
>   And apply thine heart to learn (them).

For this Amenope has:

> Give thine ears, hearken to the things I have said,
> Give thy heart to understand them.

In what immediately follows Amenope is fuller than Proverbs,
but the thought is the same. Some phrases are common to both:
where the Hebrew has 'For it is a pleasant thing if thou keep
them in thy belly, and if they be ready prepared upon thy lips',
the Egyptian gives 'Let them rest in the casket of thy belly,
that they may serve as threshold to thy heart, and that when a
hurricane of words arises, they may be a mooring-post for thy
tongue'. After one verse not paralleled in Amenope comes the
crucial passage, rendered thus in the Revised Version (Prov.
xxii. 20–1):

[1] For Proverbs I quote from the renderings of Oesterley, who bases them
on a less conservative text than that used by the Revised Version.

Have I not written unto thee excellent things
Of counsels and knowledge;
To make thee know the certainty of the words of truth,
That thou mayest carry back words of truth to them that send thee.

A marginal note to 'excellent things' says 'the word is doubtful'. In point of fact this translation rests on the slenderest of grounds. The Hebrew text has *shilshôm* 'formerly', which is unsuitable in this context, and so the original Hebrew editors have felt, for they give in their margin *shalîshîm* 'officers', which, however, is even more meaningless. By a slight change of pointing Erman read *shelôshîm* 'thirty', which yields a striking parallel to the opening words of the last section in Amenope: 'Consider these thirty chapters.' It is true, of course, that the passage in Proverbs under discussion does not contain thirty chapters, but as Gressmann has shown, it does consist of exactly thirty different precepts. Thus, if the Hebrew writer borrowed his 'thirty' from the Egyptian original, he did not do so meaninglessly or purely mechanically, but adapted its sense to his own purpose.

It is possible, of course, that Erman's conjecture may have been mistaken ingenuity, but even were it so, the parallels to the entire section in Proverbs are far too numerous to be fortuitous. Space forbids the quotation of more of them here, but when it is pointed out that the subject-matter shared in common comprises advice not to oppress the poor, not to make friends with men given to anger, not to remove ancient landmarks, and not to strive after riches, the reader will see for himself that the comparisons have real substance. Still more remarkable is the fact that both compositions give counsel as to demeanour at the table of a powerful man, and that both comment upon the way riches have of taking flight like birds.

Now, while the relationship of Proverbs and Amenope is not contested by any scholar of standing, one at least has suggested that the obligation lay upon the Egyptian side, the author of

Amenope having used an earlier Hebrew collection of precepts.
It is claimed that the Teaching of Amenope is too religious and
too truly ethical to be regarded merely as the last example of
a long line of Egyptian didactic treatises. No Egyptologist is
likely to subscribe to such a view, which takes insufficient
account of the ever-growing tendency to monotheism manifest
in all Egyptian writings of post-Akhenaton times. New evidence
of this can be found, for instance, in the maxims incorporated
in the recently published Chester Beatty Papyrus No. IV, where
reference is more than once made to the will of God and to the
kind of conduct demanded by Him. A strong argument in
favour of the priority of Amenope concerns a passage already
alluded to. The reference to behaviour at the table of a prominent man goes back to the oldest of all Egyptian moralizing
works, namely to the Precepts of Kagemni and the Maxims of
Ptahhotpe, both of them at least as old as the Twelfth Dynasty.

A well-documented and persuasive book by Paul Humbert
extends the same argument to a wider field, and discovers
Egyptian influence in Job, Ecclesiastes, the Wisdom of Ben-
Sirach (Ecclesiasticus), Tobit, the third book of Esdras, and the
story of Achikar. The author has industriously ferreted out all
passages which could lend support to his thesis, and uses them
with discretion and able self-criticism. The one thing we miss
is attention to the rival claims of Babylonia, but so far as the
restricted domain of the Wisdom literature is concerned, the
Hebrews seem unlikely to have derived much from that quarter.
It is indisputable that the Book of Job transports us into the
pessimistic atmosphere of several old Egyptian compositions,
among which the *Dialogue of the Pessimist with his Soul* is the
most interesting example. Humbert scores many good points
in matters of detail. The monster Leviathan, for instance,
seems to bear more resemblance to the serpent Apopis, the
enemy of Rêʿ, than it does to the Babylonian divinity Tiâmat;
and Job's protestations of innocence are undeniably reminiscent

of the Negative Confessions in the Book of the Dead. It is clear, of course, that any such utilization of ancient material could in no way detract from the sublime genius of the Book of Job, and in spite of the suggestive descriptions of the ostrich, the hippopotamus, and the crocodile in Job. 39–41, it is perhaps going too far to infer that the writer had lived in Egypt. As regards the other Hebrew books discussed by Humbert it is impossible here to review his evidence, but mention must at least be made of Ecclesiasticus xxxviii. 24–39, where the son of Sirach descants upon the profession of the scribe and its superiority over other callings. This theme is a commonplace of the Ramesside literary Miscellanies, which derive their inspiration from a much earlier work, the so-called 'Satire of the Trades'. The occupations characterized by Ben-Sirach by way of contrast, those of the field-labourer, the carver in stone, the metal-worker, and the potter, are all among the occupations treated in the Egyptian original.

There is no issue raised in the study of mankind more controversial or more strictly unprovable than that of the influence of one people upon another, and the well-worn debate between diffusionists and their opponents is unlikely ever to result in agreed conclusions. That fact must be borne in mind in judging the suggestions of the last few pages. This portion of my chapter may be fittingly summed up in the sober words with which the late Professor Peet closed his brilliant Schweich lectures on the compared literatures of Egypt, Palestine, and Mesopotamia:

'This literature (i.e. that of Egypt) seems to have run to seed in later times, and it was left for a greater nation, the Greeks, to make the advances in conception which alone made literature in the modern sense possible. At the same time, Greek literature cannot have sprung full-grown like Venus from the waves, any more than did Greek art, and though we may never learn the manner in which Egyptian influence made its way into Hebrew and into Greek literature, it may reasonably be doubted whether either the one or the other would have been what it is had it not been for Egypt.'

Having taken the word 'legacy' in the title of this book more seriously than was perhaps intended by the publishers of the series, I have left myself but little space for dealing with the second kind of inheritance adumbrated in my opening paragraph. This omission is the less serious, however, because the English reader has now access, not only to the lectures by Peet just mentioned, where the literary merits of three ancient literatures are carefully examined and appraised, but also to Adolf Erman's *Literature of the Ancient Egyptians* (translation by A. M. Blackman), in which all the principal pieces known up to about fifteen years ago may be read in their entirety. It will perhaps best serve the purpose of this book if I give a brief sketch of the history of literary activity in Egypt, interspersed with some observations on the value to ourselves of its manifestations.

The literature of Ancient Egypt appears to be a wholly indigenous product. That there was some mutual influence between Babylonia and Egypt near the beginning of the dynastic period is now certain, and it is even not impossible that the impulse which led to the evolution of hieroglyphic writing came from the Sumerians. But just as the art and architecture of Egypt, once started upon their course, rapidly found characteristic forms, and soon surpassed all rivals, so too, though a good deal more slowly, did Egyptian literature. What folk-tales, hymns, ritual compositions, and the like may have been current orally before the emergence of the hieroglyphs we can never know, but it seems likely that the newly acquired technique of writing was felt rather as an embarrassment than otherwise. The earliest attempts at autobiography found in the tombs are bald in the extreme, and if the letter from a king of the Sixth Dynasty to a noble who had returned from the Sudan with a 'dwarf of the dances' for his lord's delectation, pleases on account of its pictur-

esque *naïveté*, yet the intimations that we obtain of Old Kingdom literary style are far from encouraging. The semi-magical
spells of the Pyramid Texts are at once inhuman, disjointed, and
diffuse. It is possible that the moralizing books of Kagemni and
Ptahhotpe go back to the Fifth Dynasty, but such admiration
as they may excite will be a tribute to their worldly wisdom
rather than to their literary quality. The Egyptians themselves
reverenced Imhôtep and Hardedef as incomparable sages, but
nothing remains of their books, if ever they wrote any. One
autobiographical narrative, that of the Vizier Weni, incorporates
a short triumphal poem, each new thought being introduced
by a refrain:

> This army returned in peace,
> > It had hacked to bits the land of the Sand-dwellers.
> This army returned in peace,
> > It had crushed the land of the Sand-dwellers.

Such monotonous repetition is not infrequent even in some of
the finer compositions of later times, and the best that can be
said of it is that it shows a striving after literary form.

Thus it is impossible to agree with Peet's conjecture that the
lost literature of the Old Kingdom, like its art and architecture,
may well have transcended everything that came later. All the
more astonishing are the creations of the times of unrest following the close of the Sixth Dynasty. Here metaphor runs riot,
and decadent features like a deliberate preciosity are not want-
ing. One Twelfth-Dynasty writer pathetically complains of the
difficulty of finding anything new to say, in fact there is abundant evidence that literature was now an art supremely conscious of itself. Most connoisseurs of Egyptian antiquities will
have felt at some time or other that the general standard is very
low, but they will have taken comfort at the recollection of a
few pieces of incomparable beauty and grace. If it is scarcely
possible to say as much of Egyptian literature, nevertheless the
Middle Kingdom presents examples of a high order. My own

favourite remains the Story of Sinuhe, the tale of an Egyptian who, overhearing by accident the tidings of the violent death of King Ammenemes I, fled to Palestine and there rose to a position of eminence and esteem. There is a graphic account of his fight with an envious Syrian brave. In old age Sinuhe was overcome by longing for his own country, and the lyrical passage describing the way in which his desire came to the ears of Pharaoh has both poetry and subtlety. A copy of the royal letter of recall is inserted at this point, together with Sinuhe's adulatory answer to it. Could a better method have been devised of conveying an Egyptian's deep sense of the honour conferred upon him, or revealing the reciprocal attitudes of sovereign and subject? Yet Peet does not mince words in his condemnation of this passage! *De gustibus!* The narrative of the homeward journey, of Sinuhe's reception at the court, and of the honours heaped upon him, could hardly be bettered. A delicious touch occurs where it is told how the queen and the little princesses are ushered in to see the travel-stained and outlandishly clad exile:

'Then His Majesty said to the Royal Consort: Behold Sinuhe who has come as an Asiatic, the offspring of Setiu-folk. She gave a great cry, and the Royal Children shrieked out all together. And they said to His Majesty: It is not really he, O Sovereign my lord. And His Majesty said: Yes, it is really he!'

In the small compass of three hundred and fifty lines a life of adventure is recounted from start to finish, and a personality portrayed with consummate skill. We see Sinuhe alternately panic-stricken, a self-confident fighter, a humble suppliant, and then again overcome by awe in the presence of the king of Egypt. Humour and pathos are there, bombast too—and why not, since bombast was a genuinely Egyptian trait? I am not prepared to recant my former estimate of this tale.[1]

[1] I cannot refrain from quoting the letter of a great writer, to whom I had confided my belief that the Story of Sinuhe could rank as a world-classic:

There are extant from the Middle Kingdom only two more stories of any length, the Shipwrecked Sailor and the Eloquent Peasant, the former relating how a sailor was thrown on a desert island, where he conversed with a gigantic serpent, and the latter containing the long and tedious complaints of a peasant who had been robbed of his merchandise. A characteristic *genre* of the earlier part of this period is the pessimistic literature, among which the already mentioned dialogue of a disappointed man with his soul is the most interesting specimen. Another composition of the kind, the Admonitions of an Egyptian Sage, describes a topsy-turvy world in which everything is awry, the poor usurping the place of the rich, foreigners invading the land, no respect and no virtue anywhere; yet a redeemer is at hand. This is poor stuff from the literary point of view, but is interesting early evidence of the cyclic recurrence of revolutionary reversals of fortune. There are two royal 'Teachings' of King Merikarê and King Ammenemes I respectively—they might be described as political testaments. The latter is of some beauty and has a dignity of its own, but unhappily portions are too corrupt and otherwise unintelligible for us to fathom their literary worth. Reference has been made above to the Satire of the Trades. This concludes pretty well all that has survived from the Middle Kingdom, except the panegyric of a king and some fragments of songs and hymns.

How much we are at the mercy of chance for our knowledge of Egyptian literature is shown by the fact that hardly any original composition of the flourishing Eighteenth Dynasty has survived. The fragments of a tale on the insatiable greed of the sea suggests that we have lost things of real merit, and there are unpublished scraps of a book on the joys of fishing and fowling

'Semiramis Hotel, Cairo, Feb. 20. 29. Dear Mr. Gardiner, Thank you ever so much for the book of Egyptian literature, and I quite agree with you as to your estimate of the tale you specially admire. Very sincerely yours, Rudyard Kipling.'

which open up new perspectives. The Tale of Cheops and the Magicians perhaps dates from the Hyksos period. Like the stories of Ramesside times, among which the best-known are the Tale of the Two Brothers and that of the Doomed Prince, it is simpler in expression than the works of the Middle Kingdom; both the best and the worst features of that sophisticated age have been discarded. It is in the hymns of the Akhenaton period that the compositions of the New Kingdom attain their highest level, always excepting the papyrus recording the misadventures of Wenamûn in Syria and some lyrical poetry to be mentioned later. The story of Wenamûn is a puzzle. It dates from the very end of the Twentieth Dynasty, an epoch otherwise appearing completely destitute of real literary talent. We cannot tell for certain whether this story is history or fiction. It deals with the times when Herihor had just climbed into sacerdotal power at Thebes, and when the credit of Egypt was at its lowest in Syria. Wenamûn had been dispatched to fetch wood to construct the sacred barque of Amûn, and the narrative tells how he was robbed at Dor, snubbed by the prince of Byblus, and mobbed at a port to which his ship had been driven by a storm. And with it all the Egyptian envoy retains his pompous self-possession, the very image of a little effendi such as one might encounter in the streets of Cairo to-day. This tale is worthy to rank with the Story of Sinuhe.

The most extensive literary papyri which we possess from the New Kingdom are miscellanies containing model letters, and short compositions of various kinds. It is impossible to characterize or criticize these here, but in brief we may state that their interest is more psychological and cultural than literary. One effusion that gained great popularity in Ramesside times took the form of a satirical letter in which one scribe twits another for his incompetence, inventing various situations, including a voyage to Syria, wherein that incompetence is manifested. It is a clumsy production, revealing a heavy kind of humour. It will be news to some readers that the Egyptians had a sense of humour, but such is the fact, as much evidence could be brought to show.

This very incomplete sketch cannot be concluded without reference to the lyrical poetry of which we possess all too few and too unintelligible specimens. The love-songs might have been written by Heine himself. The quotation of one will be more eloquent than any description:

Seven days from yesterday I have not seen my beloved,
And sickness hath crept over me,
And I am become heavy in my limbs,
And am unmindful of mine own body.
If the master-physicians come to me,
My heart hath no comfort of their remedies,
And the magicians, no resource is in them,
My malady is not diagnosed.

. . . .

Better for me is my beloved than any remedies,
More important is she for me than the entire compendium of medicine.
My salvation is when she enters from without,
When I see her, then am I well;
Opens she her eye, my limbs are young again;
Speaks she, and I am strong.
And when I embrace her, she banishes evil,
And it passes from me for seven days.

Perhaps the only blemish in this, from the modern point of view, is the artificial introduction of the word 'seven' in the first and last lines. The poem comes from a book in which each love-song is ushered in and ended with a numeral, or with a pun upon it. A tedious device, but not enough to spoil the poem as a whole.

Another love-song runs as follows:

Mayst thou come to thy beloved quickly
Like a royal envoy whose lord is impatient for his message,

And his heart is set upon hearing it;
An envoy for whom all the stables have been requisitioned,
And he has horses at the resting-places,
And the chariot stands harnessed in its place,
Nor is there any breathing-space for him upon the road.
He hath reached the house of the beloved,
And his heart jubilates.

In quite another vein is a poem in praise of death from the wall of a Theban tomb, where it faces the famous Song of the Harper, the gist of which is: Eat, drink, and be merry, for to-morrow we die.

I have heard those songs that are in the ancient tombs, and what they tell extolling life on earth and belittling the region of the dead. Wherefore do they thus concerning the land of eternity, the just and fair, which has no terrors? Wrangling is its abhorrence, and no man there girds himself against his fellow. It is a land against which none can rebel; all our kinsfolk rest within it since the earliest day of time. The offspring of millions are come hither, every one. For none may tarry in the land of Egypt, none there is who has not passed yonder. The span of earthly things is as a dream; but a fair welcome is given to him who has reached the West.

A people that could write thus can surely lay claim to an honourable place in the fellowship of letters, even when judged by universal standards. But this is not the only value Egyptian literature has for us. The widened perspective that has been opened out by the labours of scholars is of no little intellectual importance. We can now trace the first gropings after beauty of diction, admire their achievements and regret their short-comings. A new measure is thereby obtained for estimating our own classics and for recognizing at once how little and how great our progress has been. Egyptological research will not have been in vain, if the general reader can derive from a statement of its results some part of the mental stimulus of which its adepts are conscious.

ALAN H. GARDINER

BIBLIOGRAPHICAL NOTE

For the problem of the alphabet see A. H. GARDINER, 'The Egyptian Origin of the Semitic Alphabet', in *Journal of Egyptian Archaeology*, vol. iii, pp. 1–16; K. SETHE, 'Der Ursprung des Alphabets', in *Nachrichten v. d. k. Gesellschaft d. Wissenschaften zu Göttingen*, 1916, Heft 2; and R. BUTIN's contributions to the *Harvard Theological Review*, Jan. 1928 and Apr 1932, and to *Studies and Documents*, ed. K. and S. Lake, London, 1936.

The influence of Egyptian thought upon Greek is ably studied in TH. HOPFNER, *Orient und griechische Philosophie*, Beihefte zum Alten Orient, No. 4, Leipzig 1925.

For the Teaching of Amenope and Egyptian influence in the Hebrew Wisdom literature, see P. HUMBERT, *Recherches sur les sources égyptiennes de la littérature sapientiale d'Israel*, Neuchâtel, 1929; W. O. E. OESTERLEY, *The Wisdom of Egypt and the Old Testament*, London, 1927.

Translations of most old Egyptian literary works will be found in A. ERMAN, *The Literature of the Ancient Egyptians*, translated into English by A. M. BLACKMAN, London, 1927, and for an excellent discussion of them see T. E. PEET, *A Comparative Study of the Literatures of Egypt, Palestine, and Mesopotamia*, being the Schweich Lectures for 1929, London, 1931.

CHAPTER 4

EGYPTIAN ART

MANY generations of Defoe's readers have smiled at Man Friday's amazement when his master, rescued at last from his island exile, introduced him to the noisy, glittering civilization of London. Yet any European of the fourteenth century B.C., unless he were an inhabitant of Minoan Crete, would have experienced the same feelings as Crusoe's faithful servant if he had had the chance to visit the new capital of Amenhôtep IV.

I shall ask the reader to join me in a rapid tour of this capital, Akhetaten, which rose from the desert at the will of a revolutionary Pharaoh. He will then appreciate, from the outset, the extent and originality of Egypt's achievement in the realm of art.

The city stretched along the river-bank for a good six miles, its districts grouped round the main sacred and imperial buildings, and linked by broad avenues and geometrically planned streets. On the principal thoroughfares stood the residences of the great court functionaries and imperial officials, surrounded by gardens with pools and summer-houses. Most of these dwellings were made to a set plan, with slight variations in each case, and comprised not only reception and domestic apartments, but also every additional convenience, such as bathrooms, which could minister to the comfort of the inhabitants. The temples and the main palace stood in the Royal Avenue, which ran parallel to the river. This avenue was spanned by a great brick bridge, joining the two wings of the palace, which lay on opposite sides of the road.

The architecture of these palaces in no way gives the impression of a piece of routine work, done to satisfy a client who wanted his residence enlarged by degrees. The plans show a real sense of design; there are spacious colonnaded courts, opening into magnificent reception halls, but there are also private apartments where life could be lived in comfortable and artistic surroundings. The walls were covered with large decorative designs, like veritable landscapes with green clumps of papyrus plants, thronged with many-coloured birds whose plumage lent brightness and gaiety to the ornamental waters. If the king should pass in solemn procession through one of his audience chambers, the floor-paintings would show him spurning under foot all the peoples whom he had conquered. The columns, which rose from the floor in the form of papyrus sheaves, seemed to spring from an expanse of water, full of flowers, and peopled with birds and fishes.

Further out, towards the desert, were the comfortable quarters of the police officials. Great roads branched out from the plain towards various points in the mountain. Here stood the stelae which recorded the foundation of the city, flanked by sculptures showing the king, the queen, and the princesses raising their arms towards the beneficent orb of the Sun, acknowledged as god of the universe.

One of the most interesting places to see in the city was, perhaps, the Northern Palace, which contained, among other marvels, a park with strange animals, kept there for the pleasure of the spectators.

Another sight—a special attraction, this, for art-lovers—would be the abode of Thutmose, the chief sculptor. The group of buildings included the private dwelling and workshop of the master, his foreman's house, and the quarters allotted to his work-people and apprentices. The artist's magnificent dwelling was scarcely inferior to those of the Prime Minister and the High-priest. Finally, since workmen's dwellings have been mentioned, reference must be made to the walled village near the cemetery, where the stone-masons, sculptors, and painters were housed in conditions more decent than those sometimes imposed on the workers of our great towns to-day.

It is unnecessary to pursue our imaginary visit to the City of

the Solar Disk. The point to be emphasized is that these buildings of the first half of the fourteenth century B.C., which owe
their existence to the orders and caprice of a revolutionary ruler,
are in fact, despite their novel appearance, only the full development of a technique which had been practised for twenty centuries previously. The perfection of the Amarna period was not
conceived in its entirety in the imaginative brain of Akhenaton.
He was only clothing in new forms a world which had long passed
its classical period. Two centuries later, we find a son of
Rameses II going over the Memphis cemeteries and restoring
on the pyramids of the Old Kingdom the names of kings which
had been effaced. Here lies the great mystery, the really
astonishing thing about the art of ancient Egypt; that it was
completed and brought to perfection so early, with its classical,
its revolutionary, and its romantic periods, reflecting, each in
its own way, the life of a people. A great art indeed, affording
the most complete and many-sided aesthetic enjoyment to those
who study it, an enjoyment tempered only by disappointment
that its origins should still be veiled in obscurity.

Any cultivated person who visits a large Egyptian collection
or who turns over the leaves of an illustrated book on Egyptian
art cannot fail to express some surprise at the perfection which
marks many of the works of the Dynastic period. How many
times have I not heard people say, when confronted with a real
masterpiece, 'Extraordinary—it doesn't look Egyptian at all!'
There are several excellent reasons for this attitude, and it is
worth while pausing for a moment to examine them.

Perhaps the chief reason has been an unfortunate extension
of modern theories of evolution. People imagine that they can
with impunity transfer these theories from the physical world
to the sphere of human phenomena. The inevitable result has
been that the art of classical Greece has been adopted as an
absolute standard of perfection, by which all earlier artistic

movements must be judged, and ranged in a scale of evolutionary progress. Thus none of these earlier movements could properly be placed on a higher rung of the evolutionary ladder, side by side with the perfect productions of the fifth century B.C. If we agree to use the term 'miracle' in the sphere of art, the error involved in this theory is the belief that the miracle of perfection can only occur once in the world's history.

It was actually the great discoveries made by Mariette which first induced artists and critics to pay serious attention to the problems of Egyptian art, and which led them to question the general views on the subject which had prevailed since the days of Winckelmann. It is worth while to read once again the enthusiastic notices written during the Exhibition of 1867, when Mariette was exhibiting to the Parisian public the diorite statue of Chephren and the Sheikh el Beled. It was as though the art of the Old Kingdom had revealed itself for the first time in all its splendour, though the 'Scribe' in the Louvre had been there for some years to bear witness to its magnificence. Three or even four thousand years before the Christian era, the sculptors of Memphis had reached perfection both in their unified conception of life and in their symbolic rendering of royal power. Towards the end of the nineteenth century, the unique discovery of the Dahshûr jewels added a whole chapter in itself to the history of ornament, and this chapter, also, revealed perfection.

A few years later, thanks to the efforts of English and German excavators, came the disconcerting revelation of the art of Tell el-Amarna. This revelation should have been enough to destroy, even in the minds of the most superficial observers, the fixed idea that the Dynastic art of Egypt was stationary. Finally, during the winter of 1922–3, the opening up of the tomb of Tutankhamen displayed to the entire world the splendour of the applied arts of the 18th Dynasty.

I have limited myself to recalling certain discoveries known even outside specialist circles. Yet for nearly a century the art of the ancient inhabitants of the Nile valley has constantly been revealing to these specialists—and by this I mean principally Egyptologists—new and more varied aspects of itself. But the faculties of Egyptology, still preoccupied with the perfecting of their philological technique, have hitherto failed to pay sufficient attention to the artistic aspect. In consequence Egyptian art has still to receive its due place in the general history of art; universities, even those of the leading countries, are inclined to sacrifice the achievements of Egyptian art to the handicrafts of savage races or the products of the Far East.

Certain branches of archaeology, whose existence was barely suspected at first, have been slowly formulated by an accumulation of fresh data, every addition to which makes clearer some aspect of the whole scene. Egyptian art has had a very different fate. Since the Renaissance, and, above all, since the time of Napoleon's Egyptian campaign, European scholars have claimed the right to pronounce judgement on it as a whole, to assess its achievements and define its limitations with reference to general standards of art. Europe's first contact with the art of the Pharaohs, it might perhaps be said, was made *en bloc*. In such circumstances, the most striking impression was bound to be that of continuity. In most of the works of Egyptian art permanent characteristics, it was thought, could be recognized, and these characteristics soon came to be regarded as an essential feature of this art. When they were found to be absent there was a tendency to speak of 'exceptions', of failure to conform to the rules.

Many years were needed before we first became accustomed to the extreme antiquity of these objects, and to the idea that centuries separated the periods of the most striking masterpieces. When we go back in thought over the history of western

Europe since the age of Augustus, we have necessarily to acquire a detailed acquaintance with the background in order to realize the significance of the great figures, from the first Roman emperor to Charlemagne, from Charlemagne to St. Louis, and then, by way of Louis XIV and Napoleon, to the personalities of the present time. One may grant that attempts at a history of Egyptian art are usually based on Manetho's Thirty Dynasties; but the point is that these sections taken from Egyptian life are, with few exceptions, illustrated by facts so inconsistent that we are strongly tempted to form syntheses of far too summary a kind, which obscure the true proportions of events when considered in relation to the others.

A Japanese critic, Masaharu Anesaki, has expressed very lucidly an idea which is generally admitted but which is, none the less, frequently lost sight of: 'Art is an inspiration, life is a fact. The conception and the expression of artistic inspiration are controlled, in great measure, by the conditions and circumstances of life.' Which is the same thing as saying—if we alter slightly the terms of reference—that, to appreciate accurately the art of a bygone civilization, we must first be in a position to reconstruct, in full detail, the life of the artists and of the 'consumers' of art in those far-off days.

Everyone knows that it is the ruins of tombs and temples which have done most to bring back to us the civilization of Ancient Egypt, and that the details of funeral cults have been one of the most fruitful sources of information. This has led people so far astray that they think of the Nile valley as a land of the dead, and imagine this country, where the present-day population impresses every visitor with its irresponsible gaiety, as inhabited in the past by men bowed down with thoughts of eternity. It is certainly true that the art of the tombs and of the temples is the most obvious aspect of archaeological research in Egypt; but if the delineation of the arts of life occupies such an important place in the religion and cult of the dead, it is surely an irrefutable proof of the dominating role which these arts played in everyday life. A country scene represented on the walls of an Old Kingdom *mastaba* must be regarded as evidence, not so much of the desire to transport a piece of the familiar country-side into the world beyond, as of the dead man's love of nature and of its choicest pleasures.

It is only too easy for Egyptologists, constantly delving in burial-places, and for the readers of their scholarly descriptions, to lose sight of the relation which funeral rites may bear to the everyday life of a people. Let us ask ourselves what sort of knowledge of the general appearance of Europeans during the past three centuries would be gained by excavating the principal cemeteries of our capitals—the vaults, say, of Westminster Abbey or of the Panthéon in Paris!

It is salutary, too, to reflect upon the conditions under which the remains of antiquity become available to us. It is safe to assert that, with rare exceptions, one of the essential factors of survival is the hardness of the material employed. Another factor is the degree in which the material can conveniently be used a second time. A well-squared stone from a wall, for instance, is of more immediate use than the drum of a column or a fragment of grooved cornice. The proportion of objects in metal—especially precious metal—found in all excavations in no way corresponds to the frequency with which metal was used in the actual life of the people whose customs are being studied. And the converse is equally true; it is obvious that the contemporaries of the Kitchen-Midden Folk must have had other things to eat besides the molluscs whose shells they piled up for our benefit in those huge refuse-heaps. Archaic Greek art has given us a few statues in stone; but it is common knowledge that contemporary with these there existed a large number of wooden statues (*xoana*) which must also be taken into account. Similarly, in studying the sculpture of the earliest Egyptian dynasties, we are in danger of misrepresenting the whole question if we attempt to interpret an artistic development on the basis of the statues in stone which have actually come down to us. The tombs of the Fourth and Fifth Dynasties frequently furnish reliefs which might be taken as archaic, had not the wooden panels of Hesi (Third Dynasty) already revealed to us a fully developed art—an art, one may even say, classical in its superb maturity.

So we should always keep in mind the thousands of works of art which have been destroyed, whenever we are tempted to generalize from the study of stray examples which have come down to us in circumstances which are almost abnormal. We must, in other words, base our theories of Egyptian art on general phenomena rather than on exceptional cases. I can anticipate the question which must rise to the lips of many of my readers. How, they ask, is it possible to base one's conclusions on documents which have disappeared? The answer is that for this purpose one must carefully analyse all the known data. We shall then discover a certain homogeneity in the productions of the various periods, and we shall thus realize that some of the limitations which we have imposed on the ancients are, to a large extent, the result of preconceived theories. If the general scheme of the art of any given period is enlarged sufficiently to include, besides what are known as the major arts, the infinitely varied products of the craftsman, there is more likelihood of reaching a true conception of the part played by the arts in the Pharaonic civilization as a whole. One may recall, in this connexion, the general surprise caused by the opening of Tutankhamen's tomb. It was, of course, the first time that the splendour of the kings of the Eighteenth Dynasty had revealed itself so startlingly as to destroy all the commonplace ideas of the text-books. Nevertheless, it would be easy to show that the sum total of really new facts contributed by the opening of Tutankhamen's tomb amounts to very little. Analysis of the fragments rescued from other royal tombs which had been plundered by robbers, close study of contemporary bas-reliefs and paintings, confrontation of the texts describing gifts made to the temples, tribute paid by conquered races, presents bestowed by the kings on their favourites—all this might have enabled us to foresee the luxury which was found here. Perhaps Egyptologists were too cautious and unimaginative when they treated this evidence as an indication of oriental exaggeration.

A few examples may be given to bring out more clearly this point of view, which may appear over-subtle. Let us take first a case which is exceptional in the art of the Old Kingdom. No study, however complete, of the sculptured objects, in various materials, to be found in our museums would enable us to guess that the imprint of a seal on a clay jar-sealing of the First Dynasty reveals the fact that complicated groups of figures, cast in gold, were already in existence at this period. A tiny picture on one of these seals represents King Den standing in a boat and throwing a harpoon. The tomb of Tutankhamen contained a perfect Eighteenth Dynasty replica of this design, which had been in existence as early as the First Dynasty. Here is a further example. The small ivory figures found beneath the temple of Hierakonpolis, despite the crushing which they have suffered and the damage done to them in the process, still make it possible to realize what perfect works of art they originally were. Since their discovery, the statuette of Mycerinus in the Boston Museum has ceased to be an isolated work; it becomes the culminating point of an artistic technique which was already used with skill in the time of the earliest dynasties.

One final instance may be added. Documents dating from the Ptolemaic period describe groups in which the king is represented in the act of slaying his conquered enemies. This immediately calls to mind the great bas-reliefs in the temples which depict the same scene. Can we admit that Egyptian sculpture was capable of rendering, in free-standing statuary, such ani-

mated action, bringing together figures in such varied attitudes?
The Cairo Museum has two stone statues, one of Merenpta, the
other of Rameses VI, each representing the theme of the king
triumphant, one rather clumsily, the other with a little more
artistry. But in the museum at Brussels there is a head of an
Asiatic, in crystalline limestone, worked in excellent style, the
hair of which suggests that it formed part of a group showing
the sacrifice of a prisoner. Moreover, Borchardt discovered at
Tell el-Amarna some fragments of a group which is certainly
quite as intricate, depicting Amenhôtep IV in his chariot, hunting lions. In my view, the historian of ancient art who takes no
account of the existence of these fragments, exceptional as they
are, in attempting to reconstruct, imaginatively at least, the
possible nature of such works, has failed to do full justice to the
merits of Pharaonic art.

One may justly remark that appreciation of Egyptian art has
been singularly hampered by one fact, on which it is necessary
to dwell briefly. Our Western perception and comprehension
of architecture, sculpture, and even the applied arts are, so to
speak, direct. But when we come to the graphic arts, this is no
longer the case. Faced with the problem of transferring three-
dimensional bodies to a flat surface, we must apparently resign
ourselves to a choice between two fundamental systems—
descriptive geometry, or the process of perspective. The latter,
which has become universal in modern times, represents solid
bodies as they are seen in space. The two systems are based on
principles which may be considered almost contradictory, the
first aiming at showing things as they are, and the second as they
appear to us. On the one hand we have an ideographic process,
and on the other a sensory impression. This opposition arouses
in us the feeling that any form of art which does not apply
perspective is, on the face of it, inferior and undeveloped. This
feeling is enhanced in the presence of badly executed pictures.
None the less, one should not seek to find, in imperfect

draughtsmanship, the preliminary stages of an evolution culminating in a perfect work of art, any more than one would expect spelling mistakes to reveal the origin of a correct version. If, then, we fix our attention on the most perfect examples of Egyptian draughtsmanship, in the form which was already established by the period of the earliest dynasties, we are bound to recognize in them a rigid and deliberate system which is not susceptible of any improvement. One of the greatest experts on the draughtsmanship of Dynastic Egypt formulated, some years ago, this golden rule: to appreciate Egyptian drawing, one must begin by unlearning one's knowledge of present-day technique. It is because they have failed to adopt this attitude that critics, without exception, have been convinced of the inferiority of Egyptian draughtsmanship, and they have extended this unfavourable judgement to all other forms of Pharaonic art.

Before leaving this subject, one must draw attention to the marvels of hieroglyphic calligraphy, even under the earliest dynasties. The form of the symbols, which include reproductions of animal figures, is masterly in its synthesis of the basic characteristics of each type, expressed with a perfection which has rarely been surpassed. All the descriptive technique of Egyptian drawing is here—the combination of planes revealing different parts of the figure, the insertion of details which it is desired to stress—in a word, the complete artistic convention. No one, however, would dare to claim that hieroglyphic script was the origin of this technique. It is more reasonable to suppose that writing, when it was invented, was merely a new application of the art of drawing.

Enough has been said to enable the reader to approach from the right angle the manifestations of Ancient Egyptian art, and we shall now pass on to consider its great achievements in different fields.

§ i. *The Mortuary Realm of Zoser*

Stretching along the desert plateau of Saqqâra may be seen great limestone walls, surrounding a sacred enclosure measuring 490 by 295 yards. This huge barrier, constructed of perfectly matched blocks, offers to the view, on its outer side, a complicated pattern of salients and recesses which enhances its massive appearance; its design is inspired by that of the timber construction of the royal palaces. In the centre rises a pyramid of seven stages, which covers a granite chamber. In this chamber lies the mummified body of a mighty ruler of the Third Dynasty.

This unique burial-place is really a city of palaces and sanctuaries. The entrance is by a long corridor (Fig. 1) in the south-east wall, which forms the sole means of access to this realm of death. The columns of the propylaea are shaped like a cluster of papyrus, tapering off in a style not found in later Egyptian architecture. The first impression, as one enters, is of the exquisite quality of the masonry, the harmonious proportions, the simplicity of the ornament. Here and there, carved in stone, are imitation half-open doors, showing that the main feature of this architecture is its translation into the language of stone of a method of construction designed for less durable materials.

In the south-east part of the enclosure stand the façades of two buildings with concave cornice, and showing engaged columns of a polygonal, fluted design, which are the forerunners, if not the actual predecessors, of the Doric columns with which the architects of Greece, two thousand years later, wrought such marvels.

The funeral shrine itself, projecting from the north face of the pyramid, is formed of two symmetrical blocks whose courts, with engaged and fluted columns, achieve an effect of truly classic harmony.

In the vaults, whose walls are clothed with faience decoration, are bas-reliefs of exquisite workmanship showing King Zoser performing ceremonies, the ritual of which has already been fixed by long tradition. A sealed chamber at the base of the north side of the pyramid was found to contain an admirable statue of the king, who is shown wrapped in a heavy cloak; his eyes, rendered in inlay, give him a startling appearance of life.

§ ii. *The Mother of Cheops*

More than 150 feet below the earth, at the bottom of a shaft, and completely sealed by blocks of limestone, was found a small chamber hollowed out of the solid rock, concealing part of the funeral gear of Queen Hetepheres, mother of Cheops. This included a superb sarcophagus of polished alabaster, but the queen's mummy was no longer there. The ingenious theory has been suggested that the former tomb at Dahshûr was plundered, and its contents transferred to a specially built hiding-place at Gîzeh.

The furnishings of the tomb were of exceptional quality, such as befitted one who was at once daughter, wife, and mother of kings. Every object is of precious material: we find a vase and ewer of gold; a chest, with enamel embossed ornament, holds toilet articles fashioned in most cases of gold or rare stones. There is a casket containing a set of ankle-rings in silver, on which a stylized dragonfly design has been traced in semi-precious stones. The bed and chair are of wood, covered with gold plaques with an incised pattern. The queen's palanquin bears her titles in tiny gold hieroglyphs let into the wood. They are a masterpiece of calligraphy, both in their perfect grouping and in the consummate workmanship with which every symbol has been designed and executed.

The dead woman had at her disposal everything which she was accustomed to take on a journey, including even the great jointed framework from which draperies would be hung to form a ceremonial pavilion. The inscriptions engraved on the gold

PLATE 2

FIG. 1. Entrance colonnade (restored) of Zoser's funerary monument at Saqqâra. IIIrd Dynasty

PLATE 3

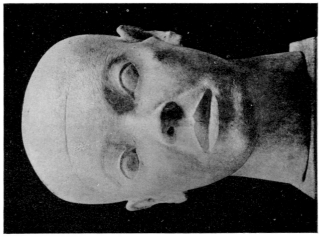

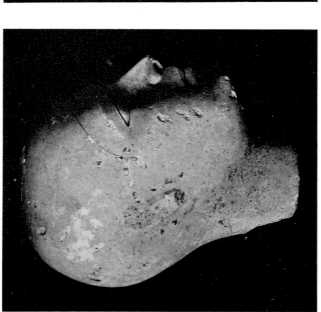

Fig. 2. Limestone funerary head from Gîza, now in Vienna.
IVth Dynasty

Fig. 3. Similar head of a negro princess, from Gîza,
now in Boston. IVth Dynasty

covering of the wooden surface are to be counted amongst the greatest achievements of hieroglyphic art.

All this impeccable technique was employed for the due honour of the mother of that Pharaoh who built the Great Pyramid.

§ iii. *The Great Pyramid*

It is hardly necessary here to give once again the dimensions of this monument, which is universally, and with justice, considered the mightiest architectural effort of the human race.

Faced with this gigantic building, the modern visitor is apt to forget what it represents as an achievement in planning and in actual organized labour. Only a part of the building material comes from the Memphis district; the granite for the sepulchral chamber was hewed from quarries more than 700 miles away. The mechanical aspect of the problem involved organized transport, creation of means of access, construction of a ramp by which to raise the building materials to the level of the desert plateau, and the arrangement of contrivances for placing the stone blocks in a convenient position. On the human side, other tasks presented themselves; recruiting the workmen, forming them into teams and sections, each under a special name, provision of food, clothing, sandals, precautions against epidemics, and so on. If Egypt had limited herself to one Great Pyramid, built by forced labour and regardless of the toll in human lives, the scale of her effort would, even so, have been overwhelming. But for whole centuries she was constructing pyramids for the rulers of the Old and Middle Kingdoms, and even those monumental tombs were far from absorbing her activities in the construction of sacred buildings, the ruins of which are still visible in every part of the country. Yet the Great Pyramid of Gizeh remains an outstanding example by which to pass judgement on the civilization whose qualities alone justify both its dimensions and its perfection.

§ iv. *The Army of the Dead*

The mortuary temples of the pyramids and the groups of *mastaba* shrines in the royal burial-places are peopled by a whole throng of life-like statues. Priests and relatives would come to visit them on days of festival, and for these statues they would perform customary rites, for by a magical ceremony the souls of the departed had been attached to them.

Frequently made of some extremely hard substance, which ensured their durability, these statues were at most periods, if not all, the work of anonymous sculptors. They were enclosed, as a rule, in small chambers, known as *serdabs*, whose only communication with the outside world was through a narrow opening.

Some of these portrait statues rank among the unquestioned masterpieces of Egyptian art. In the series of kings, the diorite statue of Chephren, the triads of Mycerinus and the remarkable copper effigy of Pepi I are sufficient proof of this.

It is possible that ritual images of the dead were originally made of wood, covered with painted stucco, and resembling closely the living being; inlaid eyes added still further to the illusion. The best known example, that of the Sheikh-el-Beled in Cairo, is sufficient in itself to prove the perfection attained by this vigorous and naturalistic art.

Important personages represented in this way were shown either standing, as in the case of Ranûfer and Ti, or sitting, as in that of Rahotep and Nofret. Sometimes they are seated on the ground, in the attitude of the Scribe.

At the beginning of the Fourth Dynasty it was usual to place a sculptured head, sometimes called a 'reserve head', in the shaft leading to the burial chamber. The finest examples are to be seen in Cairo, Boston, and Vienna (Figs. 2 and 3). They reproduce, with an intensity of expression which has rarely been surpassed, the actual features of various members of the family

PLATE 4

FIG. 4. Crossing a ford; from the *maṣṭaba* tomb of Ti at Saqqâra. Vth Dynasty

FIG. 5. Harvest scene; and the stubborn ass; from the *maṣṭaba* tomb of Ti at Saqqâra. Vth Dynasty

PLATE 5

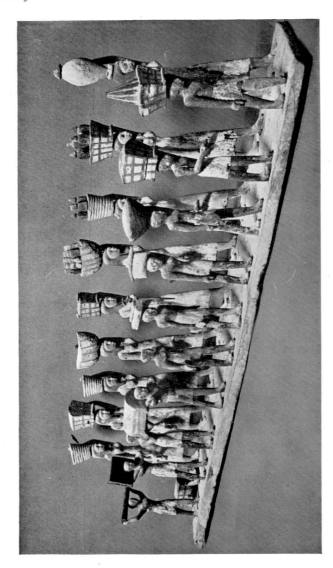

Fig. 6. Wooden model of porters, from the tomb of Karenen at Saqqâra, now in Cairo. First Intermediate Period

of Cheops. The heads bear witness to the skill of the sculptors in achieving a likeness, while the statues of the same persons which were destined for the inner shrine display a more stylized technique.

§ v. *A Pictured World*

I know well from repeated experience that one of the greatest surprises which Egypt holds for the appreciative visitor is the sudden revelation of the bas-reliefs in the tombs of the Old Kingdom (Figs. 4 and 5). The *mastabas* of Ti, Mera, and Ptah-hotep are enough in themselves to provide a faithful picture of Egyptian life as it was more than 50 centuries ago. The most striking fact is that the Egypt depicted is not that of the gods, the kings, or even the great aristocrats. The last-named figure here, it is true, but mainly as spectators. The actors in the scene are the lesser folk—peasants, hunters, fishermen, crafts-men of all kinds, boatmen, and household servants, shown crowding eagerly towards their lord's tomb to furnish it with all the things necessary to make it, in every sense, a dwelling for eternity.

Using a few main themes, but with almost endless ingenuity in their composition, the artists have also depicted the Egyptian landscape in its most characteristic aspects—the river, its boats and barges, the lakes and canals with their flowers and bird life; the desert, where every variety of wild animal is being hunted. Each scene gives the artist an opportunity of rendering different zoological types with astonishing accuracy, and of marking the line of movement characteristic of each species. The human figures are equally successful, whether it is the free attitudes of the dancer, the hunter, or the warrior, that the artist has wished to express, or the characteristic outline of a country yokel or a cripple that he desires to emphasize. Moreover these truthful and sometimes humorous sketches are accompanied by brief sentences which give, in their original pungency, the conversation of the workmen, their homely jokes and even the catchwords of the period. The wonder of the modern spectator is increased when he realizes that these scenes were first traced by draughts-men, and then completed by engravers, all of them artists of incomparable skill, which they owed to their training in tradi-tional methods.

§ vi. *The Common Folk*

We can perhaps reconstruct, in a roughly chronological sequence, the evolution which, starting from the human sacri-fice of the slaves at their lord's funeral, developed into the making of groups of tiny figures representing the 'household' of the dead man, to give him their service and company in the next world.

The burial-places of the Heracleopolitan period and of the early Middle Kingdom have given us, in this respect, an almost in-credible profusion of evidence, in the shape of what are known as 'models' (Fig. 6). Thus we find a house, or rather its front part, that is to say, the garden and the colonnade which form the entrance to the reception-rooms. Then there are scenes of various occupations—storehouses with their staffs of clerks, butchers, bakers, and brewers at work, furniture-makers, and weavers engaged on their tasks. Occasionally we find the model of a vineyard, or scenes of entertainment. But in most cases the principal subject represented is the boat, and these models have given us valuable material for the reconstruction of ancient boat-building technique. There are the boats used in funeral processions, for conveying the mummy or the ritual statue, and boats for travel on the Nile, of two distinct types, the noble-man's *dahabiyah* and the barge for the servants with the cooking utensils. One example has been found of a skiff designed for fishing and trap-laying, and we have models also of light craft, made of papyrus, manned by fishermen with drag-nets. In every case the boats found in the tombs were correctly orientated according to the direction of the Nile's flow; sailing-boats face south, and rowing-boats north.

In a few exceptional cases we find servants, or even groups of a simple kind, sculptured in stone. Thus at Cairo and Chicago may be seen dwarfs, musicians, a potter, millers, both male and female, and even children wrestling. The imaginative fancy shown by these figures must be taken into account when judgement is passed on the possibilities of Egyptian sculpture.

§ vii. *Princesses' Jewellery*

How can one describe the amazement of the archaeologist who uncovered the casket in which a princess of the Middle Kingdom had stored her most precious ornaments? The chains which linked up in a cunning design the several parts of the necklaces had perished, so that the general effect was, at first sight, that of a torrent of coloured gems mingled with tiny gold charms inlaid with enamel.

But the unique feature of the find was the discovery of some pectorals and crowns, which needed no reconstruction to display their full effect. The pectorals are perfect specimens, flawless in technique, and graceful in design. The colours are chosen with excellent judgement, and the symbolism is a masterpiece of heraldic description. The two crowns present a contrast which is worth noticing. One of them (Fig. 8), the prototype of which can be found on a statue of the Fourth Dynasty, represents a tradition in royal ornament which was never changed; the other, however, is a work of really imaginative design, in the form of a bed of growing flowers, linked by a framework of gold wire which was twined in the hair.

The admiration evoked by the treasure of Dahshûr was repeated when Mr. Brunton patiently unearthed from the mud surrounding the casket the jewellery of a princess buried at Illahûn (Fig. 7). Whether one takes the diadem, the pectorals,

4473 H

the bracelets, the mirror, or the obsidian vases, banded with gold, there is only one word that describes them—perfection.

§ viii. *Karnak*

No monument in any country in the world can bear comparison with Karnak. Passing through this sanctuary of Amûn, god of Thebes, one encounters the traces left by thirty centuries of history. Here one can decipher the annals of more than one civilization whose conquerors, after gaining the mastery of Egypt, had been assimilated by her. There are pages of history engraved on its walls which make us spectators of epoch-making events, of scenes in the struggles of rival empires for the domination of the ancient world.

These riches of the spirit are the justification for the use of material force implied by these pylons, colonnades, obelisks, and pillared chambers. One must understand the language of these great pages of history, or else risk being crushed at every step by the colossal impression of the whole. Champollion has defined this thought in authoritative language: 'It is only necessary to add that no people, whether of the old world or the new, has had such a sublime, vast and grandiose conception of the art of building as the ancient Egyptians. Their conceptions are those of men a hundred feet high. . . .'

§ ix. *Deir el-Bahari*

Deir el-Bahari is, to begin with, a place of marvels. It is literally the Land of the Dead, for there is not a single inch of ground that has not been moved, in the course of ages, to make room for a fresh grave or to plunder the treasures which the men of old laid in the tombs. The chain of hills on the left bank of the Nile forms at this point a vast amphitheatre, in which the limestone rocks rise vertically to a height of 600 feet. The action of the elements has laid bare the stone, and subsequently made great rents in it, so that when an architect came on the

PLATE 6

FIG. 7. Pectoral of Sesostris II, from Illâhûn, now in New York. XIIth Dynasty

FIG. 8. Pectoral of Amenemhêt III, from Dahshur, now in Cairo XIIth Dynasty

PLATE 7

FIG 9. Seti I adjusting the crown of the god Tum. Relief in the temple at
Abydos. XIXth Dynasty

scene, and ranged his columns at the foot of this noble mountain, man's handiwork found itself placed in a framework so harmonious that it might almost be thought to have been modelled as part of the design. For Deir el-Bahari is also the site of a temple; its modern name comes from a Coptic monastery built on the ruins of this temple. Now that the excavators have unearthed the monument and have begun to reconstruct it, the sordid, mud-brick construction of the later building has disappeared, but its name survives in connexion with one of the most perfect specimens of ancient architecture. The accurate workmanship, the harmony of the proportions, the type of columns employed, particularly on the north terraces, frequently create an impression on the uninitiated visitor which he sums up, mistakenly, in the term 'a Greek temple'.

A brief commentary, as one passes through these halls and porticoes, suffices to bring to life one of the most brilliant, but also most troubled, periods in the New Kingdom. Tuthmosis I and Tuthmosis III, the two rulers who raised the triumphal stelae on the Euphrates, were the principal figures in a contest for the supreme power. Queen Hatshepsut was the inspirer of that contest, and for a long time she profited by it. Though she dedicated this building to the memory of her father, it was her own reign that she glorified by its magnificence. Her intention was to transmit to posterity not only the record of her divine birth, but also her dazzling achievements, including the journey to the Land of Punt. All this is recounted in reliefs as delicately worked as medallions. Tuthmosis III revenged himself by defacing them, but he could neither destroy their splendour nor efface their testimony.

§ x. *Abu Simbel*

On the left bank of the Nile stands a great rock, visible a long way off, deep black in contrast with the vast stretch of golden sand which surrounds it. At a closer view, four colossal figures emerge, whose unchanging posture suggests to the imagination the idea of eternity.

To grasp the significance of Abu Simbel, one should reach the innermost part of the sanctuary, in the heart of the mountain, just as the dawn is breaking. The early sun, rising above the eastern hills, pierces it like a shaft, lighting the great statues of the gods, among whom Ramesses II, the builder of this monument, has secured a place for himself. Suddenly, for a few brief moments, the huge cave is illuminated. In the entrance chamber the columns, shaped like figures of Osiris, seem like giants issuing from the bowels of the earth. The walls, whose whole surface is now revealed, display their pictures of battles and conquests, and proclaim the protection of the gods for the Pharaoh whom they are seen exalting to a real apotheosis. Similar scenes can be viewed on the pylons of the temples; here, with their varied colours better preserved than at any other point, they stand out in all their richness and mysterious force. The impression thus given is unique; it would be useless to attempt to create it at other times of the day by the aid of electric lighting. The most extraordinary feature of Abu Simbel is that the ancient architects have deliberately, and successfully, sought to honour the rising sun by this daily victory over the powers of darkness.

§ xi. *The Norm*

Specialists do wrong to pay so little attention to the remarks of educated art-lovers evoked by their first, unbiased contact with the objects which the former have studied so long. René Francis, for example, in his *Egyptian Aesthetics*, when his eyes were opened by the bas-reliefs of Seti I at Abydos (Fig. 9), summed up his impressions in a single term: the Normal, 'that strange and most seldom met entity, the "Mean", in the Aristotelian sense'.

It seems to me that these words convey, with admirable precision, the idea that the mind, confronted with such a miraculous achievement, ceases to find any norm by the light of which it can either criticize or suggest improvement. Egyptian reliefs of other periods, it is true, earn our reasoned admiration; but in the second hypostyled chamber at Abydos, above all, one ceases to feel the need for reasoning. These gods and goddesses, this king who yields them adoration or service, these genii kneeling to offer their tribute—all seem inhabitants of an ideal world, in which elegance, refinement, and mastery of design and technique correspond to the conception of absolute ideas in the domain of thought. Here criticism resumes its sway only after the first impulse of admiration has been satisfied. And in general, after we have overcome our surprise at a method of representation so different from our own, there is nothing left to say of these reliefs, save to repeat, as in the case of the Middle Kingdom jewels, that all is perfect. What verdict shall we pass on a civilization which, not in one sphere only, produces on us the impression that perfection is the norm?

§ xii. *Theban Painting*

Situated in an obscure corner of the burial-place at Thebes, a tomb (No. 51) may be found which at first sight differs hardly at all from its neighbours. The entrance door, at the foot of a hollow place preserved from the encroaching sand by its rubble walls, leads to a room of small proportions cut out of the soft limestone of the hill-side. A rough coating of beaten earth, covered with a layer of plaster, has lent to the surface some semblance of regularity. Coming from the outside, and still blinded by the sun's brightness, the visitor has the impression of entering a cavern. It is only after some minutes that his eyes, accustoming themselves to the semi-obscurity, begin to pick out the scenes depicted on the surface of the chamber.

Along one side is seen (Fig. 10) one of the most charming subjects in the whole burial-ground, rich and varied though it is in its range of scenes. Three elegant figures, clad in folds of dazzling white, and decked with flowers and jewels, are seated on magnificent thrones. The inscriptions show them to be the high priest of a royal cult, his wife, and his mother. But for this information, we could hardly guess that the figures denoted two generations, for all three are young and beautiful, as images must be which are to serve as eternal homes for disembodied spirits. The scene is framed by a great sycamore fig-tree, its branches laden with ripe fruit at which birds are pecking. A goddess offers to the denizens of this world beyond the grave a streamlet of cool water which flows with wonderful neatness through the foliage so as to empty itself into the golden vessels held by the departed. The priest Userhêt stretches out his free hand towards a dish which the goddess is offering him, full of fruit and cakes, and surmounted by a dainty nosegay.

The unreality of the whole scene finally becomes apparent when one notices the little souls, like birds with human heads, which flutter around and perch themselves to drink at the edge of a pool, over which the goddess seems to keep watch.

The picture has suffered a few mutilations, but they do not prevent one from appreciating all the freshness, the skill in execution, and even, may one say, the *joie de vivre* which the Egyptian hoped to carry with him into the grave. A scene like this, once its full meaning has made itself felt, can never be forgotten. It takes its place with the great masterpieces of pictorial art.

§ xiii. *At the Tomb of Ramôse*

It is only in the last few years that excavators, thanks to the generosity of Sir Robert Mond, have completely uncovered the tomb of Ramôse, who was governor of Upper Egypt at the close of the reign of Amenhôtep III, and who witnessed the revolution under his successor, Amenhôtep IV.

On the great expanses of the walls of the principal chamber

PLATE 8

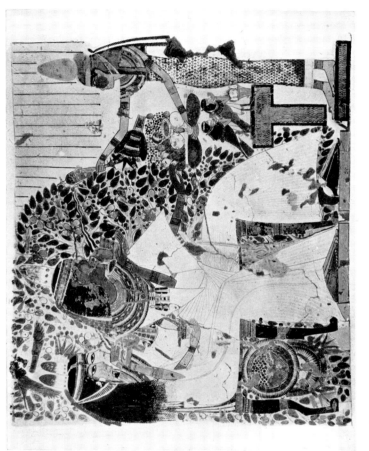

FIG. 10. Userhêt with his family beneath the sycamore. Painting from his tomb at Sheikh 'Abd el Gurnah. XIXth Dynasty

PLATE 9

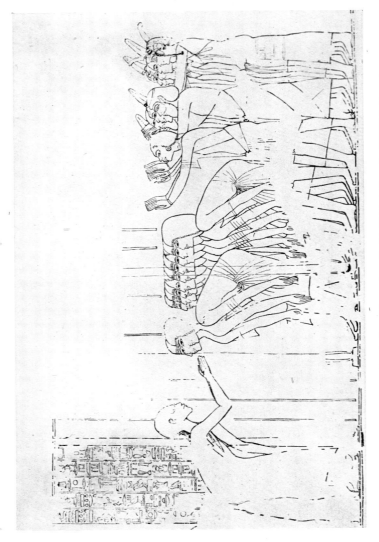

Fig. 11. Ramôse acclaimed; from his tomb at Sheikh 'Abd el Gurnah. XVIIIth Dynasty

may be viewed scenes of ritual offerings, carried out in reliefs of excellent quality. One would be tempted to say, after seeing them, that the art of this period had no more research to make in the quest for perfection. Yet, on the opposite wall, there is a series of large-scale drawings, preparatory studies for reliefs which were to be executed in the new manner, namely in what we call the 'Amarna style'.

Since Ramôse had supported the new ideas, it was fitting that his tomb should be finished in accordance with the doctrines of the revolutionary Pharaoh. From the same artistic circles which produced the creators of the reliefs came, it is probable, the man who, with astounding sureness of touch, drew the vezir first prostrate before his master, then rising to acclaim the Pharaoh as he shows himself on the balcony of his palace (Fig. 11). Ramôse, surrounded with gifts and personal tributes, turns towards his chief officers to speak the praises of his sovereign and to receive in turn their congratulations. The crowd is made up of characteristic types of Egyptians and foreigners. The whole scene, it must be repeated, is only roughly sketched out, but this makes all the more striking the power of the inspiration, and the absolute sureness of the lines traced with a reed brush on the limestone surface. Yet the master has made some corrections and at certain points he has altered a curve or tightened up a movement. There is, however, nothing automatic in this procedure, though the whole technique is based on tradition thousands of years old, and controlled by a remarkable sense of discipline.

§ xiv. *Ostraka*

The desert valley of Deir el-Medîneh sheltered, at the time of the New Kingdom, a tiny walled village in which the workers, priests, and minor officials of the burial-place lived together as a community. The pile of debris which gradually accumulated at the edge of this centre of population has provided an important series of limestone fragments and potsherds which had been used for notes, sketches, or paintings, and which are now known as *ostraka*. Many of them represent accounts; others are letters, and some give extracts from works of literature to serve as models for young writers. Large numbers of them, fortunately, have preserved for us exercises in drawing, copies from the monuments of the burial-place, and also figures and scenes portrayed with a freedom which is wonderfully attractive. Several of these works must certainly have been intended as illustrations for popular stories, including animal fables (Fig. 12). Some, too, are of such a nature that one instantly recognizes in them the results of imagination on the part of an artist who has employed a leisure moment in seeking to catch and note down the attitudes he has observed in real life. Some of the figures of female musicians or dancers created in this way have quickly won a place in the traditional subject-matter, which has thus been enlivened and transformed.

It is a long time since the figure of the acrobat at Turin (Fig. 13) revealed to the eyes of students prospects of an art more lively than that shown in the ritual scenes of the temples. To-day one can point to several hundreds of examples, all in the same manner as the acrobat, which come from Deir el-Medîneh or the Valley of the Kings, constituting an important chapter in the history of Egyptian art.

§ xv. *The Workshop of Thutmose*

In a quiet street, not far from the great *wady* which, coming in from the desert, passes through the city of Amenhôtep IV, the ruins of a brick house have been brought to light. There is nothing to distinguish it from the usual type of houses of the nobles at Tell el-Amarna, and I know many visitors who have missed having it pointed out to them by the official guides of the Service des Antiquités. Yet it is one of those places that art-lovers are wont to call a 'shrine'. From the midst of these crumbling ruins, doomed to destruction a few years hence by

PLATE 10

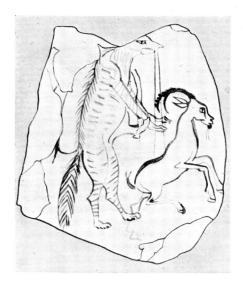

FIG. 12. 'The Fox and the Goat.' Drawing on an ostracon from Dêr el Medinah. New Kingdom

FIG. 13. Acrobatic dancer. Sketch on an ostracon in Turin. New Kingdom

PLATE II

FIG. 14. Head of Nefertiti (cast), from Tell el ʿAmarnah. XVIIIth Dynasty

the forces of wind and sand, have come the treasures now shared between the museums of Cairo and Berlin.

Here lived Thutmose, the chief sculptor; it was in his casting-room that the masks, now in Berlin, were made, and in the small chamber near the veranda the master kept his studies and his models. Thutmose based his work not only on a keen observation of nature but also on casts taken from life (Fig. 14), when he wished to record the characteristic features of a sitter. On this foundation of undoubted fact he would set himself to impose the artistic convention of the time. It is a moving experience to follow the stages in this idealization of human nature, until one sees with amazement the emergence of the Nefertiti bust of the Berlin Museum, and the head from the Cairo Museum, which comes from another studio.

Art critics have already discussed at great length what label should be affixed to the Amarna school. Naturalistic art, say some; idealistic, say others. The products of the workshops at El-Amarna have made it possible for us to gain some notion of the *naturalistic* inspiration of a group of picked artists who, in conformity with the doctrine of the Pharaoh who was their master, stamped their work with the imprint of an *ideal* quite different from that of preceding generations.

§ xvi. *Tutankhamen's Tomb*

The curiosity of the whole world during the winter of 1922–3 was centred in the Valley of the Kings at Thebes. It was an unprecedented event, and one which will doubtless never occur again. The tomb of a Pharaoh had been discovered intact. Nor was it one of those kings whom we have been accustomed to regard as one of a mere series. It was actually Tutankhamen, the ruler who ended the Amarna revolution. His tomb thus bore witness to a period when the art of the New Kingdom had not only reached its highest point but also had recently undergone a period of stress which had given it a unique character.

The tomb consists of four chambers, which were found to be full of objects of all kinds, some of them ornaments from the king's palace, others probably copies of valuable treasures which the king's successor had preferred to keep for his own use; many things had been made specially for the tomb and for the requirements of the funeral rites. This is so with the coffins, one inside the other, the innermost of which, constructed of solid gold, is a triumph of the jeweller's art, and with the shrine which encloses the Canopic chest. This shrine, of wood plated with gold and enamel, was guarded by four statuettes of goddesses, unique in their grace and movement. The chest itself, made of glistening alabaster, repeated at the corners the figures of these guardian deities. When the lid was raised, four royal heads of coloured alabaster were seen, which may perhaps be taken as idealized portraits of the young ruler. They formed the covering of the vases which contained the entrails of the dead man, enclosed in jewelled boxes.

The perfect harmony of the disposition of all these objects has to be seen in order to appreciate the degree of wealth and refinement reached by the civilization of this period. Detailed study of the furniture, the jewels, the utensils of all kinds, the sculptures, and the rest enhances this impression so strongly that a visit to the galleries of the Cairo Museum almost turns into a vision of the Arabian Nights.

§ xvii. *Cosmetic Spoons*

This is the name which has been given to the small articles, in wood or ivory, which, although destined for trivial purposes, the Egyptians made into objects of elegance and beauty (Fig. 15). The spoons have, as one might expect, a hollow part to hold the greasy substance used as ointment, and this hollow could assume various shapes, often that of a royal cartouche, or sometimes that of a little basin or shell. The hollow is also contrived like the inside of a flower, or like part of an animal's

PLATE 12

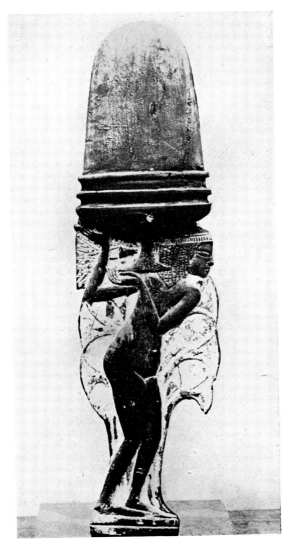

Fig. 15. Wooden toilet spoon, now in Copenhagen.
New Kingdom

PLATE 13

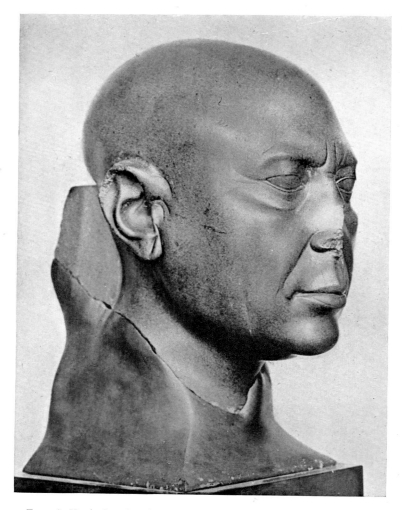

Fig. 16. Head of a priest, in green schist; now in Berlin. XXVIth Dynasty

body; sometimes it is the curving part of a vessel, and in such case the hollow is concealed by a thin lid cut in the form of a petal, a wing, or a vase.

But what gives such outstanding value to the cosmetic spoons is the fact that the craftsman usually went much further, in making them, than the practical purpose required, finding in them an opportunity for depicting miniature idylls, or even scenes of action, such as the lion bringing down its prey, or a dog in the water, seizing a fat fish by the tail. Other scenes of graceful fancy take us to an imaginary country where the lotus rears its flower-crowned stem as high as the papyrus, where tiny skiffs can be used for boating, and where life is all dancing, music-making, flower-picking, and hunting the water-fowl. Probably, if we knew more of the love-songs of ancient Egypt, we should recognize in these young men and maidens of the cosmetic spoons the characters of popular lyrics. Mention must be made, too, of the pretty nosegay-shaped spoons which ladies of fashion may, very likely, have carried to society functions, for the same reason that women of to-day carry a powder compact.

The listing of these cosmetic spoons is one of the archaeological tasks still remaining. It would produce the most unexpected, and no doubt the most brilliant evidence in favour of Egyptian art.

§ xviii. *Statues of the Saïte period*

It would be difficult to exaggerate the importance of these works, created, as they were, at a point when Egyptian civilization, in process of decline, arrested for the last time its downward course and strove for a renaissance on the basis of the traditions of the Memphis period. It was the age, too, when the Greeks, having established their power round the whole Aegean coastline, were beginning, under the influence of Eastern civilizations, to enter on their rapid ascent. Comparison of the Saïte statues with archaic Greek sculpture does not produce the impression that the relation is one of direct descent; but it shows, none the less, that the *kouroi* are difficult to account for without reference to the Egyptian figures.

Certain heads of the Saïte period in Egypt are among the works which have received the widest appreciation. The realistic character of the faces, especially of those in which attempts have been made to show the signs of old age, have reminded connoisseurs of the most accomplished work of the Pyramid age; so reminiscent are they, in fact, that attempts have been made by some scholars to attribute to the Memphite period heads which others consider Saïte, while quite recently a writer has attempted to establish a late period for certain works hitherto classed as Memphite.

The masterpiece in this style is the 'Green Head' at Berlin (Fig. 16). It is the likeness of a priest, the skull forcefully modelled, and the features accentuated by the obvious signs of old age—crows' feet at the temples, pouches under the eyes, deep lines from the nostrils to the corners of the mouth. The curious shape of the somewhat fleshy ears has been meticulously rendered. This face, which has none of that impassive character common in most mortuary likenesses, gazes at one, for all its sightless eyes, with an intensity of expression only to be found in a few outstanding Roman portraits.

§ xix. *The Tigrane Pasha Relief*

Even the most inexperienced visitor finding himself for the first time in the Alexandria Museum, and standing before the relief given by Tigrane Pasha, is struck by the distinction which marks this work. The originality of this version is at once apparent, though the scene itself is repeated times without number in the repertory of the burial-places.

It is to G. Bénédite that we owe the right term, 'neo-Memphite art', applied to this new rendering of traditional themes. The dead man is seated on a light stool, made of esparto-grass and in a shape which perhaps dates back to the earliest dynasties. He is robed in a great mantle with scalloped edges which is reminiscent of the Greek *himation*. Behind him the artist has placed a sheaf of papyrus stems, and in front there is another sheaf, combining two varieties of the plant, to which birds have been tethered by the wings, carrying lotus-buds in their beaks. This delicate decorative framework is crowned by a heron, preening itself and bearing in its beak a blue lotus-flower. The dead man, reclining at his ease, is listening to girl singers accompanied by a harpist and a maiden who plays the tambourine. The head of the old musician is more detailed than the rest of the picture; his portrait is as accurate as that of the priest of the 'Green Head' mentioned above. The women are clad in long robes, and the shoulders of the tambourine-player are draped in a shawl with rounded ends; its folds have been carefully reproduced.

One is tempted to see in this group the influence of classical Greek forms and technique, and it would be rash to deny such a possibility. At all events Egyptian art has given us, in these all too rare neo-Memphite reliefs, an exquisite flowering of its last days.

§ xx. *The Island of Philae*

Must one recall this scene, unrivalled in the world, this spot so enchanting in the days before the economic wants of modern Egypt had made necessary the construction of the Aswân Dam? The little island, enclosed in an amphitheatre formed by the rocks of the First Cataract, with its vesture of palm-trees and its buildings whose stones had taken on, in the course of ages, a patina of gold—all this now lies hidden beneath the waters. Yet in striking a true balance of the merits of Egyptian art one has no right to omit this example, on the ground that the moderns have ruined its ancient beauty. It was there that the great goddess Isis was still receiving the devotion of her worshippers at a time when the entire Roman world had become Christian. These temples, though built in the tradition of the Pharaohs, are the work of the Ptolemies, who succeeded to the legacy of Alexander the Great, and whose last heiress, Cleopatra, filled Imperial Rome with talk of her beauty and her intrigues. The civilized world had already, centuries earlier, followed the example set by the builders of the Parthenon and had adopted different architectural standards. But the architects in Egypt who, at the bidding of their foreign masters, raised these shrines in honour of the old ancestral deities, borrowed nothing from the new tendencies, and succeeded, once again, in producing a design the memory of which will never vanish from the minds of men.

The purpose of the foregoing pages has been, not so much to present a complete picture of Egyptian art, as to give some idea of the diversity and richness of its achievements. Even in 1824 Champollion, with his wide knowledge of ancient Egypt, remarked: 'The whole history of Egyptian art, it seems to me, still remains to be written. There is every indication that we have been over-hasty in estimating its technique, in defining its methods, and, above all, in fixing its limitations.' More than a century has gone by since this was written, yet in spite of the volume of research which has enlarged the material of our studies it would be premature even to-day to outline too rigidly the limits of Egyptian art. There are still many problems which ought to be attacked from a fresh angle. I may perhaps at this point be allowed to indicate some of them.

We have seen the way in which young pupils were trained— by the study of a small number of literary works which were regarded as classics. The same process was used in the apprenticeship of those who were called 'writers of outlines',—i.e. those who executed the drafts of designs for sculptors and painters to work on. These specialists in perfect draughtsmanship had acquired their skill by copying over and over again a certain number of motifs. For this purpose temple libraries were ransacked, and ancient monuments scanned, so as to discover the forms of treatment laid down from time immemorial. We can thus understand how it is that an Eighteenth Dynasty temple reproduces a scene obviously copied from an Old Kingdom monument, a scene which serves, in its turn, as model for a tomb of the Saïte period. M. G. Jéquier has recently shown that a large mural in the sanctuary of Pepi II (Sixth Dynasty) is repeated in every detail on a Karnak pylon, the relief being inscribed with the name of Amenhôtep II (Eighteenth Dynasty). The same practice explains the existence of a series of models from sculptors' workshops, both reliefs and free-standing statues, reproducing important figures from the royal or sacred monuments. The same procedure can be seen to-day in our Academies of Fine Arts, where teaching is based on the copying of models, and for this reason it is permissible to speak of an 'academic' element in Egyptian art.

This training of artists on a basis of common traditions has done much to spread the idea that art in Egypt remained stationary throughout the centuries, fixed by set rules which it was forbidden to transgress. Nevertheless, it is only necessary to compare a few scenes of the same type, taken from monuments of different periods, to see that, although the subjects are as changeless as the customs which gave birth to them, their interpretation depended on an artistic sensibility and an ideal of beauty which varied from century to century. Take, for example, the bearers of offerings from the Tomb of Ti or from the Pyramid of Pepi II; compare them with those on the tombs of Kha'emhêt and Ramôse, and finally with those of Petosiris at Tunah el-Gebel, and you will have examples which are quite characteristic of the varied aspects of Egyptian beauty. One must not, however, be deceived by this into thinking that the art of Egypt, during its thousand years of existence, had no decadent periods. On the contrary, it foundered under the stress of military and political catastrophes, and, in the periods of recovery which followed, old traditions had to be restored, and bygone splendours used as inspiration. Egypt experienced several 'Renaissances'. During the last of these, in the Saïte era, examples borrowed from the Memphite period returned to favour. Artists of this time penetrated the vaults of the Pyramid of Zoser at Saqqâra and took copies of the early Third Dynasty reliefs.

An historian who should confine his survey to a Greek original of the fourth century B.C., a copy of Roman date, a work of the Italian Renaissance, and an example of modern classical art might easily be led to think that subject, technique, and material had remained constant through all the centuries of Western civilization. He would conclude that there had been no over-throw of the ancient empires, no Romanesque or Gothic periods. He would see nothing to hint at the characteristic movements of modern times. The perspective has been similarly falsified in the case of Egypt, partly owing to the illusion that its art was static, and partly because of failure to remember the consider-able expanses of time which separate the principal periods in the history of the Pharaohs.

A closer study of the subject will dispel this idea. The artistic revolution carried out by Amenhôtep IV is now generally recognized. In this El-Amarna art we are confronted with an apparently unexpected burst of new tendencies, a desire to throw off tradition and to lay particular stress on the play of technique. These tendencies are strikingly echoed in our own aesthetic conceptions to-day. How was this revolution brought about? First and foremost, by a complete divorce between artistic representation and the age-old customs which had hitherto provided its chief reason for existence. Artists began to speak a new tongue, just as 'new Egyptian' finds a footing at this time in the language of official inscriptions. The religious and political reaction at the end of the Eighteenth Dynasty never completely succeeded in eliminating the innovations in art and language which the revolutionary period had introduced.

Further, it would be a serious mistake to maintain that the academic nature of Egyptian art precluded imagination and variety in its manifestations. Its technique was not employed only in the service of gods and dead men; it was at the disposal of the living, to give beauty to the objects of everyday use.

This brings us to the problem of the relation between beauty and utility. From the very first, the principle of the Egyptian artist was not art for art's sake, but the appeal of beauty in everyday life. We may be sure that he never dreamed of creating his elegant and graceful works for the special honour of a deity or an illustrious corpse. The reason why he offered such things to the mysterious powers which he wished to placate was that he imagined them to have tastes like those of human beings, and human beings, in those days, had learned how to fashion their household objects in forms corresponding to a particular sensibility which we call aesthetic.

It is a remarkable fact that in every period of Egyptian civilization the shapes and materials of articles of all kinds underwent changes corresponding to unmistakable waves of fashion. Bead necklaces, pottery, and seal designs display such uniformity in these changes that it is usually possible to fix their date. It was, of course, the seat of the court, with its royal workshops, which gave the lead. The product of Memphis or Thebes possessed, in the eyes of an inhabitant of the Nile valley, the *cachet* of an article 'made in Paris' to-day. But a practised eye is needed at this point to distinguish the various influences at work. Natural forms, such as the lotus flower, inspired the artists who designed drinking-cups and bowls, vases, and decorative schemes of various kinds. Subjects like that of the maiden bearing a basket laden with food gave rise to the graceful variants to be seen on cosmetic boxes. A girl swimming provided the design for spoons whose elegant form has rarely been surpassed. By the study of such objects one arrives gradually at a truer appreciation of the aesthetic sensibility shown by the Egyptians. It would be idle to discuss who, or what, played the principal part in this aesthetic development. Was it the ingenuity of workmen employed in the studios attached to the residences of kings or nobles? Or the wayward imagination of some patron, tortured with the desire for new modes of utterance, like that essayist of the Middle Kingdom who wished, we are told, to 'express' from his body words which were not in existence? We know, from the evidence of a Karnak relief, that certain rare vases were fashioned according to the personal ideas of Tuthmosis III himself. One must also take into account the influence of one workshop upon another, desiring to rival its products, and the longings of fashionable women to possess objects more beautiful or more ingenious than those of their friends. We must not imagine that the springs of human feeling were any less strong in Ancient Egypt than in civilized circles nearer to our own days. The ancients developed, even in early times, a refinement of technique which they employed for the satisfaction of all their needs. Is it a mistake to suppose that the desire for beauty, elegance, and luxury seemed essential to them? No sooner is one's attention drawn to this point than one discovers in every museum objects, often minute, in great number and variety, which prove that from the earliest period onwards the aesthetic quality was stressed, almost to the point of disregarding actual utility.

It is idle to object that the Egyptian language contains a very small artistic vocabulary, and that the words for 'good', 'beautiful', 'brilliant', and 'useful' seem strangely interchangeable. We must be careful, as Hilaire Belloc warns us, not to read history backwards; we cannot claim that the ancients, in order to attain artistic sensibility, must have discussed aesthetics, like ourselves. Chambers's exhaustive volumes on the history of taste should undeceive us on this point; he reminds us that the Greeks identified art with technique. And the Egyptians, as we know, were masters of technique.

From the moment when the inhabitants of the Nile valley emerge into the light of history, they are no longer confined within the boundaries of their own country. The earliest inscriptions preserve the traditional name of 'The Nine Bows', representing the hereditary enemies of Egypt. One of the oldest reliefs is carved on the rocks of Mount Sinai; and the records of the earliest dynasties speak of expeditions into Asia. Fragments of Egyptian stone vases have been discovered in the lower strata of Cretan sites, while on one island of the Greek archipelago a vessel has come to light which formed part of the furniture of a Solar Temple belonging to the Fifth Dynasty. At Byblus, on the coast of Syria, an Egyptian temple existed as early as the Second Dynasty, and relations between the two countries were unbroken down to the end of the Old Kingdom. The princes of Byblus, at the time of the Middle Kingdom, received gifts from the Pharaohs of Egypt, and their arms and jewellery, decorated in the Egyptian style, bore hieroglyphic inscriptions. The magical vases in Berlin and the clay figures of captured prisoners in the museums of Cairo and Brussels bear witness to the accuracy of geographical knowledge about the Asiatic world at the beginning of the second millennium B.C. The Egyptians explored the regions of the Upper Nile, and their ships traversed the Mediterranean and the Red Sea. The old idea of the isolation of Egypt is practically extinct.

Though details must be omitted here, it should be remembered that under the New Kingdom Thebes was the centre of the world, and its god Amûn was called the King of the gods. Within the walls of this capital city, representatives of all nations bore in procession their customary tribute. Egyptian traders carried the products of industrial art throughout the Mediterranean basin, while the kings of Asia begged for them as tokens of friendship, or carried them off wholesale when their victorious armies penetrated as far as Memphis or Thebes. In Nubia and in the Sudan cities were founded, and an empire was established, whose whole civilization was derived from the Egyptian. During the Twenty-sixth Dynasty the first Hellenic trading-stations were opened in the Delta; during the Twenty-seventh, the armies of Persia transformed Egypt into a satrapy of the Persian Empire. In their struggle against foreign domination the last Pharaohs were constantly appealing to the generals of Athens or Sparta.

It is scarcely credible that these continual contacts, these commercial movements and conflicts of empires could have taken place without causing a transmission of Egyptian technique both to Asia and to Europe. But this technique did not make its way only as a workshop secret; far more frequently it was spread by means of finished articles with their Egyptian individuality and their characteristic ornament. The palaces of Persepolis, the ivories of Syria or of Nimroud, the engraved bowls known as 'Phoenician', the ornaments on textiles and embroideries in various countries show the extent to which the Egyptians had spread their designs over the world, from the mountains of Persia to the shores of the Mediterranean.

When the Greeks came into regular contact with Egypt, their artistic genius received the fertilizing impulse needed to set it in motion. In two centuries Greek art was to attain a level of perfection which has remained ever since a model for mankind. Much discussion has already centred on the attitude which criticism should adopt towards Egyptian and Greek art. Some tend to exaggerate the role played by Egypt in the development of classical art; others, on principle, must one say, or out of respect for the Greek miracle, would like to reduce Greek borrowings from Egypt to a minimum. If judgement is based on the works of art themselves, it is impossible not to be struck by the rapid development of art in Greece and in Ionia from the moment when Europeans first had an opportunity of seeing the products of Egyptian art. This fact was recognized by the ancients, and Pausanias notes the survival in the old Greek sanctuaries, even in his days, of Egyptian or Egyptianising statues. But it is clear that the art of Egypt, like its writing, could not be transplanted in its entirety from one country to another. The delicate technique of Egypt might be communicated; but the spirit which animated its works of art, or rather the purpose which brought them into being, was completely different.

But why should one attempt to classify in order of merit the products of these two arts which have bequeathed to us so many masterpieces? Why should one denounce everything in Egyptian art which does not conform with our traditional rules? Why should one credit Greek art, as if it were one of its greatest titles to fame, with having achieved what the Egyptians never attempted? In both these civilizations there were men, artists of genius, confronted with similar problems. What solutions did they produce, and in what degree do these solutions find an echo in the hearts of their contemporaries and of later generations, an echo that stirs their deepest feelings? No treatise on aesthetics, applied as a standard common to Egyptian and Greek art, can supply the answer to these questions.

Quite recently a highly cultivated French politician, not thinking at all to discover Egyptian art, has at all events expressed very happily the impressions made upon him by the great monuments of the Nile valley. Note his characteristic reactions. 'The admiration which I feel for the sculptures of the Parthenon, with their noble humanity, is in no way impaired; but I remain in ecstasy before a diorite statue of Chephren. . . . In its accuracy of line, its balance of composition and its serene attitude such a work is as near to us as the celebrated examples of classical art.' And if these are the emotions aroused in him by Egyptian sculpture, the same feelings are excited by the drawings in the tomb of Ramôse, the bas-reliefs in the temples, and, still more strongly, perhaps, by Egyptian architecture. 'Even though one loves Greece to distraction', writes M. Édouard Herriot, 'it is no longer possible to deny that the purest classicism flourished in this country on the banks of the Nile, some thousand years before the fifth century B.C. which witnessed the glory of Athens.' What won him over to this view in the temple of Deir el-Bahari was the order, the purity of line, the sense of proportion which gives full satisfaction to the mind. Thus he does not fall into the mistake of seeking to determine the relative position of Egyptian and Greek works of art in a chronological series, in which perfection would be marked only by the time which had elapsed. 'Between the ideal represented by this conception [the Egyptian] and the Hellenic ideal there is no contrast; there is rather a close relationship.' It is clear that this can hardly be explained on the principle of genealogical descent; it is comprehensible only by assuming a 'close relationship' in the realm of the noblest and purest creations of the human spirit.

Thus the problem presented by Egyptian art takes on at once an entirely different aspect. At a period when the rest of the world, with the possible exception of Mesopotamia, was plunged in barbarism, Egypt had already developed a complete civilization. At least as early as the beginning of the Third Dynasty, the kings of Egypt were raising monuments as magnificent and as elegant as the temples of Zoser at Saqqâra. Even at this time the art of drawing had reached a level which has hardly been surpassed, although its system of notation was different from that which the West adopted thousands of years later. In the sphere of applied art, the wealth of the country found expression not only in the working of precious materials but in the richness of the designs, and in a taste for ornament which found new utterance in each generation. Revolution, on several occasions, shook the foundations of this empire of the Pharaohs, but it did not shatter the artistic traditions, nor the religious beliefs and funerary cults which maintained the life and activity of these traditions. The expansion of the political, military, and commercial power of Egypt placed the outer world, from an early date, in contact with the technique, the forms, and the subject-matter of Egyptian art, and familiarized it also with the expression of Egyptian thought. Thus if we deny that the world of Egypt was, for some thousands of years, one of the most active centres in the spread of civilization, we shall have to admit that in the ancient world all the causes which operated in more recent periods had not yet begun to produce their normal effects. It will never be possible to define precisely which were the elements which, after their first appearance on the banks of the Nile, were diffused over the whole world, and which will undoubtedly never again vanish from the memory of mankind. (It has been shown that the use of mud-bricks, dried in the sun, passed to the New World; the name 'adobe' came with them—a form hardly differing from that which was current in Pyramid times.)

Egypt gives us the opportunity to study and to follow the development, over more than forty centuries, of the artistic manifestations of man's activity in the most varied fields. As one writer can say: 'No known art has been so complex in its ideas and yet so great in the simplicity of its expression.'[1] Our final conclusion may be that Egypt reveals to us the knowledge of one of the sources—perhaps the source—from which the great river of beauty has flowed continuously through the world.

J. CAPART

[1] F. H. Taylor, *Worcester Art Museum Bulletin*, xxiii, 1932, p. 16.

CHAPTER 5

MECHANICAL AND TECHNICAL PROCESSES. MATERIALS

THE 'Legacy of Egypt', as applied to Mechanical and Technical Processes, should strictly mean such processes as have passed directly into medieval and modern Europe almost unchanged. Stone building certainly seems to have originated in Egypt, but the methods of construction used then have no connexion whatever with those of the Greek or Roman architects. Mathematics, Astronomy, Art, Science, and Literature can be shown to have left a more or less direct and definite legacy, but to trace the practical means of their expression—which is the aim of this chapter—is a complicated task. Herodotus, who visited Egypt about 450 B.C., is astounded (Book II, 35) at the extraordinary difference between the manner in which the Egyptians did the everyday things of life, and that adopted by his own countrymen, and this difference appears to apply even more to the mechanical and technical processes, of which he speaks little except as regards weaving. Glass-making seems undoubtedly to have originated in Egypt, but blown glass, which is the basis of most medieval and modern glass-work, definitely did not originate among the Egyptians. The *cire-perdue* process of casting seems to be the only exception.

The method which I propose to adopt in the following pages is to describe briefly the rise of the crafts as civilization progressed in early Egypt, and discuss how the technical and mechanical processes were carried out during the whole of Egyptian history (for there was little radical progress from the Third Dynasty until nearly Ptolemaic times); and from this survey perhaps an estimate can be formed of our debt to Egyptian craftsmanship.

The literature dealing with the mechanical and technical

processes employed by the ancient Egyptians is very considerable indeed, but suffers much from being diffused over a multitude of works in English, French, and German, most of which are quite inaccessible to the general public, and even more from serious mis-statements of facts and wild assertions which archaeologists have made in the past without consulting experts in any particular trade. Even worse are the statements and theories printed by engineers, architects, and other technicians, after a brief visit to the monuments of Egypt, which would never have appeared had they consulted the archaeologist. The public, ever ready to believe something startling or quaint, is from time to time informed that the Egyptians knew the incommensurable value of π, that chariot wheels were tyred with rubber, that iron weapons were used by the Egyptian troops in the Eighteenth Dynasty, that the pyramid blocks were tested for rectangularity with a mason's square before being laid, and that stone was drilled by tubular drills of copper set with jewels; and having no means of checking such theories, believes them.

Petrie's *Arts and Crafts in Ancient Egypt*, published in 1909, did much to stimulate general interest in the various mechanical and technical processes, but it is too brief and very much out of date, and often does not take into account observed facts. His *Tools and Weapons* (1917) is also a very valuable record of the fine collection in University College, London. In 1930 the late Mr. Somers Clarke and the present writer endeavoured to give an outline of the mechanical methods of the ancient Egyptians in a work entitled *Ancient Egyptian Masonry* (Oxford University Press), in which the whole subject is examined, with the object of passing on to future workers the information gathered from our unrivalled opportunities for studying the monuments. In 1934 Mr. Alfred Lucas, late Director of the Chemical Department in Egypt, and now honorary chemical adviser to the Antiquities Department, brought out a work entitled *Ancient Egyptian Materials and Industries* (Edward Arnold and Co., London), which met a long-felt want. This not only contains an immense amount of original research but incorporates much material on the working of stone from our volume on *Masonry* and gives an abundance of references. A very large portion of the material in this chapter has been drawn from the two last-mentioned works.

The earliest Egyptian civilization at present known is that whose remains were recently discovered at the villages of Abu Ghâlib and Beni Salâma, known as 'Merimda'. The site lies some fifty miles north of Cairo at the western edge of the Delta. Its flint implements resemble very strongly those of the neolithic period long known in the Egyptian deserts. Houses were built up with lumps of mud, shaped by hand, in the form of beehives, with low narrow doors. Metal seems to have been completely unknown, but a basalt vase of rather crude form (Fig. 1, *d*) shows that the Merimda people were at any rate attempting to gain mastery over hard rocks. The pottery is very rough but of a fair diversity of forms, and was made entirely without a potter's wheel (Fig. 1, *a–c*). Glazing and glass were unknown, and no baskets, matting, or linen have been found. Skins, possibly roughly tanned, were used as garments, and corn had been cultivated and stored in granaries in the settlements. The next oldest known evidence comes from the cemeteries on the eastern desert edge near the markaz town of El-Badâri, in Upper Egypt. This culture is now known as the Badarian. No direct connexion with the Merimda culture can be noticed, except in its flint implements, but it is closely connected with a somewhat similar civilization from the Faiyûm. The Badarian civilization is directly followed by a series of what are known as predynastic cultures, which, in turn, develop without break into those of the protodynastic and dynastic periods. The crafts had made considerable progress by Badarian times. Wonderfully fine burnished pottery, with a surface

PLATE 14

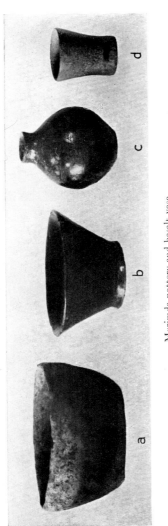

Merimda pottery and basalt vase

Badarian ripple-surfaced pottery

FIG. 1.

PLATE 15

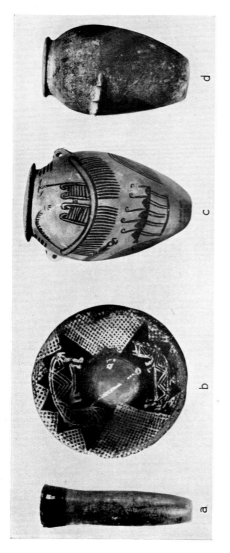

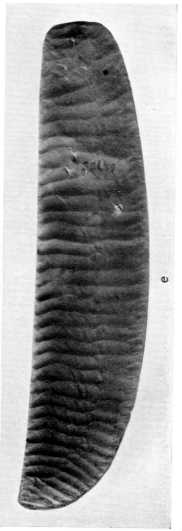

Fig. 2. Predynastic pottery and flint knife

decorated with fine ripples (Fig. 1, *e–g*), makes its appearance beside rougher types used for cooking and other household purposes. Copper was known, and used as a precious material for beads. But the fact that hard stone beads, perforated by what was probably a metal tool, are also found, seems to show that the use of copper as a tool was already known. Glazed beads are also found, but whether this craft was known to the Badarians or whether these beads were imported is still uncertain. Basketry, mat-making and weaving of small pieces of linen are first observed in this period, and although vases of hard stone have not been found, palettes of schist for the grinding of copper carbonate eye paint show that the schist out-crop in the Wady el-Ḥammâmmât was known, while the copper carbonate shows that the Badarians had connexions with the peninsula of Sinai, and also with the Red Sea. Flint and bone still remained the material *par excellence* for implements.

The predynastic cultures which followed the Badarian have left traces all over Upper Egypt. The chief advance in the crafts was that which resulted from using copper, perhaps still imported, for carpentry and cutting the hardest rocks. In the middle prehistoric period, pottery is found on which are somewhat crude drawings of boats of considerable size, with cabins and apparently propelled by paddles (Fig. 2, *a–d*). Similar types of pottery are found in far-removed districts along the Nile, showing that there was trade between different tribes, and objects such as malachite and turquoise from Sinai, schists and porphyritic rocks from the Wâdy el-Ḥammâmât, and shells from the Red Sea increased in number as time passed. Metal adzes, axes and borers were freely used; faience was made and glazed, and the technique of the stone vases reached a standard of excellence unsurpassed in later times. Linen increased in fineness and size of pieces, and pottery, still made without the wheel, showed a great diversity of types, the earlier being the shiny red ware with a black rim round the neck, and the red vases with white designs superimposed. Next followed the decorated vases of light ware, and the so-called red-polished ware was common almost until the dynastic period. Basketry, already long known, flourished, and bodies are sometimes found wrapped in matting or buried completely in baskets. Flint-working during the middle half of the pre-dynastic period reached a peak of excellence never again seen in Egypt or elsewhere, knives being made of this material, with hundreds of flakes struck off accurately, herring-bone fashion, from the centre line; these flakes were in turn divided again and again until the edge had the form of a very fine saw (Fig. 2, *e*). Many have 'explained' how this flaking was done but none, to my knowledge, has produced even a small sample as proof. We may call this one of the lost arts of Egypt. The predynastic races hunted and domesticated animals. There is little reason to believe that they were in any way war-like.

At some period the graves of the predynastic people of Middle Egypt begin to reveal a proportion of skeletons with skulls much larger than the average, which are remarkably small. At or about this time inscriptions either incised or in ink, begin to appear on pottery. These inscriptions, though crude and brief, give proof of a long period of progress behind them. Certain signs appear already to have been set aside as purely alphabetic, while class-signs, or determinatives, are in use. The origin of the 'writing people', who later developed into the dynastic race, is still the subject of controversy. Some maintain that a Delta tribe, possessing the art of writing, conquered the other tribes. The main reason for the Delta being chosen is that in reality practically nothing is known of its early history, except that its large towns go back to the remotest times. I can only suggest that, first, in a hot climate it is unlikely that a single tribe inhabiting an over-rich river-bed would develop war-like and energetic tendencies, yet the progenitors of the dynastic race were men of almost incredible energy. Secondly, if the art of writing had been known to one of a series of trading tribes, it would soon have become generally known, and evidences of a previous stage would appear on vases up country. Thirdly, the dynastic peoples were different from those on their commemorative palettes whom they are represented as slaughtering. Fourthly, their language was Semitic in grammar, though there are comparatively few definitely Semitic words in the language of the Old Kingdom. An invasion, preceded no doubt by peaceful penetration, seems to my mind to be indicated; and though it is by no means clear as to whence the invaders came, I suggest the highlands of Palestine or Syria. At any rate, the introduction of new and energetic blood, together with the art of writing, produced an immense effect on the inhabitants of Egypt, who already had gained complete mastery over stone and, moreover, possessed an abundance of excellent clay for ceramic work, and experience in its use.

After the appearance of writing in the protodynastic graves of Egypt there is no abrupt change in the type of household utensils or other objects found in them, though a change was to come. Our earliest written record of the progress of the country under the protodynastic kings is a monument known as the Palermo Stone, fragments of several copies of which are known, which shows that records were kept until the Fifth Dynasty. Although ceremonies and battles are recorded as the first consideration, we also find that the measurement of the Nile was regularly kept, that some form of cattle census was taken, that shipbuilding went on, and that buildings were constructed. In other words, the country had been brought under a powerful administration. A ruling class had developed, which insisted on the greatest possible luxuries being provided for it, and this, no doubt, gave great impetus to the crafts, especially stone-working. The rulers and nobles were buried at Abydos in brick-lined graves, and at Saqqâra in large *mastabas* with elaborate brick super-structures.

Although there is little mention of agriculture on the Palermo Stone, the immense importance attached to it from the Old Kingdom onwards leads us to suppose that the cultivation of food was one of the chief concerns of the dynastic race, while the predynastic race had only cultivated enough for their needs, or so it appears. In the protodynastic period and throughout the Old Kingdom there seems to have been a comparatively small ruling class, holding in subjection a relatively enormous artisan and serf class. The effect of intensive cultivation in a fertile country like Egypt must have been to increase the population very greatly. Where currency did not exist, nor a system of export, a time would come when the population would exceed the maximum that could be employed for the growing of cereals, their transport, distribution, and storage, the digging and maintenance of canals, the breeding of domestic animals, in fact the needs of subsistence. Later still the population would be in excess of the number that could be employed to gratify every whim of the kings and ruling classes, even after they had sent parties, with reckless disregard for human life, to distant mines and quarries to obtain precious materials. By the Third Dynasty matters seem to have reached such a pass that the nobles, rather than have about the country a huge population unemployable for any useful purpose, had to put its vast numbers to work on large monuments of benefit only to the souls of the kings and their relatives; and it is a surprising fact that the relatively small aristocracy could keep in subjection hundreds of thousands of serfs for upwards of 500 years, until the end of the Sixth Dynasty, when there appears to have been a revolt and the Memphite dynasty fell.

After a few small stone buildings the Step Pyramid, with its extraordinary dependencies and full-blown architecture, springs

PLATE 16

FIG. 3. Plan of typical Zoser masonry from the Step Pyramid at Saqqâra

FIG. 4. Casing-blocks from the north face of the Great Pyramid

PLATE 17

Fig. 5. Imitation of matting in faience and stone on a panel from a gallery in the Step Pyramid at Saqqâra. IVth Dynasty. Cairo Museum

suddenly into existence. Saqqâra was certainly the home of fine masonry, since limestone of such good and tractable quality occurs nowhere else than in the Muqattam-Tura-Ma'sara hills immediately across the Nile. To discuss the artistic forms, seemingly of mushroom growth, observed in the Saqqâra masonry is somewhat outside the range of the present chapter. It is enough to point out that all the forms observed, with the exception of the mass of the pyramid itself, are derived from brickwork and plants. The panelling of the temenos wall is a direct copy of the brick panelling of the *mastabas* known for some centuries before. The ribbed columns seem to have their origin in bundles of reeds tied together, the roofs imitate undressed logs, while reed mats form the motif of the panelling of the underground galleries, and so on. It is in the quality of the masonry that progress can be observed from the Saqqâra blocks to those of the Fourth Dynasty pyramids and *mastabas* which followed them. Shorn of details, the Saqqâra blocks are small, and their joints, though fine as far as the eye can see, only remain so for a very short distance from the facing; within the wall the masonry is poor (Fig. 3). The progress in megalithic masonry is seen in the perfect joints between the immense casing blocks weighing 10 tons or more of the Great and other Pyramids (Fig. 4). The methods by which stone buildings were constructed will be discussed later.

In the earliest predynastic times (Merimda and perhaps Badari) rectangular mud-bricks do not seem to have been known. As I have already said houses of beehive type were made by building up, spirally, lumps of wet clay moulded in the hand. By late predynastic times, however, the rectangular mud-brick is found. The method used thenceforward has hardly differed until modern times. The clay was sometimes, although not always, mixed with chopped straw or dung and put into moulds open at the top and bottom and fitted with a handle (see Fig. 14, *e*, facing p. 137); the mould was lifted off the tacky clay, placed alongside it and another brick 'struck'. The bricks were left for some days to dry, stacked, and were then ready for use. In building the mortar was simply the same clay from which the bricks were made. Another form of brick, longer and flatter, was used for making barrel-roofs, without

FIG. 6. Method of constructing an arch without centring by means of special bricks.

'centring', over rooms and galleries. Each half-ring of brick was leant against its neighbour (Fig. 6). Burnt brick, although known at a very early date in Mesopotamia, was not used in Egypt until Roman times. Although after the advent of stone this material began to enter into the construction of the houses and palaces of the nobles, brick continued to be the material *par excellence* of residences, walls, and temple dependencies (Fig. 7).

A real legacy from the crafts of ancient Egypt is found in

the word *Adobe*, which passed into English from South American Spanish, and which means, according to the *Concise Oxford Dictionary*, 'unburnt sun-dried brick'. It passed into the Spanish through the Arabic-speaking conquerors of Spain, being a transcription of Ṭûb (singular Ṭûba), which is the colloquial Arabic word for this material, derived from the Coptic ⲧⲱⲱⲃⲉ (Tôôbe) and the ancient Egyptian *db.t* which had the same pronunciation as the Coptic.

The art of basketry antedates that of weaving. Mats and baskets were made from the fibres and leaves of date-palms, from dôm-palms, from grasses and from other plant stems. Basketry is known from neolithic times, and by the time of the New Kingdom baskets are found made of differently coloured grasses in a great variety of forms. Mats are equally ancient and by the Third Dynasty they are found represented on the walls of the Step Pyramid galleries, translated into stone and faience (Fig. 5). The subject of basketry has received so little study from experts that any statement on

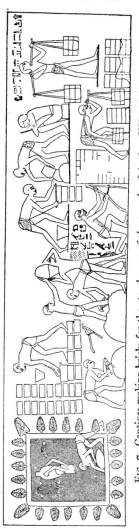

Fig. 7. Captives making bricks for the storehouses of the temple of Amûn. XVIIIth Dynasty. (After Newberry *Rekhmara*, Pl. xxi.)

the progress of the technique of this craft would be premature.

Hides were used for garments in the earliest predynastic (Merimda) period, and tanning seems to have been practised almost, if not quite, as early. Apart from articles of household use—sandals, bags, braces, chairs, seats, tents, &c.—leather was used for binding blades of axes and adzes on to their hafts and for the tyres of chariots, those on the miniature chariot of Sitamûn being still in perfect condition. The largest leather object known is the tent of Isimkheb, composed of squares of fine leather painted alternately red and green. Appliqué work in colours was practised, and leather cut into fine network. It was also used for armour, the narrow overlapping scales of the remains of Tut'ankhamûn's corslet being specially remarkable (Fig. 8). Leather was also used as a material to write upon. In the tomb of Rakhmirê', of the Eighteenth Dynasty, it is stated that the laws were written on forty rolls of leather.

Weaving dates from the predynastic period and is depicted on tomb walls as early as the Twelfth Dynasty The material employed for weaving was almost exclusively flax. The thread was spun by hand on small spindles just as it is in Egypt to-day, and the looms were of the simplest type (Fig. 9); in spite of this the women, even at an early period, succeeded in weaving cloth of admirable fineness. Tapestry weaving is known from the time of Tuthmosis IV, and many examples of this art are seen in the robes and gauntlets of Tut'ankhamûn. Wool was rarely used in Egypt until Christian times; cotton, originating in India, and silk from China do not appear until Graeco-Roman times.

Pottery is first found in the Merimda civilization. Here the pots are coarse-surfaced and made without a wheel. With the Badarian civilization comes a great advance, the surfaces of the better specimens being red with a smooth polish, and often decorated with very fine ripples. The thinness of the pots is

PLATE 18

Fig. 8. Fragments of a leather corselet. Tomb of Tutʿankhamūn. Cairo Museum

PLATE 19

FIG. 9. Model weavers' workshop. XIth Dynasty, from the tomb of Meketrē'
at El-Deir el-Baḥari. Cairo Museum

also often remarkable (see Figs. 1 and 2, facing pp. 122–3). The later predynastic ware shows an immense variety of forms, the earlier often having a polished surface with black tops, the slip being a red iron compound completely polished, with designs in white. Subsequently pots of a light ware make their appearance carrying designs of ships, houses, men, and so on, also some with a polished or rough red surface (see Fig. 2, *a–d*, facing p. 123). At this period also small handles for suspension are found. At this time, and for an indeterminate period after, the pots were baked on the ground in a mixed heap of pots and fuel, perhaps covered with dung to conserve the heat. The kiln had been well established by the Fifth Dynasty, when one is shown in a tomb at Saqqâra. As to the wheel, the only technical process, apart from the true kiln, which seems to have developed after the predynastic period, there is a considerable divergence of opinion as to the earliest date of its use, some authorities asserting that it was known in the First Dynasty, others that it was a later evolution. 'Wheel-marks' on pottery are apt to be misleading; for a most elementary advance in pottery-making would be to put the pot on a table which could be made to revolve as the pot was gradually being built up by hand, or to smooth it off when shaped; this would leave concentric rings on the pot. The wheels depicted in a Fifth-Dynasty tomb at Beni Ḥasan show that they were turned by hand. To shape a pot by the swiftly moving wheel, modern fashion, requires both hands free; the wheel has to be turned by foot, as Egyptian potters do to-day, or by an assistant. Until further evidence is available we must leave the date of the introduction of the true 'potter's wheel' with its quite special technique as an open question.

Much has been written by excavators and others, who are not themselves acquainted with pottery technique, on the subject of slips, polishes, washes, and other processes when attempting to describe the surface of a pot. While the predynastic pots had obviously been covered with a separate material, and those of the Eighteenth Dynasty were clearly often painted before firing, many, indeed most, of the shiny surfaces of Egyptian pots were not always due to the application of a different material to them, although red ochre is known to have been employed for this purpose. Shiny surfaces can be made on suitable clays when the pot is nearly but not quite dry, and the surfaces thus treated often lead one to suppose erroneously that a 'slip' has been added. Furthermore, a common error is the belief that an unglazed pot will not hold liquid. As a matter of fact, the porosity depends entirely on the nature of the clay used and the way it is kneaded. A porous pot can, however, be made watertight by glazing, or by coating it internally with pitch or a similar substance. Egypt provides a great variety of clays, and even during the predynastic period the pots show that clays were exchanged between different districts and that the potters were well acquainted with their natures.

Ropes of enormous size must have been made from pyramid times onward for use in the hauling of large monuments, though the largest at present known, of rather doubtful dynastic date, is one of palm-fibre of about 5 inches diameter. The palm-ropes of ancient Egypt are precisely similar to those used on the *saqya* wheels to-day. Other types of rope are found made of flax-fibre, one of which dates back to the predynastic period. A rope of halfa grass is known in the Sixth Dynasty and one of flax in the First. A piece of rope of $\frac{3}{4}$ inch diameter of the Eleventh Dynasty, made of twisted flax threads, compares favourably with the finest modern products. Two rope-making scenes are depicted on the tombs, one in the Fifth and one in the Eighteenth Dynasty.

The art of netting dates back to very ancient times, to judge by the fishing and fowling scenes. The earliest net extant which I have personally examined is of Twelfth Dynasty date; its knots are precisely the same as those in modern nets. Netting needles are common, especially in the New Kingdom and Roman times.

Faience was made as early as predynastic times, and by the Third Dynasty had reached a high degree of excellence (see Fig. 5, facing p. 127). It consists of a body material of very fine, clean, angular grains of quartz without any visible admixture of clay or other ingredient. The quartz has the appearance of having been artificially powdered. The adhesive most probably used was natron from the Wady Natrûn. In the experiments conducted by Mr. Lucas a mixture of quartz powder strongly fired with 10 per cent. of natron produced a mass closely resembling ancient faience. After heating, only about 3 per cent. of the natron remained in combination, the rest having volatilized. Since the number of analyses of ancient faience are still comparatively few, this may account for the adhesive not having been recorded. The usual method of making faience objects was by casting them in pottery moulds, of which thousands have been discovered of all periods. It is possible, however, that in certain cases the fused mass of quartz and natron was carved as if it were stone. Faience was used for vases, statuettes, amulets and inlay. It can take a high glaze, but the method of its application is still uncertain; in fact, although most careful experiments are now being carried out, we are still only able to give the broad lines of the process of faience manufacture.

The chemical composition of glass and glaze is identical (Fig. 10, facing p. 134), namely the result of a complete fusion of quartz sand containing calcium carbonate with natron or plant ashes and colouring matter. The term *glaze* is used when the substance is applied to some material such as stone or faience, while *glass* is applied to objects made entirely of this substance. Glazed beads are known from the predynastic period, but the specimens of glass ascribed to periods earlier than the beginning of the Eighteenth Dynasty are all of somewhat dubious date. Blown glass is not known until the Roman period; the Egyptian glass objects, such as vases, having been made by winding drawn rods of glass round a sandy clay core, reheating, rolling and polishing, or by casting. Beads were made by winding thin glass threads round a copper wire, which was later withdrawn, while pieces for inlay, mosaics, and so on, were made by flattening the rods into strips and subsequently cutting them up. The advent of glass largely displaced the use of hard stones for inlay in jewellery. The colouring matters were generally manganese, copper, cobalt, and iron compounds.

Gold occurs in Egypt in the Eastern Desert south of the Qena–Quṣeir road as far up country as Merowe in the Sudân, and was used from the predynastic period. Expeditions were sent out from early times in search of it. It is found in the quartz-veins running through the granite, and the ancient workings are enormous, their galleries having been pounded by balls of dolerite for hundreds of yards into the living rock. It was also imported from Asia and elsewhere. The process of making gold leaf was known, but ancient specimens are as thick as 0·004 to 0·036 inches, more than a thousand times as thick as that which we use to-day. The foil was used for plating all kinds of objects. By the New Kingdom, an immense quantity of gold was available, at any rate to the royalty and nobility. The gold coffin of Tutʿankhamūn weighs 300 lbs. avoirdupois. Even in the times of Shesonq of the Twenty-second Dynasty, the weight of gold and silver dedicated to the temple runs into more than a score of tons! Many of the gold ores contain such a large proportion of silver that the lighter colour is perceptible. This alloy, much used in Egypt, is known as electrum.

Silver ores do not occur in Egypt except in conjunction with gold ores. The chemical knowledge of the Egyptians was not sufficient to separate the two. Silver was rarer than gold in Egypt and was used for the same purposes. The source of the ancient supply is unknown.

Generally speaking the tools of the Old Kingdom and earlier

PLATE 20

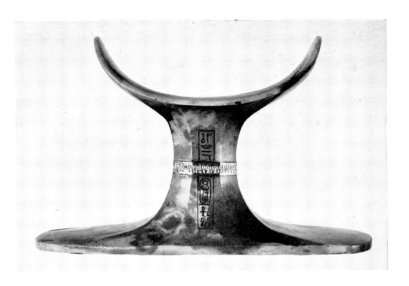

Fig. 10. Imitation head-rest of glass from the tomb of Tutʿankhamūn; glass vases from Saqqâra and El ʿAmarna. All XVIIIth Dynasty. Cairo Museum

PLATE 21

FIG. 11. Model carpenters' workshop from the tomb of Meketrē' at El-Deir el-Baḥari. XIth Dynasty. Cairo Museum

are of more or less pure copper; those of the New Kingdom of bronze. The transition seems to have occurred gradually in the Middle Kingdom, particularly during the Twelfth Dynasty. Native copper is very rare and the chief ancient source of supply of copper ore seems to have been Sinai. The copper was smelted by comparatively primitive methods, the fundamental principle being to mix the broken ore with charcoal in a heap on the ground or in a shallow pit, and to apply a simple form of forced draught by means of blow-pipes (Vth Dyn.) or by bellows, which were apparently not known until the Eighteenth Dynasty. To give a résumé of the processes of refining is outside the range of this chapter and, indeed, much is still conjectural. Metal was, however, both wrought and cast as early as the middle predynastic period. Ancient Egyptian copper objects, especially tools, show that the metal was still crystalline and that it had never been raised to the annealing temperature. Bronze is a term used for a mixture of copper with from 3 to 16 per cent. of tin. Its advantages over pure copper are its hardness, its lower melting-point, and the fact that it flows better than copper in the process of casting. It can also be hammered cold. The source of ancient tin is still in dispute. It may be added that brass, an alloy of copper and zinc, is not found in Egypt until the first century B.C.

Although known as the 'Ore of Heaven' from the New Kingdom iron ore does not appear to have been smelted for general use as tools and weapons until the Twenty-fifth Dynasty. In fact the problem of the use of iron in Egypt has formed the subject of much controversy. The earliest definitely dated specimens of iron are a number of small tubular beads found in a small predynastic cemetery at El-Gerza. Although completely converted into rust, chemical examination showed that they contained $7\frac{1}{2}$ per cent. of nickel, and thus were almost certainly of meteoric origin. The evidence of date put forward for the piece of iron supposed to have been found in the stonework of the Great

Pyramid by Vyse, the piece of a pickaxe of the Sixth Dynasty from Abuṣîr, the fragments of the same date from Abydos, and the spear-head of the Twelfth Dynasty from Nubia are very doubtful, in spite of very definite assertions to the contrary on the part of their finders. The assignment to the time of Tuthmosis III of a very large number of iron weapons found by Petrie in the mounds of Gerar in Palestine, depends almost entirely on the dates of the levels in the mound, an extremely dangerous procedure unless objects of indisputable date are also constantly found. Tut'ankhamūn had an iron dagger, which it has not yet been possible to examine chemically, also an *udjat* eye, a model head-rest, and some extremely light blades in wooden handles. The shaping of these specimens reveals clearly the lack of mastery over the material. The Cairo Museum does not possess, other than these, a specimen of iron of a date prior to the Twenty-fifth Dynasty. Iron is stated in the Book of the Dead to be the necessary material for certain amulets, but until the Twenty-fifth Dynasty it seems to have been a rarity only obtained from meteorites, though perhaps occasionally imported as well. The commonest iron ore in Egypt was haematite, which was made into beads, amulets, and so on, from predynastic times.

Tin, derived from an unknown source outside Egypt, was used in forming bronze and as a colouring agent. Lead was known from predynastic times, being easily reduced from its metal-like ore, galena, which, together with malachite, a green ore of copper, was commonly used as eye-paint in Egypt. Antimony, which does not occur in Egypt, was known as a rare metal for beads in the Twenty-second Dynasty.

The papyrus plant (*Cyperus papyrus*) was used by the Egyptians for baskets, rope, matting, brushes, and above all for writing material. The ancient method of making sheets of papyrus, wrongly described by Pliny, seems to have been as follows: fresh green stems of the plant were cut into suitable lengths and the

PLATE **22**

FIG. 12. Wooden box inlaid with over 20,000 pieces of ivory and ebony
Tomb of Tut'ankhamūn. XVIIIth Dynasty. Cairo Museum

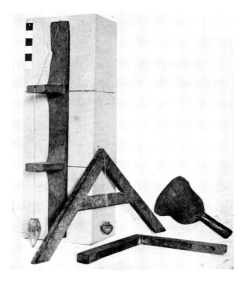

FIG. 13. Square, level, and plumb-rule from the
tomb of Sennūtem at Thebes. XXth Dynasty.
The mallet is from Saqqâra, its date being uncertain. The scale is in inches

PLATE 23

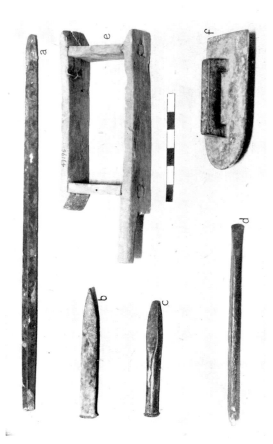

Fig. 14. Ancient tools: *a*, Quarrymen's chisel; *b*, *c*, Mason's chisels; *d*, Mortise chisel; *e*, Wooden brickmaker's mould; *f*, Plasterer's tool. All New Kingdom. Cairo Museum. The scale is in inches

green rind stripped off; they were then cut into thick slices and laid parallel to each other, and slightly overlapping, on an absorbent cloth. Another similar layer was laid above and across them and the whole covered by another cloth. It was then hammered with a mallet for about two hours, which caused the sheets, without the addition of any adhesive, to become welded into a single mass, which was finally pressed and dried. Papyrus sheets date from the First Dynasty, and inscribed sheets are known from the Fifth Dynasty.

The native Egyptian woods which have been definitely identified as having been used by the ancient carpenters are sidder (Arabic *nabq*), sycamore fig, tamarisk, willow and persea. The last was a sacred tree but was occasionally used in the Eighteenth Dynasty for making funerary objects. Among the imported woods were cedar and cypress (predynastic), ebony (Ist Dyn.), juniper (IIIrd Dyn.), fir (Vth Dyn.), yew (VIth Dyn.), oak (XVIIIth Dyn.), and box and beech (Roman times).

The advent of carpentry (Fig. 11) very naturally followed at once the application of metal for tools, but specimens of the craft from predynastic times are extremely rare. By the First Dynasty a complete mastery over wood had been obtained, elaborately decorated boxes were being made, and scenes were being carved on labels. Boat-building had been in full swing for many ages before. By the Third Dynasty the carpenters had even invented ply-wood consisting of six alternate layers of different woods! In the earliest coffins (IIIrd Dyn.) the halved, mitred and concealed mitre joints were freely used. By the Fourth Dynasty statues were made of wood, one, a masterpiece in any age or clime, the 'Sheikh el-Beled', being of this date. The art of veneering, inlaying with ivory and ebony, and overlaying with gold, silver, and copper appears early and reaches an almost incredible perfection in the marquetry work of the Eighteenth Dynasty (Fig. 12). Nails usually consisted of wooden pegs, but very minute nails of metal, such as gold, for affixing, have been found in the remains of the coffin in the Step Pyramid. Hinges, at least by the Eighteenth Dynasty, differ little from those used to-day. Tenons and mortises are known from the Third Dynasty, and their use reached a high perfection since broad planks were unobtainable from the native timber such as sycamore fig. A technique obviously learned from Asia was that of chariot-building, where a vehicle of the utmost lightness consistent with strength and stability was required. The double spokes and the joints between the spokes and the rims were of a quality entirely their own.

The carpenters' tools were the simple chisel, the deep and narrow mortise-chisel, the axe, the adze, the awl (used as a borer in conjunction with a bow), a club-like hammer, the mallet, the scraper, the saw, the square, the plumb-rule and the cubit measure, the last measuring about 20·6 inches, divided into 7 palms and 28 digits. The chisels vary little in form throughout the dynasties, and the dates of axe and adze blades, in the absence of other definite evidence, can be only partially estimated by their shape. The adze did the work now done by the plane, a tool unknown until Roman times, and with it even to-day native carpenters can achieve astoundingly delicate and accurate work. Although ancient saws, apart from models, are very rarely found, it is certain that the cut was made by the pulling and not the pushing stroke. The adze-blades were bound on to wooden hafts by interlaced leather thongs, probably of donkey-hide applied wet. The Cairo Museum has an unsurpassed collection of carpenters' and other tools (Figs. 13 and 14).

The art of boat-building developed early, and even in predynastic times we find crude representations of boats of very considerable size, though the details are somewhat obscure. In the reign of King Sneferu of the Third Dynasty there is a record of a boat 100 cubits (172 feet) long having been constructed. By the Twelfth Dynasty a pyramid chamber, of one block of quartzite, was transported by water to Hawâra by King Amenemḥēt III,

PLATE 24

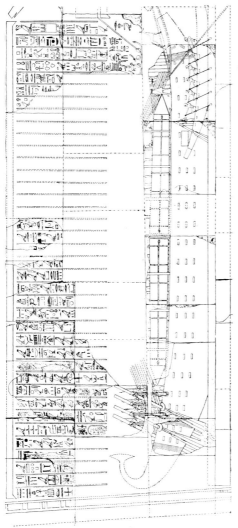

Fig. 15. Great barge of Queen Hatshepsut carrying her two obelisks mounted on sleds. Temple of El-Deir el-Baḥari. XVIIIth Dynasty

and by the Eighteenth Dynasty craft had been constructed to carry weights of 650 tons and upwards (Fig. 15). Tomb scenes and models show that during the ages a multitude of types of craft were used. Some had cabins, others pens for cattle, while

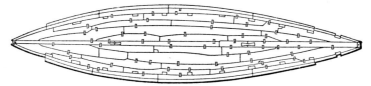

FIG. 16. Plan of a royal barge from El-Lisht showing its construction of small pieces of wood. XIIth Dynasty; Cairo Museum.

FIG. 17. Boat-builders, from the XIIth-Dynasty tomb of Khnemḥotpe at Beni Ḥasan.

many seem to have been constructed for merchandise only; others were warships pure and simple. The model ships give little detail of the construction of the hulls apart from their shape, but two large Twelfth Dynasty boats from El-Lisht, now in the Cairo Museum, and several boat-building scenes, notably one of the Middle Kingdom from Beni Ḥasan (Figs. 16 and 17),

show that the statement made by Herodotus regarding the
methods of construction was based on personal observation. He
states (Book II. 96) that 'they cut a quantity of planks about
2 cubits (41 inches) in length, arranging the planks like bricks,
and attaching them by ties to a number of long stakes or poles
till the hull is complete. They give the boat no ribs, but caulk
the seams with papyrus from inside.' The hull was prevented
from collapsing outwards under a load by a series of thwarts,
while longitudinal rigidity was maintained by one or more stout
cables attached at each end and passed over fixed stays at one-
third and two-thirds distance along the hull. Tension was
achieved by means of sticks used like a tourniquet, the device
known nowadays as a 'Spanish windlass'. Boats can also be
made entirely of papyrus, and such craft are in use on the Upper
Nile to-day. Their form, with upturned bows, was copied and
perpetuated in wood, especially for sacred craft. Even the giant
barge of Queen Ḥatshepsut, depicted at El-Deir el-Baḥari (Fig.
15, facing p. 138) as loaded with two obelisks butt to butt, is
represented as being of the traditional shape, but here, and in
the other cases of barges used for carrying enormous weights, we
have to be on our guard against taking the artist's information
too literally. For instance, the obelisks are represented up on
deck, which would certainly make the ship top-heavy, since
each obelisk weighed about 300 tons. Attempts have been
made by retired naval officers and shipbuilders to show that
such a boat as the ancient artist depicts might have had an
internal construction which could have done the required work.
Such attempts, postulating a construction dependent on calculations of stress and strain far beyond the ancient Egyptians'
mathematical knowledge, only leave one as firmly convinced
that the weight-carrying craft were but rafts made of logs or
tree-trunks, such as were used for levers, built up round the
object to be floated. In the Sixth Dynasty, a boat was constructed under the direction of a noble named Uni for the

transport of stone, which he records was made from acacia-wood and measured 60 cubits (103 feet) in length, and 30 cubits (51 feet 6 inches) in width, and which was constructed in 17 days. This would seem almost an impossibility if the construction were like that described by Herodotus or shown on the Lisht boats. On the other hand, a raft of logs could easily have been made in the time.

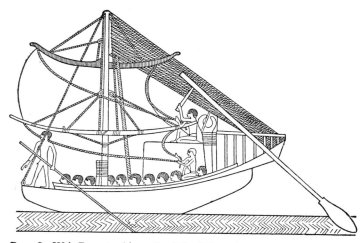

FIG. 18. IVth-Dynasty ship under full sail from the tomb of Ipi at Saqqâra. Now in the Cairo Museum.

Sails were of rectangular form, and the halyards did not pass through pulleys but either through holes pierced in the mast, rectangular frames lashed to the mast, or rings attached to the mast (Fig. 18); these devices would cause very great friction when the halyards were pulled. A feature of most Egyptian sailing-boats is the seemingly unnecessary number of ropes which hold up the lower yards. My explanation of them is that, lacking pulleys, the Egyptian crew had to stand on the lower yard and push the upper yard and sail up into place so that the function of the numerous halyards was merely to hold them up and not to hoist them. The rudders of the ancient ships, if of the traditional papyrus type, consisted

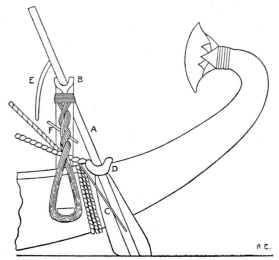

FIG. 19. Steering gear of the trading ships of Queen Ḥatshepsut. XVIIIth Dynasty. Temple of El-Deir el-Baḥari.

of two fixed paddles, one on either side of the stern, which could be rotated by a small lever fixed near the tops (Fig. 19). Other ships had a single paddle—with a similar method of rotation—reaching far astern.

The subject of the ancient methods of shaping stone for use in various handicrafts has been extensively studied, although several problems remain open to controversy. Egypt is prolific in stone, which may be divided for the purpose of consideration of the methods of working it into hard and soft varieties. The hard rocks are the diorites, the dolerites, the schists, the

PLATE 25

FIG. 20. Left to right: Fashioning a wooden or soft-stone statue by means of copper chisels; pounding the details of a hard-stone statue; polishing a stone vase. From the Vth-Dynasty tomb of Kaemreḥu at Saqqâra. Now in the Cairo Museum

FIG. 21. Unfinished schist statuette of Saite date showing marks made by a blunt pointed metal tool. Cairo Museum. The scale is in inches

PLATE 26

Fig. 23. Back of a basalt triad of King Menkewrē' showing the marks left by a saw. IVth Dynasty from Giza. Scale $\frac{5}{12}$

Fig. 22. Limestone quarry face at Ma'ṣara

porphyrys, the basalts, the granites, the quartzites, and certain varieties of marble-like limestone. The soft rocks are most other varieties of limestone, sandstone and alabaster.

Generally speaking the soft rocks could be *cut* with a chisel and mallet; the hard rocks could not (Figs. 20 and 21), but had to be

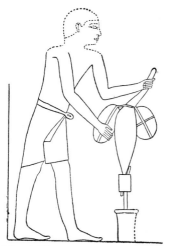

FIG. 24. Man drilling out the interior of a stone vase.
VIth Dynasty, from Abuṣîr.

pounded with balls or hammers of dolerite, jarred by an instrument like a mason's pick, with a comparatively blunt point, drilled (Fig. 24) or sawn, both in conjunction with an abrasive material.

The principal sources of stone used in the building craft are as follows. Limestone extends from Cario to a little beyond Esna. The finest building variety is found in the Ṭura-Maʿṣara-Muqaṭṭam hills, just south of Cairo. A very fine-grained limestone, hard and of marble-like texture, is found near Qâw and Beni Ḥasan, and there are other quarries of different qualities too numerous to mention. Sandstone occurs south of Esna and extends, though not continuously, as far south as Wâdi Ḥalfa. The finest quarries are at Gebel el-Silsila, a few miles south of Kôm Ombo. Granite occurs at Aswân, which was the chief source of supply, but other quarries known to have been worked are found near the Wâdi el-Ḥammâmât, between Qena and El-Quṣeir. Pink, grey, and almost black varieties occur in close proximity. Alabaster is found in many isolated places, the chief ancient quarry being that known as *Ḥat-nūb*, somewhat south of Tell el-ʻAmarna. Basalt is found in many places, such as Khanqa, Abu Zaʻbal, and the Faiyûm, the last being probably the ancient source of supply. There is an outcrop of quartzite close to Cairo, known as El-Gebel el-Aḥmar or the Red Mountain. This, however, was not the sole source of supply in ancient times.

When quarrying limestone, as at Ṭura or Maʻṣara (Fig. 22), where the best strata are far below the surface of the outcrop, galleries sometimes extending for several hundred yards in length were driven into the required stratum, and a ledge was cut near the roof to enable a man to work with a chisel there, first to make a narrow vertical trench behind the block to be extracted, and then to separate it from the stone on either side. Finally the block was released by driving a series of small horizontal wedges along its lower edge. In this manner the blocks left the quarries with a regularity of size almost like bricks from a brickyard. In a surface quarry the method was much the same but involved less labour. The hard rocks were quarried by means of a hard, blunt-pointed tool in conjunction with metal or wooden wedges, the technique varying with the period and with the locality.

With certain minor exceptions all the rocks of Egypt had been worked to a certain extent by middle predynastic times. In the Old Kingdom and afterwards the stones mentioned above were used as follows. Limestone was employed for all kinds of

buildings, but had the disadvantage of being useless for archi-
traves of more than about 3 yards span. By the Eleventh
Dynasty limestone began to give way to the Silsila sandstone
for buildings because, though softer and less pleasing to the eye,
it could provide architraves spanning 8 yards or more without
giving way. In the Old Kingdom granite had to be used for
spanning large spaces; it was used for statues, gateways,
sarcophagi, vases, &c., much less commonly for entire buildings;
and the same applies to quartzite and alabaster. In the Old
Kingdom basalt was much used for pavements and linings of
limestone buildings.

Other rocks worked by the ancient Egyptians were the porphyritic rocks, schists, and other igneous rocks from the Wâdy
el-Hammâmât; diorite, the ancient quarries of which were
re-discovered in 1931 about 50 miles west of Tushka, in the
Western Nubian Desert. Many other rare stones are found in
the watershed between the Nile and the Red Sea, some of which
are mentioned on page 155.

It has often been asserted that the Egyptians tempered copper
to a hardness unknown nowadays. Of this there is no proof.
Copper can be brought, if not previously annealed, to the
temper of mild steel, by heating, chilling and hammering. To
use copper on stone in the form of a chisel is a very wasteful
process, even in working soft limestones like those from Tura;
and the expenditure of copper in the construction of a pyramid
must have been immense. To *cut* a stone like diorite is almost
an impossibility. The Egyptian method of making, let us
say, a granite colossus, was somewhat as follows. The block was
detached from the parent mass first by pounding with balls or
hammers, made of some hard, resilient stone such as dolerite,
held in the hand, and then by the use of wedges. In this connexion it must be remembered that the pounding-ball does not
pound or bruise away the stone any more than does the blunt-
pointed pick of the modern mason. It jars off pieces of stone

by vibration and the efficiency of the work depends on the quality of the blow; one strength alone does the job: harder or lighter blows have no effect. The same result can be seen to-day in boring holes to take blasting charges in the hard rocks by a 'jumping-iron'. As for wedges, traces of wedge slots can be seen in thousands in the Aswân quarries and elsewhere, some of enormous size. Many of these functioned together with metal wedges flanked by thin sheets of a softer metal (now known as feathers) and struck with a heavy hammer. Another method was to split the granite by means of wooden wedges made to expand by wetting them. A method I have used in an experiment on granite has been to cut the slots with sides nearly parallel, hammer in wedges of a non-oily wood, such as beech, which had previously been wetted for an hour or more, split the wedge with an adze or chisel, and hammer in another on the top of it. The wood expands in about 10 hours. My reason for believing that the Egyptians used this method is that here and there wedges have functioned in positions where no heavy blow could have been delivered. To-day wedge slots are made with steel points which have to be frequently re-tempered and re-sharpened. The ancient examples all seem to have been made with a tool akin to a mason's pick. I have never found any traces of one which had been drilled. The colossus, once clear of the parent rock, was pounded into shape by the dolerite balls or pointed hammers, but parts too deep for the balls to strike were operated on by a metal pick-like tool. Once the colossus had been reduced to its required shape it was left in its rough form and put on a sled, which was either dragged directly over sleepers or, if the colossus was very large, over sleepers in conjunction with rollers. In the tomb of Thut-nakht at El-Barsha such a colossus is depicted being dragged by 172 men. Once the colossus had arrived at its destination or workshop, the picking was continued with tools of ever reducing size. A point was reached, however, where a metal pick in chipping away certain parts would be likely to damage others (for example, the eyes, if they were to be subsequently inlaid, and the corners of the hiero-glyphs). Drills of tubular form were next brought into use; if small they were presumably made to revolve by means of a bow; if large they were rotated by hand and loaded with large weights. Although no tubular drills have been found, the eyes of several statues show traces of them, of graduated sizes, and the bottoms of the holes prove that the metal must have been of extraordinary thinness. The nature of the abrasive is a matter for speculation; indeed, the whole technique is still imperfectly understood, and a great deal of practical experiment would be necessary before any further assertions could be justifiably made. For the final process, the cutting out of corners, a pointed tool would have to be used, and it would be during this process that the expenditure of metal would be enormous. That this was so can be inferred from the fact that drilling was always carried as far as possible for economy's sake. We are equally short of in-formation on the method and the material used for bringing the stone to the wonderful polish which many monuments exhibit.

The ancient Egyptians could saw the hard stones, at any rate granite and basalt (Fig. 23). Here again the nature of the abrasive is quite unknown and the technique in general more than doubtful. Cases are known of a saw-cut over a yard long, implying the use of a saw nearly 2 yards long!

The Djoser architects had discovered, we do not know how, that Ṭura limestone was unsuitable for free-standing columns if they had to support a roof of any great weight; secondly they had also realized that this limestone could not provide archi-traves to span a space of more than about 3 yards if roof-slabs of stone had to be laid over them. Hence the extreme narrowness of the passages and chambers of the Djoser masonry. The pyramid builders acted on this knowledge and, if they wished to span large spaces, used granite from Aswân. Such roofs can be seen in the 'King's Chamber' of the Great Pyramid and in the so-called Temple of the Sphinx. Apart from architectural forms, it can almost be said that, after the Great Pyramid, the masonic craft remained static as regards mechanical and technical processes until the advent of the Greeks and Romans. One factor greatly affected the dimensions of the halls of the buildings, as I have already mentioned, namely the exploitation, in the New Empire, of the sandstone quarries at Gebel el-

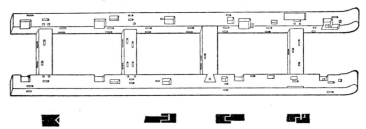

FIG. 25. Wooden sled, 14 feet long, on which a royal barge (Fig. 16) had been transported; XIIth Dynasty, Dahshûr. Cairo Museum.

Silsila, near Aswân. This stone, though not as beautiful as the Ṭura limestone, is very easily worked; large flawless blocks can be obtained near the river edge, and, lastly, it can be used as architraves to span spaces of 8 yards or more without risk of collapse.

We can only understand the methods used by the Egyptians from the Third Dynasty until Roman times in the construction of their buildings by putting entirely out of our minds any preconceived notions, and examining, first the tools known to have been used by the Egyptians, and secondly the existing monuments.

The implements used in building, apart from those already discussed, for shaping the stone, were the lever, the sled (Fig. 25), ropes, rollers, sleepers, water for levelling, vast embankments of rubble, plumb-rules, boats, and unlimited man-power. The question of the mason's square is discussed later. Modern and medieval masonry is intimately connected with the pulley, acting in conjunction with a 'lewis' or 'tongs'; the block is cut, tested for rectangularity by means of a square, lifted above the course, which is duly mortared, and finally lowered into position and tested by the square and plumb-rule. In Egyptian masonry a difficult point arises at the outset, namely that the Egyptians did not use the pulley. That none has been found is not sufficient evidence (see my remarks above on the tubular drills), but other considerations make this fact certain. In the numerous representations and models of large sailing-ships (see p. 141), where the pulleys should be, at the masthead, none exists; men had to stand to push up the yard. No trace of the use of lewises or tongs is seen on the laid blocks in the monuments. The size of the blocks proves that they were therefore not lifted as we understand the term; they had to be levered on to a sled and hauled up an incline leading to the course. Traces of such ramps can be seen in the Great Pylon of Sheshonq at Karnak and elsewhere. In the monuments, statues, blocks and even obelisks are represented on sleds, one of which 14 feet in length has been found, and is now in the Cairo Museum (Fig. 25). Rollers and sleepers have also been found, though admittedly not very big. Since blocks of great size could not be lifted, they had to be handled from the side by means of levers, and bosses are common on blocks in pyramid and other times. Assume that a block had been hauled up to the course: it had to be handled from the front, otherwise, if it once projected too much, there would be no means of getting it back. We therefore have to assume that not only were there supply slopes of earth or rubble leading up to the course being laid, but also an embankment outside the course on which the builders could not only stand, but use their levers, if only for disengaging the block from its sled! If these considerations are not perplexing enough we have another even more so, namely, the fact that in the majority of the great blocks used in pyramids and *maṣṭabas*, the joints between the blocks are neither vertical to the ground nor at right angles to the line of the building. In other words, the joints (or 'rising joints' as they are now called) are askew in every sense, but in good masonry the fit is perfect from front to back. We have to face the fact that block *A* had to fit block *B*, block *B* had to fit block *C*, and so on (Figs. 26–28). If we assume that two blocks were brought up to the course and laboriously fitted one to another, we have to believe that they were lowered on to the course and tested against each other several times. In the absence of pulleys, however, the lowering of the blocks on to the course would involve raising it again to correct any errors, an impossibly long process when levers alone were used. The only explanation which meets the case in a general way is that the blocks were lined up elsewhere than on the course, and that parallel planes were cut between each pair, and that they were then pushed together and perhaps a saw-cut made between each pair to make the joint perfect. The problem is indeed a perplexing one!

Several other points can be noticed in the best masonry with large blocks. One is the very fine top-surface of each course, those of the pyramids being almost dead flat. It is also clear that mortar was put into each joint. With such a fine fit and with blocks of great sizes, the use of mortar would seem superfluous, but a consideration of the laying of the blocks opens up a new vista of inquiry. Once off its sled on to the course there is no conceivable method by which a block of several tons could have been pushed 'home' against its neighbour, unless it were, so to speak, floating on a thin bed of wet, viscid mortar. I believe that this is the explanation of the mortar and the almost perfect smoothness of the tops.

The remains of unfinished temples and walls show that the front surfaces of the building were finished last, when the mason's square was of necessity used in making the corners

PLATE 27

Fig. 26. Granite casing-blocks only partly faced, near the entrance of the Third Pyramid at Giza, showing the bosses into which the levers could engage during the laying process. IVth Dynasty. The average height of the courses is about four feet

PLATE 28

FIG. 27. Granite blocks in the Third Pyramid at Giza showing the oblique joints

rectangular. In the case of a Great Pyramid we cannot suppose that when all was complete the whole was scaffolded before the dressing was carried out. The absence of traces of 'putlogs' in the masonry in places such as the top casing of the Second Pyramid makes this almost certain. The only explanation for the method of dressing large buildings is that it was done while the embankment which, as we have seen, must have covered the whole building, was being removed, to measured lines or other indications left when the building was being erected. From a close study of this point I believe that the top outside edge of each course was dressed in to the eventual surface—a kind of bevel, as it were.

If the above sketch is not sufficient to illustrate the vast difference between Egyptian masonry and that with which we are familiar I can cite one other. In some of the less carefully constructed buildings, one course is not quite parallel with those above and below it. This, and other considerations, particularly the Egyptian habit, at times, of building with blocks of irregular height, lead me to believe that the top of the course was dressed *after* the blocks had been laid. Their only method of levelling was by running a watercourse, the water being banked up with Nile mud, along and about the surface to be levelled, and then measuring down from the surface at many points simultaneously, thus establishing datum points to which the complete surface would be eventually reduced. One instance can be cited to show the likelihood of some such method having been adopted. The platform which runs partly under the Great Pyramid was examined very carefully by the Survey of Egypt, who found that, although the exposed parts lie on an almost perfect plane, the whole slopes up about 6 inches from the north-east to the south-west corner. If, when the points were being simultaneously checked, a north-east wind had been blowing, such a result might occur; indeed no other explanation seems possible.

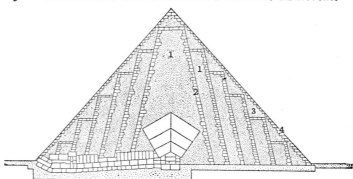

FIG. 29. Section of pyramid of King Sahurê' at Abuṣîr; Vth Dynasty
(after BORCHARDT; *Das Grabdenkmal des Königs Sahurê'*, p. 29).

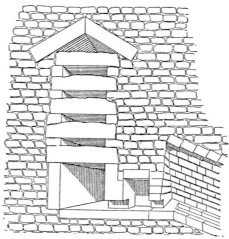

FIG. 30. Section of the relieving chambers above the King's Chamber in
the Great Pyramid (after PERROT and CHIPIEZ, *Histoire de l'Art dans
l'Antiquité*, p. 227).

The relieving devices in the pyramids are easy to explain; the
interior blocks, except those next to the casing-blocks or to

PLATE 29

Fig. 28. Masonry in the wall of the funerary temple of the Vth-Dynasty pyramid of Unas at Saqqâra. The angle *ABC* is a right angle but the plane of the joint *AB* is not at right angles to the face of the wall. Similarly, though the angle *DCE* is a right angle the plane the joint below the joint is at a slant with the bedding joint

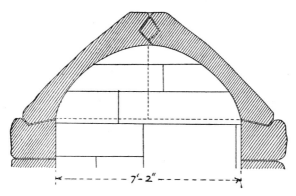

Fig. 31. Corbelled arch in the central sanctuary of the XVIIIth-Dynasty temple at El-Deir el-Baḥari.

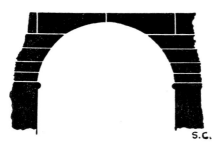

S.C.

Fig. 32. False arch, cut from two granite blocks; in a Middle Kingdom *maṣṭaba* at Dahshûr (from DE MORGAN, *Fouilles à Dahchour, mars–juin,* 1894, p. 55).

chambers and galleries, are hardly bonded at all. Furthermore, for some obscure reason, they all seem to have internal facings (Fig. 29). This strange method of construction might result in a huge mass of masonry slipping down *en bloc* on the chamber, which in bonded masonry could not occur (Fig. 30).

Before leaving the subject of masonry the arch remains to

be considered. The arch was known both in brickwork and in rough stonework, but in monumental masonry no example of the arch as we know it—the voussoirs mutually supporting—has been preserved before Roman times. A round roof was obtained by the Egyptians either by bringing each course slightly inwards until the two walls met and afterwards cutting the round roof (Fig. 31), or by constructing a pent-roof and cutting the 'arch' in that (Fig. 32).

The subject of masonry in ancient Egypt leaves many problems unsolved. When one reflects on the considerations that I have brought forward, incomplete as the length of this article of necessity makes them, it is a mystery how the great pyramids could each have been constructed in the lifetime of a man. The *reasons* for many of the strange masonic fantasies are even more perplexing—if reasons there ever were. For instance, why did Sneferu and Amenemḥēt III build two pyramids each; what were the reasons for Djoser's apparent continual changes of mind while the superstructure and galleries of the Step Pyramid were being constructed? Lastly why, in the first gallery of the Great Pyramid, do we pass, at regular intervals of 10 cubits (17 feet), clean through the middle of a vast block?

Apart from gold beads and beads of semi-precious stones, the earliest jewellery dates from the First Dynasty, the outstanding example being the armlet found on the arm of the Queen of Djer. This consists of a 'banner-name' sign, surmounted by a hawk, alternating in gold and turquoise and supplemented by amethyst beads. By the Sixth Dynasty the celebrated cloisonné jewellery appears, the gold cloisons being filled with hard stones cut to fit. This form of jewellery reached a height of excellence in the Twelfth Dynasty, some of the pectorals from Dahshûr and El Lâhûn containing several hundred pieces of inlay. The proportions and fine taste of some of these pieces are unsurpassed in later periods. By Tutʻankhamūn's time, although the motifs multiply to an enormous extent, the inlay is almost entirely of glass, and elaboration robs many of the pieces of a great deal of their beauty. Cloisonné work continues until the Roman period. A more detailed description of ancient Egyptian jewellery belongs to the realm of art rather than to the subject of the present chapter, and is provided elsewhere.

From predynastic times agate, amethyst, green felspar, rock crystal and chalcedony were obtained from the Eastern Desert, malachite and turquoise from Sinai, and lapis lazuli from western Asia. Haematite and even jade or jadeite were also employed, but the source of supply is unknown. In the Middle Kingdom red and green jasper make their appearance, both of which seem to come from the Eastern Desert. Beryl, of which emerald is the jewel form, does not occur until Ptolemaic times. Other materials used in jewellery are a resin, resembling but not identical with amber, which was used from the earliest times. Coral was used from about the seventh century B.C. Mother of pearl was known early, at any rate in Nubia, but pearls are unknown until Ptolemaic times. The diamond, ruby, sapphire, and opal are not found in ancient Egyptian jewellery.

Egyptian paintings, in general, were crude. Very little blending of colours was attempted by the painters, though some of their efforts show the most astounding amount of detail. Their colours were derived from the naturally occurring substances and were of the following composition. The black was always some form of carbon, such as soot or charcoal, the blue was either azurite from Sinai (IVth Dyn.) or an artificial frit made by heating silica, malachite, calcium carbonate and natron. This is also known in the Fourth Dynasty. The brown was ochre, a naturally occurring oxide of iron; the green was powdered malachite (from Sinai) or a frit analogous to the blue frit, possibly a mixture of blue frit and yellow ochre. Grey pigment is comparatively rare, and consisted either of a mixture of gypsum and charcoal or of yellow ochre and lamp-black. Pink was a mixture of red and white pigment in dynastic times. Madder does not appear until the Roman period. The red was a natural red ochre, and the white either chalk or gypsum. In early times the yellow was also ochre, but by the Eighteenth Dynasty orpiment was also used.

Analyses to determine the paint vehicles have not been satisfactory. Beeswax was certainly used, however, both for painting on and for coating finished work. Gesso, a mixture of whiting and glue, was freely used for painting on and for gilding, especially when the material to be coloured was plaster or wood. The usual bases for paint work were canvas, papyrus, plaster, pottery, mud, stone and wood.

Scenes of brewing beer are numerous, especially in the Old Kingdom, where each process is sometimes accompanied by a brief description; while grape picking, treading, pressing and bottling the wine are depicted on tombs of the New Kingdom with great frequency and detail. In certain scenes the artists go as far as to depict the disastrous effects of over-indulgence. The details of brewing, involving the discussion of the chemical principles of fermentation in general, are rather beyond the scope of this chapter. It suffices to say that the ancient beer was made from barley, without any admixture of hops, the general process of manufacture being almost identical with that by which *bûza* is now made in Egypt for the lower classes of the population. This to-day has an alcoholic content of some 7 per cent.

Mr. Lucas describes the preparation of modern *bûza* in Cairo as follows:

1. A good quality wheat is taken, the dirt removed, and the wheat coarsely ground.
2. Three-quarters of the ground wheat is put into a large wooden basin or trough and kneaded with water into a dough, yeast being added.
3. The dough is made into thick loaves, which are lightly baked so as not to destroy the *enzymes* or kill the yeast.

PLATE 30

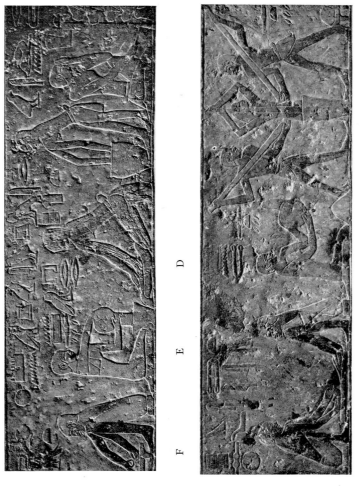

Fɪɢ 33. Brewing beer from a scene from the *maṣṭaba* of Kaemreḥu from Saqqâra. Vth Dynasty. Now in the Cairo Museum

PLATE 31

G   H   I

FIG. 34. Remainder of the brewing scene shown in fig. 33. The scenes run from right to left

4. The remaining quarter of the wheat is moistened with water and exposed to the air for some time, after which, while moist, it is crushed.

5. The loaves are broken up and put into a vessel with water and the crushed moist wheat added; the mixture ferments on account of the yeast present in the bread, though in order to induce a quicker fermentation a little old *bûza* from a previous brewing is added.

6. After fermentation, the mixture is passed through a hair sieve, the solid material being pressed on the sieve with the hands.

In the brewing scenes shown in Figs. 33 and 34 the processes are depicted from right to left. The inscriptions are a mixture of the remarks made by the brewers and terse descriptions of what is being done. They are as follows (after Mr. Alan Rowe):

A. (Words spoken to a woman) '. . . thee! Hurry! It is hot.'
B. {'Crush well. I have finished with the grain.'
   {'Oh! I am crushing with all my strength.'
C. 'Selecting the grain.'
D. 'Sifting the grain.'
E. 'Kneading the fresh dough.'
F. 'Beating the *pesen* bread for brewing.'
G. 'Straining.'
H. 'Mixing.' (With names of the mixers.)
I. 'Filling with beer.'

The scene showing two men and a woman pounding in a mortar bears no description. It may represent the process described by Mr. Lucas under No. 5.

Wine was not only imported, but vines were grown in Egypt both in the western oases and the Western Delta. As in the case of beer, there were a great many varieties of which we do not know the differences. In the New Kingdom wine was bottled in amphorae with mud seals, on which traces can generally be seen of the hole left in the seal for the escape of the gas during fermentation. They were then inscribed with the quality and place of origin of the contents, and the name of the chief of the vineyard.

Palm wine was known in the Old Kingdom. This appears to have been made by tapping the body of the tree near the head and permitting the liquid to run out and afterwards ferment, while date wine was known in the same period.

The process of distillation was unknown until late times; the first mention of it is by Aristotle in the fourth century B.C.

Sugar from the sugar-cane was just known by Roman times, the cane being a native of the Far East. Sweetening in Egyptian times was by honey extractions from grapes or dates.

The cultivation of the cereals, wheat, barley and spelt, being the staple industry of the country, one would expect that we should have a vast mass of information about the making of bread and cakes. Indeed, from the Old Kingdom onwards we have the names and can see the shapes of scores of types of these, yet their actual nature is rarely revealed. The corn was cut with a wooden sickle into which saw-edged flints were inserted, specimens of which have recently been found in the First Dynasty tomb of Ḥemaka at Saqqâra; and this primitive form of implement is known to have been used as late as the time of Sheshonq. Mills seem to have been unknown in ancient Egypt. In the Middle and New Kingdoms we find representations of great mortars in which one or two men are 'pounding the corn' with heavy pestles. The flour was next rubbed finer between two stones. In the tomb of Tutʿankhamūn a model grinder was actually found. In the Old Kingdom the lower and larger stone was placed on the ground sloping towards the front, so that the finely ground flour ran down into a little hollow there; and the woman who ground the flour knelt before it. During the Middle Kingdom a table hollowed out in front of the rock took the place of the lower stone; the woman could then stand and her work was thus made lighter. After the grinding followed the kneading of the dough. In the nobles' houses the dough was placed in a basket and kneaded with the hands; the water was pressed out into a pot placed underneath the basket and the dough was then shaped into the form required and placed on a conical stove, and apparently not in an oven, although what is believed to be an oven has been found at Tell el-'Amarna. For very large kitchens the dough was kneaded with the feet. On the subject of leaven we are almost without information.

In conclusion, I would point out that the title of the present chapter, 'Mechanical and Technical Processes', can be made to cover an even larger range of subjects than those enumerated in the previous pages; this particularly applies to the materials known to the ancient Egyptians. A multitude of organic substances such as cosmetics, perfumes, resins, incenses, oils, fats and waxes were known and many of them have been definitely identified. Most of these, with one exception, can hardly be considered to be definitely connected with mechanical or technical processes except as regards their manufacture, and here we are mostly very short of information. The exception is the process of mummification. After considerable hesitation I have decided to omit this entirely, since the technique varies from period to period, sometimes from dynasty to dynasty, and a discussion of the materials employed would occupy a space far beyond the range of the chapter; furthermore, some points in connexion with mummification are still in dispute, and anything short of a complete *exposé* of the subject would mislead rather than instruct.   R. ENGELBACH

CHAPTER 6

SCIENCE

It is with science in the making rather than with science as we understand the word to-day that we have to deal in the present chapter. Modern science implies not only the collection of observed facts and the application of those facts to practical problems, but a study of the underlying principles and their formulation into natural laws. Meteorology, for instance, is far more than either weather lore or weather statistics.

It seems hardly legitimate to apply our present conception of science in dealing with the older civilizations of Egypt and Mesopotamia. The majority of writers on Greek science assume that the scientific idea suddenly emerged with the Ionian Greeks. The Egyptians taught orally; the Greeks by writing. For this reason, far less is known of the Egyptians than the Greeks, and the writer on Egyptian science starts at a disadvantage. The Egyptians never had the consuming intellectual curiosity which is characteristic of the Greek spirit. In their enthusiasm for the marvel of the Greek achievement many writers have been apt to forget the debt Greece owed to Egypt—a debt the Greeks themselves acknowledged in no uncertain terms.

Thales and many others after him were profoundly impressed and stimulated by the Egyptian civilization. In Egypt they found an immense store of practical and useful knowledge, if not exactly science in the full sense in which we use the word to-day, at any rate the raw material of science. Yet future research may reveal a more developed scientific attitude in Egypt than has hitherto been suspected.

A study of the beginnings of science in Egypt enables us to gain some idea of the processes of thought which underlie the remarkable development which took place among the Greeks. The material available for study is relatively meagre, and fresh discoveries may necessitate considerable modification of the conclusions expressed in this chapter.

The Calendar

The outstanding achievement of the Ancient Egyptians in science was the introduction of the first practical calendar. It is dealt with in Chapter 1.

Astronomy

Star diagrams were made at a very early date, the stars being grouped in constellations according to a fancied resemblance to some animate or inanimate form. The grouping, however, was not the same as our own, which derives from the Babylonians. Several examples of star diagrams survive on the ceilings of temples and tombs and on the interior surfaces of coffin lids. They were supposed to be of some use to the deceased in his journeyings in the netherworld. They do not exhibit the differences one would expect, had they been intended for horoscopes as some writers have suggested. Generally speaking, they conform to a standard pattern with comparatively minor variations.

The keeping of the calendar being in the hands of the priests, special value was attached to the selection of the proper days for religious observances. The sun and moon played a large part in priestly cosmology and mythology. In the literature available are references to the planets ('the stars who never rest'), and in particular to Venus ('the morning star' or 'the evening star'— in early times probably differentiated); Jupiter ('the resplendent star'); Saturn ('Horus, the Bull'); Mars ('the red Horus'), and possibly Mercury.

A map of the heavens, specially prepared to show the positions of the principal stars as seen from Memphis about 3500 B.C., enables us to identify some of the star groups figured in the ancient star maps. At that date the 'Great Bear' was conspicuous in rotating round the pole and was named the 'ox-leg'.

The Bedawiyyîn of the Sahara still call it *Er-Rigl*—'the leg'. Other constellations which can be identified are *Bootes* (crocodile and hippopotamus); *Cygnus* (a man with outstretched arms) which played an important part in Egyptian cosmology; *Orion* (represented as a man running and looking backwards over his shoulder); *Cassiopeia* (a figure with arms extended); *Draco* and possibly the *Pleiades*; *Scorpio* and *Aries*. *Sirius* was 'The Great Star'. An early myth regarding Thoth and the injured eye of the sun-god may point to an underlying conception of the part played by the moon in eclipses. Particular sanctity was attached to the circumpolar stars, visible throughout the year—'the never vanishing ones', 'the imperishable stars'.

The twelve zodiacal signs are entirely absent from the sacred astronomy of Egypt before the Greek period. Instead, the 'dekans' were used to divide the year. These are groups of stars, or a conspicuous star, rising at particular 'hours of the night' during the 36 successive periods of 10 days each, constituting the year. They are situated within a wide equatorial belt and commence with Sirius ('the mistress of the year'). Some of the names survive in Greek.

Each period of 10 days was marked by the heliacal rising of the next dekan on the eastern horizon. Lists of dekans were prepared for ascertaining the time of the night if the calendar date was known, or for determining the dekan, if the hour of the night was known. Dekan calendars in a much debased form and full of copyist's errors appear on the lids of Eleventh-Dynasty coffins (*c.* 2100 B.C.).

The 36 dekans form the old year of 360 days, ignoring the five additional or epagomenal days. They therefore fell at different periods in successive years. The tables give the days and months on which a dusk culmination, a dusk setting or a dawn rising of the corresponding dekanal constellation occurred. They could therefore be used to fix the day and season and the hour of the night by anyone who observed the positions of the constellations in the night sky. Additional tables were used to show how far the calendar had shifted through the seasons. The two calendars existing side by side presented no great difficulty. In Egypt to-day three calendars are in general use—the Arabic (or lunar) for religious purposes; the Coptic (or Ancient Egyptian) for agricultural operations; and the European for business dealings with Europeans and Americans. An almanack showing all three can be purchased for half a piastre and a surprising interest is taken in the calendar by all. Those who are able to read are appealed to by those who cannot—the vast majority.

The dekanal system can be traced back at least as far as the Third Dynasty (*c.* 2800 B.C.) and may be older. In later times the names of the stellar deities were forgotten and became mutilated beyond recognition. New interest in them was aroused when the Greeks introduced the twelve signs of the zodiac (derived from the Babylonians), which were then represented intermingled with the older pictures of the dekanal stars. Later the dekans played an important part in astrology, which developed independently of Graeco-Roman influences.

The day was divided into 24 hours—12 'hours of the day' and 12 'hours of the night'. Observations of the stars were made by a simple sighting instrument, the *merkhet*, used (as the inscriptions record) as an 'indicator for determining the commencement of a festival and for placing all men in their hours'. Some star diagrams in the tomb paintings of the Twentieth Dynasty (*c.* 1200 B.C.) attempt to show the position of the stars during the 12 hours of the night at intervals of 15 days.

The *merkhet* instrument was also used for alining the axis of a temple in the ceremonial observed during the laying of foundation stones. In wall scenes depicting the ceremony, the cord, pegs, and hammers used are represented, and the accompanying inscriptions refer to observations of the stars determining the position of the axis.

The hours of the night were determined by water clocks

specially used 'when the dekan stars are not visible'. The oldest water clock dates from about 1300 B.C. An account of one specimen, of the same type, in an Eighteenth-Dynasty tomb is of special interest as the earliest record of physical observations. It gives a relation between the lengths of the summer and winter nights.

The water clock, later called by the Greeks the *clepsydra*, took the form of a vessel shaped like a flower-pot. In use, it was filled to a certain mark with water, which flowed out gradually through a small aperture near the base. On the interior surface a series of marks corresponding to the water-level at the various hours of the night indicated the 'hours'. These 'hours' were not of uniform length, but in the absence of regularly moving mechanism or precise methods of observing the movements of the stars, the irregularities were probably not noticed. Clep-sydrae were used in temples to enable the hours of duty of the attendants to be apportioned. The 'hour', being thought of as the twelfth part of the night, varied according to the season of the year, and a scale of markings for each month was pro-vided.

Some unusual features of the only inflow type of water clock extant (*c.* 100 B.C.) seem to point to the Egyptian origin of several passages in classical literature dealing with the rate of increase in the length of the day from winter to summer. In this type of water clock, water was allowed to drip in from a reservoir, and time intervals were gauged by the rise of the water-level against a scale of markings on the interior surface— the Nilometer in miniature.

The hours of the day were very roughly determined by simple shadow clocks, evolved independently of the clepsydra. Shadow clocks are still in use in country districts and to this day the 'servant gapeth after the shadow' (Job vii. 2 margin), when it is nearing time to knock off work. In the East, except in towns, there is still little need for mean solar time, and clocks and watches in Arabia are altered daily at sunset to agree with the time of sunset as shown by the almanack. The day begins at sunset. (Cf. Gen. i. 13.)

Observations of the directions of shadows during the day time as well as observations of the night sky enabled early observers to acquire a sense of direction and to mark the meridian[1] dividing the period of daylight conveniently into morning and afternoon. The orientation of the faces of the Great Pyramid to the cardinal points of the compass to a very high degree of accuracy points to exact observations of transits of stars across the meridian. There is no direct evidence that the Egyptians determined the summer (or winter) solstice, when the sun reaches its highest (lowest) point in the heavens, and its noon shadow is shortest (longest): or the equinoxes, when the sun rises due east and sets due west. It is difficult, however, to imagine that these features passed unnoticed.

No records of continuous observations have yet been brought to light. Should any be discovered in the future, it might be possible to decide many points, at present matters of conjecture: such, for example, as to whether the shadows cast by pyramids and obelisks were actually used to measure time. Vexed questions of chronology might be settled if dated records of celestial phenomena as, for instance, eclipses were available.

Mathematics

The sources of our knowledge of Egyptian mathematics are meagre. The Greeks are commonly spoken of as the first mathematicians, but that is only because a considerable amount of literature on the subject has survived.

The Egyptians achieved astonishing results in the practical applications of their knowledge, but no written records as to

[1] An observer standing with his face to the north is in the plane of the meridian. The sun crosses the meridian at the highest point of its daily journey across the sky. It then casts the shortest shadow.

how they accomplished them have come down to us. Such theoretical knowledge as there was, was mainly in the hands of a privileged class—priests and scribes—whose interest it was to keep it secret.

As early as the First Dynasty (*c.* 3200 B.C.) a decimal system of numeration was in use involving high numbers running into millions. There were separate signs for unity and for each power of 10 up to a million. There was no sign for zero and therefore no positional notation, which even the Greeks did not develop and which was introduced later by Indian mathematicians. As there were no separate signs for numbers between 1 and 10, signs were repeated to the number required. Thus the number 142,857 comprised 27 separate hieroglyphic signs. The cursive hieratic, however, employed abbreviations.

The Egyptian notation and methods illustrate the principle that, ultimately, all arithmetical processes are based on counting. Addition is simple counting. Multiplication is a special form of counting. (The Egyptian word means 'to nod', namely to count by nodding, a perfectly natural process. Primitive peoples and children to-day sometimes find it difficult to count without sympathetic movements of the hand or fingers.) Subtraction is merely counting backwards. Division is the reverse of multiplication. To the Egyptian, all four processes were simply forms of counting. To multiply 9 by 6 was to 'calculate 9 to 6 times'. To divide 88 by 11 was to 'reckon with 11 to find 88'. Squaring was a special form of multiplication and square root was a form of division. The square roots of $6\frac{1}{4}$ and $1\frac{1}{2}\frac{1}{16}$ were correctly evaluated, but there was no general method of finding a square root.

The Egyptian dispensed with multiplication tables. He could double any number without calculation, and he could also multiply by 10 simply by substituting 'ten' signs for units, 'hundred' signs for 'tens', and so on. Thus, each sum usually involved a number of successive doublings or halvings. If, in the course of the work, it was necessary to multiply 15 by 13, the Egyptian proceeded as follows:

$\diagup 1 \times 15 =$ 15   The multipliers which added up to 13
   $2 \times 15 =$ 30   were ticked off and the corresponding
$\diagup 4 \times 15 =$ 60   products added together.
$\diagup 8 \times 15 = 120$

   Total

   $13 \times 15 = 195$

The method of proportion was frequently employed, but never explicitly formulated. A typical method was to assume a trial result and then find what alteration was necessary to fulfil the requirements of the problem. Thus, to quote an actual case: 'What number added to its one-seventh part gives 19?' To 7 is added its seventh part. Result—8. The figure 19 is then divided by 8 and the result is multiplied by 7 giving the correct result $16\frac{1}{2} \frac{1}{8}$, or $16\frac{5}{8}$ as we should now write it.

This is the method of 'false position' (*regula falsi* or *positio falsa*) much used by Diophantus of Alexandria (*c.* A.D. 250). It continued in use in our early arithmetical text-books, until displaced by algebraic methods.

With the exception of $\frac{2}{3}$ and $\frac{3}{4}$ no mixed fractions were used, but only those with unity in the numerator—unit fractions. A fraction which we should now write as $\frac{7}{12}$ was expressed by the unit fractions $\frac{1}{3} \frac{1}{4}$ written side by side, implying addition, just as we now write $1\frac{2}{3}$. Tables were drawn up for fractions with 2 in the numerator, with their equivalents in two or more unit fractions. A typical entry in such a table is:

     Division of 2 by 89   : $\frac{1}{60}$ $\frac{1}{356}$ $\frac{1}{534}$ $\frac{1}{890}$

If, in the course of the work, it was necessary to double $\frac{1}{89}$ the writer would refer to the table and set down the series of unit-fractions given above.

In this way, the Egyptian avoided the trouble of evolving a more complex fractional notation, which would greatly have simplified his work. He knew that $\frac{2}{3}+\frac{1}{15}$ made 11 unit-fractions each $\frac{1}{15}$, and that 4 more were required to complete the whole, yet he made no attempt to evolve any notation to express the 11 unit-fractions as $\frac{11}{15}$. To him, it was a collection of 11 unit-fractions. The first examples of mixed fractions are not found until Demotic times. Thus: 'my $\frac{1}{3}\frac{1}{15}$ part, which makes 2 parts of 5 of the houses', which is merely another way of writing $\frac{2}{5}$.

The limitations of this notation made necessary the use of special tables. For measuring out grain, a unit (*hekat*), approximately a bushel, was in use. This was divided into fractional parts $\frac{1}{2}$, $\frac{1}{4}$, $\frac{1}{8}$, $\frac{1}{16}$, $\frac{1}{32}$, and $\frac{1}{64}$ each with its own name, and at some

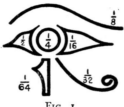

Fig. 1.

stage identified with a part of the picture of the magic eye of Horus, which (according to the ancient myth) was torn in pieces by the wicked Set. Fractions below $\frac{1}{64}$ were expressed in terms of the *ro* ($\frac{1}{320}$ part of the *hekat*). The Egyptian never used any other fractional parts, but if in the course of his work he wished to express a fraction such as $\frac{1}{7}$ he immediately reduced it to a series of dimidiated parts, as above. In the same way to-day, we should not write $\frac{1}{11}$ ton, but express it in cwt., qrs, and lb.

A table was then drawn up, expressing the various fractions of the *hekat* in terms of the recognized units. Two examples from such a table may be given:

$$\frac{1}{11}\ hekat = \frac{1}{16}+\frac{1}{64}\ \text{and}\ 4\frac{1}{11}\ ro$$
$$\frac{1}{13}\ hekat = \frac{1}{16}\ \text{and}\ 4\frac{1}{2}+\frac{1}{13}+\frac{1}{26}\ ro$$

Two-thirds seems to have been a primary concept, and the Egyptian could write down $\frac{2}{3}$ of a number without calculation. One-third was obtained by halving $\frac{2}{3}$, which was regarded as 'the two parts' of a length divided in three parts, $\frac{1}{3}$ being 'the third (and last) part'. (Cf. Genesis xlvii. 24.) Even now, we say 'three parts full', where division into four parts is tacitly assumed. It should be noted that $\frac{2}{3}$ is, in fact, equivalent to $\frac{1}{1\frac{1}{2}}$, and that, as for $1\frac{1}{2}$, both the Greeks and the Romans had a special word for it. (Cf. German—*anderthalb*.)

With such a cumbrous system of fractional notation, calculation was a lengthy process, frequently involving the use of very small fractions, e.g. $\frac{1}{5432}$ occurs. There was a danger, too, that a number of fractions might be set down without realizing that they would readily combine to form one or more simpler fractions.

The system of unit fractions survived long after the use of mixed fractions had become general. It is found, with the same exceptional treatment of $\frac{2}{3}$, in the papyrus of Akhmîm, written in Greek about A.D. 600. Modern Stock Exchange quotations in Cairo are still often given in the same form, e.g. $98\frac{1}{2}\frac{1}{32}$. $\frac{1}{32}$ in excess of $\frac{1}{2}$ conveys a clearer meaning than $\frac{17}{32}$.

It is not difficult to see how the fractional notation originated in practical problems dealing with division of food and other commodities. The word 'division' originally meant partition in two. Suppose 5 loaves are to be divided among 6 persons— an actual problem. The primitive method, still in use in remote parts of the world to-day, is to divide each loaf in half, and give one half to each person. The remaining 4 half loaves are again divided. Of the 8 portions, 1 is distributed to each individual, leaving 2 quarter loaves over. Each of these is divided in three, giving one portion to each person, who has thus received $\frac{1}{2}\frac{1}{4}\frac{1}{12}$ of a loaf. To the Egyptian, this was a complicated process, because of the limitations of his notation. To us, who can write $\frac{5}{6}$, it presents no difficulty.

As no symbolic notation was developed, there are no general formulae, with one possible exception: 'To make $\frac{2}{3}$ of a fraction take $\frac{1}{2}\frac{1}{6}$.'

Stated in modern terminology, the following are examples of the types of problem successfully solved:

1. Subtract $\frac{1}{4}\ \frac{1}{8}\ \frac{1}{10}\ \frac{1}{30}\ \frac{1}{45}$ from $\frac{2}{3}$. (*Ans.* $\frac{1}{9} + \frac{1}{40}$.)

2. To a number $\frac{2}{3}$, $\frac{1}{2}$ and $\frac{1}{7}$ of it are added. The result is 37. What is the number? (*Ans.* $16 + \frac{1}{56} + \frac{1}{679} + \frac{1}{776}$.)

3. Divide 10 measures of barley among 10 men, in such a way that each gets $\frac{1}{8}$ more than his neighbour.

   This amounts to finding an arithmetical progression of ten numbers, whose sum is 10 and common difference $\frac{1}{8}$.

4. Divide 700 loaves among 4 men in the proportion of $\frac{2}{3}$, $\frac{1}{2}$, $\frac{1}{3}$, and $\frac{1}{4}$. (*Ans.* $266\frac{2}{3}$, 200, $133\frac{1}{3}$, and 100.)

5. The area of a rectangular enclosure is 12 acres. The breadth is $\frac{3}{4}$ of the length. Find the length and breadth.

   This example involves the solution of a simple equation with one unknown quantity.

6. A triangle of given area has the perpendicular height $2\frac{1}{2}$ times the base. Find the base and the height.

   It seems certain that the properties of the isosceles, if not of any, triangle, now expressed by the formulae which follow, were known; but it is not easy to prove this conclusion from the material available.

$$A = \frac{bh}{2}; \qquad b = \sqrt{\left(2\frac{Ah}{b}\right)}; \qquad b = \frac{b}{h}\sqrt{\left(2A.\frac{h}{b}\right)}$$

where A = area, b = base and h = height.

7. Find the area of a circular field 9 cubits in diameter.

   The working implies the use of the following rule: 'Subtract $\frac{1}{9}$ from the diameter and square the result.' This is equivalent to a value of π (ratio of circumference to diameter) of 3·1605. The fact that the area is expressed as a square points to the method of counting squares on a surface ruled in squares. The value of π now known to be 3·1415. . . . The Babylonians used 3, as did the writer of 1 Kings vii. 23.

8. Find the content of a cylinder of diameter 12 and height 8 cubits.

The area of the base is found as in No. 7 above. This is then multiplied by the height.

The question whether the Egyptians knew that a triangle whose sides are proportional to 3, 4, and 5 is right-angled has been much discussed. It seems inconceivable that they should not have made this discovery. Yet there is no direct evidence that they did so. We find equations of the form $3^2 + 4^2 = 5^2$, but there is no statement of the general relation nor any evidence such as three rods of lengths 3, 4, and 5 cubits bundled together, or a cord knotted at points dividing it in the same ratios.

One example indicates that the Egyptian had a clear conception of the nature of a geometrical series, of which the first term is unity. The sum of 5 terms is correctly given. It is not clear from the solution that any general formula was known.

Problems dealing with pyramids illustrate the Egyptian method of measuring an angle of slope by the horizontal offset per unit vertical height (the *seked*), a measure of what we now call the co-tangent of the angle. In the practical application to the cutting of casing stones to the required angle, the stone mason would mark off one cubit vertically and then set out the *seked* horizontally. He then drew the line indicating the direction in which the stone should be cut. Such lines have often been found on stone blocks.

The problem most widely discussed in modern times is one dealing with the volume of a truncated pyramid. It is far in advance of anything we know of Egyptian geometry. Many attempts have been made to reconstruct the mental processes required for the sequence of operations, which follows the use of the modern formula $V = \frac{1}{3}h \ (a^2 + ab + b^2)$, where h is the

height, and *a* and *b* are the sides of the squares forming the top
and the bottom surfaces.

The truncated pyramid was a familiar sight during the construction of a pyramid and, no doubt, calculations had to be

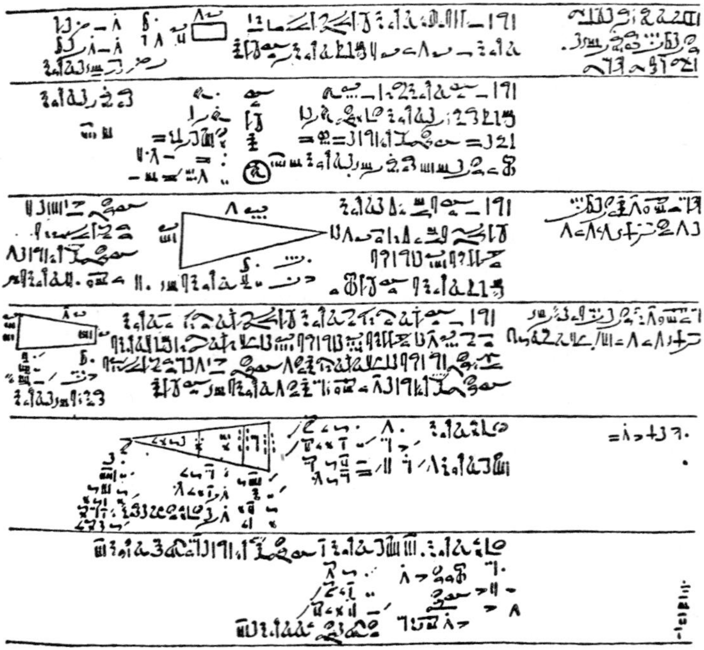

FIG. 2. Rhind Mathematical Papyrus (Brit. Mus. Pl. XIV). Problems
dealing with rectangles, circles, and triangles.

made in connexion with questions of labour and material. An
obelisk is a small pyramid on top of a truncated pyramid.

It is possible that the result was arrived at by experiments
with models. For the purpose, Nile mud in a half-dried, semi-
plastic state would serve as well as the modern plasticine. The

general method might have been discovered by cutting up a solid model into simple solids of easily determined volumes. Perhaps the volumes were found by a weighing method similar to that used later by Heron of Alexandria (*c.* 250 B.C.).

There is no direct evidence that the Egyptians knew how to calculate the volume of a pyramid, yet it is difficult to imagine that they did not. The volume might have been determined by constructing a pyramid in model blocks and then rearranging the blocks in the shape of a solid prism. The formula 'Volume = $\frac{1}{3} \times$ area of base $\times$ height' is first used by Democritus (*c.* 460 B.C.). Heron uses various formulae for the volumes of cones and pyramids—some correct, others incorrect. It is significant that the incorrect formulae were derived, in part, at any rate, from Babylonia, where they originated in problems of everyday life, such as the contents of baskets, tree-trunks, and dikes. These incorrect formulae lingered in use for a long time, for practical purposes.

If the Egyptian *did* know how to find the volume of a pyramid, the volume of a truncated pyramid would have been easily determined as the difference between the volumes of two pyramids.

The statement is frequently made that one problem indicates with certainty that the Egyptian of 2000 B.C. knew the formula for the area of a hemisphere. There are sound reasons, however, for rejecting this interpretation, which would place Egyptian mathematics on a far higher level than the evidence from other sources warrants.

From the foregoing summary, it will be clear that mathematical knowledge in ancient Egypt was essentially practical in character and must have developed as occasion arose in dealing with problems encountered in daily life. Most of the problems deal with the concrete—7 loaves, 5 men—rarely with abstract numbers. While the Egyptian knew how to deal with particular cases, there is little evidence that he realized the underlying principles. The examples employ, for the most part, simple numbers and must be regarded as illustrations of method, model solutions, easy to learn by heart and apply to other similar problems. The methods employed were evolved by experiment in special cases and tested by experience to be of general application.

Three technical problems mentioned in a papyrus (*c.* 1200 B.C.) illustrate the sort of practical problems encountered. One scribe rallies another on his inability to deal with problems connected with the building and erection of monuments such as a 'royal scribe in command of the soldiers' might be called upon to solve:

1. The number of bricks required to construct a ramp of given dimensions.
2. The number of men required for the transport of an obelisk of which the dimensions are given.
3. The number of men needed to effect the removal of sand from a magazine in a given time.

By the Fourth Dynasty (*c.* 2700 B.C.)—the age of the Pyramids—Egyptian mathematics had probably completed its development and had reached the stage in which we find it in the papyri of the Twelfth Dynasty (*c.* 2000 B.C.), from which period we derive the material available for study. Thereafter, it simply stagnated, for the reason that the Egyptians did not study the subject for its own interest, but because they wanted simple working rules to enable them to deal with their practical problems. They were not particularly interested in theory or philosophy, and so long as a method met their immediate need, they were content, and that method continued in use without thought that it might be improved or simplified.

It has been the custom of many writers to emphasize what the Egyptians did *not* achieve rather than what they accomplished. This method of presentation of the facts is economical in words but is apt to disguise what was actually effected. The

PLATE 32

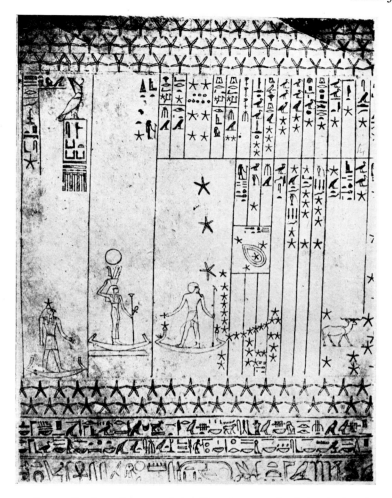

FIG. 3. Portion of astronomical ceiling (Sen-n-mut). (*Isis*, xiv (1930),
Pl. 19.) Jupiter, Sirius, and Orion are shown in three successive columns
starting from the left. The three conspicuous stars almost in a vertical line
seem to be δ, ε, and ζ *Orionis*. The 'Egg' near the centre may represent the
Pleiades and the V-shaped group—between Orion and the 'Egg'— the *Hyades*.
Above is part of the dekan list

PLATE 33

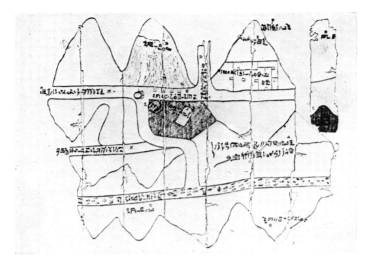

Fig. 4. Early map of a gold-mining region (site unknown) of the time of Seti I, *c.* 1320 B.C. (Lepsius, *Auswahl*, Pl. xxii). The mountainous nature of the country is shown in primitive fashion. A water cistern, plans of houses and buildings, and entrances to the galleries are indicated. Inscriptions give details such as: 'These are the mountains where the gold is washed; they are of a red colour.' They are coloured red on the map. 'Roads leading to the sea.' 'The well of King Seti'

Egyptian has not always been given full credit for what he did. Before 2000 B.C. he had developed a practical system of numeration and could carry out arithmetical calculations (involving the manipulation of complicated fractional expressions) with ease and accuracy. He evolved methods of solution, some of which survive in modern text-books—in particular those connected with division in given proportions, and 'work' problems (by the method of adding reciprocals). He could solve problems involving two unknown quantities and had elementary notions of arithmetical progression using fractions, as well as of geometrical progression. He was familiar with the elementary properties of rectangles, triangles, circles, and pyramids. Thus he could deal successfully with mathematical problems encountered in his daily life. The examples we have throw light on the methods of trading, the feeding of live stock, the raising of taxes, and the determination of the values of food and drink in terms of the amount which can be made from a given quantity of material.

How far, if at all, Egypt was indebted to Babylonia in regard to mathematics and astronomy is a matter for conjecture in the present state of our knowledge. In both subjects there are indications of independent evolution and as yet there is no evidence that the early Egyptians owed anything to other sources.

Weights and Measures

The prototype of the beam balance is frequently represented in scenes depicting the weighing of precious metals in Egypt, from the Fifth Dynasty onwards. It is sometimes accompanied by a tray with numbered weights. The earliest examples employ a simple beam drilled at the centre for a loop suspension, as well as near the ends for a single cord and hook on which hangs a basket or pan to take the weights on one side and the object to be weighed on the other. The design shows gradual improvement with time. The plummet makes its appearance about 2500 B.C. Later four suspension cords for each scale pan are used. A small balance from Tell el-'Amârna consisting of a beam and two pans (*c.* 1350 B.C.) may be seen in the South Kensington Museum. The four strings from each pan pass through an aperture bored in the end of the beam and are brought out through a hole in the upper surface of the beam, where they are knotted together. In the larger standard balance the beam ended in a flange in the form of a lotus which served to keep the beam-radius the same whatever the tilt of the beam, and made for greater accuracy. This type persisted until Roman times.

Large numbers of weights have been discovered, but only a few of these are stamped with the weight value, and with the exception of two or three specimens, the standard is not indicated. A study of the available material points to the use of several standards at the same time in different parts of the country. A complex system of weights exists in Egypt to the present day.

The most important lineal unit was the royal cubit[1] of 20·62 inches, divided into 7 palms or 28 digits. This was the side of a square of which the diagonal was 29·161 inches, the basis of land measure—the principal unit being the *remen*, half this diagonal. The relation enabled areas to be halved or doubled without altering the proportions. The short cubit (17·72 inches) was divided into 6 palms. Hence the 'cubit and an hand-breadth' of Ezekiel (chap. xl, verse 5) emphasizing the use of the royal cubit.

The principal capacity measure (the *hen*) held water weighing 5 *debens*. The *deben* was the weight (1,470 grains) of the anklet of the same name, of which the tenth part was the *qedet*, the weight of the finger ring.

Despite the variety of standards, the importance of maintaining standards of reference was recognized. The deceased

[1] From Lat. *cubitum*, elbow. The cubit being the length from the elbow to the tip of the middle finger is represented as a hieroglyph by the forearm and hand ⤙

PLATE 34

Fig. 5. Gold rings being weighed against a bronze weight in the shape of a ram's head (*c.* 1380 B.C.). (*Proc. Royal Inst. of Gt. Brit.* 29 (1936), Pt. 1)

arraigned before the judgement seat of Osiris bears witness that he has not 'diminished the cubit measure' nor 'falsified the corn measure'. The inter-relationship of measures and weights is of particular interest and is evidence of considerable thought and ingenuity. The same principle was not again made use of in Europe until the introduction of the metric system.

The ancient Egyptians had a wide knowledge of plants and herbs—especially of their medicinal uses—as well as of agriculture and stock-breeding. Their knowledge was traditional and in the nature of farm-lore. Calculations dealing with daily food rations for different kinds of poultry and cattle point to organized farm life, and a fragmentary papyrus dealing with the treatment of diseases of animals shows that attention was paid to veterinary science.

The training of the educated classes was carried out in the temple precincts, out of touch with manual work which was relegated to a despised class. Learning was valued not so much for its own sake, as for the fact that it provided a means of entry into the civil service and escape from a life of manual toil. The scribe developed an enthusiastic reverence for books and looked down on the cultivator and artisan, who remained largely illiterate. Thus it is hardly surprising that we have so little recorded material for estimating the scientific value of the work of the ancient Egyptians.

The reader may be disappointed to find here little encouragement for the belief, fairly widespread among the general public, in the wonderful scientific knowledge attributed to the ancient Egyptians and now lost. There is no positive evidence for its existence and it is not in keeping with what we do know of the mentality of the people. Nevertheless, the Egyptian achievement must not be underrated. They were pioneers. They laid the foundations of mathematics and science, and in the early period of their history they made astonishing progress in the practical applications of their knowledge, centuries before the Greeks, who were primarily theorists in all the arts and sciences.

Our concepts of the origin of scientific knowledge have had to be revised in the light of recent discovery. It is now recognized that the contribution of the Greeks to world knowledge was not entirely original. Greek colonists, settled in Asia Minor, travelled widely. Thales and others full of enterprise and love of adventure, and athirst for wonders in strange lands, came to Egypt. There they saw the Egyptians at work and marvelled. There they found the beginnings of mathematics and science which they developed and brought to greater perfection.

Through the Greeks, the legacy of Egypt was transmitted to the rest of the world.

R. W. SLOLEY

BIBLIOGRAPHICAL NOTE

A summary of our present knowledge of ancient Egyptian astronomy is given by DR. HERBERT CHATLEY in *The Observatory*, vol. lxii (1939), p. 100.

A general account of ancient Egyptian mathematics, fully referenced, is to be found in an article by T. E. PEET in the *Bulletin of the John Rylands Library* (Manchester), vol. xv (1931), p. 409.

Details of clepsydrae and shadow clocks are given in articles by R. W. SLOLEY in *Ancient Egypt* (1924), p. 43, and in the *Journal of Egyptian Archaeology*, vol. xvii (1931), p. 166.

CHAPTER 7

MEDICINE

§ i. *Introductory*

IN classical times the Egyptians had a great reputation for their medical knowledge. In the *Odyssey* it is said that the physicians of Egypt were skilled beyond all others, and Herodotus several times mentions the medical practitioners of Egypt, each of whom, he says, was a specialist, applying himself to the study of one particular branch. The same writer relates that Cyrus sent to Egypt for an oculist and that Darius held that the Egyptians enjoyed the highest reputation for their medical skill: elsewhere similar references are to be found. The 'wisdom of the Egyptians' is indeed proverbial, and although they were incapable of true philosophy and abstract thought, there is no doubt that they were a highly gifted people, with a great capacity for practical achievement. That the foundations of medical science were laid in Egypt more than fifty centuries ago there can no longer be any reasonable doubt. Although many modern writers have credited the Egyptians with scientific medical knowledge of profound extent, others have denied this claim almost to the point of asserting the non-existence of any such knowledge. But the truth lies, as always, between these two extremes; and, indeed, a nation which had evolved sufficient knowledge and skill to plan and accomplish feats of architecture and engineering as early as the fourth millenium before Christ, and whose mathematical knowledge, whilst wholly practical in aim, involved the principles of cubic capacity, angles, fractional notation, and the square-root, must clearly have been far ahead of its contemporaries in intellectual capacity. Time has spared for our admiration not only the tangible proofs of what the Egyptians could do but, in addition, a mass of documentary evidence. As regards medicine and surgery, we are fortunate in having a relatively large number of original documents—the so-called Medical Papyri.

§ ii. *The Medical Papyri*

The contents of these papyri fall into two main groups: (i) those which may claim to be called medical books, and (ii) those which are rather magical in purport or are collections of popular recipes. Tradition has ascribed to various gods, to certain early kings, and to sages such as Imhôtep (the Imouthes of the Greeks) the authorship of medical treatises. Whilst we have no indications of the authenticity of such attributions, nevertheless we have definite proof that at least one or two of such treatises did exist and extracts from them have come down to us in several papyri.

It will here be convenient to enumerate the principal medical and medico-magical papyri and to indicate the nature of their contents, since these documents are the foundation upon which most of our knowledge rests, and they constitute, indeed, the oldest body of medical literature in the world.

(1) *The Ebers Papyrus.* This is the longest and most famous of these documents; it was found together with the Edwin Smith papyrus in 1862, and was acquired a few years later by the Egyptologist whose name it bears. It is now preserved in the University of Leipsic and is in almost perfect condition. Its contents are medical and magical throughout, except that on the verso, and quite unrelated to the recto, is written a calendar which has been of the utmost importance in the study of the difficult problems of Egyptian chronology. The Ebers Papyrus was written about the beginning of the Eighteenth Dynasty, but there is abundant evidence, based on philological and other grounds, that it was copied from a series of books many centuries older. It is not a book in the proper sense of the word: it is a miscellaneous collection of extracts, recipes, and jottings

collected from at least forty different sources, and is exactly analogous to the books of medical and household recipes of Europe in later times. The text covers 110 large columns in the original roll, which a modern editor has conveniently divided into 877 numbered sections of varying length. It consists mainly of a large collection of prescriptions for numerous ailments, most of which are named but not diagnosed, specifying the drugs to be used, the measures of each, and the method of administration. A few of the sections are extracts from a general medical treatise of the kind already referred to, other parts of which have survived in the Edwin Smith and Kahûn papyri, and these excerpts can readily be recognized by their structure and the distinctive formulae employed in them. These extracts in the Ebers Papyrus relate to diseases of the stomach, to the action of the heart and its vessels, and to the surgical treatment of cysts, boils, carbuncles, and similar conditions. Freely interspersed amongst these elements are magical spells and incantations.

(2) *The Hearst Papyrus* was discovered at Deir el-Ballâs in Upper Egypt in 1899 and is now preserved in the University of California. The outermost folds of the roll are fragmentary, but otherwise the document is in good condition and contains fifteen almost undamaged columns comprising 250 prescriptions or sections. This papyrus is somewhat later in date than the Ebers, and may be assigned to the time of Tuthmosis III (XVIIIth Dynasty). Its contents are very similar to those of the Ebers Papyrus, and in some cases the matter is derived from the same archetypes, certain passages being common to both documents.

(3) *The Edwin Smith Papyrus* is now in the possession of the Historical Society of New York and a sumptuous edition of it was published a few years ago by the late Professor J. H. Breasted. The greater part of it belongs to the above-mentioned Group I and is devoted to the surgical treatment of wounds and fractures, extracted from the same general medical treatise as

the before-mentioned sections of the Ebers Papyrus. It contains forty-eight long sections, each dealing with a particular case, i.e. the affection of a particular region or organ, and in addition to these it contains thirteen medico-magical incantations and prescriptions. These latter fall into the same class (Group II) as those which constitute the greater part of the Ebers and other papyri.

(4) *The Chester-Beatty Papyrus.* The sixth papyrus in this collection (British Museum, No. 10686) is likewise bi-partite in character, and dates from the Nineteenth Dynasty. The recto contains a series of prescriptions and remedies for affections of the anus and rectum, and might almost be called an early treatise on proctology. Although the general arrangement resembles the unscientific medico-magical recipes, yet there is an important difference from these which will be alluded to in the sequel. The verso is filled with spells and incantations of the popular pattern.

(5) *The Berlin Medical Papyrus* (XIXth Dynasty; Berlin Museum, No. 3038). It contains 204 sections and is similar in character to the Ebers and Hearst papyri, of both of which it contains some duplicate passages. It is mostly of the popular type, but contains some elements drawn from the medical sources of Group I.

(6) *The Kahûn Papyrus* was discovered at Lâhûn in the Faiyûm in Lower Egypt in 1889. It is older in date than any other published medical papyri[1] and must be assigned to the Twelfth or Thirteenth Dynasties. Although very fragmentary, it contains the remains of thirty-four sections, all dealing with one subject—gynaecology. A considerable part of this document consists of extracts from the same general medical treatise as that represented by certain parts of the Ebers and Edwin Smith papyri, such sections being readily recognized by the standard-

[1] Two unpublished medical papyri of the Middle Kingdom are known to the writer.

ized formulae employed in them (Group I). The rest is made up of medico-magical recipes and incantations brought together because of their subject-matter (Group II).

(7) *The London Medical Papyrus* (Brit. Mus., No. 10059) is a badly written palimpsest assignable on palaeographical grounds to the latter part of the Eighteenth Dynasty. It is entirely medico-magical in its contents and contains nothing assignable to Group I.

(8) *Other documents.* The Chester Beatty Papyri Nos. 10, 15, and 18 (Brit. Mus., Nos. 10690, 10695, 10698) contain medico-magical prescriptions and spells belonging to Group II, No. 10 being wholly concerned with aphrodisiacs. The museums of Paris, Leiden, Turin, Berlin, Budapest, Rome (Vatican), and elsewhere contain considerable numbers of magical papyri, which, although not generally therapeutic in character, are medical in so far as their object is the treatment and cure of disease and personal injury. The papyri in the Chester Beatty collection (other than those mentioned above) also include several documents of the same nature.

(9) *Later documents.* The papyri enumerated above are all of the Pharaonic period, that is to say, of the Middle and New Kingdoms, but in addition to these we have some documents of later date. An important magical papyrus (The London-Leiden Demotic Papyrus) written in the demotic script and of the third century A.D., contains a good deal of medical matter, but all of it belongs to Group II. Of Coptic material, the great medical papyrus of Mashâykh (9th or 10th cent. A.D.) is, in the main, similar to the documents of Pharaonic times, but Greek and Arabic elements have to some extent obtruded themselves. Other Coptic medical fragments of much smaller extent exist in the British Museum, the John Rylands Library, the Vatican, and in the museums of Berlin and Michigan. From various sites in Egypt has come to light a series of medical fragments wholly Egyptian in character though written in Greek. These are now

deposited in various museums. But amongst the Graeco-Egyptian medical papyri there are some which are clearly of Greek and not of Egyptian origin. These latter fall into our Group I, and amongst them may be mentioned the Golenischef Papyrus (gynaecological; 3rd cent. A.D.) and the Cattaui Papyrus (surgical; also 3rd cent.).

It is mainly from an analysis of the foregoing material that our knowledge of Egyptian medicine is derived.

§ iii. *Magic and Medicine*

Magic played a very prominent part in the social and religious life of the Egyptians: it affected not only the relations of men with their living fellows but with the dead and with the gods. By the Egyptian, magic was believed to be a sure means of accomplishing all his necessities and desires and of performing, in short, everything that the common procedure of daily life was inadequate to bring about. Amongst the numerous purposes for which magic was employed, the activities of the magician are most commonly met with in the prevention and cure of sickness and injury, the bites and stings of noxious animals, and other misfortunes and accidents affecting the individual. These medical applications of the magic art, besides being the most numerous, well exemplify the procedure of the practitioner. In the numerous medico-magical texts which have come down to us the idea of possession is very evident, for diseases are usually treated as if personified and are harangued and addressed by the magician. It is generally stated or implied that disease or suffering is due to the actual presence in the patient's body of the demon itself, but almost as often it is implied that the suffering is due to some poison or other evil emanation that the demon has projected into the patient's body.

In such cases the simplest method of procedure was the recitation of a spell in which the disease-demon was summarily commanded to quit, or the poison to flow forth, and leave the patient's body. These spells, of varying length and elaboration, are full of references to the gods and contain fragments of myths of the highest interest. Some of the more elaborate spells embody threats and exorcisms of a very daring character. In these simplest cases, the magician operated merely by word of mouth only, but in most spells the spoken words are accompanied by a ritual—by gestures, or by the use of amulets and other objects. These two essential parts of the magician's art have been aptly defined by Dr. Alan Gardiner as the *oral rite* and the *manual rite,* respectively. It is usual in the medico-magical texts to find a rubric at the end of the oral rite giving directions as to the performance of the accompanying manual rite. The manual rite often took the form of reciting the words over an image of wood or clay, a string of beads, a knotted cord, a piece of inscribed linen, an amulet, a stone, or some other object. These objects, thus magically charged, were generally placed upon, or attached to, the patient's body. In cases of illness or injury, the manual rite often takes the form of repeating the oral rite over a mixture of substances which were then given to the patient to swallow or for external application, the medicine so given being thus rendered efficacious. The medical papyri, which are filled for the most part with prescriptions of drugs, are interspersed with magical spells the object of which was to give efficacy to the prescriptions which follow them. Such spells are the oral rites belonging to each group of prescriptions, the preparation and administration of which constitute the corresponding manual rite. Many of the doses contain noxious or offensive ingredients, and the object of such is manifestly to be as unpalatable as possible to the possessing spirit, so as to give it no encouragement to linger in the patient's body.

It is characteristic of the magician at all times that he should have more than one string to his bow, for if one remedy fails another may succeed, and his prestige and reputation must at all costs be maintained. Consequently in the medical papyri are found numerous alternative prescriptions for each ailment and in the magical texts many alternative spells for every kind of sickness and calamity. Some of the remedies contain drugs that are really beneficial and appropriate, and such prescriptions, actually accomplishing their purpose, would tend to survive their more fantastic fellows. By such means more and more reliance would come to be placed upon the drugs themselves (i.e. upon the magician's manual rite) and less and less upon the recited spells (i.e. his oral rite), whence the persons, therefore, who would be most in request in cases of sickness would be those who were skilled in the knowledge and preparation of drugs and in manipulative treatment. Such men were no longer mere magicians, but were becoming physicians—and thus out of magic grew medicine.

But it must not be supposed that the evolution of the physician extinguished magic. It is rare in human experience for the new completely to supersede the old. The first physicians kept magic as a stand-by in case of need: magical methods continued to be employed side by side with the more rational procedure, as the medical papyri of Pharaonic times plainly show. Moreover, the existence of many magical papyri, dating from Ptolemaic times and later, written in demotic Egyptian, in Coptic, and in Greek, reveal that magical practices for the cure of disease were in active operation long after the influence of scientific medicine, which was mainly due to the Greeks, had made itself felt. Magic maintained powerful sway throughout the early centuries of the Christian era and throughout the Middle Ages: it persisted into the sixteenth, seventeenth, and eighteenth centuries, and is by no means extinct to-day, even amongst civilized nations. The magician has survived: he has merely changed his role from time to time, becoming successively the palmer, the merry-andrew, the quack, and the advertiser of patent medicines. The ancient magician, when, *malgré lui*, he had become physician, was loath to part with the mysticism of his craft, and he often disguised his more rational treatment under a veneer of mystery, a method which has been followed throughout the ages by his successors.

The very multiplicity of the prescriptions is of itself a confession of their purely arbitrary and unscientific character; the fact that numerous alternative prescriptions are provided for each ailment implies that if one failed, another might be tried. Thus the procedure in most of the medical papyri amounts to this: Try A, *or* B, *or* C. An advance on this method is marked by the treatment prescribed in the Chester Beatty Papyrus No. 6, where the plan is: Do A, *then* B, *then* C; that is to say the prescriptions for each case were to be *all* employed in series progressively, and not merely selected at will from many alternatives. It is for this reason that I would place this text in the Group I defined above.

§ iv. *Anatomy and Physiology*

The custom of embalming the dead in Egypt, involving as it did the removal and handling of the viscera, had a profound influence upon the growth of medicine, although it was not carried out by physicians but was primarily a religious observance. Not only did the practice of mummification familiarize the Egyptians with the appearance, nature, and mutual positions of the internal organs of the body—opportunities that were denied to all peoples who inhumed or cremated their dead—but it made them acquainted with the preservative properties of the salts and resins they employed for the purpose. The custom provided for the first time opportunities for observations in comparative anatomy, for it enabled its practitioners to recognize the analogies between the viscera of the human body and those of animals, the latter long familiar from the time-honoured custom of cutting up animals for food and for sacrifice. It is a noteworthy fact that the various hieroglyphic signs representing parts of the body, and especially the internal organs, are pictures of the organs of mammals and not of human beings. This shows that the Egyptians' knowledge of mammalian anatomy is older than their knowledge of that of man, and further that they recognized the essential identity of the two by devising signs based on the organs of animals and using them unaltered when referring to the corresponding organs of the human body.

The extent of the knowledge of a people in respect of any technical subject can be gauged by the richness or otherwise of its terminology. In the ancient language of the hieroglyphs there are considerably over one hundred anatomical terms, and this fact alone shows that the Egyptians were able to differentiate and name a great many organs and organic structures that a more primitive and less enlightened people would have grouped together or would have failed to perceive. Whilst, however, the Egyptians' terminology for the gross anatomy of the body is fairly accurate, they entirely failed to understand the nerves, muscles, arteries, and veins. They had but one word to denote all these structures: they appear to have regarded them all as various parts of a single system of branching and radiating cables forming a network over all parts of the body. The word used for the blood-vessels communicating with the heart is the same as that employed for the muscles in the prescriptions for stiff-joints and rheumatoid complaints. In such cases the context alone allows us to perceive what is meant.

As regards physiology, the most important document we have is a long passage in the Ebers Papyrus that deals with the heart and its 'vessels'. The passage is obscure, corrupt, and very difficult to understand and the second copy of it in the Berlin Medical Papyrus is so faulty and incorrectly written that it affords but little help, while a third duplicate text, that in the Edwin Smith Papyrus, is too fragmentary to be serviceable. The Egyptians themselves must have felt the difficulty of understanding the passage, for many glosses were introduced for the purpose of explaining the meaning of the sentences. These glosses may have helped the Egyptians of the Eighteenth Dynasty, but for us they add to, rather than diminish, the difficulties. The title of the passage is: 'The beginning of the science of the physician; to know the movement of the heart and to know the heart; there are vessels attached to it for every member of the body.' An explanatory gloss follows, stating that by placing the fingers upon the region of the heart and upon the head and limbs, the action of the heart will be perceived through the vessels leading to each member, that is to say, the pulse can be felt in various parts of the body because of the vessels that radiate from the heart. There is, of course, no hint of any knowledge of the circulation of the blood (although some writers have read this meaning into the text),[1] nor indeed is there any mention of blood: all that was perceived was the sympathy of the pulse with the beating of the heart itself. The Egyptians certainly regarded the heart as the most important organ of the body. It was held to be the seat of intelligence and of all the emotions (they attached no importance at all to the brain), and its presence in the body was so important that it was not even removed from the body during mummification, but was carefully left, together with its great vessels, in its place in the thorax, although all the other viscera were removed. The text, after this introduction, proceeds to enumerate the vessels that communicate with each part of the body, stating what was conveyed by them, and continues with a description of the behaviour of the heart under various conditions.

Nothing like a system of physiology can be reconstructed from this obscure and garbled passage, although one or two facts emerge quite clearly. One of them is the importance of

[1] It is scarcely necessary to say that this modern view is absurd, for long ages were destined to pass before the difference between arterial and venous blood was either observed or appreciated, and before the discovery of the lymphatic vessels.

the heart as the centre of the vascular system, and the other is the belief that the 'vessels' were not exclusively concerned with blood, but were the vehicles also of air, water, mucus, semen, and other secretions. This erroneous conclusion doubtless arose out of the condition of the vessels observed during the post-mortem manipulations of the embalmers, and could not have been derived from the functional vessels of a living body. It was believed also that the ears, besides being the organs of hearing, were part of the pulmonary system, for it is stated that the breaths of life and death enter them, on the right and left sides respectively.[1] Beneath all this jumble of statement that fills several pages of the papyrus, much of which is erroneous, there remains a nucleus of correctly observed truth which suggests that in very early times a serious attempt was being made to understand the structure and functions of the body and its organs, and the effects of injury upon them. It was observed, for instance (as we learn from the Edwin Smith Papyrus), that the brain is enclosed in a membrane and that its hemispheres are patterned with convolutions; that injury to the brain causes a loss of control over various parts of the body, the tension of the facial muscles and other manifestations; that injury to the spinal column may cause priapism and involuntary emission; that such an injury also may cause meteorism; that certain injuries can be confidently cured, whilst others are only doubt-fully curable, and others again are definitely hopeless.

A passage in the Ebers Papyrus dealing with affections of the stomach, and another in the Kahûn Papyrus dealing with uterine and other female disorders, introduce a novel feature in that they describe symptoms and give a diagnosis. In nearly all the other medical texts the diagnosis is assumed and only treat-ment is provided. These passages, together with the concluding part of the Ebers Papyrus, are evidently drawn from quite a

[1] Compare the association of the left side with death and the right side with life in Apollodorus, III. x. 3.

different source from that of the bulk of the medical writings and belong to a type that has been designated above as Group I.

§ v. *Pathology and Therapeutics*

As already indicated, there cannot be the slightest doubt that Egyptian medicine had its origin in magic and that magic never lost its hold on medicine even when rationalism was pervading it to a greater and greater extent. Many of the drugs in the pharmacopoeia, even when wholesome and rational, were clearly adopted in the first instance for purely magical reasons; their very use was but a development of the manual rites of the magician. A study of the medical papyri demonstrates quite clearly that all illness and disease was believed to be due to possession, and the art of the physician had its beginnings in the various attempts that were made to coax, charm, or forcibly expel the demon from its involuntary host. It was originally only in cases of illness and injury that had an evident and palpable cause that purely rational methods of treatment were employed. Thus wounds, which are inflicted by visible human agency, are dealt with by more or less rational therapeutic methods, but diseases and pains (even when they had such obvious external manifestations as sores, boils, or swellings) were submitted more often to magical than to medical treatment. In the medical papyri the prescriptions are each headed by a title, and in these titles instead of the simple phrase, 'prescription for curing' such and such a disease, we have 'prescription for driving out', 'banishing', 'terrifying', or 'killing' such disease, and even in the more rational surgical treatment of wounds a formula commonly used by the surgeon is, 'it is a condition I will contend with', or 'wrestle with'. In such phraseology the notion of possession is manifest. The therapeutic treatment consists always of liquid or dry medicines for internal consumption, or of ointments or lotions for external use.

When we come to the pathology of the papyri we meet with

a host of difficulties. The texts are full of lexicographical problems, and it is often extremely difficult to find English equivalents for the Egyptian names of the diseases, owing to the usual lack of diagnosis and symptoms and to the inherent difficulties in Egyptian modes of expression. As in anatomy, so also in pathology, the terminology is large and varied, but a very large number of terms, even common ones, we cannot yet translate. A very considerable number of terms has, however, been identified with certainty, and a still larger number with considerable probability, and we can accordingly perceive that, in general, the maladies with which the papyri are concerned are those which attack the fellahin of to-day. Intestinal troubles due to bad water; ophthalmia and a large number of other affections of the eyes; boils, sores, and bites of animals; dermatitis; bilharzia infection; intestinal worms; mastoid and naso-pharyngeal diseases —such are amongst those for which the ancient practitioner had to find remedies. We meet also with prescriptions for treating diseases of the lungs, liver, stomach, intestines, and bladder, for various affections of the head and scalp (including such complaints as alopecia and ointments to prevent the hair from falling out or turning grey), for affections of the mouth, tongue, and teeth, and of the nose, throat, and ear. There is a long series of remedies for rheumatoid and arthritic complaints and for diseases of women. Added to these medical prescriptions there are household remedies for getting rid of fleas, flies, snakes, and other vermin. In short, the general make-up of the papyri closely resembles the leech-books of the Middle Ages and the household recipe books of later days.

§ vi. *Surgery*

Mention has already been made of the Edwin Smith Papyrus which deals with wounds in the head and thorax, with the concluding portion of the Ebers Papyrus which deals with boils, cysts, and the like, and with the Kahûn Papyrus which is concerned with gynaecological cases. All these are clearly extracts from one and the same book and their form and arrangement is far in advance of those of the greater part of the medical papyri, which consist merely of prescriptions. The surgical texts are drawn up with certain definite formulae in a fivefold form: (i) title, (ii) examination (symptoms), (iii) diagnosis, (iv) opinion (i.e. whether curable or not), and (v) treatment. In many cases glosses are added which help us to understand the meanings of the terms and idioms of the text. From the rational and almost methodical way in which these texts are drawn up, the late Professor Breasted claimed that the former belief in the magical origin of medicine was no longer tenable, and that there is now evidence that anatomy was studied for its own sake, and that the Edwin Smith Papyrus is in the true sense a scientific book. He failed to recognize, however, that the Edwin Smith Papyrus is only a part of a larger body of texts into which magic enters to no small extent, as it does, indeed, into that very papyrus itself. It does not in the least detract from the importance and interest of this text to prefer the opinion that whilst it un-doubtedly affords evidence that an attempt was being made to understand the elements of anatomy and physiology, yet it must be clearly borne in mind that it deals only with wounds and fractures—injuries of palpable and intelligible origin—and not with diseases, the cause of which was to the ancients invisible, impalpable, and unknown. A wound or injury caused by a fall or other accident, or by a weapon or tool, was well understood and generally treated by rational means: but the causes of headache and fever, of skin eruptions or swellings, and of countless other maladies, were wholly mysterious and attributed to supernatural agencies. Two brothers might on the same day come before a doctor at Memphis or Thebes, the one for treat-ment of a dagger-wound in his breast, the other for an irritating rash affecting the same region of the body. The cause of the one was self-evident; the cause of the other was a mystery, and the treatment of the two cases differed in its nature accordingly. The medical and the magical marched side by side and the same age produced both the Edwin Smith and the Ebers Papyri with their widely differing contents. Indeed, in the Edwin Smith Papyrus there is an incantation in the body of the surgical text itself, and on the back of it there is written a collection of charms and prescriptions similar to those that fill page after page of the other so-called medical papyri. The ancient owner of the Edwin Smith Papyrus saw no incongruity in copying into the same note-book elements that appear to us of to-day as absolutely antagonistic in nature and content. One might imagine, as a parallel, a modern medical student taking simultaneously and equally seriously the utterances of John Hunter and of Culpeper.

§ vii. *Materia Medica*

The same difficulty confronts us when dealing with the drugs as has already been mentioned in connexion with the maladies, namely our inability to identify many of them. Some hundreds of ingredients are mentioned in the prescriptions, and they were derived from the animal, the vegetable, and the mineral kingdoms. Most of the animals can be determined: usually their fat or blood is employed, but if small enough, the whole animal is often used. Thus we find the fat of the ox, ass, lion, hippopotamus, mouse, bat, lizard, snake, and others used, also the blood of these and other animals, as well as many birds and invertebrates. Hartshorn, tortoise-shell, and calcined horns, hides, bones, and hoofs are likewise employed. In the case of vegetables we are unable to identify with certainty more than a relatively small proportion of the very large number whose names abound in the prescriptions. We find the whole plant, or its leaves, fruit, seed, juice, pith, or root employed as drugs.

The vehicles for liquid doses are usually water, milk, honey, wine, or beer. For emollients and ointments the basis is honey or fats of various kinds, goose-grease being specially frequent.

Dry medicines are crushed or ground and some of the remedies are boiled, warmed, or cooled, as the case may be. Medicaments for external use are generally applied by rubbing, bandaging, or poultice. The quantities of each drug are meticulously specified in the prescriptions, minute fractional notation being employed.

The form in which these prescriptions was drawn up was copied, down to the smallest details, by the Greeks and passed thence into the medical literature of other countries. Egyptian influence, often quite unequivocal, can be recognized in Greek, Latin, Arabic, Syriac, and Persian medical books as well as in those of western Europe of the Middle Ages and later times. To prove this generalization an army of instances might be produced, but space forbids a further elaboration of this aspect of the question, which has already been fully discussed elsewhere

§ viii. *Conclusion*

What, then, is the legacy that Egypt has bequeathed to Medicine?

In general terms it may be said that the popular medicine of almost every country of Europe and the Near East largely owes its origin to Egypt, and in its various migrations it has preserved its ancestral form almost intact throughout the ages. Not only were many well-known drugs of universal vogue first used by the Egyptians (such, for instance, as hartshorn, castoroil, mandragora, cumin, dill, and coriander), but in addition to these more obvious examples, many of the drugs, as well as the properties and traditions ascribed to them by the Egyptians, that occur in the works of Pliny, Dioscorides, Galen, and even in the Hippocratic Collection itself, are clearly borrowed from Egypt. These later writers, and others who followed them, are the sources from which the compilers of herbals and books of popular medicine mainly drew for their material, and the works of classical writers are therefore often merely the stepping-stones by which much of the ancient medical lore reached Europe, apart from direct borrowings. When a drug really possesses the virtues attributed to it and is an effective remedy its survival into modern times is natural enough, but the fact that many quite fantastic and arbitrary remedies have been carried on almost to our own days is definite proof of the slavish copying from the works of one writer to the works of another in a continuous line that originated many centuries ago on the banks of the Nile. The use of certain arbitrary and distinctive preparations, the use of the same formulae, idioms, and colophons in the popular medical literature of many countries through as many centuries, are all indications with an unmistakable interpretation.

But if Egypt bequeathed her popular and largely magical knowledge to the later world, she bequeathed also a heritage more valuable than this. From Egypt we have the earliest medical books, the first observations in anatomy—human and comparative—the first experiments in surgery and pharmacy, the first use of splints, bandages, compresses, and other appliances, and the first anatomical and medical vocabulary, and that an extensive one.

In two other ways, most important of all, has Egypt served the history of medical science. First, through the distinctive custom of mummification, aided by the favourable climatic conditions, hundreds of actual bodies, many of them accurately datable, have carried down to us the earliest actual cases of the effects of disease. The history of the incidence of many diseases and conditions can be thrust back farther and farther into antiquity from the evidence provided by mummies and skeletons: of calculi, bilharzia, arterial diseases, tuberculosis, arthritis and other bone-diseases as well as many inflammatory and countless other conditions. And secondly, and most important of all, the Egyptians, by that same custom of mummification, had the greatest of all influences on the history of medicine—and this was the fact that mummification familiarized the popular mind for over twenty centuries with the idea of cutting open the dead human body. It was in Egypt, mainly in Alexandria, that it became possible for the Greek physicians and anatomists of the Ptolemaic age to practise for the first time the systematic dissection of the human body, which religious and popular prejudice forbade in their own country and in all other parts of the world. To this fact alone the true science of medicine ultimately owes its origin and the possibility of its development.

WARREN R. DAWSON

CHAPTER 8

LAW

COMPARED with other ancient civilizations the Egyptian era
prior to the time of Alexander the Great has yielded very little
evidence of its legal institutions. In particular, to this day,
hardly any statutes have been traced. We know that there were
statutes in very early times, but we do not know what they contained. We must therefore try to deduce the nature of the
law from the documents of that era. But only a few legal documents from the Old Kingdom have been preserved in their original
form on papyrus. The oldest known at present is a judgement
from the period of the Sixth Dynasty (2420–2294).[1] This means
that the evidence for the law of Egypt begins several centuries
later than that of the land of Sumer. That is, however, a mere
accident. Any new excavations may change the picture in
favour of Egypt, for we know that as early as the time of the
Third Dynasty (2815–2690) certain formal documents were
required for important legal transactions. From that time
onwards mention of legal transactions is made in inscriptions
in tombs and on stelae. Thus, together with Sumerian law,
Egyptian law is the oldest legal system about which we have
any information.

Further, from the moment that we can trace the system at
all we find it already in an advanced and civilized state, never
in a primitive one. It would be a great mistake if, in a survey
of the legal history of the world, one were to treat Egyptian law
as being on a low level of development, merely because it is very
old. In its early stages, as far as we can know them, it can claim
full equality with ancient Greek law or with much early medieval
law. The development from a primitive to a civilized state of

[1] Papyrus Berlin 9010.

society in Egypt must be sought for in a period which is not covered by the sources available to us.

Old and Middle Kingdoms (*3188–c. 1700 B.C.*)

During the period of the Old Kingdom Egypt was governed by a strictly absolute monarchy. The king was the sole legislator. The cult of the Ruler raised him to a divine status and made it a religious obligation to perform his commands. Not only had he full power over the life and death of his subjects, but he could also control their labour and their property. But this 'superior ownership' of the king did not impede the development of a system of private law. At any rate not all land was administered as Crown property, for there were estates which could be the subject of legal transactions concluded between private persons. To an even greater extent chattels could be the subject of private ownership.

A person could validly acquire the ownership in any object only either by giving some consideration for it or under a special document, the so-called 'house-document',[1] drawn up by the former owners and setting out the transfer of ownership. Thus Egyptian law distinguished between acquisition for a consideration and acquisition by gift, and it checked the making of gifts through its insistence upon the necessity for such a document. This 'hostility to gifts' is a peculiarity which is to be found later in the Germanic codes and also in the code of the Akkadian King Hammurabi (1791–1749 B.C.); but so far as we know it makes its first appearance in the law of Egypt.

Such 'house-documents' were also drawn up in the case of a sale of valuable objects. The declaration of the former owner that he was willing to transfer the ownership in the object was noted on a piece of papyrus, followed by the names of three witnesses who had heard the declaration. Some high official then rolled up and fastened the papyrus with a seal, so as to make

[1] *imy·t pr*—an accurate translation of this word has not yet been found.

further additions impossible. At the time of the Third Dynasty
a special 'royal document' was added to the 'house-document'.
That was possibly a confirmation of the transaction by the king
in his capacity of superior owner. But later, the 'house-document' alone was undoubtedly sufficient.

Whenever it was intended to undertake an obligation which
was to be fulfilled in the future, the debtor confirmed it by an
oath in which the king, as a god, was usually invoked. Whether
an obligation which was undertaken without such an oath was
regarded as valid we do not know. The theory has been put
forward in respect of certain ancient legal systems, e.g. those
of Greece and Rome, that the whole institution of transactions
creating an obligation developed from an oath. It is to be hoped
that this question, which is of great importance for the whole
history of law, will one day be answered with certainty by the
help of Egyptian texts.

Coinage was unknown to the Egyptians. Payment was made in
kind by the handing over of such objects as the creditor was
willing to accept. Up to this point it was a system of barter.
But since, for the purpose of such payment in kind, all objects
were valued according to a general standard, and since they were
accounted for by the creditor in accordance with such valuation,
it is a law of sale rather than a law of barter which we find
developed at that time in Egypt.

The religion of the Egyptians provided them with a firm
belief in a life after death. To make that life pleasant it was
essential that the body should lie in a well-appointed tomb, and
that the dead should receive regular offerings. The Egyptian
therefore tried to ensure by contracts that such offerings should
be made to him for ever. For that purpose he used to settle
some profit-bearing part of his properties upon a body of
'Ka-servants',[1] subject to a continuing obligation to provide in
perpetuity such offerings after his decease. A property which

[1] The Egyptian name for these 'priests' specially appointed for this purpose.

had been handed over to Ka-servants was called 'eternal property', *ḏt*. These contracts are very similar to the medieval *donationes pro anima* by which pious persons used to bind some monastery to read masses on feast-days for the salvation of their souls. Medieval law regarded the lord of the monastery which was thus bound, or the saint of the monastery, as the owner of the property, who held it upon trust to carry out the terms of the endowment. The Egyptians may have regarded their 'eternal property' in the same way. The Belgian scholar Pirenne has advanced the theory that they had gone even further than that conception and that they had treated the 'eternal property' as a legal personality, a construction which even the Romans accepted only very reluctantly and which has not been clearly developed until we come to modern legal systems.

A will, either in its Roman or in its modern sense, was as unknown in Egypt as it was to the Code of Hammurabi. If a man desired that after his death part of his property should go to some other person, he gave it to that person by means of a 'house-document', *inter vivos*. But we do not know how he ensured that the things thus given away remained his own property until his death. He may possibly have secured this by retaining the 'house-document'.

As in the early Middle Ages procedure was, it would seem, closely hedged about by the strictness of the law of evidence. In one action, a record of which has been preserved, the decision depended upon the genuineness of a document. The court decided that if one party were to bring three witnesses who would swear to its genuineness, he should be successful, otherwise he should lose the action. There was thus no independent weighing of the evidence; a rigid formalism prevailed. Three witnesses were to take the oath, but the question whether they had been present when the document had been drawn up was not raised. As in the case of the medieval oath-helpers, all that was required was that the witness should have sufficient faith in the veracity of the party to swear to the genuineness of the document.

We must not leave the discussion of the law of the Old and Middle Kingdoms without mentioning the revenue law which was already developed at that time. Beside other taxes there existed then a personal tax which was probably a poll tax. Some amusing returns relating to that form of taxation have been preserved. In them the head of the family declared all the persons who belonged to his household, but the document was doubtless written by a revenue officer. The names of the tax-payers were neatly written, one under the other, in one column. Now, as is well known, every word in Egyptian ends with a determinative sign. Thus the name of a man, e.g, ends with the seated male figure (𓀀). The revenue officer, when drawing up the lists, made use of that fact in order the more readily to summarize the results of his survey. He separated the determinatives from the rest of the spelling of the names and put them into a column of their own in which one could then see at a glance how many men (𓀀), women (𓁐), and children (𓀔) were present in one household. He even added to the names of some women the symbol of birth (𓁑), presumably to indicate that a new taxpayer was soon to be expected. A revenue authority which caused such detailed returns to be made must surely have kept a tax roll as well.

New Kingdom (1573–712 B.C.)

The number of legal records surviving from the New Kingdom is very much greater and among these some laws are now preserved. In the tomb of Rekhmirê' at Thebes we have not only a representation of a sitting of the court of the vezir, with the whole *corpus juris* of Egypt in force at that time displayed before the vezir on papyrus rolls, but also the text of two important fragments of the great Code of Ceremonial at the court of the king. In one of the fragments the solemn words have been preserved which the king had to speak at the investiture of a vezir; in the other one we find regulations concerning the duties of the vezir. In the latter fragment particularly, many legal rules of general significance can be found. Finally, we possess, on a stele in the temple of Karnak, a statute enacted by King Haremheb (1349–1314) against arbitrary actions of officials, with penal sanctions.

As compared with the Middle Kingdom the administration has become more centralized. Thus the regulations concerning the duties of the vezir contain the rule that all 'house-documents' are to be taken to the vezir to be sealed—a task which in the Middle Kingdom had been performed by some of the higher provincial officials. That, however, seems to have been an exaggeration: it was asking too much of every villager to go to Thebes if he wanted to sell his house or settle it upon his children against his death. Thus the only examples we possess of that type of document come from Thebes, the official residence of the vezir, and none of these are later in date than the Nineteenth Dynasty. In its stead a different kind of document developed, the 'scribe and witness document' which from this time remained the principal type of document current in Egypt. As opposed to the 'house-document' it was not sealed, but the place of the seal was taken by the invariable form of the instrument. It began with the date and ended with the name of the scribe (which was absent in the 'house-document'). It was thus protected against later additions and consequently did not require to be sealed. The drafts of such documents were not written on papyrus, which was too expensive, but on cheap material such as potsherds or fragments of limestone, and by chance many of these have been discovered.

Records of loans of various kinds have also come down to us. In these transactions the rate of interest amounted usually to 100 per cent. per annum; at the end of each year the interest was added to the capital and a further 100 per cent. was charged on the resulting total. Nor was it unusual for a person to give security for the performance of a future obligation by declaring that he was ready to receive a hundred strokes should he break his promise; but such shocking penalties for breach of contract as we find in Assyrian law (where the debtor promised to 'sacrifice his eldest son to the god') do not occur in Egypt.

We do not know how marriages were contracted at this time, but we have evidence of the custom of making marriage settlements at the time of the marriage which safeguarded the financial position of the wife and the children. As is well known the Code of King Hammurabi regarded the making of such a settlement as essential to the validity of a marriage, and that remained the law in the Near East until Byzantine times. It is possible that a similar rule was in force in Egypt under the New Kingdom, but this is still uncertain. A man who wanted to re-marry after the death of his wife had to come to an agreement with the children of the first marriage, by which two-thirds of the property of the first marriage was given to the children of the first marriage, and one-third to the father. It was also possible to divorce a wife by simple repudiation.

In the law of succession we find a rule which again must be explained by the religious belief that the burial of the body was essential for the after life: only a person who has buried the testator can become his heir.

The courts of law consisted of meetings of the local dignitaries under the chairmanship of an official who presided over the trial. The highest court consisted of a meeting of the dignitaries of Thebes, the capital, sitting in council and presided over by the vezir. But in exceptional cases, such as the great conspiracy against Rameses III (1192–1161), the king established special courts.

In the law of procedure there had been development and progress since the time of the Old Kingdom. The idea of eliciting the truth had taken the place of rigid rules of evidence. All kinds of proof were admitted, considered, and weighed by the judges. Thus in one case we find that a party had to swear to the truth of his assertion and that at the same time a penalty was agreed upon in case the assertion should prove untrue. Then the witnesses for the other side were sworn and testified to the opposite of the first party's evidence, so that oath stood against oath, one of which was necessarily perjured. No objection, however, was felt to this; under the then prevailing law of procedure all means could be employed which might help to ascertain the truth. An important part was taken by documentary evidence. In questions of personal status and of ownership the official tax rolls were frequently used as a means of evidence. Thus the tax rolls at that time performed a function which was to be assumed in Roman times by a land register. Decisions were given in the form of a declaration by the court that 'X is right, Y is wrong'. Such decisions could not, of course, be put into execution immediately, as that would have cast upon the responsible officer the burden of studying the files so as to ascertain the meaning of 'X is right'—whether it meant that Y had to hand over a chattel or whether he had to pay a sum of money. From this it may be assumed that according to the law of the New Kingdom, just as under the later law and under Babylonian law, the case did not end with the judgement but that the judgement had to be followed by a declaration of submission by the defeated party, contained in a separate document. The defeated party declared therein that he was bound to do such and such a thing or that he had not such and such a claim against the other party, and that he undertook to pay a fine should he renew the claim put forward by him in the action. But it was regarded as a sign of special skill on the part of the judge if he could persuade the parties to settle the action before any judgement was given.

From the Nineteenth Dynasty onwards, perhaps as a sign of reaction against the unsuccessful religious reforms of King Amenophis IV (1375–1358), we see quite a different kind of procedure developing, a procedure which may be described as a deterioration and which was later abolished. A god was made the judge in the action and his will was ascertained by ceremonies which it is difficult for us to understand, and which possibly consisted of rhythmical dances. Take, for instance, the case of a man whose garments have been stolen. He would appeal to King Amenophis I, who had been long dead and who was worshipped as a god. A list of all the inhabitants of the village was read aloud before a statue of the deified king. Upon the reading of one name the god would make a sign to indicate that this was the thief. The person indicated would deny the accusation and appeal to another god, who might also decide against him. He would then continue to deny everything, but might be condemned again by Amenophis. Thereupon he would be beaten until he confessed and swore never to repudiate his confession. Judgements rendered by a god have existed in many nations at various times; but it would appear that the Egyptians of the Nineteenth and following dynasties made the most consistent attempt to build up a whole law of procedure upon the omniscience of the deity.

Criminal law and criminal procedure were inhuman. In contrast to the Jewish law which limited corporal punishment to forty strokes, one hundred strokes was the ordinary punishment in Egypt. Torture was often used, not only upon the accused but also upon independent witnesses. Strange forms of capital punishment seem to have been practised, such as leaving the prisoner to be eaten by crocodiles. It was a special favour to allow a convicted criminal to commit suicide. Numbers of criminals, with their ears and noses cut off, were condemned to forced labour in concentration colonies on the frontiers of the country. A thief furthermore had to pay a multiple of the value of the stolen chattel—a penalty which also can be paralleled in the Code of Hammurabi and in the oldest Roman law.

We further possess treaties dealing with international law.

The finest surviving example is the treaty of Rameses II (1297-1231 B.C.) with the king of the Hittites, Hattušiliš III. According to the Akkadian text of this document it is a treaty of peace and of alliance, with the obligation to give armed assistance. Fugitives from one country who came into the territory of the other country were to be extradited to their home country, but were not to be punished there. It is interesting to observe that the religious dogma of the divinity of the Egyptian king, compared with whom a foreign king was only a miserable human being, prevented the publication of an unexpurgated version of this treaty. While in the original text both kings call each other 'Great-king', on a footing of complete equality, in the Egyptian version which can still be seen in the temple of Karnak the 'great-god' Rameses fixes the frontiers of his country according to his choice, granting the treaty to the 'great prince' of the Hittites who has come to ask for peace.

The literature of this period depicts the Egyptians as a nation which takes great interest in legal decisions. Law-suits before the courts take a larger part in Egyptian literature than in the literature of other nations. When a fragment relates a 'dispute for supremacy between the members of the body' we may see in it a forerunner of the fable told by Menenius Agrippa when the Roman Plebs had seceded to the Mons Sacer to show the rebels that the various social classes in a State supplement each other as do the members of the human body. Since that time this comparison of a State with a living organism has continuously made its appearance in the speeches of statesmen of every nation.

Another kind of literature is represented by the Wisdom books or ethical rules of life. They give us a lofty idea of the Egyptian conception of justice. The 'investiture of the vezir' from the tomb of Rekhmirê', which formed part of a Law of Court Ceremonial, is in many parts reminiscent of these 'Teachings'. When the king tells the vezir: 'if a suppliant approaches thee, thou shalt see that everything is done according to the rules, helping everyone to his right' he anticipates the *suum cuique tribuere* which Justinian, following the jurist Ulpian, put as *praeceptum juris* at the beginning of his Institutes and of his Digest.

Late Egyptian and Persian Period (712–332 B.C.)

A great number of legal documents of the late Egyptian era have been preserved. In Upper Egypt at first the hieratic cursive script was used, in Lower and Middle Egypt the demotic. Later on, the demotic character alone was employed. Therefore at first the forms of documents were not all of the same pattern. Inasmuch as at the beginning of the late Egyptian period Lower Egypt and Upper Egypt were often governed by different rulers, it is possible that these differences in form indicate different legal systems for the two parts of the country, which were only gradually superseded by a new unity.

But the documents in hieratic as well as the demotic legal documents were only new forms developed from the unsealed 'scribe and witness documents' of the New Kingdom.

A document is now always retained by the person who is in possession of the objects to which it relates. A person when selling a house would hand over at the same time all the documents relating to that house so that the purchaser could trace back the chain of former owners for a long period. There was therefore no need for an 'abstract of title' when the property changed hands.

Stereotyped forms were developed at that time for various legal transactions such as an agreement not to sue, contracts of sale, leases, division of property held jointly, marriage settlements and divorces, and these forms, with slight modifications, were preserved down to Roman times.

A peculiar form of transaction were the 'self-sales' of free persons into servitude, which can be paralleled from the oldest

German law as described by Tacitus. There are also 'self-sales' into the position of a son, which lead us to assume that a father possessed a certain *patria potestas* even over a grown-up son, as otherwise the purchaser in such a case would not have received any consideration.

Only two types of marriage settlements are known to us—the settlement made by the husband for the benefit of the wife, and that made by the wife for the benefit of the husband. If it was the husband who made the settlement, he very often transferred his whole present and future property to his wife and to their children. That of course implies that by law he had such a wide right of usufruct and of administration over the wife's property during marriage that it was not a matter of practical importance to him if he was no longer the owner of his property: that was the case so long as he did not divorce his wife. During his marriage he could not transfer any valuable object to a third person without the express consent of his wife and possibly of his eldest son as the representative of the children. That is why in many contracts of sale we find a declaration of consent by the wife and by the eldest son. As in those cases the wife and the children had already during the lifetime of the head of the family become the real owners of the property, there was no succession at his death. When he died, the ownership was not changed, only the right of usufruct and administration was extinguished.

In the law of procedure appeal to oracles was preserved for a considerable period. The decision of Amun of the Siwa oasis concerning the divine descent of Alexander is perhaps the last historical evidence of it. But the majority of actions were presumably decided by a purely secular procedure which was conducted entirely in writing. An action consisted of statements of claim, defence, and one further pleading on each side. Oral argument was not admitted. At this time we already find it customary for litigants to go, not directly to the courts, but first to a high official who attempts to settle the dispute by agreement between the parties.

The conquest of Egypt by the Persians did not bring with it any fundamental changes in the law, although the Greek tradition represents Darius as a great Egyptian legislator. Up to the present it has been impossible to prove that during the Persian period any part of the law of the Near East was adopted by the Egyptians. We find on the contrary that certain Aramaic documents drawn up by Jewish soldier colonists at Aswân, where they formed the Persian garrison, were literal translations into Aramaic of clauses taken from Egyptian forms of contract.

Ptolemaic Period (332–30 B.C.)

The case was very different under the Macedonians and the Greeks when, as a result of the conquest of Alexander the Great, they had become the masters of the country. Just as Psammeticus I (663–609) had allowed the Greeks to form a πόλις in Naucratis, in which they could live purely under Greek law, so the Greeks in the newly founded Alexandria and Ptolemais were governed entirely by Greek law, which, for instance, took over several provisions from Solon's Athenian legislation. Thus some provisions of the old Greek law have only become known to, or clearly understood by, us through the papyri. Further, those Greeks who were scattered through the country were, in their relations with each other, governed entirely by Greek law. But Egyptian law was preserved for the use of the Egyptian population. The demotic documents of the Ptolemaic period show at first the same law as those of the Saïte period. A third system of law was added: the royal law. The government proclaimed new statutes which were binding both on its Greek and Egyptian subjects, especially statutes dealing with taxation, customs, monopolies, and other matters of public law.

There was a certain amount of mutual reception of legal institutions. Thus the Egyptians took over from the Greeks the so-called 'double document' for loan transactions. In this case the whole text was written out twice on the papyrus, one copy beside the other. One copy was rolled up and then sealed by the person who had drafted it and sometimes by the witnesses as well, and it was thus protected against subsequent alterations. The second text, which was identical with the first, remained unsealed and could be read at any time. In an action the seal could be broken so as to discover whether the text which had been protected by the seal was identical with the unprotected version. Conversely, the royal law incorporated Egyptian customs. Although the Ptolemaic kings filled the highest offices with Macedonians and Greeks, the titles of those officials were often nothing but translations of Egyptian titles which we know as early as the New Kingdom. The division of the country into nomes remained the same. The Ptolemaic administration took over from the Egyptians their financial organization with its treasury and storehouses (θησαυροί), as well as the tax returns, which are framed precisely as are those known to us from the Middle Kingdom except that they are written in the Greek language. The taxes were farmed, but the tax-farmer was assisted by a staff of government inspectors. Even in minor details we can trace the Egyptian tradition in the royal statutes—the farmer of a monopoly who had searched a house for the purpose of inspection but who had not found anything was bound to assure the master of the house on oath, sworn in Egyptian fashion in a temple, that he had not searched his house out of malice or without justification. The increasing intermixture amongst the Greek and Egyptian population helped towards a greater assimilation of these three coexisting legal systems.

The Ptolemaic kings altered the Egyptian organization of the courts. They appointed special inspectors (εἰσαγωγεῖς) to all courts, alike to those with jurisdiction over Greeks and those with jurisdiction over Egyptians. These inspectors took no part in determining the judgement of the court, but without them no action could be brought. They were present at the sitting and supervised the execution of the judgement. The Ptolemies further had to define the extent of the jurisdiction of the different courts of law. For actions between Greeks there were Greek courts in the Greek towns and special itinerant courts in the country. Egyptians came before the Egyptian courts. For actions between Greeks and Egyptians at first a 'joint court of law' was instituted. Later it depended upon whether the documents upon which the plaintiff sought to rely were written in Greek or in Egyptian, the corresponding court having jurisdiction to try the action. Special courts in which special officials, mostly Greek, acted as judges were established for all matters which in any way were connected with public revenue.

It was not too easy to initiate an action. Application had to be made, by way of petition, to a high official (the petition being often addressed to the king in person). That official in the first instance, either himself or through a lower official, tried to bring about a settlement, and only if those efforts were unsuccessful did he hand over the case to the courts for a decision. This procedure was based on the Egyptian conception that settlement is better than judgement, an idea which was quite contrary to the Roman procedure of the same time, which aimed at a quick decision.

So far as our present knowledge goes, the Ptolemies do not appear to have interfered to any great extent with the private law of the Egyptian people. Criminal law had, it seems, become slightly more humane in the course of time.

Roman and Byzantine Period (30 B.C.—A.D. 640)

Even the conquest of Egypt by Augustus did not at once bring with it a complete change. The Romans were far from forcing the law of the city of Rome—the 'classical' Roman law —upon a conquered country, and so the number of legal systems which co-existed in Egypt was merely increased. Only the few Roman citizens who had come over from Italy were governed by the Roman 'imperial law'. In addition to this the Romans had developed a completely different legal system which was applied only in the provinces and which was adapted to the needs of each province, the 'Roman provincial law'. The third legal system which was in force among the native population was the 'national law', which was not, however, a uniform system, inasmuch as the Greeks lived under Greek law as before, and the Egyptians under Egyptian law. The Roman provincial law, which may be regarded as the most interesting of these legal systems, was the one system which was best capable of further development.

This law, which ran parallel with the 'classical' Roman law of the age of the great Roman jurists, was in its own way a classical law too. It displays the great administrative and colonizing qualities of the Romans and their capacity for seizing on essentials. The style of the documents of this period was terse and clear, while in the post-classical period it became digressive and pompous. The provincial law has a special value for legal history inasmuch as it very often anticipated the development of the imperial law. To give one example: in the city of Rome at this time the classical law of civil procedure, which we know from Gaius, was in force. The litigants went to a magistrate who clearly summarized the legal issues in a formula, but who could not himself pronounce judgement. That was done by a private person who was chosen as 'judge' by the parties. That was a procedure which corresponded to the republican form of government but which Augustus left untouched, out of his respect for tradition. But he had no interest in introducing republican institutions into Egypt which had always been under a monarchic form of government. The law of procedure which he introduced into Egypt was related rather to Roman practice in other provinces. The governor was to be the supreme judge.

He held a *conventus*—an assize court—every year for that purpose in three towns (Alexandria, Pelusium, and Memphis) and occasionally in other places. The local authorities had to prepare the case in advance very carefully so that the proceedings could be disposed of during the few days of an assize. If a decision could not be obtained during the *conventus*, then the case was referred to a *judex pedaneus*, who had always to be an official and who received his instructions from the governor. Such instructions bore a certain, though only a superficial, similarity to the formula of the Roman procedure. In other matters, too, this procedure differed materially from that of the classical Roman law. The summons issued from a public authority and not from the plaintiff. Accordingly judgement by default could be given against a party who did not enter an appearance. We hear nothing of the Roman rule that judgement could be given only in terms of the payment of a sum of money: under provincial law judgement could be given for the specific restitution of property and was so executed. Looked at from the Roman point of view this was procedure by *cognitio*, as opposed to the formulary procedure. The Roman jurists from whom we derive our knowledge of Roman law dealt almost exclusively with the formulary procedure, and thus the importance of the Egyptian papyri lies in the fact that they give us a clear conception of the procedure by *cognitio* as it was practised under the early empire. Furthermore, with the strengthening of the imperial power in Rome between the second and fourth centuries the *cognitio* procedure became finally the only form of procedure in Rome itself. There too, judgement by default could now be given against the party who failed to appear, there too, a person could be compelled to make specific restitution of property. Thus the experience of the provincial procedure by *cognitio* which we can trace in the papyri was of value as the experimental stage from which the subsequent practice developed throughout the empire.

The remarks made above about the law of procedure can be applied quite generally to other branches of law. Thus, as a result of recent researches by the Italian scholar Arangio-Ruiz, it appears that the provincial law came very near to attaining the conception of negotiable instruments for money debts. At any rate a record of a trial[1] shows us how the plaintiff in that action relied entirely on the fact that he was in possession of a promissory note which had been drawn in favour of a third person.

The Romans tried to facilitate dealings in real estate because they were fond of investing their capital in provincial land. But here Egyptian national law, which was still in force, presented an obstacle: if a husband had transferred his property to his wife by a marriage settlement he could not dispose of any land without the consent of his wife and of his eldest son. If the consent was not given the property could not pass. But the Roman speculators in real estate were not always aware of the matrimonial affairs of the Egyptian vendors. Therefore the governors introduced the βιβλιοθήκη ἐγκτήσεων, the land register, the only one of its kind which we know in antiquity. All title-deeds concerning real property were collected in one centre, indices (διαστρώματα) facilitated reference. The purchaser of a piece of land could search these archives, and presumably he might rest assured that a right did not exist if it could not be found here. Nothing corresponding to this land register existed in Roman imperial law.

Here we have proof of the creative power of the early provincial law which thus introduced an institution which had to be reinvented in the Middle Ages and in modern times. But we do not know how far this land register served also for taxation purposes and how far it was therefore developed from the old Egyptian tax rolls. Diocletian abolished it in connexion with his great tax reform.

[1] Papyrus of the R. Università di Milano, 25.

In the course of time the different provincial legal systems were fused with the imperial law. It has been thought that the *Constitutio Antoniniana* (212) (the text of which we know from an Egyptian papyrus) which granted Roman citizenship to the whole population of the empire caused the immediate abolition of national and provincial law, but that is not so. Even as Roman citizens the natives were still living under their former laws, though the process of gradual fusion which had begun before that time continued, and reached its culminating point under the Emperor Diocletian (284–305). At this time it is but rarely that we can trace any local peculiarities: the same law is applied throughout the empire. Legal documents in demotic script ceased to exist. In Egypt as well as elsewhere the literature upon the classical Roman law was studied. It is due to that fact that several important fragments of works by Roman jurists (e.g. Gaius) have been preserved by the papyri of Egypt.

Coptic Law

After Diocletian a certain renaissance of Egyptian national law set in. But its extent and importance must not be overestimated. Under the influence of Christianity the Egyptians again became more fully conscious of their national characteristics. The Coptic script could be easily read, and the development of a Coptic literature created a new foundation for an independent development of law in Egypt. But the old Egyptian law had been forgotten. It is true that legal documents were once more drawn up in the Egyptian—i.e. now the Coptic—language, but on closer examination it becomes evident that the phrases used there were nothing but translations of those used in Greek documents during the Byzantine period. Coptic law is fundamentally only a development of Roman law, and therefore Coptic documents very often show a surprising similarity to the contemporary Frankish documents. During the Arabic period the influence of the Qur'ân, especially on the law of procedure and on public law, is added to that of Roman law. It is rather in certain details that Coptic law showed its own peculiar character. Under Roman law litigation *could* be ended by putting a party on his oath or by a settlement. Under Coptic law this was considered to be the normal end of an action, much more common than a judgement. It would be illegal under Roman law to give a free child to a monastery to spend his life there, not as a monk, but as a servant: but gifts of that kind were attested by Coptic notaries. But it is extremely doubtful whether one can see herein any connexion with the 'self-sales' into slavery of the Saïte period. The same must be said of the similarities which may be found between demotic and Coptic legal documents, both in the law of marriage and the law concerning sureties.

After the conquest of Egypt by the Arabs legal documents written in Greek soon disappeared; the Coptic country population, however, preserved its writing and language down to the eleventh century. Only then the Coptic legal documents disappeared and with them the last relic of the richly variegated history of Egyptian law.

ERWIN SEIDL

CHAPTER 9

EGYPT AND ISRAEL

I

In dealing with the relations between Egypt and the Hebrews a preliminary matter which calls for brief mention is the geographical position of Syria, of which Palestine, which lay to the south of the Lebanon ranges, formed part. The Mediterranean sea on the west, and the Arabian desert on the east, made Syria-Palestine a kind of corridor about four hundred miles long and less than a hundred broad. With Mesopotamia to the northeast and Egypt on the south-west, the land formed a highway between the continents of Asia and Africa. Its possession was, therefore, of the greatest importance to the leading Powers of the two continents, both for military purposes and also because of the trade routes, used also, of course, for the march of armies. Of these routes there were four main ones which ran north and south, that along the maritime plain being the most important; they were crossed in the southern parts of the land by others running east and west, but these were of less importance. It needs no further words to show the unique geographical position held by Syria-Palestine, and the importance of possessing it.

The earliest references which we have of contacts between Egypt and Syria-Palestine are not, for obvious reasons, concerned with the Israelites; nevertheless, inasmuch as racially, and possibly even more closely, the Israelites were connected with, at any rate, a portion of the people of Syria-Palestine during the second and third millenniums B.C., it will not be out of place if we begin by drawing attention to some of the indications which we have of the earliest contacts between Egypt and Syria-Palestine. There are not many, but, such as they are, they deserve mention.

Belonging to the time of the Fifth Dynasty (c. 2560–2420 B.C.)

there is, in a tomb, a representation of Egyptians attacking villages which were evidently in southern Palestine, since these towns or villages are called 'the enemy town Nedya, the enemy town ʿEn-Ka . . .', the latter evidently 'Ain-Ka, 'the spring of Ka . . .', clearly a Semitic name. Somewhat later (about 1950 B.C.) we have the interesting story of Sinuhe, an important official who had accidentally become acquainted with a secret communication intended only for his royal master; he, therefore, thought it advisable to escape from the king's wrath and fled to southern Palestine; there he settled down among the Bedawîn. It is the account of his sojourn among these 'plunderers' or 'sand-dwellers', as they were called by the Egyptians, that throws light on the relationship between Egypt and these Asiatics; the picture given of the life and conditions in Palestine corresponds with those of the time of the Tell-el-Amârna letters (14th century, see further below). Among other things, Sinuhe refers to the building of a wall 'to prevent the Asiatics from going down into Egypt', which shows that incursions into Egypt from Syria-Palestine had begun long before the time of the Hyksos invasion (see below).

Again, one of the inscriptions in a tomb of Beni-Ḥasan (near Hermopolis), belonging to about 1900 B.C., tells of how a body of thirty-seven Aamu, or Bedawîn, from the desert, brought tribute of green eye-paint; their leader has the name of Ibsha or Abshai (cf. the Biblical Abishai, 1 Sam. xxvi. 6, &c.), who is called a 'prince of the desert'. The scene depicting this presents the facial characteristics of these Aamu as clearly Semitic, and thus witnesses again to the contact between Egypt and the Asiatic dwellers of Syria-Palestine. This is further illustrated by the discovery, made some years ago now, of a small Egyptian statuette found on the site of ancient Gezer, belonging approximately to 2000 B.C.; it has on it a short inscription in hieroglyphics, containing a formula, as Professor F. Ll. Griffith points out, which 'is usual on statuettes dedicated in temples or tombs, or perhaps for the cult of ancestors within the house'.[1] There are other early indications among Egyptian 'finds' of this contact; but those mentioned will suffice.

A time of deep humiliation for Egypt began soon before the end of the Thirteenth Dynasty, somewhere about the year 1800 B.C. This was when the Asiatic Hyksos, or 'Shepherd' kings (cf. Gen. xlvi. 34: 'for every shepherd is an abomination unto the Egyptians') invaded the Delta region, where, according to Manetho,[2] they established themselves and founded their capital, Avaris. Their victory may have been due, as has been suggested, to their use of bronze weapons. There are some grounds for the contention that the Hyksos came originally from Asia Minor, their conquest of Syria-Palestine being but the first step towards their real objective. In their invasion of Egypt they were then joined by the Semitic peoples of Syria-Palestine. In support of this view as to the original home of the Hyksos is the existence of many non-Semitic proper names which are met with during the succeeding centuries in Syria-Palestine; for these may well have been the names of the Hyksos invaders. On the other hand, Manetho speaks of them as Phoenicians and Arabians. The name of Jacob-el, which occurs on the scarabs of a Pharaoh of the Hyksos period, suggests the possibility that the head of one of the Jacob-tribes among the ancestors of the Israelites occupied a position of leadership at one time during this period.

It is often contended that the Hyksos invasion of Egypt, and their expulsion from there, is reflected in the traditions of Abram going down into Egypt (Gen. xii. 10–18), followed by his return to Palestine (Gen. xii. 19, 20, xiii); and also in the traditions of Jacob, who likewise went there (Gen. xlvi. 2–7), and came back to his native land with a large following (Gen. xlix. 28, l. 9–24). It is impossible either to prove or disprove

---

[1] Palestine Exploration Fund, *Quarterly Statement*, April 1906, pp. 121 f.

[2] The Egyptian priest-historian who wrote in 280 B.C.; he is quoted by Josephus, *Contra Ap.* i. 73 ff.

conjectures of this kind; nevertheless, though the narratives in question can hardly be held to be reliable history, it may be regarded as certain that Hebrew traditions always had some basis in fact; so that there may well be some justification for believing that these narratives do contain an echo, expressing the Hebrew point of view, of the Hyksos period.

The supremacy of the Hyksos in Egypt lasted till about 1580 B.C., though the opinions of experts differ regarding the length of their rule in Egypt. Their expulsion took place with the rise of the Eighteenth Dynasty. Ahmose, the first ruler of this dynasty, drove them out, and pursued them into Southern Palestine, conquering the city of Sharuhen (this city is mentioned in Joshua xix. 6).[1] This was, however, only a beginning; wars continued under his successors Amenhôtep I and Tuthmosis I, and went on for many years. The real destroyer of their power was Tuthmosis III (1506?–1461 B.C.), whose great victory at the battle of Megiddo (1478 B.C.), though not decisive, was of prime importance. On a commemorative inscription of this victory there occur names of conquered cities which are familiar to us from the Old Testament, such as Taanach, Jaffa, and others. Although there were further wars to almost the end of the fifteenth century, the power of the Asiatics was no more a menace. The mention of the Hittites on this inscription, though it does not concern the present inquiry, is worth noting, for it is the first mention that we have of them; they are often spoken of in the Old Testament.

We come now to what is often described as the Tell-el-Amârna period. 'All the powers', says Breasted, 'Babylonia, Assyria, Mitanni, and Alasa-Cyprus, were exerting every effort to gain the friendship of Egypt. From the Pharaoh's court, as the centre, radiate a host of lines of communication with all the great peoples of the age. The Tell-el-Amârna letters, perhaps

[1] Breasted, *Ancient Records of Egypt: The Historical Documents*, ii. 13 (1905).

the most interesting mass of documents surviving from the early East, have preserved to us this glimpse across the kingdoms of hither Asia as one might see them on a stage, each king playing his part before the great throne of the Pharaoh.'[1] Nevertheless, in spite of this widespread recognition of Egyptian overlordship, the actual hegemony of Egypt over Syria-Palestine was little more than nominal. This, after the victories of Tuthmosis III and his immediate successors, mentioned above, sounds strange; but the fact is that the Tell-el-Amârna letters make it abundantly clear that a new menace to Egyptian suzerainty over Syria-Palestine had arisen. Among these letters, most of which are addressed to Amenhôtep IV (1376–1359 B.C.),[2] there are a large number from the vassal kings to the Pharaoh which contain reiterated requests for help against the attacks of enemies. And here we come to what, from the point of view of the present essay, is of particular importance. Among these enemies were those who are called the *Habiru*. The question as to who the *Habiru* were has occasioned a great deal of controversy; to discuss it here would take us too far afield;[3] but we may without hesitation adopt the conviction of the majority of experts, namely that the name is equivalent to the 'Hebrews'; the ideographic form of the name is SA.GAZ (which occurs more frequently than *Habiru*), and it is equivalent to the ʿprw occurring on Egyptian inscriptions. This is not to say that the *Habiru* are to be identified with the Hebrews, or Israelites, as we know them; the people of Israel of later times were the descendants of the union of *Habiru*—Hebrews with Aramaic tribes; but it

[1] *A History of Egypt*, p. 332 (1912).

[2] A blue porcelain ring, with the cartouche of this king, was found at Tell Zakariya, in the vale of Elah.

[3] See, e.g., Winckler, 'Die Hebräer in den Tel-Amarna-Briefen', in *Semitic Studies in memory of Alexander Kohut*, pp. 605 ff. (1897); Burney, *The Book of Judges*, pp. lxxiii ff. (1918); Peet, *Egypt and the Old Testament*, pp. 115 ff. (1922); Jirku, 'Die Wanderungen der Hebräer im 3. und 2. Jahrtausend v. Chr.', in *Der alte Orient*, xiv. 2 (1924).

may well be that some of the *Habiru* were the people of the Egyptian bondage, and that in later Israelite tradition they were held to be the ancestors of the Israelites; that the tradition reflected the truth is extremely probable. It must only be added that the Biblical evidence makes it clear that the people in bondage did not represent the *entire* ancestry of Israel. When all that is said about the *Habiru* in the Amârna letters, and in the Egyptian inscriptions, is compared with the narratives in the Old Testament, these latter are seen to be substantiated in a surprising manner; as Jirku truly remarks: 'Whatever the Old Testament narrates about the Hebrews can be brought into connexion with what is said about the *Habiru* or about the *ʿprw* in the ancient oriental records.'

We turn now to the vexed question of the date of the exodus. Here, again, want of space forbids discussion;[1] we can but offer a few general remarks upon the subject without discussing the various arguments for and against the suggested dates. There are three periods during which the exodus might have taken place: (*a*) from the time that the Hyksos were driven out of Egypt to the conquests of Tuthmosis III, roughly from 1570 to 1500 B.C.; (*b*) from the decline of the Eighteenth Dynasty to the time of Seti I, and Rameses II, approximately from 1400 to 1300 B.C.; (*c*) after the end of the Nineteenth Dynasty, i.e. from 1200 B.C. onwards. None of the data adduced in support of these dates, respectively, are conclusive; all that can be said is that the last is the least probable, and that there is something to be said in favour of the second. This conclusion is disappointing; but the fact is that unless, and until, more definite data are forthcoming, the matter must remain in the realm of conjecture.

While it will be allowed that what has so far been said has a bearing on our main subject, it is all of an indirect character;

[1] See Peet, op. cit., pp. 105 ff.; J. W. Jack, *The Date of the Exodus* (1925); Oesterley and Robinson, *A History of Israel*, i. 68 ff. (1934).

we come now to the time when the contact between Egypt and Israel becomes definite and direct.

II

Soon after Merneptah came to the throne of Egypt (1225) a widespread revolt against him arose in Asia; among those who revolted were the various States of the whole of Palestine-Syria, including the Israelites. The revolt was quelled, and Merneptah set up a stele to commemorate his victory; part of the inscription runs:

> The kings are overthrown, saying, Salam!
> Not one holds up his head among the nine nations of the bow.
> Wasted is Tehenu,
> The Hittite Land is pacified,
> Plundered is the Canaan, with every evil,
> Carried off is Askalon,
> Seized upon is Gezer,
> Yenoam is made as a thing not existing.
> Israel is desolated, her seed is not,
> Palestine has become a (defenceless) widow for Egypt.
> All lands are united, they are pacified;
> Everyone that is turbulent is bound by King Merneptah.[1]

This is the earliest direct mention of Israel on an ancient inscription; it is worthy of note that they are spoken of as a people, and must, therefore, have been settled down in the land for some time. This shows, by the way, the untenability of the contention that the exodus took place under Merneptah; a contention further weakened by the fact that his body has been found in Thebes, so that he cannot have been drowned in the Red Sea.

Soon after the time of Merneptah a period of continuous decline began to set in; this is well illustrated somewhat later by the story of Wen-Amon, the envoy of the Pharaoh Hrihor

[1] A German translation of this important document is given by Gressmann, *Altorientalische Texte zum Alten Testament*, pp. 71–7 (1926).

(1090–1085) to Byblus, on the Syrian coast; from this it can be seen that Egyptian influence over Syria-Palestine had entirely ceased. 'During this period of Egypt's total eclipse', says Breasted, 'the tribes of Israel gained the opportunity to consolidate their national organization, and under Saul and David they gradually gained the upper hand against the Philistines.'[1] Soon after this begins the time, about 1000 B.C., when we are able to obtain a good deal of information from the Old Testament about the relationship between Egypt and Israel. Here it must be premissed that it is sometimes difficult to be sure about the exact sequence of events; the Old Testament narratives are not always strictly chronological, and authorities differ with regard to Egyptian chronology.

It is recorded that Solomon (*c*. 976–936) 'made affinity with Pharaoh, king of Egypt, and took Pharaoh's daughter, and brought her into the city of David' (1 Kings iii. 1); this Pharaoh is held, with much probability, to have been Sheshonk I (945–924); Egypt is thus seen to be entering once more into active relationship with Palestine; and the sequel shows that Sheshonk aimed at making Syria-Palestine part of the Egyptian Empire again. His alliance with Solomon was a first step towards this, and it was strengthened by the wedding-gift of the city of Gezer to his daughter on her marriage with Solomon. It is said that 'Pharaoh, king of Egypt, had gone up and taken Gezer, and burnt it with fire, and slain the Canaanites that dwelt in the city, and given it for a present to his daughter, Solomon's wife' (1 Kings ix. 16). This points to a regular campaign which Sheshonk must have undertaken, for to capture Gezer meant that the Philistine coast-land had been subdued, as Gezer lay right to the north of Philistia. It is possible that Sheshonk's alliance with Solomon was in reality only a means to lull, for the time being, any misgivings that Solomon may have had regarding this conquest of Philistia; for we read presently of

[1] *A History of Egypt*, p. 526.

some rather suspicious action on the part of Sheshonk. In 1 Kings xi. 18–21, 25 there is the account of Hadad, of the seed royal of Edom, taking refuge in Egypt after David's conquest of this land (2 Sam. viii. 14). When Solomon comes to the throne Hadad leaves Egypt for Palestine where, as it is briefly narrated, he does 'mischief'; the account, it is true, is laconic, but, in any case, the Egyptian king, Sheshonk, does not prevent him from his undertaking; indeed, one may well ask, where did Hadad get his troops from for doing 'mischief', if not from Egypt? Similarly, somewhat later, under Solomon's successor, Rehoboam, Sheshonk harbours another fugitive, Jeroboam, who likewise, when the opportunity occurs, returns to Palestine, with grievous results for Judah (1 Kings xi. 40; xii. 20). This all suggests a settled purpose on the part of Sheshonk of creating trouble in Palestine, and thus preparing for direct action. And very soon this takes place. In 1 Kings xiv. 25 ff. we read: 'And it came to pass in the fifth year [*c.* 930 B.C.] of king Rehoboam, that Shishak [= Sheshonk], king of Egypt, came up against Jerusalem; and he took away the treasures . . .'; this is also referred to in 2 Chron. xii. 2–9, where there is a certain amount of overstatement, characteristic of the Chronicler. The details of this campaign are recorded by Sheshonk on the walls of the Karnak temple at Thebes;[1] from these it is clear that his objective was not confined to the southern part of Palestine; among the cities plundered are several which lay in the Northern Kingdom. The Biblical account does not mention these because it is concerned here only with the Southern Kingdom.

From what has been said it is evident that Sheshonk intended that Syria-Palestine should, after a lapse of nearly three centuries, become once more part of the Egyptian Empire. But internal troubles in Egypt prevented this, and Egyptian influence over Syria-Palestine did not again play any decisive rôle until the rise of the Ptolemaic dynasty in 323 B.C. This does

---

[1] Breasted, *Ancient Records* . . ., iv. 709–24.

not mean to say, however, that attempts were not made to assert that influence. About twenty-five years or so after Sheshonk's victory we read in 2 Chron. xiv. 9–15 (8–14 in Hebr.) that in the reign of Asa, king of Judah, Zerah[1] the Ethiopian invaded the land; a battle is fought 'in the valley of Zephathah at Mareshah', at which the Ethiopians were defeated, 'and Asa and the people that were with him pursued them unto Gerar . . .'. Doubts have been cast, not without some reason, on the identification of Kûsh with Ethiopia (in southern Egypt), as it is held (though this is not certain) that there was a Kûsh in Arabia; it must, however, be noted that the flight of these Ethiopians south-westwards to Gerar points to the shortest route into Egypt; moreover, in 2 Chron. xvi. 8, where this battle is referred to, the Lubim (Libyans) are mentioned together with the Ethiopians; and further, there are a number of passages in which Kûsh is quite clearly to be identified with Ethiopia (e.g. 2 Kings xix. 9; Isa. xi. 11, xliii. 3; xlv. 14; Zeph. iii. 10, and others). So that the passage referred to (2 Chron. xiv. 9–15) certainly seems to point to an invasion from Egypt which was repulsed. The date of this would be a little before 900 B.C.

Soon after this the reinvigorated power of Assyria began to assert itself, with momentous consequences for Syria-Palestine. The movement westwards was begun by Ashurnasirpal II (889–859 B.C.), who invaded Syria and subdued various north-Syrian States; he also received tribute from important Phoenician coastal towns, such as Byblus, Tyre, and Sidon. His successor, Shalmaneser III,[2] similarly came westwards with the intention of reducing the whole of the Mediterranean coast-land of Syria-Palestine. In the sixth year of his reign there was fought the important, but indecisive battle of Qarkar on the Orontes (853 B.C.), where he was opposed by a coalition of western

---

[1] His identification with Osorkon I is very doubtful.

[2] According to Winckler, Shalmaneser II, *Keilinschriftliches Textbuch zum Alten Testament*, i. 18 (1909).

States; and here we find Egypt and Israel fighting side by side against the common foe. The former was doubtless actuated by alarm at the growing power of Assyria. Of this battle no mention is made in the Old Testament, but on Shalmaneser's inscription, 'The Black Obelisk', among the allies the name of the Israelite king occurs: '2,000 chariots and 10,000 men of Ahab of Israel.' The silence of the Old Testament is difficult to account for; an Egyptian inscription mentions the contingent sent to aid the allies.

It is rather more than a century before we have the next mention of contact between Egypt and Israel. In 733 Hoshea came to the throne, and of him we read in 2 Kings xvii. 1–6 that he reigned in Samaria over Israel nine years, and that 'against him came up Shalmaneser (i.e. the Vth), king of Assyria; and Hoshea became his servant, and gave him presents. And the king of Assyria found conspiracy in Hoshea, for he had sent messengers to So, king of Egypt (Mizraim), and brought no present to the king of Assyria, as he had done year by year; therefore the king of Assyria shut him up, and bound him in prison. Then the king of Assyria came up throughout all the land, and went up to Samaria, and besieged it three years. In the ninth year of Hoshea the king of Assyria took Samaria, and carried Israel away unto Assyria . . .'. The Egyptian king here called So, or Sewa, was, as Breasted surmises, 'an otherwise unknown Delta dynast'; the point of interest for our present purpose is that 'unable to oppose the formidable armies of Assyria, the petty kinglets of Egypt constantly fomented discontent and revolt among the Syro-Palestinian states in order, if possible, to create a fringe of buffer states between them and the Assyrians'.[1] It would thus appear that Egypt's one objective now was to secure herself against Assyrian aggression. In illustration of this we have, under Egyptian incitement, the rebellion of Ashdod, and other cities against Assyria, in 715 B.C.; but it

[1] *A History* . . ., p. 549.

was in vain; Ashdod fell, and the revolt was quelled (Isa. xx. 1). The prophet graphically describes the futility of relying on Egypt (Isa. xx. 2–6): '. . . And they shall be dismayed and ashamed, because of Ethiopia their expectation, and because of Egypt their glory. And the inhabitant of this coastland shall say in that day, Behold, such is our expectation, whither we fled for help to be delivered from the king of Assyria; and we (i.e. Judah), how shall we escape?' But the prophet's warning was disregarded; and a few years later another and more formidable alliance against Assyria, in the reign of Sennacherib (705–681 B.C.), was formed. The allies included Phoenicia, Philistia, Judah, Edom, Moab, Ammon, with various Bedawîn tribes, and Egypt; a host 'without number' as Sennacherib records. At the battle of Eltekeh (701 B.C.), not far from the Egyptian frontier, the allies were defeated,[1] and for the third time the Assyrians stood on the borders of Egypt without invading it, being forced to retire because of troubles elsewhere. Egypt as an ally of Judah had, however, again disappointed expectations. With truth did Sennacherib's officer send the mocking message to Hezekiah, king of Judah: 'Now, behold, thou trustest upon the staff of this bruised reed, even upon Egypt; whereon if a man lean it will go into his hand and pierce it; so is Pharaoh, king of Egypt unto all that trust on him' (2 Kings xviii. 21).

During the next twenty years or so there is nothing to record so far as Egyptian activity in Syria-Palestine is concerned. On the death of Sennacherib in 681 (680) B.C. his son Esarhaddon ascended the throne; and after having quelled the civil war which arose after the murder of his father, Sennacherib (2 Kings xix. 37), and otherwise settling affairs in his empire, his attention was called westwards. In 677 B.C. the king of Sidon, Abdimilkutti, in all probability instigated by Egypt, revolted; Esarhaddon was soon on the spot, captured Sidon, and sacked it.

[1] For the details concerning Judah, see 2 Kings xviii. 13–37, xix.

The constant activity of Egypt in stirring up the various rulers in Palestine against Assyria determined Esarhaddon to invade Egypt, and by conquering the land, to establish Assyrian suzerainty over the west without further interference. The first attempt, in 673 B.C., failed; but in 670 B.C. Egypt was invaded, Memphis was captured, and the whole of the Delta region occupied by Assyrian troops. For a brief space the fortune of war once again favoured the Egyptians; the Pharaoh Tirhakah, who had fled to Thebes, gathered an army and reconquered Memphis, the Assyrian king having in the meantime returned to his own country. No sooner, however, did he hear of what had happened than he set out for Egypt again; but on the way thither he died. The respite for Egypt did not last long. In 668 B.C. Ashurbanipal, Esarhaddon's successor, invaded the land, re-took Memphis, and Thebes was also occupied. After a few years Tirhakah's successor, Tanutamon, tried once more, in 663 B.C., and with some initial success, to gain possession of Lower Egypt; in 661 B.C., however, Ashurbanipal was again in Egypt; Tanutamon fled to Thebes, but was pursued; he himself escaped. Thebes was captured and sacked. Egypt was now entirely under Assyrian control. The fall of the great city of Thebes (No-Amon) had a resounding effect upon the peoples, and half a century later it was recalled by the prophet Nahum in describing the nemesis which had overtaken the Assyrians; in reference to Nineveh, the capital, he says:

> Art thou better than No-Amon that lay by the streams,
> Her rampart the sea, waters her wall?
> Kûsh was her strength, and limitless Egypt;
> Pût and Lubim, they were her help.
> Yet was she taken, went into captivity;
> Her children were killed at the top of the streets;
> As for her nobles, the lot was cast,
> All her great ones were bound in chains.[1]

[1] Nah. iii. 8–10; the Hebrew is in verse, with four beats to the line.

Assyrian control over Egypt seemed to be consolidated when Ashurbanipal set his own nominee, Psammeticus, on the Egyptian throne as Tanutamon's successor (663 B.C.). But Psammeticus threw off his allegiance when in 654 B.C. war broke out between Assyria and the rising power of Babylon. The result was that for some time Egypt was again independent; Psammeticus even sought to renew Egyptian influence over Syria-Palestine by invading Philistia (640 B.C.); nothing came of this, however, owing to the Scythian attack on Syria.

It will be readily understood that the conditions being what they were during the seventh century, there was not much scope for direct contact between Egypt and Judah. Towards the end of this century, however, this contact became ominously pronounced.

The course of events leading to the final downfall of the Assyrian Empire has been much illuminated by the Babylonian document published within recent years by C. J. Gadd.[1] Taking this into consideration, we may give the following brief record of what happened. Soon after the death of Ashurbanipal, in 626 B.C., the ruler of the vassal State of Babylonia, Nabopolassar, asserted his independence; similarly the Medes in the north-east, and the western States. A long-drawn-out struggle followed during the reigns of two sons of Ashurbanipal. Of particular interest is the fact that Egypt fought on the side of Assyria; the Scythians, too, supported Assyria at first, but before long they joined forces with Nabopolassar and the Medes. Two victories were gained by the latter in 616 B.C., and then they, in turn, were defeated. But in 614 B.C. the Babylonian and Median armies surrounded Nineveh; at first they were repulsed, but ultimately, in 612 B.C., Nineveh fell, and according to the Babylonian Chronicle the city was 'turned into a mound and a ruin'. Nevertheless, the Assyrians struggled on; Harran, about a hundred miles west of Nineveh, was fixed on as the new capital.

[1] *The Fall of Nineveh; the newly discovered Babylonian Chronicle,* No. 21,901 in the British Museum (1923).

Late in 610 B.C. this city was attacked and captured; but the Assyrian army fled before the attack began, with the purpose, as the sequel shows, of joining up with the Egyptians. Together they sought to recapture Harran in the following year, 609 B.C., Pharaoh-Necho having succeeded to the throne of Egypt; in this they were unsuccessful, but they were able to withdraw to Syria. Presumably the Egyptians returned to their own country; but the Assyrians occupied Carchemish, on the Euphrates. For four years hostilities ceased; for what reason is not known. Assyria was, in any case, not in a position to exercise any authority, and of this Egypt took full advantage, so far as Syria-Palestine was concerned. The Old Testament gives evidence of this, though it must be confessed that some chronological confusion is evident in 2 Kings xxiii. 29, 30 and 2 Chron. xxxv. 20–4; at any rate, what is said in 2 Kings xxiii. 31–5 shows that Palestine was wholly subject to Egypt; this passage must be quoted; in reference to Jehoahaz it is said: 'And Pharaoh-necho put him in bands at Riblah, in the land of Hamath, that he might not reign in Jerusalem; and he put the land to a tribute. . . . And Pharaoh-necho made Eliakim, the son of Josiah, king in the room of Josiah his father, and changed his name to Jehoiakim; but he took Jehoahaz away; and he came to Egypt and died there. And Jehoiakim gave the silver and the gold to Pharaoh; but he taxed the land to give the money according to the commandment of Pharaoh; he exacted the silver and the gold of the people of the land, of everyone according to his taxation, to give it unto Pharaoh-necho.' This supremacy of Egypt was of but short duration. In 605 B.C. the Babylonian army, now under the command of Nebuchadnezzar, gained a decisive victory over the Egyptians at Carchemish; and Egypt lay at the feet of Babylon. This battle is described in Jer. xlvi. 1–12; and in 2 Kings xxiv. 7 it is said: 'And the king of Egypt came not again any more out of his land; for the king of Babylon had taken, from the brook of Egypt unto the river Euphrates, all that pertained to the king of Egypt.' Syria-Palestine was thus incorporated in the Babylonian Empire.

We reach now the last occasion in pre-exilic times on which there was a contact between Egypt and Judah. Jehoiakim, the king of Judah (608–597 B.C.), was, of course, forced to acknowledge Nebuchadnezzar as his suzerain, and 'became his servant three years; then he turned and rebelled against him' (2 Kings xxiv. 1). It is impossible to doubt, in view of subsequent events, that Jehoiakim's rebellion was prompted by Egypt. Before Nebuchadnezzar could take action Jehoiakim died, and his son Jehoiachin succeeded him (2 Kings xxiv. 6). In 2 Chron. xxxvi. 6 we read that Nebuchadnezzar bound Jehoiakim in fetters 'to carry him to Babylon'; but nothing of this is said in 2 Kings. Scarcely was Jehoiachin seated on the throne than Nebuchadnezzar appeared with his army before Jerusalem; Jehoiachin immediately surrendered and was carried off to Babylon. In his place Nebuchadnezzar appointed Zedekiah (597 B.C.).

The events during Zedekiah's reign are passed over in silence in 2 Kings xxiv. 18–20; but from what we read elsewhere it is evident that there was a strong pro-Egyptian party in the State; and it was doubtless owing to Egyptian influence that, as it is said in 2 Kings xxiv. 20, 'Zedekiah rebelled against the king of Babylon'; and in Ezek. xvii. 15 it is recorded of Zedekiah that he 'rebelled against him in sending his ambassadors into Egypt'. The king of Egypt was now Apries, who came to the throne in 588 B.C.; in Jer. xliv. 30 he is called Hophra. Nebuchadnezzar quickly marched westwards; he made his head-quarters at Riblah, on the Orontes, and sent a detachment against Jerusalem. But the Babylonians were forced to retreat owing to the advance of the Egyptian army: 'And Pharaoh's army was come forth out of Egypt; and when the Chaldeans that besieged Jerusalem heard tidings of them they brake up from Jerusalem' (Jer. xxxvii. 5, see also v. 11). This was but a respite, and the prophet's words (Jer. xxxviii. 3) came true; in the following year Jerusalem fell, and the kingdom of Judah ceased to exist.

It should be added that the recently discovered Lachish letters throw some interesting light on this tragic event; they are 'the first personal documents found, reflecting the mind, the struggles, sorrows and feelings of ancient Judah in the last days of the kingdom'.[1] A further reference will be made to them below.

III

Judging from the purely political standpoint, as outlined above, the relations between Egypt and Israel were of a character far from profitable to the latter. It must not, however, be concluded from this that Israel gained nothing through her contact with Egypt. There must have been much intercourse between the two peoples, the details of which we know but little, see, e.g., Gen. xii. 10–20, and Hagar was an Egyptian (Gen. xxi. 9; xxv. 12); see also Gen. xlvi. 3–7; l. 22 ff.; for, as will be seen, the marks of Egyptian influence in certain cultural respects were very significant.

It will be instructive to note, first, the indications we have of Israelites making their permanent home in Egypt. It is, of course, impossible to say to what period the earliest settlement of Hebrews in Egypt is to be assigned; though such a passage as Gen. xlvii. 27 is suggestive: 'And Israel dwelt in the land of Egypt, in the land of Goshen; and they gat them possessions therein, and were fruitful, and multiplied exceedingly', cp. Gen. l. 8; though belonging to the latest, Pentateuchal, document (P), this reflects the idea of a permanent settlement according to the tradition. Further, the possibility can hardly be excluded of some of those who were in bondage in Egypt having remained in the country, whether forcibly detained or of their own accord; the nucleus of a permanent settlement

[1] *Lachish I (Tell ed Duweir): The Lachish Letters*, by Torczyner and others, p. 18 (1938).

might thus have been formed. Adaptation to environment and the propagation of the race have always been characteristic of the Hebrews. This is, however, pure surmise. Although the first indisputable references to Hebrew settlements in Egypt do not appear until the time of Jeremiah, it can be proved, as will be seen, that long before this time Israelites were living as permanent settlers in Egypt.

We may point first to an indirect indication. In Jer. xxvi. 20–3 it is told how, following Jeremiah's example, Uriah the son of Shemaiah of Kiriath-jearim 'prophesied against this city (i.e. Jerusalem) and against this land, according to all the words of Jeremiah'; in consequence of this the king, Jehoiakim,[1] sought to put him to death. Uriah therefore fled to Egypt. It is not inappropriate to ask why he should have fled to Egypt, and the obvious answer is that it was because he would find people of his own race there, which, as will be seen, was actually the case. In passing, it is worth mentioning that this episode is dealt with in one of the Lachish Letters, where further details are given, a most striking corroboration of the Old Testament record. That there were Israelite settlements in Egypt is made clear from Jer. xliv. 1, where reference is made to 'all the Jews which dwelt in the land of Egypt, which dwelt at Migdol, and at Tahpanes, and at Noph, and in the country of Pathros'; these places were widely separated; Migdol was in the extreme north-west, Tahpanes in the north-east, Noph (Memphis) on the Nile, about a hundred miles to the south, and Pathros farther south in Upper Egypt.[2] Although we know nothing further about these settlements, nor yet when they were founded, their widely separated positions suggest that they had existed long before the time of Jeremiah. Of particular interest is the colony at Elephantiné, of which the Aramaic

[1] It is recognized by all authorities that 'Jehoiakim' is erroneously written for 'Zedekiah', as in Jer. xxvii. 1.

[2] On this last, see Condamin, *Le Livre de Jérémie*, p. 291 (1936).

papyri, discovered in 1906, give us detailed knowledge.[1] The immense importance of these, over seventy, papyri, can hardly be overestimated; we can, however, do no more here than mention one or two points.

Elephantiné (its Semitic name is Yeb) was situated on an island in the Nile, on the frontier of Southern Egypt, so that, as far as we know, it was a military colony from the beginning. The papyri contain a record of historical events connected with the settlers during the years 525–407 B.C. as well as many details concerning their private affairs. As to the date of the first founding of this settlement, we have the following indication in one of the documents: 'Already in the days of the kings of Egypt (i.e. before the Persian conquest) our fathers had built that temple in the fortress of Yeb, and when Cambyses came into Egypt he found that temple built.' Cambyses came into Egypt in 525 B.C., so that if the temple was already built then, the colonists must have been settled there for some time previously; and this is borne out by what Aristeas says in his Letter, § 13—and he is well informed on Egyptian matters—that Jewish mercenaries had entered Egypt and fought in the army of Psammeticus, no doubt the second of this name is meant (593–588), during his campaign against the Ethiopians; after this war the Jewish soldiers were settled in Elephantiné as a protection to the southern boundary of the kingdom. But a still earlier date for the original settlers is suggested by the fact of the existence of the temple, just referred to; for this implies ignorance of the Deuteronomic legislation; moreover, the colonists worshipped other gods besides Yahweh; both facts look like a continuation of pre-exilic customs and religious beliefs. In this case the original settlement must be dated some time during the seventh century B.C.

[1] See especially, Sachau, *Aramäische Papyrus und Ostraka aus einer jüdischen Militärkolonie zu Elephantiné* (1911); Cowley, *Jewish Documents of the time of Ezra* (1919), and *Aramaic Papyri of the Fifth Century B.C.* (1923).

The next mention we have of a Jewish colony in Egypt is in connexion with the founding of Alexandria by Alexander the Great, in 332 B.C. There is no reason to doubt the truth of Josephus' statement that Alexander gave the Jews 'equal privileges in this city with the Greeks themselves' when he founded the city (*Bell. Jud.* ii. 487, cf. *Contra Ap.* ii. 35); for this is borne out by the edict of the Emperor Claudius, in which it is said that 'the Jews of Alexandria, called *Alexandrians*, have been joint-inhabitants in the earliest times with the Alexandrians, and have obtained from their kings equal privileges with them, as is evident by the public records which are in their possession, and the edicts themselves . . .' (*Antiq.* xix. 281). It is not to be supposed that Josephus invented this! The Jews were assigned a special quarter in the city by Alexander's successors, 'who set apart for them a particular place' (*Bell. Jud.* ii. 488); this is also mentioned by Strabo (quoted by Josephus, *Antiq.* xiv. 117). But by the time of Philo this isolation no longer existed, for he says that they lived in all parts of the city (*De Leg. ad Cajum*, § 20). Regarding their organization, Strabo says: 'There is also an ethnarch allowed them, who governs the nation, and distributes justice to them, and takes care of their contracts, and of the laws belonging to them, as if he were the ruler of a free republic' (*Antiq.* xiv. 117). Space forbids our following out further the history of the Jews in Alexandria under Ptolemaic rule,[1] and later under the Roman Empire; but we cannot think of the Jews of Alexandria without recalling the fact that this city was the home of the Septuagint. The account of the origin of this profoundly important work, as given in the Letter of Aristeas, is the embellishment, with a number of imaginary details, of the fact that among the Jews of Alexandria a Greek translation of the Pentateuch (the Law) was made for use among

---

[1] See Büchler, *Die Tobiaden und die Oniaden* . . ., pp. 212–38 (1899); Schürer, *Geschichte des jüdischen Volkes* . . ., iii, pp. 24–52 (1909); and for the Temple in Leontopolis (162 B.C.) see Büchler, pp. 239–76; Schürer, pp. 144–8.

the Greek-speaking Jews; their ignorance of both Hebrew and Aramaic rendered this necessary. The Aramaic-speaking Jews of Palestine, also for the most part ignorant of Hebrew, had their interpreter (*methurgeman*) to explain the readings of their Scriptures in the synagogues; but as the Alexandrian Jews did not know Aramaic, it was necessary for these readings to be in Greek. A discussion on the date of this version would be out of place here; it will suffice to quote Swete's words: 'It may fairly be argued that a version, which at the beginning of the third century had won its way to acceptance among the literary Jews of Alexandria, probably saw the light not later than the reign of Philadelphus'[1] (i.e. Ptolemy II, 285–245). At first only the Pentateuch was translated; the whole Old Testament was completed probably by the beginning of the Christian era. It became the Bible of the early Church, and for this reason fell into discredit among the Jews.

IV

A brief consideration is called for regarding the question as to whether any Egyptian influence on the religion of the Hebrews is to be discerned. It is certain that no lasting signs of such influence are to be discovered; but it may be asked whether in the early periods of the history of the Hebrews, during the close relationship between Egypt and Syria-Palestine, religious influences may not have been brought to bear upon the subject-peoples by the dominating Power. On the face of it, this might have been expected; 'abundant evidence', says S. A. Cook, 'for the prevalence of Egyptian religious ideas in Palestine is afforded by the innumerable seals and scarabs, and by representations of Osiris, Isis, Ptah, Anubis, Sebek, Bes (with moulds), Hathor etc. . . . Not only did Egyptian and Semitic thought share much in common, but a considerable amount of religious

[1] *Introduction to the Old Testament in Greek*, p. 18 (1900, 4th ed. 1920).

syncretism (as was only to be expected) is proved by the archaeology of Syria (e.g. the figurines of Astarte, seals etc.).'[1] Remains
of Egyptian temples have been discovered in Ras Shamra, Byblus,
Bethshean, Megiddo, Taanach, Lachish, and elsewhere; Rameses
III (1194–1163) built a temple in the south of Palestine (Pe-
Kanan) 'like the horizon of heaven which is in the sky'; there
was a great statue of the god to which 'the Asiatics came bearing
tribute before it, for it was divine'.[2] And many other illustrations could be given. With the many proofs of the existence of
Egyptian forms of worship, it is not unreasonable to surmise that
the Israelites during, at any rate, the pre-prophetic period may
have been influenced by Egyptian religion. We venture to
suggest that such influence is to be seen in the worship of the
'Golden Calf'. The record of this is contained in Exod. xxxii.
1–6; as belonging to the Elohistic document, this passage is
interpreted in the light of Canaanite bull-worship; but if, as
seems probable, this episode reflects something that actually
happened—and Hebrew traditions usually contain a kernel of
truth—then the worship of the 'Golden Calf' cannot have been
of Canaanite origin. In Exod. xxxii. 4 it is said: 'These be thy
gods, O Israel, which brought thee up out of the land of Egypt';
here we have the over-working due to the later standpoint, for
according to 1 Kings xii. 28 the 'Golden Calf' was only one
deity, and an Egyptian one. We hazard the suggestion that this
deity was the goddess Hathor. There is a perfect image of this
cow-goddess belonging to the time of Amenophis II (*c.* 1460–
1420); the head, neck, and horns were originally covered with
gold; it is now in the Cairo Museum;[3] this image is strongly
suggestive of the 'Golden Calf'. She is described elsewhere as
the goddess whose necklace shines 'like heaven with its stars; she
is called "the golden" one, or "the gold of the gods"';[4] this, too,

---

[1] *Camb. Anc. Hist.*, ii. 345 (1924).   [2] Op. cit., p. 343.
[3] Gressmann, *Altorientalische Bilder zum Alten Testament*, plate 266 (1927).
[4] Grapow, *Der Alte Orient*, 1920, Heft I, p. 13. Erman, *Die Religion der*

is suggestive as the reason why the 'Calf' was called 'golden'. Figures of this goddess have also been found at Bethshean, Gezer, and Jericho;[1] and the goddess Astarte is sometimes represented with the head-dress of Hathor. Some justification, therefore, it must be allowed, exists for identifying the 'Golden Calf' with the Egyptian goddess Hathor.

The widespread forms of Egyptian worship in Palestine raise the question as to whether in the ritual of the New Year festival which, as the Old Testament shows, played an important part in ancient Israel, Egyptian influence may be discerned in any particulars? But it must be confessed that the evidence is definitely against this, and solely in favour of Mesopotamian influence. On the other hand, it is possible that belief in the divine kingship in Israel may have been influenced by Egypt. Such influence on Canaanite ideas is visible in the Tell-el-Amârna letters, and may have indirectly affected those of Israel; but, in any case, not deeply; for none of the mummification or immortality elements connected with the divine kingship in Egypt seem to have come in.

V

Knowledge of some branches of Egyptian literature on the part of certain circles of Israelite thinkers is proved beyond doubt by the discovery of many Egyptian literary compositions of various types. It is not unreasonable to postulate intercourse from time to time between those of kindred spirit belonging to the two nations. The presence of Egyptians in Palestine and of Israelite settlements in Egypt, to which reference has been made above, would have offered plenty of opportunities for like-minded men to consort together and exchange thoughts on

Ägypter, p. 30 (1934), where mention is also made of dancing in connexion with her worship, cf. Exod. xxxii. 6.

[1] S. A. Cook, *The Religion of Ancient Palestine in the light of Archaeology*, p. 125 (1930); Gressmann, *op. cit.*, plates 281–4.

subjects of mutual interest. But inasmuch as the Egyptians were, in most respects, more highly cultured than the Israelites, literary influence would naturally have been exercised by the former on the latter. Literary activity among the Egyptians goes back to a time probably a couple of millenniums before anything of the kind arose among the Israelites. On the other hand, it is to be noted that with the rise of the new literary epoch in Egypt, which dates from about 1300 B.C., and lasted for some five hundred years, it is found that one of the outstanding characteristics of the literature is the presence of alien words; these, as Erman tells us, 'are almost all borrowed from Canaan, and show, as is well known, what a close connexion existed between Egypt and Palestine'.[1] The point is of interest; but it does not, of course, imply any Canaanite influence on Egyptian literature as such. With the prose writings of Egypt we are not here concerned, for the indubitable marks of Egyptian influence on Hebrew literature are confined to poetical compositions.

In the poetical literature of Egypt there are certain characteristics in structural form, mentioned by Erman,[2] which are of particular interest in the present connexion on account of the presence of precisely similar phenomena in Hebrew poetry. Thus, poems are divided into strophes, or verses, not necessarily of equal length as to the number of lines, but clearly indicating divisions. The frequent use of parallelisms is another feature; a thought receives twofold expression, so that a line consists of two short sentences in each of which the same thought occurs in different forms. Then, again, it is evident that poetical lines have a definite and regular number of rhythmic beats. Wordplays are of frequent occurrence, similar-sounding words occurring close together. The Egyptian poets were also fond of alliteration. A curious usage which occurs at times is that a

[1] *Die Literatur der Ägypter*, p. 5 (1923); Engl. transl. by Blackman (1927).
[2] Op. cit., pp. 9 ff.

word in one line is taken up and repeated in the next line
(*anadiplosis*). The use of metaphors is also frequent. Now when
it is seen that all these features occur in Hebrew poetry, it is
difficult to resist the conclusion that the Hebrew poets were to
some extent, at any rate, indebted to Egyptian patterns for
structural form in their poetic literature. It will be instructive
if we give an illustration of each of these features. The Egyptian
illustrations, both here and in what follows, are taken from the
writings of various experts (Griffith, Erman, Ranke, Grapow,
Lange, and Anthes). We omit an illustration of strophic form,
as this would take up too much space.

Parallel thoughts occur in the following quotation from an
Egyptian poem:

> Then spake these friends of the king,
> And they answered in the presence of their god.

Similarly in one of the most ancient Hebrew poems which have
come down to us:

> Adah and Zillah, hear my voice,
> Ye wives of Lamech, hearken unto my speech (Gen. iv. 23).

In each case the thought of the first line has its parallel in the
second. These quotations offer also an illustration of rhythmic
beats; in the former each line has three rhythmic beats; according to Erman, in Egyptian poetry the lines have either three or
four of such stresses. In the second, each line has four beats in
the Hebrew. The beats fall, of course, on the dominating words.

Word-plays, as Erman says, cannot be illustrated in translation, but he refers to an ancient ritual poem concerning the
presentation of offerings in which the name of each offering is
followed by a word-play on it. As an instance of alliteration
we have:

> The flood flows to thy fields,

which corresponds to the original. For Hebrew poetry, here is
an example of both word-play and alliteration combined:

Shā'alu shelom Yerushālaim

  Yishlāyu 'ohabāik.

Oh, pray for the peace of Jerusalem

  May they prosper that love thee (Ps. cxxii. 6; the rhythmic beats
  are 3 : 2).

For the way in which a word in one line is taken up and repeated in the next line we are unable to give an Egyptian illustration; but in Hebrew we have an instance in Ps. cxxi: in *v.* 1 it is said that from the mountains comes 'help'; this word is taken up in the next verse, where it is said that 'help' comes from Yahweh; in *v.* 3 'he that keepeth' is repeated in the next verse; in *v.* 7 'he shall keep' is again repeated in the next verse; Ps. cxx is another good example. As an instance of metaphor we may give the following; it is said of the god Chnum:

  He (it is) that constructeth on the potter's wheel,
    And formeth the body;

with this we may compare Isa. lxiv. 8 (7 in Hebrew), where it is said of Yahweh:

  We are the clay and thou the potter,
  And we are all the work of thy hand (the rhythmic beats are 4 : 3).

So far, we have been concerned mainly with structural form. We come now to what is of much greater importance, namely, the indebtedness of Hebrew writers to Egypt for thought and content in their writings. This must be considered under three heads: religious poems, wisdom writings, and non-religious poetry.

Many religious poems are to be found in the Old Testament, but the *Psalms* are, of course, the religious poems *par excellence*. And here attention must be directed, first, to some striking parallels which exist between the Egyptian poem in praise of the sun-god, Amon-Re, and various passages in the *Psalms*; and also between the celebrated hymn of Amenhôtep IV (Akhenaton), in praise of the sun, and Ps. civ. The former belongs to the middle of the fifteenth century B.C., it is written on papyrus, and is now in Cairo Museum. What strikes one as especially noteworthy here is the way in which words addressed to the sun-god are paralleled with those addressed to the God of Israel, in a number of passages in the *Psalms*; the impression is gained that Israelite psalmists, to whom this hymn must have been known, have adapted thoughts from it and applied them to Yahweh; the parallels seem to be too many to be fortuitous; just a few may be offered.

Amon-Re is addressed as 'the greatest one of the heavens, the most ancient of the earth, the lord of all that exists'; it is said that he is unique among the gods, 'the chief of all the gods'; he is 'the lord of truth, father of the gods, he that formed men, and created the animals'; and he is further described as the creator of all things. He is also spoken of as 'he who rides, exulting, across the skies'; and is called 'the righteous one'. With all this we may compare the following passages from the *Psalms*, which are far from being exhaustive (the verses are as in the English Version, in the Hebrew they often differ): 'For who in the skies can be compared with Yahweh? Who is like Yahweh among the sons of gods?' (Ps. lxxxix. 6). 'There is none like thee among the gods, O Lord' (Ps. lxxxvi. 8). 'For great is Yahweh, and highly to be praised, to be feared is he above all gods' (Ps. xcvi. 4). In Ps. xxxi. 5 it is said: 'Yahweh, thou God of truth.' Again: 'By the word of Yahweh were the heavens made, and by the breath of his mouth all their host' (Ps. xxiii. 6). 'From the end of the heavens is his going forth, and his circuit unto the ends of it' (Ps. xix. 6). Many other parallels could be given, but these will suffice to show the community of thought. It goes without saying that all the psalms quoted were written centuries after the Egyptian hymn, so that it is difficult to avoid the conviction that the Hebrew psalmists knew it and utilized it. But even more convincing is the identity of thought, sometimes there seems to be almost verbal identity, between the

hymn of praise to the sun, offered by Amenhôtep IV, and
Ps. civ.[1] To appreciate this fully it would be necessary to place
the two side by side; unfortunately, want of space forbids this.[2]

Reference has been made above to the New Year festival, and
to the belief in the divine kingship. In the latter of these the
presence of Egyptian influence, though indirect, may be discerned, so that the references to this in the *Psalms* come into
consideration here; and these references are probably more in
number than is often held to be the case. But to deal with this
would take us too far afield, for it would involve giving quotations from Egyptian mythical texts as well as from the *Psalms*.[3]
It must, therefore, suffice merely to draw attention to the
fact that we have here, in all probability, further evidence of
Egyptian influence upon the literature of the Hebrews.

We turn now to the Wisdom literature. That the wisdom
of Egypt was proverbial among the Israelites may be gathered
from the mention of it in 1 Kings iv. 30, where it is said that
'Solomon's wisdom excelled the wisdom of all the children of
the east, and all the wisdom of Egypt'; and the prophet Isaiah,
in prophesying the utter break-up of the kingdom of Egypt, is
represented as saying (text slightly emended): 'Nought but fools
are the princes of Zoan, the wisest counsellors of Pharaoh are
an ignorant counsel; how say ye to Pharaoh, A son of the wise
am I? . . . Where, then, are thy wise men? Let them make
know, let them declare unto thee. . . .' Of the Wisdom literature of Egypt some highly interesting specimens have come
down to us: *The Teaching of Ptah-hotep*, not later than the
middle of the third millennium B.C.; *The Teaching of Ka-Gemni*,
of which only a fragment is extant; these belong to what is

[1] On the subject in general see Blackman's interesting essay in *The Psalm-ists*, ed. D. C. Simpson, pp. 177 ff. (1926).
[2] See the present writer's *A Fresh Approach to the Psalms*, pp. 16–19 (1937), where both are given in full.
[3] The matter is dealt with in *Myth and Ritual*, ed. S. H. Hooke (1933).

known as the 'Prisse Papyrus' (after the name of the French Egyptologist); *The Teaching of Amen-emhet*, about 1300 B.C., but it is the copy of an older form; *The Teaching for King Meri-Ka-Re*, about the middle of the fifteenth century B.C.; *The Teaching of Duauf*, about 1300 B.C. in its present form, but the original is earlier; *The Wisdom of Anii*, about 1000 B.C.; and, most important of all from the present point of view, *The Teaching of Amen-em-ope*, about the middle of the eighth century B.C., but the extant copy is a couple of centuries later (Griffith).[1]

A comparison with these and many passages in the Old Testament Scriptures shows at times a remarkable community of thought, and suggests the presence of Egyptian influence; but this becomes a matter of absolute certainty when we find in the book of *Proverbs* literally dozens of sayings to which there are parallels, sometimes almost verbal, in the *Teaching of Amen-em-ope*, as well as, though to a less extent, in other Egyptian Wisdom writings. Among these *Psalms*, too, i.e. those which partake of a Wisdom character, there are also parallels; to a less extent, but also noticeably, in the book of *Deuteronomy*. To illustrate this fully would take up many pages; we shall, therefore, restrict ourselves to some of the most interesting parallels between the book of *Proverbs* and *The Teaching of Amen-em-ope*. Among the various collections of wise sayings gathered together in the former is a short one comprised in xxii. 17–xxiii. 14; it is to this that we now draw attention; the most profitable way of illustrating the parallels will be to place the relative passages side by side (we omit the verse-numbering in each case):

Proverbs.	*The Teaching of Amen-em-ope.*[2]
Incline thine ear, and hear my words,	Give thine ear, and hear what I say,
And apply thine heart to apprehend;	And apply thine heart to apprehend;

[1] For translations and further details see Griffith, *The World's Best Literature* (1897); Erman, *Die Literatur der Ägypter*, and Gressmann, op. cit. 38 ff.

[2] For our rendering of the passages from *Amen-em-ope* we are indebted to

Proverbs.	*The Teaching of Amen-em-ope.*
For it is pleasant if thou keep them in thy belly, That they may be fixed like a peg upon thy lips.	It is good for thee to place them in thine heart, Let them rest in the casket of thy belly; That they may act as a peg upon thy tongue.
Have I not written for thee thirty sayings Of counsels and knowledge! That thou mayest make known truth to him that speaketh, That thou mayest carry back words to him that sent thee.	Consider these thirty chapters; They delight, they instruct. Knowledge how to answer him that speaketh, And how to carry back a report to one that sent him.
Rob not the poor, for he is poor, Neither oppress the lowly in the gate.	Beware of robbing the poor, And of oppressing the afflicted.
Associate not with a passionate man, Nor go with a wrathful man, Lest thou learn his ways And get a snare to thy soul.	Associate not with a passionate man, Nor approach him for conversation; Leap not to cleave to such an one, That the terror carry thee not away.
A man who is skilful in his business Shall stand before kings.	A scribe who is skilful in his business Findeth himself worthy to be a courtier.
When thou sittest to eat with a ruler, Consider diligently what is before thee; And put a knife to thy throat, If thou be a man given to appetite. Be not desirous of his dainties, Seeing they are deceitful meat.	Eat not bread in the presence of a ruler, And lunge not forward (?) with thy mouth, before a governor (?) When thou art replenished with that to which thou hast no right, It is only a delight to thy spittle. Look upon the dish that is before thee, And let that (alone) supply thy need.
Toil not to become rich, And cease from thy dishonest gain;	Toil not after riches; If stolen goods are brought to thee,

the translations of Griffith, Ranke (in Gressmann), Lange, *Das Weisheitsbuch des Amen-em-ope* (1925).

Proverbs.	*The Teaching of Amen-em-ope.*
For wealth maketh to itself wings, Like an eagle that flieth heavenwards.	They remain not over the night with thee. They have made for themselves wings like geese. And have flown into the heavens.
Speak not in the hearing of a fool, For he will despise the wisdom of thy words.	Empty not thine inmost soul to everyone, Nor spoil (thereby) thine influence.
Remove not the widow's land-mark. And enter not into the fields of the fatherless.	Remove not the land-mark from the bounds of the fields . . . And violate not the widow's boundary.
Apply thine heart unto instruction And thine ears to the words of knowledge.	Give thine ears, hear the words that are said, Give thine heart to interpret them.

Other parallels occur, but these must suffice.

Unfortunately, space forbids our dealing with the many points of contact between Egyptian love-poems and the *Song of Songs*.

W. O. E. OESTERLEY

CHAPTER 10

THE GREEK PAPYRI

PAPYRA, *throned upon the banks of Nile,*
Spread her smooth leaf, and waved her silver style.
—The storied pyramid, the laurel'd bust,
The trophied arch had crumbled into dust;
The sacred symbol, and the epic song,
(Unknown the character, forgot the tongue),
With each unconquer'd chief or sainted maid,
Sunk undistinguished in oblivion's shade.
Sad o'er the scatter'd ruins Genius sigh'd,
And infant Arts but learned to lisp and died.
Till to astonish'd realms PAPYRA *taught*
To paint in mystic colours Sound and Thought,
With Wisdom's voice to print the page sublime,
And mark in adamant the steps of Time.
ERASMUS DARWIN, *The Loves of the Plants* (1789).

IN the year 1778 a commercial traveller in Egypt was offered
by the fellahîn some forty or fifty rolls of papyrus; one of them
he bought as a curiosity for a small sum and left the rest to be
burnt by the natives, whose noses were tickled (so the story goes)
by the aroma of burning papyrus. The survivor found its way
into the hands of an Italian and was by him presented to Cardinal
Stefano Borgia. The hopes cherished by many savants, Winckelmann among them, that here was one of the lost treasures of
Greek literature were soon disappointed. The roll was found to
contain nothing more than a list of peasants who had performed
in the village of Ptolemais Hormou in the Faiyûm their quota
of compulsory labour on the neighbouring canals and dykes, and,
as the age of social history was still far in the future, it is no
matter for surprise that the roll and the circumstances of its
discovery were soon forgotten. And yet the incident is significant, for the Charta Borgiana was the first papyrus to reach
Europe since the trade in what had been the primary writing

material of the ancient world flickered out in the Dark Ages. Though more than a hundred years were still to pass before excavations were undertaken for the definite purpose of discovering Greek papyri,[1] the number of texts which were found by natives and, passing through the hands of travellers and private collectors, eventually found their way to the museums of Europe steadily increased throughout the nineteenth century. That the first literary papyrus to be found should be a manuscript of part of the *Iliad* was both proper and symbolic of the enormous, indeed unwelcome, preponderance of Homeric texts; of more promise for the future was the discovery in 1847 of fragments of six speeches, hitherto unknown, of the orator Hypereides. Not long after the plundering of the Greek rubbish-heaps of Arsinoe (Medinet el-Faiyûm) had flooded the market with thousands of papyri (often very fragmentary)[2] the age of scientific excavation began, and though it is not yet over it seems certain that no site will rival the riches of Oxyrhynchus which rewarded the pioneers in this field, B. P. Grenfell and A. S. Hunt. With it began that minor renaissance which has affected nearly every department of classical studies; to-day, when social and economic conditions are the recognized material of history, even the Charta Borgiana has come into its own.

For the legacy of the papyri is in its nature indirect, a legacy to civilization's knowledge of its own past rather than directly to the world of to-day, except in so far as modern institutions —the Church is an obvious example—are modified by increased knowledge and insight into their own origins. Nor are papyri *objets d'art*, or only very rarely (we may think of the one or two

[1] The term 'papyrology' is commonly used to describe the study of all written material from Egypt, except inscriptions on stone, i.e. parchment, ostraka, or potsherds, and tablets of wood or lead, and is so used in this essay. The great majority of the texts are on papyrus.

[2] It is so rare for a literary text to be found entire (though documents often are) that it must be assumed that the literary texts mentioned are, in very varying measure, incomplete.

illuminated papyri, such as that of the jockeys of Antinoe,[1] or of a few superb examples of calligraphy); though they have added a new chapter to the history of Greek palaeography, it is their contents that is our main concern. This legacy is a novel one in that the information we derive from the papyri is often not merely new but often of a new kind; in what this novelty consists it is the purpose of this essay to discuss.

By way of introduction a little may be said of the material. Centuries before Alexander's conquest had made the Greeks the masters of the country, Egypt had manufactured papyrus out of the pith of the marsh plant of that name which once grew plentifully in the Delta swamps, and the Egyptians by their carefully guarded processes (at no time in the ancient world was the preparation of papyrus for writing purposes carried on outside Egypt) had made of it the finest writing material known. Throughout the classical age of Greece it was commonly used; indeed, without such a relatively cheap and convenient material literature and the sciences could scarcely have developed as they did, or at least their diffusion and survival would have been rendered much more difficult. Egypt supplied the whole Roman Empire, from Hadrian's Wall to the Euphrates and from the Danube to the First Cataract, and papyrus was used as naturally by Irenaeus in Gaul as by Origen in Alexandria. Its last recorded use is in the Chancery of Pope Victor II in 1057, but whether the papyrus was Egyptian and, if so, whether it was recently imported, we do not know. Just as papyrus was of immense service in the creation and transmission of classical culture, so in the last hundred years it has been the means of renewing and increasing the legacy of Greece and Rome. The account is not yet closed; every year brings with it the publication of new texts, and their range is no less surprising than their number.

Until the Egyptian discoveries our knowledge of this material,

[1] See S. J. Gąsiorowski, *Journal of Egyptian Archaeology* xvii, 1.

and consequently of the form and methods by which literature was transmitted, was limited to a few papyrus codices of the sixth century, the small and late group of Papal and Ravenna documents, and the damaged rolls of Herculaneum. To-day we have specimens of writing, both literary and documentary, in a series which, if not unbroken, has few serious gaps from the fourth century B.C. down to the eighth century A.D.; we have some fragments of a roll of the *Phaedo* written less than a century after Plato's death, a papyrus of Cicero probably anterior to the Christian era, and what may even be the relics of a contemporary roll of Polybius. We should note, too, that here is what we may call a direct legacy from Egypt to the West, whose character has been more clearly defined by the discoveries of papyri; it was only to be expected that the country which produced the material should also exercise a marked influence on the form and organization of the ancient book—for example, it is highly likely, though not proven, that the papyrus codex, the precursor of the parchment book, has its origin as a regular vehicle for literature in Egypt. In these matters Egypt means Alexandria, and it is to Alexandria that we owe the illuminated manuscript of the Middle Ages; but here the actual evidence of the papyri, valuable though it is, is scant.

Yet to term this gift of Egypt a legacy is, in a sense, a misnomer and a paradoxical one; for never was a testator less conscious of what he was doing or a bequest more fortuitous. The great mass of our Greek papyri have been salvaged from ruined towns and villages of Upper Egypt and the adjacent rubbish-dumps abandoned to the desert when, in Byzantine and Arab periods, the irrigation system broke down. Occasionally the digger is fortunate enough to find some family or official archive, carefully stored in a jar or a box (Dioscorus of Aphrodito has earned our double thanks for choosing to wrap up his papers in the leaves of a codex of Menander); a few of our literary papyri have been found in tombs, as for example the Hawara Homer found resting under the head of a mummy of a young girl. (This practice results not from a sentimental feeling for a favourite author but from an adaptation by the Greeks of an Egyptian habit they failed to understand; that anyone should select a copy of Isocrates' speech *Against Nicocrates*, which was found lying between a mummy's legs, as a companion for the next world is a strain on our credulity. If, however, they are Greek substitutes for the Egyptian Book of the Dead, it would explain both this and why the Timotheus roll was already fragmentary when it was placed in the grave.) However, the mass of them (for example the papyri from Oxyrhynchus and Arsinoe) were thrown away as so much waste paper; this is why they are so often broken and torn. But the oddest transformation has been suffered by those papyri which were converted into a kind of papier mâché, and used to form the covering or stuffing of mummies, whether of men or crocodiles; from one such emerged the earliest fragments of any manuscript of the Bible, the Manchester papyrus of Deuteronomy, which were found covered with glue and wrapped in some pieces of the first book of the *Iliad*—as nice an example of cultural fusion in the second century B.C. as could be wished. We should note that the survival of papyri is determined, generally speaking, as well by the absence of rainfall as by height above inundation level, and that consequently almost all our papyri come from Egypt south of the modern Cairo. Since then, as now, the Delta was economically the most important part of the country, while Alexandria was the fountain-head of its intellectual and artistic life, as far as this was Greek, we must be prepared to allow for a certain provincial bias in our texts, literary as well as documentary.

So, while from one point of view papyri are so much waste product, miscellaneous contents of a gigantic waste-paper basket steadily filled up in the millennium between Alexander and the Arab conquest, from another they are the raw material from which a civilization can be reconstructed. Indeed it is only because they are the first that the second is possible; it is just because the material was not consciously selected (if we except for the moment the literary texts), was not intended to survive, that they are of unique value to the historian. Our knowledge of the ancient world rests primarily, and must always do so, on our literary authorities; but it is not their function to give us the raw material of history, nor can we always tell what are their principles of selection, nor, when we do know them, can we always share them. So to free ourselves from the aristocratic and political bias common to most of the ancient historians and to study the economic and social factors commonly of little interest to them, to catch the inhabitants of this part of the ancient world not posing in public attitudes but off their guard in their ordinary business and in their private correspondence, to look at government from the point of view of the governed, for all this these ephemeral and humdrum, sometimes tedious, documents are invaluable. To select two out of the many themes that the documentary papyri illustrate: we can observe in a way impossible before what Greek colonization meant, how far the settler adapted himself to his surroundings and what were the effects of this invasion in social and political life, and we can watch what was the actual practice of Roman administration in Egypt, its methods and its spirit.

Before attempting to outline the kind of contribution that the papyri have made to historical studies, something must be said of what is certainly the most startling result of the excavations—the additions to Greek literature. When, after Alexander's conquest, there flooded into Egypt from every corner of the Greek world soldiers, business men, farmers, and administrators, they brought their literature with them. The Greeks were already a literary people in the sense that the literature of their own past had become a vital part of their own existence; when all else that had been characteristic of the classical civilization disappeared or changed almost out of recognition in the new empires of Alexander's successors, their education—literature and the gymnasium—remained. In provincial Egypt, at any rate, no attempt was made to keep the race pure; to be a Greek soon meant to speak Greek and to have had a Greek education. Hence it is no accident that so many literary papyri have been recovered from Egypt. The oldest papyrus yet found in Egypt is that of the *Persae* of Timotheus, and that a work so exotic and sophisticated should have come from the earliest period of the Greek occupation is significant of the endless variety of the literary texts. Not only is every branch of Greek literature from Homer and Hesiod down past the lyric poets and satirists, the Old and the New Comedy to the novelists and the Christian Fathers, represented by fragments however small, but there is scarcely an author of whom we can assuredly say that he was not read in Egypt. The greatest of these discoveries have now taken their place in the ranks of Greek literature, and are no more the preserve of the papyrologist. First among them is perhaps the codex of Menander owned by that Dioscorus of whose own attempts upon the Muse his editor wrote 'At no moment has he any real control of thought, diction, grammar, metre, or meaning'. Thanks to this and other smaller papyri Menander is no longer merely a source of indiscriminate apophthegms but is seen as a playwright capable of dramatic power and delicate characterization. Among the other discoveries notable in extent and in intrinsic merit are those of the odes and dithyrambs of Bacchylides, a poet all but unknown before, the *Athenian Constitution* of Aristotle, the *Ichneutae* of Sophocles (the only satyric drama which we have from his hand), the *Hellenica Oxyrynchia*, probably from the hand of Ephorus, and several manuscripts of the early lyric poets and of Callimachus. The latter, as is proper for a poet whose home was Alexandria, has come into his own with the discovery of considerable parts of the *Iambi* and *Aitia*, types of his work of which no specimens were extant; no one would have appreciated better than he the irony of such a casual resurrection. But of the writers of that generation none has emerged more startlingly or to more effect than Herondas, whose mimes are vignettes of city life drawn with vigour, realism, and a marked preference for the seamy side; they unite vivid powers of characterization with a highly sophisticated attitude and great technical ability. One of his most successful mimes, *The Schoolmaster*, affords a good commentary on the school texts which are also found among the papyri. A contemporary text-book which has recently been published (probably one from which the master dictated to his class) provides interesting parallels; just as the boy in the mime is made by his father to spell out a proper name (and makes a hash of it), so the school-book contains lists of proper names, some of them regular tongue-twisters. When he is asked to recite a piece of poetry for the edification of the family, he can't get beyond the first two words and stammers at that—even his illiterate old grand-mother, says his mother, could do better than that; sure enough in the schoolbook are two pieces of Euripides, doubtless to be copied and learnt by heart. The mime ends with the school-boy receiving a sound flogging; this is not specified in the book, but the motto, 'Work hard, boy, or you'll be beaten' copied out on a piece of papyrus six times as an imposition, tells its own tale.

To the grudging work of Egyptian schoolboys we owe not a few texts, though we may wish that Homer had not been quite such a staple article of diet. Ostraka were frequently used in schools—they were the cheapest material, since to the supply of broken potsherds there was no end—and so, it may well be, from this source has come the latest ode of Sappho's to see the light; the uncertain hand and the mistakes in spelling which indicate that the copyist had only an imperfect grasp of what he was writing lend colour to this view. The poem is an invitation to the poet's friends to attend a solemn but joyous rite to which Aphrodite is invoked—

'Where is a lovely grove of apple-trees and altars therein smoking with frankincense; there too cool water plashes through the apple boughs, with rose trees all the place is shaded and from the dancing leaves deep sleep steals down; there a meadow where horses graze is rich with the flowers of spring and sweet is the scent of the dill. Hither come, O sovran Aphrodite and at the dainty feast pour out the nectar mixed in cups of gold.'

From this scene to the parched land of Egypt is a far cry and many a reader by the waters of the Nile must have remembered Zion; but its presence in Egypt is at once a measure of the strength of Hellenism and an explanation of it.

These are a few of the more important accessions that we owe to the papyri; to give any but the most cursory description of them would take us far beyond the limits of this essay.[1] The majority of the finds are small and, as papyri were torn down rather than across, more often yield a row of broken lines than a few complete ones; but even a small fragment may have a contribution to make. So a small and nearly contemporary fragment of the grammarian Harpocration supports an emendation of Sauppe's in a speech of Lysias, confirms a quotation of some anthropological interest from the comic poet Theopompus which had been needlessly emended, and, for the first time, puts a citation from the historian Ephorus in its proper place in his work; and all this in some twenty-five incomplete lines. To take two instances of dramatic texts somewhat more substantial but small enough: a single parchment sheet at Berlin from *The Cretans* of Euripides has restored to us Pasiphae's sophistic but spirited apologia for her crimes, while from an Oxyrhynchus papyrus we learn the plot of Cratinus' comedy *Dionysalexandros*,

[1] An alphabetical list of those published before 1923 will be found in C. H. Oldfather's *The Greek Literary Texts from Greco-Roman Egypt*: since then all texts of importance are recorded in the annual bibliography in *The Journal of Egyptian Archaeology*.

with the added explanation that the play was a hit against
Pericles; it was a parody of the Trojan War with Dionysus
playing the part of Paris and included a Falstaffian scene in
which Dionysus, hearing of the approach of the Greeks, hides
Helen in a basket and metamorphoses himself into a ram. It is
not that the drama has been particularly favoured; there is
scarcely a branch of Greek literature that has not gained similar
unexpected additions. At times, indeed, the scraps are so small
that they merely tantalize; such for example are the few 'silly-
boi' or tags which were attached to the top of the roll as titles.
One of these bears the complacent inscription 'The Complete
Works of Pindar', another 'The Female Mimes of Sophron'.
Yet even these are an assurance that the books from which they
have strayed still circulated in Roman Egypt and therefore may
still have left some *disiecta membra* in the sand.

The art or science of textual criticism is another study that
has benefited from the discoveries of papyri;[1] not far short of
half the literary texts from Egypt belong to works already
extant. With very few exceptions these papyri are much older
than the oldest of our medieval manuscripts (e.g. for the greater
part of Xenophon's *Cyropaedia* we have no manuscript earlier
than the twelfth century, while our earliest papyrus fragments
are of the second), and as a rule were copied before the families
into which our manuscripts divide were formed; in consequence
their evidence, as it stands outside the common tradition of the
manuscripts, is often of particular value. To generalize on the
relation of the papyri to the medieval texts is only possible
within wide limits, as the text of each author has its own history
and its own problems, but with this qualification some comments
are possible. On the whole the papyri support the general *con-
sensus codicum* to a surprising extent; that our tradition is
generally sound cannot be doubted unless far-reaching changes

[1] The best discussion of this subject to which I am indebted here is still
that by B. P. Grenfell in *The Journal of Hellenic Studies* for 1919.

were made or corruptions occurred at a date earlier even than the papyri, and the very fact that some of the cruces in the medieval manuscripts were already recognized as such by the editors of the papyri supports the soundness of the tradition as a whole. The corollary to this is that the wider flights of fancy in emendation on the part of modern scholars receive singularly little encouragement; the palmary emendation dreamed of by scholars has only very rarely obtained confirmation. (A classic exception is Wilamowitz's correction of the senseless καρπὸν εἰς ἀθάνατον in Diogenes Laertius v. 7 to καρπὸν ἰσαθάνατον which was later confirmed by the Didymus papyrus.) On the whole, the influence of the papyri has been towards a soberer and more cautious handling of texts. Again, we have learnt, rather paradoxically, that in assessing the value of a manuscript too much stress should not be laid on its antiquity: firstly because some of the early Ptolemaic papyri are conspicuously careless and sometimes worse than careless; secondly, and more important, because it is by no means uncommon for a papyrus to agree with a reading in one of the so-called *deteriores* against an earlier manuscript. That they support the earlier and better manuscripts more often than the *deteriores* is true; what is important is that they should support the latter at all. So although the text provided by the papyri may not always be as sound throughout as that of the best medieval manuscripts, this eclecticism they display has had a marked effect on textual criticism.

The view that the function of the critic was to find, where possible, the best (and generally this was the oldest) manuscript of his author, and adhere to that as far as possible at the risk of dismissing attractive readings of other manuscripts as due to the ingenuity of scholars or the ignorance of scribes, has received a severe setback. In as far as the eclectic principle implies that the critic must rely more on his knowledge of the language and of the author and on his common sense and less on external criteria, the change has been wholly beneficial.

That some of our earliest texts are both slovenly and eccentric might seem a reason for doubting the general soundness of our tradition; but we should note that these texts are relatively few in number, that they mostly come from one or two village sites and so may be regarded as 'provincial' texts not necessarily representative of the best then in existence; further, that several of them are anthologies and in all ages anthologies are notorious corrupters of texts, and finally that (except in the case of Homer) their eccentricity has been exaggerated—there are several quite 'normal' texts of this age. But when all this is said, a real difference remains between the early and the late texts, and the explanation of the change is to be found in Alexandria. The deep influence exercised by the scholars of the Museum and Library at Alexandria in establishing the texts and often the authenticity of classical works has always been recognized; now the papyri, and above all the papyri of Homer, allow us to observe this influence at work.

In the earlier papyri we find marked divagations from the received text and not merely in single words; whole lines are omitted or more commonly added (though these new lines are as a rule 'repeats' from other parts of the poems and make little or no difference to the context); in one *Odyssey* papyrus there are as many as nine additional lines out of seventy. That this 'eccentric' text is inferior to the received tradition is clear; it is equally clear that in the third century B.C. the text of Homer was in a confused and fluid state, at any rate in Egypt. But after about the middle of the second century B.C. these eccentric texts tend to disappear and in the several hundred papyri of Homer later than this the text is in all essentials that of the medieval manuscripts, is in fact far closer to them than in the case of any other author; indeed, the Homeric papyrus of the Roman period is rarely more than a witness to the poet's popularity. There can be little doubt that this is due to the skill and thoroughness with which the Alexandrian scholars did their work.

We can watch, too, to a limited extent in the papyri the process by which a classical tradition was formed, a result partly of the work of the critics and scholars of Alexandria, though originally they had no such object in mind (to the pre-Alexandrine age the idea was entirely alien), in part of the schools and the conservatism of the school tradition. In the Ptolemaic period we find that the new literary fragments greatly exceed in number those of known authors; in the Roman period the balance is fairly equally held between the two, while in the Byzantine age the known and standard texts predominate. But this was no single or even a deliberate process, at least in the early stages; that the Byzantines were not limited to the standard authors that survived in medieval times is clear from the discovery of the texts of Eupolis and Sappho to mention two names alone. Nor could any discovery offer clearer proof of the survival of Hellenism or suggest more markedly the continuity between the ancient and medieval worlds than does that of a treatise on Aristotelian physics, written after the Arab conquest of the country, and forming as it does a visible link between the philosophy of Greece and that of Averroes and Aquinas.

Christian literature has been enriched no less than pagan by the Egyptian discoveries. Here again we find the same variety in kind, in age, and in condition; side by side with the canonical books of the Bible have been discovered non-canonical and apocryphal works, stories and sayings of the saints, homilies, liturgies, prayers, and hymns. Taken together they present us with a fair picture of the reading and culture of the Christian community in Upper Egypt, at least in the later centuries; the impartial spade will turn up now a few verses of the Psalms scrawled on papyrus and carried round the owner's neck as an amulet, now a primitive hymn with musical notation, now part of a treatise by Origen or the letters of St. Basil. The additions to Christian literature need a chapter to themselves; all we can do is to note in passing that they include such famous texts as the so-called *Sayings of Jesus* and the Unknown Gospel in the British Museum, a work whose sober and narrative character as well as its early date distinguish it alike from the theosophical fantasies of the Gnostics (the earliest representative of which is a leaf of the *Gospel of Mary*, now in Manchester) and from such romantic hagiographies as the recently published *Acta Pauli*, which provided the pious with a satisfactory substitute for the pagan novel.

But in Christian studies the history of the Bible text occupies a place of unique importance, and their debt to the papyri would still be great even if no new works had been found at all. As it is, we have witnesses to the text of the Bible from Egypt far earlier than those from any other source; recent discoveries enable us to follow the history of the text back to the second century A.D. The oldest fragment of the New Testament is the small fragment of St. John's Gospel in the Rylands Library, of importance not merely because we can infer that the Gospel was read in Upper Egypt in the first half of the second century, but because the text of this fragment, small as it is, is in essence that of our later manuscripts. But incomparably the most important event in recent Biblical scholarship has been the publication of eleven codices of the Old and New Testaments ranging from the second to the fourth century, the majority of them being the property of Mr. Chester Beatty. It will be some time before the new material is thoroughly assimilated and the full effect on textual criticism seen, but that they support the general integrity of the text of the Bible is certain. As Dr. H. I. Bell points out, whatever doubts may surround the historicity and origins of the New Testament books, 'it is probably true to say broadly that no vital Christian doctrine, no basic saying of Christ, no central incident in His life, depends on a reading about which there is any serious textual doubt'.

The relevance of these documents, those vast masses of official, business, and private papers, to New Testament studies is less obvious and the help they give certainly less spectacular; but the connexion is there and is a striking instance of the relationship between vastly different types of material. We might hope to find among the documents direct evidence of the expansion of Christianity and of the way of life of the early communities; but here the papyri fail us, probably for the obvious reason that as long as Christianity stood in danger of persecution its adherents would be careful not to leave in writing evidence that might always be used against them. Even so, the distinctively Christian formula 'in the Lord' is found in several letters of the third century; one of these, from a boy to his mother, is revealing because the formula he uses shows that they were not orthodox, but members of some Gnostic Christian sect. The letter runs thus:

'To my most precious mother Mary, Besas, very many greetings in God. Before all things, I pray to our Father, the God of truth, and to the Spirit of Intercession, that they may preserve you in soul and body and spirit, giving to your body health, to your spirit cheerfulness, to your soul life eternal. Whenever you find anyone coming my way, do be sure to write to me of your health, that I may hear and rejoice. Don't forget to send me the coat against the Easter holiday, and send my brother to me. I salute my father and my brothers. I pray for your lasting health.'

And the so-called Decian *libelli*, certificates issued by local officials of the government at the time of the Decian persecution as evidence that their holders had duly sacrificed to the pagan deities, are an eloquent reminder of the dangers to which the ordinary Christian in the remotest village might be exposed, although there is nothing to prove that those we have were issued to recanting Christians. Later, as we should expect, the evidence is more plentiful and more detailed; here we can only refer to the archive of Meletian letters preserved in the British Museum.[1]

[1] See H. I. Bell, *Jews and Christians in Egypt.*

Of more importance is the indirect contribution made by the documents. From no other country of the ancient world have we such a wealth of varied material relating to all the complex forms of social and economic life. Although the bulk of this evidence is strictly relevant to Egypt only, it is fair to recall that at the time when the books of the New Testament were written, the neighbouring lands of Egypt and Palestine were both provinces of the Roman Empire, that both were partially hellenized with a large non-Hellenic population, that contact between the two was easy, and that the official and business language of both countries was Greek. This Koine Greek, derived from Attic, but influenced by other dialects, was the lingua franca of the Roman East and though different parts of the empire produced their local variations, though within one country the spoken language differed from the written, and that of the educated from that of the half-educated, yet it was unmistakably a single language and the degree of uniformity in the written Koine was high. The publication of numerous contemporary documents, both papyri and inscriptions, has radically altered the views formerly held about the Greek of the New Testament; in particular, the idea that its language was something peculiar and divinely unrelated to other forms of Greek has disappeared.

It is true that the Semitic element is strong in parts of the New Testament, that no letter remotely like the Epistles of St. Paul has been found in Egypt, and that the characteristic words of New Testament religion cannot be paralleled from the papyri; not only are few of our documents directly concerned with religion, but a new religion will commonly create its own vocabulary and Christianity deliberately avoided the usages of pagan cults. Yet these books were designed to be intelligible to and to appeal to the ordinary Greek-speaking public, and were not all intended for Jewish or Judaized audiences. Hence the resemblances between the language of the papyri and that of the New Testament books have given a new direction to the study of New Testament Greek and, particularly in the case of the Gospels, have brought it more into touch with the world from which it sprang; even St. Paul, whose style and thought is most his own, had to make concessions to the reader of the day. Such words as παρουσία (used of the Second Advent) or συνείδησις (conscience) can be placed in their contemporary setting, and we can form some idea of the overtones and associations they carried with them; while others such as ἀρχιποίμην (chief shepherd) or ὀρθοποδεῖν (to walk uprightly), are seen to be not eccentric neologisms but normal, if infrequently used, expressions.

More difficult and more elusive is the question how far the conditions of life as the papyri represent them provide an appropriate background for the events described in the New Testament. Here, though we must guard against the tendency to press every chance parallelism into the service of exegesis, we must remember that even such specifically religious works as the Gospels, which have their own canons to obey, yet had to fit into the framework of the society of their day. A single example must suffice. When in a report of legal proceedings of A.D. 88 we find the prefect C. Septimius Vegetus admonishing the plaintiff for imprisoning on his own initiative a man probably his debtor (a practice to which there are plenty of parallels in the papyri), it is legitimate to recall the parable of the unmerciful servant; and when the prefect summing up observes 'you deserve scourging (for this action) . . . but I make a present of you to the crowd and will show myself more merciful than you', the story of Pilate and Barabbas forces itself upon our minds.

Just as the Christian letters and the Christian literary texts supplement each other in that they combine to give a picture of the Church in Egypt, so a similar relation may be asserted between the Greek literary papyri and some of the documents. Even in isolation the former have their value for the historian. A phrase such as 'Hellenization of the Near East' takes on a more definite meaning when we reflect that on the site of the small Egyptian village of Socnopaiou Nesus, perched up on a rock above Lake Moeris and separated by miles of desert or water from the next village, centring round and dominated by the temple of the crocodile god Sobk, were found fragments of the *Hector* of Astydamas and Plato's *Apology*, while among the authors whom we know were read at the neighbouring Karanis are Chariton, Isocrates, and a Latin grammarian (? Palaemon). Taken together, the literary texts give us a fair idea of the extent and variety of the literature available to the Greeks of Egypt and constitute a kind of barometer of Hellenic culture in Egypt which steadily sinks from the third century A.D. onwards. But of the subjects and methods of education we learn far less from the documents than we could wish or might expect. It was privately organized (if we except the foundation of the Museum and Library of Alexandria by the first Ptolemy and the official recognition of the gymnasia in the Roman period), but it seems likely that the Ptolemies were interested in the establishment of the gymnasia both in towns and villages. Among the numerous papers of Zenon, who was agent to Apollonius, Chancellor of Egypt under the second Ptolemy, and in close touch with him, are several references to the gymnasia; he is consulted about the building of one at Philadelphia, where Apollonius had his country estate, and on another occasion he writes to the trainer Hierocles to ask whether a young protégé of his is really worth his keep and whether his athletic achievements justify Zenon in taking him away from his books. The trainer's answer is that the boy is making excellent progress in his sport and in his other studies—only he would like Zenon to send him some more equipment. In another letter Zenon is informed that another protégé of his has been successful at the Ptolemaic games in the little village of Holy Island; the trainer who writes the letter improves the occasion by asking for a cloak 'thicker and of softer wool' for the boy to use at the Arsinoeia (games in honour of the late Queen Arsinoe). Here, though Zenon's interest is no doubt financial, we see that the institution of these games (which would be organized by the local gymnasia) was closely bound up with the cult of the royal house and was obviously not a matter to which government circles were indifferent. Just as the gymnasia had served the purpose of the Ptolemies, so in later times we hear of the city of Oxyrhynchus celebrating the *Ludus Capitolinus*, originally founded by Domitian; there is extant a letter from the gymnasiarch to the head of the athletic organization requesting him to round up as many competitors as possible; no doubt for these games to prove a failure would savour of disloyalty.

It was typical of Rome to substitute for the informal and perhaps casual encouragement of Greek education a defined and organized system; so Augustus, wishing on the principle of *divide et impera* to encourage the hellenized elements in Egypt against the Egyptian influence which had grown in power under the later Ptolemies, gave official recognition to the office of gymnasiarch, and by abolishing the village gymnasia and granting financial privileges to the metropolites, made the towns strongholds of Hellenism to a greater degree than they had been before. Education was the road to a career for a Greco-Egyptian; so Apion writes back from Misenum, where he has joined the Roman fleet, to his father in the Faiyûm:

'On reaching Misenum I received three gold pieces for my travelling expenses from Caesar and all is going well. I beg of you, my Lord father, write me a letter, first that I may learn how you are, secondly how my brother is, thirdly that I may kiss your hand [the Greek word has the double sense of hand and handwriting], for you have given me a good education and with the gods' favour I hope to get on fast . . . I have sent you my picture [presumably in uniform] by Euctemon.'

Most of the letters relating to education which have reached us insist on the industry and application of the boys; one boy goes so far as to rebuke his parent for not coming to see whether his tutor is paying sufficient attention to him, but the inner meaning of this may be elucidated from another letter in which the lady of the house gives instructions for some pigeons and chickens, which she doesn't eat herself, to be sent to her daughter's tutor, 'that he may work hard with her'. This attitude is natural; but it is a relief to see the other side of the picture in a letter of a Byzantine parent withdrawing his son who had proved an unsatisfactory pupil (it is possible, but I think less likely, that the boy was not at school, but apprenticed).

'You have written to me about little Anastasius, and as I am in your debt, be sure you will be paid in full. Nothing of what has been told you is true except that he is stupid and a child and foolish. He wrote me a letter himself quite in keeping with his looks and empty wits. And since he is a child and stupid, I will fetch him home. I am keeping his letter to show you when I come. Chastise him; for ever since he left his father, he has had no other beatings and he likes getting a few—his back has got accustomed to them and needs its daily dose.'

So few are the allusions to higher education among the papyri that the following letter deserves quotation. The writer, who was probably at Alexandria to complete his education, after relating how he has had an accident with the family chariot (which may be connected with some discreditable incident in the theatre to which he makes several references), expatiates to his father on the difficulty of finding good tutors:

'He has also persuaded the sons of Apollonius to attend Didymus' school. For they and he since the death of Philologus have been looking for an abler tutor right up till now. For my part, I'd pray never to see Didymus, even from a distance, again, if only I had found tutors worth the name. What really depresses me is that this fellow, who was a mere provincial schoolmaster, has seen fit to compete with the rest. So as I know that apart from paying more and more fees all to no purpose there's no good to be had from a tutor, I've other resources of my own. Write and tell me soon what you think about it. . . . By attending the lectures of the professors—Posidonius is one of them—with the gods' favour I shall do well for myself. The worry over these matters is such as to compel me to neglect my health—I have the feeling that those who are still unsuccessful ought not to concern themselves with it, particularly when there is no one bringing in any money.'

He then dwells on the enormities of a certain Heraclas, probably his *paedagogus* or attendant slave, and suggests that he might be set to earning some money, and after saying that when a young brother joins him they will move into more spacious lodgings, he ends by thanking his father for the usual supplies from home.

But, as we have seen, the idea of the gymnasium included education of the body no less than education of the mind. We have already mentioned the village games of the Ptolemaic period; in the Roman age, though towns such as Oxyrhynchus and Hermopolis ran their own games with considerable display and expense, the emphasis had changed and the really important events were the great international contests. The standardization of culture under the Roman Empire has its counterpart in the highly professionalized and international sport of the age. The documents from Egypt show us these professional athletes (they describe themselves as members of 'the sacred athletic international union, under imperial patronage') touring the world to take part in games at Sardes, at Sidon, or at Naples, and returning home to receive the grateful thanks of their fellow citizens and, more important, exemption from taxes, a monthly pension, and, in some cases, freedom from public burdens for themselves and their descendants. Not quite in the class of the world champions, but no less mercenary, was a certain Dios whose letter to his wife Sophrone has been preserved. He had gone to Alexandria with some friends to look for someone (probably a debtor) who had disappeared: 'we did not find the fellow', he writes, 'instead we found our lord the king'. Games were held at royal command and Dios contrived to get himself admitted 'by an act of favour' (probably he was not qualified); he was, however, badly beaten in the *pancratium* by the professionals. Nothing daunted, he hit on the bright idea of challenging his own companions (with whose abilities he was doubtless acquainted) to a kind of all-in wrestling match, was victorious, and received a money prize from the emperor while the others were awarded clothes for consolation prizes. He repeated his success on a day when the emperor led the procession to the Lagaion (it is interesting to find a Roman emperor honouring the memory of the father of the first Ptolemy) and concludes his letter: 'so don't be vexed; though we haven't found the fellow, fortune has given us something else'.

But the great mass of the documents, whether public or private, have no direct connexion with education or the history of Greco-Roman culture. Although these may be reflected in the description of people as illiterate, or in the style, the syntax, and the orthography of the documents (for example, the stilted and repetitive language of Byzantine documents is proof enough that Greek was a dying tongue, kept alive by artificial stimulants), the documents are primarily sources for the economic, social, and administrative history of the country. These documents are now counted in their thousands; and embarrassing though their number sometimes is, in it lies no small part of their value. One tax-receipt or a single account may not be very informative (though it is to a single papyrus of A.D. 359 that we owe the knowledge that the government was taking steps at that time to revive the trade between Egypt and India); its value is greatly enhanced when it can be treated as one of a series in which normal can be distinguished from abnormal practice, the incidence of the tax and its local variations calculated, or, in the case of accounts, the price-level of an article observed over a number of years. The same holds good of contracts which form one of the largest classes of documents; we have enough leases, for example, to follow the development of the system of land-tenure from Ptolemaic times down to the end of the Byzantine period, though evidence may be more plentiful for one period than for another, and as a lesson in social history few things are more instructive than to read through a series of deeds of marriage or divorce and to observe in the former the varying obligations assigned at different periods to husband and wife, in the latter the purely business-like character of the earlier documents and the somewhat long-winded pretexts of the later ones. Or we may compare an ordinary will of the Roman period with, for example, the *donatio mortis causa* of the fourth century in which Flavius Abraham, an ex-*praepositus* in the Roman army, binds himself to bequeath half his property to the holy Church, his wife to have the use of the other half until her death when it reverts to the Church, and gives instructions for all his slaves, male and female, to be freed (this, however, is not uncommon in pagan wills). Such dispositions of a man of high rank are an epitome of a whole social revolution.

To the social historian few documents are more valuable than contracts; if we take a representative selection,[1] we shall find that each gives a vignette of life in the ancient world. In one, a deed of adoption, the adoptive parents promise the real parents that the child shall inherit their estate and not be reduced to slavery; in another, two brothers set free 'under sanction of Zeus, Earth and Sun' the third part of a female slave which they hold jointly, the other two-thirds being already emancipated; in a third, a father apprentices his son to a weaver, the latter to feed and clothe him and the father to pay a drachma for every day that the boy plays truant, while under the terms of another such agreement the boy is 'to sit at his teacher's feet from sunrise to sundown', but to enjoy twenty days' holiday with pay. Somewhat similar is the contract by which a man places his slave with a certain Apollonius to learn shorthand, two years being allowed the slave to learn to read and write it perfectly. Many, as we should expect, relate to agriculture; in

[1] Each of those cited below with the exception of the last will be found in vol. i of the *Select Papyri* in the Loeb Library.

one, for example, two men undertake to lease for one year all the operations connected with a vineyard and we have a detailed description of what this entails. They even provide some evidence about the lighter side of life, as when Onnophris and some friends of his at Oxyrhynchus hire a whole company of flute-players and musicians (the word used is συμφωνία) for the five feast-days, donkey transport to be provided, and part of the substantial fee to be paid in advance. From the darker side of ancient life we may quote a Berlin papyrus in which a widow contracts with her prospective mother-in-law to expose the child of her previous marriage; what is surprising to us is not that the exposure (which we know was common) should take place, but that it should be provided for by a legal document.

Much of the material that the papyri have provided for the historian is of this indirect character, though a date attached to a contract may effect a vital change in chronology, just as the geographical particulars in a deed of sale or lease may inform us of the existence of some unsuspected temple or cult; direct evidence, that is reference to persons or events of historical importance in contemporary documents, is rarer than we might expect. But examples of this are to be found; in the Zenon papyri, for example, historical personages occasionally figure. In one letter a garrulous and unknown correspondent reports to Zenon that he has called in an expert to 'cure' some dice made of gazelle bone; the expert thinks poorly of them and to confirm his judgement refers to his practice at the court, where he has 'cured' dice for Alexander the Etesian—a man who had once been king of Macedon for forty-five days (hence his nickname) and now some twenty years later appears as a pensioner playing knuckle-bone at the court of Ptolemy Philadelphus. Again, a scrap of a decree of no more than three lines is sufficient to show that Antiochus Epiphanes of Syria, when he invaded Egypt in 170 B.C., did, as our ancient authorities say, dethrone the reigning Ptolemy, while the fact that the Faiyûm is not called the

Arsinoite but the Crocodilopolite nome may indicate that Antiochus wished to suppress a name that honoured the Ptolemaic house. From the Roman period we have the two edicts of Germanicus of A.D. 19, in one of which he rebukes the Alexandrines for paying him the semi-divine honours proper to the emperor alone (his threat that, if they continued in this course, he would be obliged to show himself less frequently to them, may have seemed inadequate to his uncle Tiberius): the famous letter of the emperor Claudius to the Alexandrines: a copy, though incomplete, of the revolutionary *Constitutio Antoniniana* of Caracalla, conferring the Roman citizenship on all the inhabitants of the empire, apart perhaps from the *dediticii*: the text of the proclamation issued by the prefect of Egypt introducing Diocletian's changes in the method of assessment for taxation, and so fundamentally changing the economy of the empire, which proves conclusively that the *capitatio humana* was extended to Egypt. One result of Diocletian's monetary reforms can be seen in a letter in which an official who has inside information of a measure to reduce the face value of an imperial coin writes to his agent 'to make haste to spend all the Italian silver that you have on purchases, on my behalf, of goods of every description at whatever price you find them'. From the same period comes a copy of a circular letter, probably from the chancery of the bishop of Alexandria, denouncing the tenets, and above all the practices, of the new sect of the Manichees —the earliest witness that we have to the spread of the religion of Mani; that the danger to the Church remained is shown by the recent discovery in the Faiyûm of a number of Manichaean codices in Coptic.

But these, after all, are the exceptions; the subject of the documentary papyri is the ordinary rather than the extraordinary, government seen not with the eyes of the statesman or the political historian, but as it affected the masses of the people. To describe the intricacies of the administrative system as applied by the Ptolemies and adopted from them and made more rigorous by their Roman successors is beyond the scope of this essay; it has been justly described from the evidence of the papyri in a pregnant phrase as *l'exploitation pratiquée sous le signe de l'absolutisme*. Countless papyri show how the principle that the subject existed for the benefit of the State was ruthlessly applied in every department of life; the position of the king in the Ptolemaic age as in theory the sole owner of all land in the country is but one instance of a principle of almost universal application. Individual kings or prefects might profess, and sincerely, their desire to see the taxpayer meet with fair treatment, but the system was too strong for them, nor did any remedy, such as, e.g., setting one official to watch another, materially change the situation. A Tebtunis papyrus has preserved for us a memorandum with detailed instructions on the management of certain departments of the royal revenue; it was probably intended for the *oeconomi*, treasury officials stationed in each nome, and had we not the evidence of petitions, letters, and legal reports we might take it that the following quotation was typical of the administration:

'In your tours of inspection try in going from place to place to cheer everybody up and to put them in better heart; and not only should you do this by words but also, if any of them complain of the village scribes or the comarchs about any matter touching agricultural work, you should make enquiry and put a stop to such doings as far as possible.'

Such handbooks of official instructions appear in the Greek world for the first time in the Hellenistic kingdoms, and the editors of this text point out that they were the model for the Roman *mandata principis*; in this, as in other matters, Rome built up the structure of her empire on Hellenistic foundations. A similar document of the Roman period is the Gnomon of the Idios Logos, regulations for the department of the Special Account originally drawn up by Augustus and preserved in an abbreviated form by a Berlin papyrus. No document gives a better picture of the spirit and practice of Roman administration than this, with its detailed instructions how this or that breach of the regulations (if, for example, a priest wears his hair long or wears a woollen garment, thus infringing the priestly law) might be turned to the financial advantage of the government.

The principles of administration were clearly recognized by the people; it is significant that petitions and complaints of robbery, injustice, or maltreatment commonly conclude by imploring the competent authority to take action 'lest any harm accrue to the state (or treasury)'; even where the dispute is purely private and no official is involved, the petitioner asks for assistance on the ground that if it is not forthcoming he will be unable to pay his taxes. A petition of A.D. 280, alleging abuse of his powers by a financial official, has been endorsed by the prefect of Egypt to this effect: 'With a view to what is expedient for the revenues . . . his Excellency the epistrategus shall sift the matter with the utmost equity.' Such petitions might be addressed to a variety of authorities from the king or emperor down to the local police commandant and deal with a great variety of topics; but when they are used for evidence of the state of the administration, it is necessary to remember that no petitions are written to express satisfaction with the government. The incidental information they contain is varied and often valuable, particularly that circumstantial detail which a petitioner trusts will give verisimilitude to his claims. To take two from a group of Ptolemaic petitions addressed nominally to the king, though in fact decided by subordinate officials; from one, in which a widow of a soldier complains that her neighbour is interfering with her building of a wall, we learn that her husband had erected a shrine to the Syrian goddess and Aphrodite Berenice, and, as the lady's name is Asia, we may suspect that his predilection for a foreign deity was due to his wife's influence and that the neighbour perhaps objected to these foreign ways, just as we hear of Egyptians attacking Greeks because they were Greeks and vice versa. The second, in which a man complains that now he is old and suffering from a disease of the eye (still to-day one of the plagues of Egypt) his daughter, in spite of all he has done for her, will not support him, lets us see that education for women was not unknown in Ptolemaic Egypt.

One of the difficulties of the study of documentary papyri is that of finding a unifying principle by which to treat them. This may be done by considering together a group of documents such as petitions or leases, and though temporal and local variations may be considerable, yet the results gained, particularly from the diplomatic and legal standpoint, will be valuable; as an alternative to this vertical view we can occasionally take a horizontal cross-section of miscellaneous documents. Such archives—large groups of documents from the same place and approximately of the same date, and relating in the main to one group of persons—are not very numerous; the largest and richest is that of the papers of Zenon, and second to it, at least among the earlier papyri, the large collection relating to the affairs of some inmates of the Serapeum at Memphis in the second century B.C. Among the smaller archives none is more homogeneous or more attractive than that of Apollonius, strategus of the nome of Apollonopolis Heptakomia at the end of Trajan's reign and the beginning of Hadrian's.

The papyri of this archive number nearly 150 and all fall with a period of seven years; they are a part, if only a small part, of the collected papers which Apollonius took with him when he laid down his office and retired to his property at Hermopolis. It is very rarely that we get such a clear view of anyone as we do of Apollonius both in his private and in his public life. It so happens that he held his office—in spite of its title, the office of strategus was a civil one whose holder was responsible for the general administration of his nome and in particular for the proper functioning of the taxation system—at the time of the great Jewish revolt in the eastern provinces which almost assumed the proportions of a civil war and caused widespread damage and loss of life. The position grew so desperate in Egypt that the strategus had to call out a levy *en masse* of the peasants and place himself at its head to hold the rebels till reinforcements of Roman legionaries could arrive—an incident which has no parallel in the history of the office. We find him writing to the prefect requesting sixty days' furlough to set his own affairs in order after his long absence (his tenure of his office was unusually long) and the havoc caused by the revolt of the 'godless Jews'. His immediate superior was the epistrategus of the Thebaid, who sends him instructions about the inspection of lands and adds a hint that the 'natives' are not to be subjected to extortion or false accusation. It is another epistrategus, Flavius Philoxenus, who writes, in a letter which is that of a man whose mother tongue is Latin rather than Greek, to introduce to Apollonius a friend of his: he concludes 'Treat him as you would myself. Need I say more? You know my disposition. Farewell.' Hadrian's accession to the throne was celebrated in the nome with speeches and dramatic performances, and among Apollonius' papers is a draft of the libretto of the pageant in which Demos and Phoebus announced the good news to the people and which hints that the festivities were also to include a fountain flowing with wine.

The routine business of his office is represented by long reports from the land surveyors on the state of the irrigation, by sworn attestations from village officials or peasants that so much land will be cultivated, by a report from the city clerk on men suitable to act as city police in which the names of the streets— Isis Crescent, Street of the Women's Bath—are of interest. Public baths, both for men and women, were a Greek innovation;

to the Egyptian peasant, then as now content with the Nile, the idea was as alien as was that of the gymnasium; to the Greek these things meant civilization. The metropolis of the nome was small in comparison with a town such as Arsinoe; but though it had only 1,173 houses, we know that sometimes quite small fractions of houses were leased so that the population may well have been larger than at first sight would appear. To him, too, came the returns of the fourteen-yearly census in which every householder had to return all members of his household, their ages, sex, and status; for this purpose, as St. Luke tells us and the papyri confirm him, every man had to go to his own place. As strategus, he held a court of first instance, and consequently complaints and petitions figure among his papers; among them is one accusing the royal secretary (the next highest official in the nome) of illicit exactions, and another from a group of peasants who, suspected of implication in the murder of a Roman centurion, attempt to involve others in the charge; the case itself would be heard at the *conventus* of the prefect. It is no wonder that he was, as he himself says in a letter to the inspectors of the nome, 'distracted by the collection of the corn dues and all the other unfinished business of his office'.

Of his family circle we have in the private letters an unusually intimate picture. He and his sister Aline were deeply attached to each other; she was also his wife, a practice which, after it had received the sanction of the Ptolemies, had become quite common among the hellenized population of Egypt. No concession by Hellenism to oriental manners is more striking than this; it is noteworthy that in the Gnomon of the Idios Logos it was found necessary specifically to forbid such marriages to Romans. Such a marriage carried no social stigma with it and did not prevent Apollonius from having many Roman friends. During the Jewish war Aline writes to him begging him to put the burden of the work on to his subordinates as other strategi did and not to run into unnecessary danger; when he went away, she says, she could taste neither food nor drink, nor could she sleep. Equally moving and sincere is the following letter from Taus, a woman who was perhaps a family servant:

'Taus to Apollonius her lord very many greetings. Before everything I salute you, master, and I pray always for your health. I was distressed, my lord, not a little to hear that you had been ill, but thanks be to all the gods that they keep you safe from harm. I beg you, my lord, if it please you, to send for me; else I die because I do not behold you daily. Would that I were able to fly and come to you and make obeisance to you; for it distresses me not to behold you. So be friends with me and send for me. Goodbye, my lord.'

We may mention too among his private papers some letters from Herodes, the architect of his new house; in one of them he explains that owing to a death in the foreman's family they can't work for a few days and so he asks leave to go and visit his brother. Herodes' references to his work and the details of the house are reminiscent of another letter, not of the same archive but not far distant in date, in which Capito writes to his friend Teres about the decoration of the latter's house which he is superintending; he discusses the problem of the colonnade which needs repair, and suggests that some mural paintings— scenes from the *Iliad*, or whatever his friend would like—would be very suitable; it is, he says, just what the place demands (ὁ γὰρ τόπος ἀπαιτεῖ).

One other letter from the Apollonius archive may be quoted, of interest both for the reference to home weaving (the most primitive form of an industry which was highly organized in Egypt) and labour troubles, and for the vivid picture it gives of the writer herself. It is from the hand of Eudaemonis, mother of Aline and Apollonius, and was probably written during the Jewish troubles:

'Eudaemonis to her daughter Aline, greeting. Before all else I pray that you may be safely delivered and that I get news of a male child. . . . It was only with difficulty that I got the wool from the dyer's on

Epeiph 10th. I am working together with your slave-girls as best I can. I can't find any able to come and work with me, they are all working for their own mistresses. For our people are marching round the whole city demanding higher wages. Your sister Souerous has given birth. Teeus wrote and told me how grateful she was to you; so I realise, my lady, that my commands are still good, for she has left all her own people and has travelled in your company. The small one (Aline's daughter, Heraidous) sends her love and is working hard at her lessons. I tell you that I shall have no time for God, unless I get my son back first. What did you send me the 20 drachmas for, when I'm so badly off? I've already the prospect before my eyes of spending the winter without a rag. Good-bye. P.S. The wife of Eudemus is inseparable from me and I'm most grateful to her.'

In another letter she refers to some difficulty that she is having with a relative named Discas, probably about some family property, and writes as follows:

'I have already performed my part, and I have neither bathed nor worshipped the gods because of my fear about your unsettled case, lest I too be driven to the law-courts.'

Her postscript is revealing:

'At your wedding the wife of my brother Discas brought me 100 drachmas; and now that her son Nilus is about to marry, it is right that we should make a return gift, even if we have got grievances against them.'

This attitude to religion, though it finds clearer expression here than is usual, was no idiosyncrasy on Eudaemonis' part; it is an attitude which goes far to explain the widespread use of magical practices in Egypt for all the purposes of life, trivial and serious alike. The papyri have brought us a large number of magical texts, actual amulets and incantations or magician's handbooks such as the great London or Oslo papyri, the premiss of all of them being that the appropriate acts can bend the heavenly powers to the service of the agent. Some of the spells recommended in these handbooks have a touch of the modern advertisement and their psychological appeal is not so different: for example—

'A magic formula that restrains anger, secures goodwill, success in the lawcourts, works even with kings; there is absolutely nothing better. Take a silver plate, inscribe on it with a bronze pencil the figure drawn below and the names, carry it in the folds of your dress and you will win' (then follow the names and the actual formula).

Among all varieties of public religion which we find in the papyri, magic and the attitude it expresses remain constant.

Not many of the private letters are so full of character and life as Eudaemonis'; they are excellent examples of the type of material for ancient history with which only the papyri can supply us. More typical of the ordinary letter, both in its concern with Egypt's abiding interest, agriculture, and its unpretentiousness, is this:

'Ammonius to his dearest Aphrodisius, greeting. I wrote a letter to the herdsman Heracleus that he should supply you with a donkey, and I bade Ophelion to supply you with another and to send me the loaves. You have sent me three artabae; I ask you therefore to do your utmost to send the remaining three artabae immediately and the relish, as I am on board a boat. As to the pigs' fodder and the rest of the price for the hay, make provision until I come; for I expect to make up an account with you. I have given you every allowance. Urge your wife from me to look after the pigs and do you also take care of the calf. Be sure, Aphrodisius, to send me the loaves and the relish. . . .'

Such unconsidered trifles may seem beneath the dignity of Clio; but if we have enough of them they can provide us with a background against which the historical events of the period assume their proper proportion.

No exact classification of documents, except by their formal character and not always then, is possible; they have the variety, the confusion, the irrational complexity of life itself. If, as the elder Pliny thought, written records are of the essence of civilization, then to form a picture of an age, however imperfect and biased it needs must be, documents of all kinds are welcome; 'cum chartae usu maxime humanitas vitae constet et memoria'. If we think of *humanitas* in the sense which Pliny gave it, we may claim that the literary papyri have added some pages in the history of Greek literature and so enriched our perception of it; but there is a different sense too, in which we may assert a real relation between *humanitas* and the study of the papyri. Our view of life in the eastern Mediterranean in the millennium that separates Alexander from Mohammed has indeed been rendered more 'humane' by the concreteness and the vividness which papyri have brought to almost every branch of ancient studies, and with them our idea of what *humanitas* as applied to history can mean has developed. If a sense of the continuity of history, of the fundamental resemblances between civilizations, among their more obvious and very real differences, is an attribute of a civilized society, then we can claim that this is a legacy for which we may own a proper gratitude.

C. H. Roberts

CHAPTER 11

EGYPT AND ROME

IF one of the emperors had been asked what were the principal contributions of Egypt to the Roman Empire, he would undoubtedly have answered: corn and money. Egypt furnished few recruits to fight in the Roman armies; the natives were assessed so low in the social scale that they were even forbidden to enlist in the legions. It contributed yet fewer members to the governing aristocracy of the empire: the Egyptians were excluded from the Roman citizenship and *a fortiori* from the equestrian and senatorial orders, from which were selected the officials who ruled the empire; and even Alexandrians were, until the third century A.D., debarred from the senate. Apart from the three Greek cities which were in Egypt but not of it, it produced very few men of learning and culture, such as were the pride of Greece and Asia Minor. In religion its influence was on the whole regarded as pernicious: for though the Romans were awed by the immense antiquity of the Egyptian gods and cherished a belief that their priests were the guardians of a profound esoteric philosophy, they were moved to contempt by the superstition of the natives, particularly by the worship of sacred animals. They frequently repressed the magicians and astrologers who were the chief representatives of Egyptian religion abroad, and even regarded with suspicion the widespread cult of Serapis and Isis. In the eyes of the Roman government Egypt had no intellectual or spiritual contribution to make to the life of the empire—or none that the empire would not be better without—and its people were unfitted to fight for Rome, much more to take any share in its government. The value of Egypt was purely material; its rich soil, watered and fertilized each year with unfailing regularity by the Nile and laboriously tilled by its docile inhabitants, provided an abundance of corn for export to the hungry city of Rome, and its trade and industries brought in a revenue in cash which far exceeded the costs of administration and was a welcome asset to the imperial exchequer.

As an afterthought our Roman emperor might have mentioned papyrus. For though papyrus was a negligible item in the economic life of the empire as compared with the corn and money which Egypt provided, it remains true that the swamps of the Delta supplied the whole ancient world from Britain to Mesopotamia with the only writing material which was at once convenient, durable, and reasonably priced. The existence of such a material must have contributed not a little to the relatively high standard of literacy achieved under the Roman Empire, and the cessation of the supply after the Arab conquest of Egypt—papyrus was still imported into France under the Merovingian kings—must have increased the darkness of the Dark Ages of Europe.

Now that the corn has been eaten and the money spent, the papyri which the dry climate of Egypt has preserved remain its great contribution to our knowledge of the Roman Empire. Elsewhere we know only what the ancients thought it worth while telling us, either by writing it in books, which have been copied and re-copied and some of which have eventually come down to us, or by inscribing it on stone. What the ancients thought important we often find uninteresting; we could, for instance, well spare the diffuse orations of Aelius Aristeides, which were so passionately admired in antiquity, and the scores of inscriptions which record the banal virtues of local worthies. On the other hand, much that we should greatly like to know they either took for granted, or considered beneath the dignity of literature or epigraphic record. The papyri dug from the rubbish-heaps of Egyptian towns and villages have been subjected to no selective editorship. Many, perhaps most, of them are, taken by themselves, extremely dull reading. But their cumulative testimony enabled the historian to draw a picture of the Roman administration of Egypt with a wealth of detail which is, and always will be, impossible for any other province of the empire.

Many of the topics illustrated by the papyri are of more than local bearing, and the contribution made by the Egyptian documents to these well illustrates the incomparably larger scale on which the picture of ancient life can be drawn in Egypt than elsewhere. The Romans were essentially a military people and have left many records of their army. Its greatest work was achieved along the banks of the Rhine and Danube: yet it is the militarily negligible province of Egypt that furnishes us with our only intimate glimpse into army life. Here we can read the pay-sheets of the soldiers, and see how much they had left when all deductions for rations, uniforms, and arms had been made, and how they spent it. We possess the daily records of the units, which enumerate the several duties to which the men were detailed day by day. We see them going out to the villages to requisition corn, wine, oil, and meat for rations, and horses and camels for remounts. Finally we can follow their careers when, after their discharge, they settled down on the farms which the government granted to them as a reward for faithful service.

Roman law is again a subject on which we are, thanks to the literary tradition, exceptionally well informed. Yet even here the papyri have added enormously to our knowledge, more especially of the practical workings of the Roman legal system. The papyri tell us how contracts were drawn up, how plaintiffs instituted proceedings, how evidence was heard; we possess many dossiers of actual cases. They illustrate moreover one topic on which the literary legal texts tell us practically nothing, the way in which the Romans administered the Hellenistic law of the East, gradually infusing into it some of their own principles, and the complementary process whereby, after Roman law had in A.D. 212 become officially of universal application, it, in its turn, was influenced by Hellenistic practice.

Perhaps the most curious anomaly is that it is from Egypt, the home of bureaucratic absolutism, where civic autonomy was tardily and grudgingly bestowed, that we get our most intimate glimpse of how the affairs of a city-state were conducted. We have, it is true, from the Greek world countless decrees, inscribed on stone, but it is only in Egypt that we can read the actual minutes of council meetings, and hear the councillors electing the magistrates and discussing the supply of oil to the gymnasium or the execution of a contract for cloth by the local guild of weavers.

Our knowledge of Egypt is, in comparison with the rest of the empire, so detailed that it is often very difficult for us to tell whether an institution recorded in the papyri but unknown elsewhere was in fact peculiar to Egypt, or if it is merely our information that is deficient. To take an instance trivial in itself but typical of many others, no one would guess from our literary records of travel—which include the exceptionally circumstantial narrative of the Acts—that a passport system existed in the Roman Empire. Yet we know from the papyri that no one could leave Egypt without a passport. Did St. Paul have to show his papers wherever he travelled, and has the author of the Acts not troubled to mention the fact? Or was the regulation peculiar to Egypt? Egypt was in many ways a peculiar province—and in this particular case the unique rule that Roman senators might not set foot in it without imperial permission may suggest that the passport system was confined to it—but its peculiarity can easily be exaggerated. The fact that papyrology is a separate science, which demands of its students such specialized skill that they cannot be at the same time historians, has encouraged the tendency to treat Egypt as a country apart. Papyrologists too often do not look beyond the boundaries of the province; and Roman historians, daunted by the bulk and complexity of the papyrological evidence, are only too willing to brush it aside as merely of local import. Yet it is certain that much is lost by the failure of the two to co-operate. The fiscal system of Egypt was admittedly highly peculiar: yet even here the papyri probably would, if full use were made of them, contribute much to the solution of a problem of general bearing and of great intrinsic interest, the reason for the breakdown during the third century of the regular taxation instituted by Augustus, and its supersession throughout the empire by the arbitrary 'benevolences' and requisitions in kind, which were ultimately crystallized by Diocletian into the Byzantine fiscal system.

The Egyptian evidence has made a great contribution to our knowledge of the Roman Empire at large, and might make a yet greater if it were studied with an eye to its analogies with the rest of the Roman world rather than to its peculiarities. Yet the fact remains that Egypt was a peculiar province. Its anomalous status is brilliantly summarized by Tacitus in one of those epigrammatic sentences which it is unfortunately impossible to do more than paraphrase in English. 'Egypt and the forces with which it has to be kept in subjection have been, ever since the days of the deified Augustus, ruled by Roman knights as viceroys; it has been thought expedient thus to keep under home control a province difficult of access and productive of corn, distracted and excitable owing to its superstition and licence, ignorant of laws and unacquainted with magistrates.'

The first sentence gives in brief the unique status of Egypt in the Roman Empire, that alone of the major provinces it was governed not by a senator, but by a member of the second order of the Roman people, who furthermore had, alone of his class, the prerogative of commanding legionary troops. The sting in the tail of the sentence, the allusion to the vice-regal position of the prefect, is a typical piece of Tacitean innuendo, and of less real importance. The *princeps*, the elected first magistrate of the Roman people, was, it is true, a king in Egypt; one may still amuse oneself by picking out on the walls of Egyptian temples representations of such prosaic figures as Vespasian or Antoninus Pius, arrayed in the Double Crown and adorned with the many picturesque titles of the Pharaohs. But this was a ritual matter only; the religious life of Egypt was built up round its divine king, and without a king the whole mechanism of Egyptian life would have stopped. In the public law of Rome, however, Egypt was a province of the Roman people, and even the exceptional power of the prefect was ratified by a law passed in the *comitia*. And if the emperor's will was in fact absolute, was it not equally so in any of his provinces?

The first pair of adjectives with which Egypt is qualified sufficiently account for the anomalous position of the province. The career of Ptolemy, son of Lagus, was proof enough how easily a governor of Egypt could, secure behind his desert frontiers and commanding the vast economic resources of the country, defy his overlord, and it was probably these considerations, which are stressed elsewhere by Tacitus, that moved Augustus not to entrust Egypt to a senator, who might cherish political ambitions, but to a man of too humble a station to hope for independent power. But the choice of a knight was probably dictated by other reasons also, suggested in the third pair of epithets. Egypt was 'ignorant of laws' in the sense in which a Greek or Roman understood laws; it was governed by administrative regulations enacted by the Crown. And it was 'unacquainted with magistrates' who owed their authority to the people and were responsible to them for their exercise of it; it obeyed the officials of the king. Egypt was in fact a bureaucratic state, and as such required of the governor a business-like grasp of administrative detail which was more likely to be found in the equestrian order, with its long financial and commercial experience, than in the Roman nobility.

This bureaucratic absolutism, which had been from time immemorial characteristic of Egypt, remained throughout the

Hellenistic and Roman periods its salient feature. Ptolemy, son of Lagus, when in 323 B.C. he came to Egypt as satrap of the heirs of Alexander, found the system in working order: we know at any rate that under the rebel Pharaohs who ruled the country for much of the fourth century B.C. the nomarchs, who governed the several departments or nomes, were appointed by the Crown and operated an elaborate fiscal system which can only have been based on detailed statistical data provided by those officers so characteristic of Egypt, the royal scribes. Ptolemy accepted the system, and he and his successors gradually elaborated and refined it, till it became one of the most perfect examples of a totalitarian state that the world has ever seen. The whole life of the country was regimented down to the minutest detail with the single object of securing to the government, and the government alone, the control of its vast material and human resources, in order that with these resources the dynasty might maintain the armies and the fleets and pay the subsidies and bribes whereby it conducted its ambitious and expensive foreign policy. Augustus, when in 30 B.C. he annexed Egypt, again preserved the system in its main outlines, only too thankful to acquire a means of rehabilitating the tottering finances of the empire. And the later emperors did their best to maintain it, until their own excessive exactions and the incompetence of their officials forced them gradually to modify it.

The bureaucratic absolutism of the Ptolemies undoubtedly had some influence on the other Hellenistic monarchies, and, both through them and directly, on the Roman Empire. How far this influence is to be accounted distinctively Egyptian it is more difficult to say. We know so little of pre-Ptolemaic Egypt that it is in many cases impossible to say whether a given institution is of native origin or a Greek invention, and some of the most characteristic features of the Ptolemaic system were undoubtedly transplanted from the Greek cities. But they were so profoundly modified in their new environment that they may

U

be regarded, when they were re-exported, as Egyptian products.

The theological basis of the absolutism of Egypt was the divinity of the king. This conception was not, it has been proved, so common among the people of the Near East as it was once thought. The kings of Assyria and Babylonia were not gods, nor did the Persians worship their kings, though the Greeks thought that they did. Egypt was in fact the only important monarchy where the theory was held. It is tempting therefore to attribute to Egypt the rapid growth of the divine monarchy in the Hellenistic age. A careful investigation of the problem has, however, recently established that this was not the case. Alexander and the Ptolemies were of course gods in the Egyptian pantheon, like every ruler of the two lands. But the worship of kings by Greeks grew from Greek roots. The anthropomorphic spirit of Hellas had never drawn a very clear line between gods and men. Some of its gods, Heracles for instance, had by universal consent once been men, and according to a theory which was popular in the Hellenistic age all the gods were great rulers of the past whom their grateful subjects had deified; with the growth of rationalism in the fourth century it was not difficult to apply this reasoning to modern benefactors. Yet Egypt did play a small part in the spread of the doctrine. One of the most curious incidents in the story of Alexander is his journey to the oracle of Zeus Ammon. We shall never know what motives prompted his romantic spirit, whether it was the example of his ancestor Heracles, or that yearning which he felt to explore the mysterious and unknown. Nor shall we ever know what words passed when Alexander entered the sanctuary alone, save for the high priest, and questioned the god. But it is tolerably certain that the god, through the mouth of his priest, must have addressed him as a god and a son of Amen; for the temple was an Egyptian temple, and Alexander was king of Egypt. And it is certain too that this answer must have impressed Alexander's mind: for Zeus Ammon was more than an Egyptian god and his oracle had been for generations famous and respected in the Greek world.

It was probably this incident which convinced Alexander of his divine nature. At any rate when in later times representations were made of the god Alexander, he was generally portrayed with the ram's horns of Amen, and in the legends of Islam he is still He of the Two Horns. It moreover gave to the Greeks the oracular sanction necessary for what was to some extent a new departure in religion; it is worth noting that when in 304 B.C. the Rhodians wished to deify another king of Egypt, Ptolemy I, they first consulted Zeus Ammon. Egyptian practice thus perhaps gave the first impetus to a theory which was to have a long history. Quickly taken up by nearly all the Hellenistic monarchies, it was adopted, at first with hesitation but soon with conviction, by the Roman Empire. When that empire became Christian it did not die: Constantine and his successors still called their palace, their laws, even their treasury, sacred, and did not hesitate to dub as sacrilege any opposition to their will. Thence, in the modified form of the Divine Right of Kings, it passed to the Middle Ages and even to modern times.

The chief source of Egypt's wealth was then, as it still is to-day, the land. The land therefore was systematically exploited in the interests of the king. In principle the Crown claimed ownership over the whole surface of Egypt. A certain proportion was granted on favourable terms to privileged classes or individuals. The gods were, for instance, allowed to retain, in return for a quit-rent, their ancient holdings, and were even given new estates; the king, however, administered their lands for them, and paid them what he thought fit out of the profits. The king's friends, his ministers and principal officials, were allotted lands 'in gift'; but those gifts were probably for life only. His soldiers also were rewarded with estates; their tenure also was for life only and was subject to a quit-rent. The rest of Egypt—and it must have been a very considerable proportion

—formed the 'royal land' proper, and was rack-rented in small farms to the peasants, the 'royal cultivators'. The Crown controlled every stage in the agricultural year. Not only did it regulate, as every Egyptian government must, the water supply: it determined what the crop should be, loaned the seed, and, after collecting its rent, usually in kind, claimed its share of the second crop of animal fodder. The system is incredible in its complexity, but thanks to the labours of an army of scribes it worked: bales of papyri testify to the precise information which was available to the government on every tiny plot of land—its legal status, its dimensions, its position, the name of its holder, the rent due from it, the state of its irrigation, the nature of the crop sown on it.

The basic theory of the royal ownership of the soil, which justified this system of exploitation, appears to have been prevalent in Pharaonic Egypt. But whether it was or not, the Ptolemies probably derived their claim from Greek ideas. In the eyes of the Greeks an oriental king was the owner of his kingdom; his subjects were his slaves, and all that they possessed was in the ultimate analysis his property. By the Greek laws of war the persons and property of the vanquished passed to the victor and his heirs. Ptolemy therefore as the heir of Alexander, the conqueror of Darius, was the owner of Egypt. Royal ownership of the soil was thus a theory common to all the oriental Hellenistic kingdoms. But nowhere but in Egypt could the theory be exploited. Elsewhere the kings might expropriate some of the old landowners in favour of their own followers, but they had not the statistical data or the administrative machinery necessary for organizing the cultivation of the land themselves. They had to content themselves with charging the owners, now officially their tenants, with a customary rent, which was in effect the old taxes under a new name. Royal ownership therefore meant little in practice, and even the theory was gradually abandoned, except in a few limited areas. In

Egypt, though the tenure of the military settlers became hereditary, and certain classes of land were granted on perpetual leases, the theory seems to have survived intact until the Romans came: and though they modified it, allowing to the gods and to the privileged classes full ownership of their estates and claiming as the property of the Roman people only the royal land proper, their general conception of land tenure was probably influenced by it. A modern authority on the subject has suggested that the example of Egypt was an important factor in the growth of the famous doctrine current under the principate, that all provincial soil was in the ultimate resort the property of the Roman people.

Besides appropriating the products of the soil the Ptolemaic government exacted a heavy toll from commerce, both foreign and internal, by a complicated system of customs dues, levied on the frontiers and at various points within the kingdom. It furthermore absorbed the greater part of the profits of industry by a comprehensive series of monopolies, which covered almost every article of common use from textiles to beer, the normal drink of the natives, and the vegetable oils which served them for lighting, for cooking, and for soap. Whether monopolies were exercised by the Pharaohs is uncertain; but they were a familiar, if rather disreputable, financial device in the Greek cities, and it was probably from them that the Ptolemies borrowed the idea. The method whereby they were operated, the farming system, was certainly of Greek origin. This system was in the Greek cities merely a lazy device for fobbing off on to a private entrepreneur the troublesome task of collecting the public revenues, and it has so frequently been abused that it is often regarded as something evil in itself. But it could be, and in the hands of the Ptolemies was, an effective and legitimate device for securing to the government the full return from a source of revenue whose exact value could not be calculated in advance. Its purpose can best be seen in the regulation of the oil monopoly, which a papyrus has preserved. The whole process is minutely supervised from beginning to end. The government determined the acreage to be sown with the plants whence oil was extracted, and through its officials furnished the seed and saw that it was planted. It fixed the price at which the culti-vator sold the plants to the contractor. Its officials established factories and provided labour, whose rate of pay and working hours were determined by royal decree. Finally the govern-ment fixed the price at which the finished product was retailed to the public. It is clear that the farming system was not adopted to save the government trouble; its officials did the greater part of the work themselves and supervised the contractor's share at every stage. Yet the contractor was no sleeping partner in the concern. He had bid, at competitive auction, as high a price for the profits of the monopoly as he dared, and it was to his interest to see that the profits should if possible exceed that price. He could therefore be relied upon to keep a careful watch on all concerned to see that no unnecessary loss was incurred, and he was given wide powers of inspection and search to pre-vent illicit private manufacture by the public and to check negligence or corruption among the royal officials: he was, for instance, entitled to damages from any official who failed to provide seed to the cultivators in proper time. The government thus secured itself against leakages at a small cost; for the con-tractor obviously could not make any large speculative profit in so minutely regulated a concern. The general public were protected by the publicity given to the prices, and their interests could in case of need be protected by the officials, who had no cause to favour the contractor as against their own charges.

No such elaborate scheme of monopolies seems to have been operated in any other Hellenistic kingdom, and in Egypt itself it was abandoned by the Romans, who substituted for it licences on manufacturers. The mixed system of farm and régie is, however, found elsewhere applied to percentage taxes. It is a disputable point whether these systems were inspired by Egyptian practice or evolved independently, but in one instance, the *Lex Hieronica*, whereby the tithe of Sicily was collected, the analogies with Ptolemaic technique are so close that it seems plausible that King Hiero, who had close relations with the second Ptolemy, profited by Egyptian examples. The *Lex Hieronica* was taken over by Rome when she annexed Sicily, and its principles seem to have been applied later to the tithe of Asia and other provinces. Unfortunately, owing to collusion between the provincial governors and the tax farmers, the system, which was according to Cicero in theory a model of ingenuity, giving full protection to the government, the contractors, and the cultivators, became under Roman rule an instrument of gross extortion, and was ultimately discredited and abandoned save for a few indirect taxes. Even in this limited sphere it was long before the Roman government regained a Ptolemaic standard of efficiency: it is an amazing fact that Nero was the first emperor to give publicity to customs tariffs, and it was not till the second century A.D. that imperial procurators were appointed to check the contractors.

As lords of Egypt the Ptolemies had a right to the personal labour of all its inhabitants. It was a right which they exercised little, less probably than had the Pharaohs. Their army was at first composed of foreign mercenaries, and when later natives were enrolled there is no evidence that conscription was applied. Their civil service was professional and a government post seems to have been greatly coveted, whether for the salary attached or for the perquisites which invariably fell to officials in antiquity; such was the competition even for the humble position of a village scribe that applicants were prepared to pay for it. Even agricultural labour was in the main voluntary: leases of royal land were allocated by competitive auction, the applicant who offered the highest rent securing the farm till he was outbid. The only purpose for which forced labour was normally used was the maintenance of irrigation works; and even to-day the government of Egypt is entitled to call out every able-bodied man to guard the banks of the Nile in flood.

Nevertheless the right of the government to the labour of its subjects remained latent, and on emergency the Ptolemies did not hesitate to use it. Thus when they failed to lease royal land at a rent agreeable to their ideas they are known on occasions to have conscripted the peasants to cultivate it. Such measures were rare under the Ptolemaic régime, but under Roman rule they became about normal. The Ptolemies squeezed the last penny of revenue out of Egypt, it is true, but they did allow a sufficient margin of profit to their subjects to make them willing to work for them. The Romans were more exacting: whether they over-estimated the productivity of Egypt or whether its prosperity declined for other reasons under their rule, the demands of the Roman government often left so small a balance to their subjects that they had no incentive to work. Undeterred, the Romans, instead of adjusting their demands, resorted to compulsion. In agriculture this took two main forms. Public land for which no tenant would bid the rent demanded by the government might be compulsorily allocated to the village community, which sublet it on the best terms it could get and shared out the deficit. Alternatively it might be allocated to a private landowner, who had to pay its rent out of the profits of his own more lightly taxed land. Both methods were in the Byzantine age applied extensively throughout the empire to the problems of collecting the rent on imperial estates and the tribute on private land: and as economic decline and the consequent difficulty of keeping land under cultivation, or rather of extracting the revenue due from uncultivated land, began far earlier in Egypt than elsewhere, it is a reasonable presumption that the imperial officials of the Byzantine age were inspired by the precedents set by the Roman administration in Egypt.

The doctrine of compulsory service was also applied by the Romans to the work of administering the country. The origins of this change are obscure. The Ptolemies had governed Egypt through a professional bureaucracy, checked in certain departments by public contractors. It was the contracting system which seems to have broken down first under Roman rule. The Romans refused to accept lower tenders when the revenues shrank, but instead compulsorily imposed the contract on their own terms on persons of suitable means, or, abandoning even the forms of the farming system, instituted direct collection, again insisting on their own estimate of the revenue. The bureaucracy ceased for similar reasons to attract voluntary applicants. Officials had always been liable to make good deficits arising from their own negligence, and as the Romans refused to believe that a decline in the revenues could be due to anything but negligence, the lot of an official became an unhappy one. From about the end of the first century A.D. the administration of Egypt came to be conducted by agents compulsorily appointed for a short term of years, who combined the responsibility of the official to carry out the work and of the farmer to guarantee the full return.

The word used to describe this compulsory service, liturgy, is derived from the terminology of the Greek city. Athens and many other democratic cities had since the fifth century B.C. devolved on to their richer citizens certain troublesome and expensive departments of the administration, such as the production of choruses for the musical and dramatic festivals or the fitting of ships of war and the training of their crews. The system was widely applied in the Hellenistic age, but seems to have been modified inasmuch as persons were no longer nominated to liturgies by the magistrates but elected by the people. Appointments were in fact generally voluntary, for the standard of civic patriotism was high; but an elected candidate could not refuse except for a reasonable cause. The liturgy of the Hellenistic city has obviously certain features in common with that of Roman Egypt, enough to justify the use of the word. But the Egyptian liturgy was something very different both in form and more especially in spirit. In Egypt those who had to fulfil them were not elected by the community but nominated—by the Roman imperial officials assisted by the ubiquitous scribes. And they did not work and spend on behalf of a city of which they were members and in whose welfare they took interest and pride, but for the imperial administrative machine. The institution is typically Egyptian and could only have been evolved in that home of absolutism.

The reciprocal influence of Egypt and the city in the later development of the imperial liturgy, which came to be the dominating feature in the Roman administrative system, is a difficult and obscure problem. Certain features of the later system are certainly of civic origin, notably the responsibility of the community for its nominees. This principle was introduced into Egypt by Septimius Severus, who created in the capitals of the nomes pale imitations of Greek cities, whose principal function it was to appoint officials to serve the central government. The reason for the change was that the property of the individuals who were nominated to serve the state was sometimes inadequate to meet its claims and they themselves were difficult to catch and punish if they ran away: from henceforth the community which appointed them had to make up any deficit and supply substitutes. Whether Egypt made any contribution to the evolution of the imperial liturgy is, owing to our ignorance of the early history of the institution elsewhere, difficult to determine. The cities had always been responsible to the central government for the performance of certain imperial services, notably the collection of the tribute, and they had presumably elected officers to conduct these services. What is uncertain is whether these officers were personally responsible to the central government, and in particular whether they had to make good deficits from their own property, as they did in the third century. It is possible that they did not, and that the personal responsibility of civic officers, particularly on the financial side, to the central government was an idea which originated in Egypt. The eventual system, whereby the liability of the individual was backed by the guarantee of the community, would in that case be a combination of the Graeco-Roman principle of the responsibility of the city with the Egyptian idea of the service owed by the individual to the state.

The contribution of Egypt to the political theory and practice of the Graeco-Roman world is difficult to assess because we know so little of contemporary developments elsewhere in comparison with the abundant evidence we possess for Egypt. The most that we can say is that on our evidence certain institutions which later became common to the Roman Empire seem to develop first in Egypt, and that though some of them were in origin foreign importations, the form which they ultimately took and in which they became universal was essentially Egyptian. It can at any rate be said that Egypt was already in the Ptolemaic and still more in the Roman periods dominated by the baleful notion which in the Byzantine age casts its shadow over the whole empire, that the individual exists for the state and not the state for the individual.

A. H. M. Jones

CHAPTER 12

THE EGYPTIAN CONTRIBUTION TO CHRISTIANITY

I. EGYPT AND THE CHRISTIAN CHURCH

No country has affected the development of the Christian religion more profoundly than has Egypt, or rather—to speak more exactly—no city has affected the development of the Christian religion more profoundly than has Alexandria, the Greek-speaking capital of Egypt. Native Coptic-speaking Egypt did indeed itself come to play no small part in later Christian history, for at a very early date Coptic Christianity produced pioneers in the ascetic life whose influence was felt throughout the Church as Christian monasticism established itself. This contribution of native Christian Egypt will be dealt with in this book by another hand. Then again the later development of the Monophysite Coptic Church and the story of its chequered relations with the Imperial Church and the Patriarchal See of Constantinople constitute a significant chapter in the history of the Church in the Nearer East. But though the part which Egypt played through each of these movements is noteworthy in a high degree, in neither case would it justify the claim which I have advanced for Egyptian influence in Christian history. The outstanding legacy of Egypt to the Church, the legacy which has coloured all later history, has been the scientific Platonizing theology which the catechetical school of Alexandria was beginning to fashion at the close of the second Christian century and which the comprehensive genius of Origen carried to a successful issue in the first half of the third century.

Let it be said at once that Origen's bold speculative system of Christian doctrine has never commanded the allegiance of the Church at large. In his lifetime he appears to have incurred no formal censure on the ground of his teaching, but his own writings testify to the uneasiness which he occasioned to some of his hearers, and in the half-century which followed his death his views encountered vigorous opposition from able writers. Again at the close of the fourth century his doctrines gave rise to a lively and unedifying controversy in the course of which Origenism was anathematized by an evil Patriarch of Alexandria and by a Pope of Rome. Finally, in the sixth century, the imperial champion of orthodoxy, Justinian, formally condemned many passages from his writings as heretical. The stigma on his name lasted throughout the Middle Ages, though books were written to defend the belief that in spite of the anathemas of the Church Origen might yet be saved. It was not till the Platonic revival of the Renaissance that his teaching again received serious attention. To the Christian humanists, notably Erasmus, Origen was a congenial spirit, but Luther repeats once more from an angle of his own the condemnation of his name and memory.

This recurrent suspicion and even hatred of Origen's doctrine is not, however, the whole story nor is it the most important part of the story of Origen's influence in the Christian Church. 'There has been no truly great man in the Church', wrote Charles Bigg, 'who has not loved Origen a little.'[1] If we do not forget Luther we may probably accept what Bigg has said. Certainly no one man did more than Origen to determine the whole subsequent history of Greek theology, for, even when his views were repudiated, his formulations of the problems remained of decisive importance, and this was recognized by some of the greatest of the Fathers. The great Athanasius, though he makes no use of some of Origen's most characteristic thoughts, and though he could not be satisfied with his Christology in its entirety, yet spoke with reverence of his name. To the Cappadocian Fathers Origen was the master, and in token of their

[1] Charles Bigg, *The Christian Platonists of Alexandria*, p. 279.

veneration for his work Basil and Gregory Nazianzus compiled an anthology from his writings—*Philocalia*—which has come down to us. This excellent compilation includes extensive and precious fragments from the Greek original of Origen's great work on Christian religious philosophy, περὶ ἀρχῶν, a book which survives as a whole only in the faulty Latin paraphrase of Rufinus. It is no doubt significant that Basil and Gregory selected extracts from the third and fourth books only, dealing with the relatively uncontroversial subjects of free-will and the method of Scriptural interpretation, while the first two books, which contain the more daring of Origen's speculations on the Godhead, the world, and the origin and destiny of man, were not represented. It was not only in the East that Origen's influence endured; in the West, too, through the writings of Hilary of Poitiers, of Ambrose, and of Jerome, Origen's exegetical labours remained current.

The tradition of Christian Platonism had already struck roots in Alexandria before Origen appeared upon the scene, and the earlier phase is represented for us in the writings of Clement, Origen's predecessor and teacher. Clement, who was probably himself a native of Athens, had been converted to Christianity in mature life and brought with him a wide, if somewhat desultory, acquaintance with the achievements of Greek literature and Greek philosophy. He had wandered in quest of wisdom through Greece, southern Italy, and the East, but it was an Alexandrine Christian, Pantaenus, who brought to him the religious and the intellectual satisfaction for which he craved. Pantaenus is known to us only through the writings of others, especially of Clement. He is reported to have been a Stoic in philosophy and he is said to have journeyed as far as India as a missionary of the Christian faith. To us he is chiefly of importance as Clement's forerunner at Alexandria and Clement's father in the Faith. In the writings of Clement we gain for the first time a direct reflection of the life of the Christian Church at Alexandria, or at any rate of certain sections of that Church. We note that Clement writes for a public which is plainly in possession of some wealth and leisure and of a not inconsiderable measure of mental cultivation.[1] To present the Christian faith in relation to the thinkers of the age is a paramount necessity if it is to hold its own in the society amid which Clement lives and moves. His own Christianity is sincere and deep; he is a convinced believer in the Church's rule of faith, and he appeals continuously to the Scriptures both of the Old and the New Testament. But he is so far influenced by the great Gnostic teachers, who in the earlier part of the second century had grafted upon the common Christianity of the multitude an esoteric doctrine of redemption, that he, too, made a distinction between the simple believers who were the body of the Church and those fully enlightened Christians who for him were the true Gnostics. Clement's Gnostic is not less truly a believer in the common faith than others, but he has learned to advance from mere faith to a higher stage in the knowledge of God in virtue of which he and his like constitute the Church's soul. This exaltation of Gnosis, 'knowledge', combined with a rejection of the heretical tendencies of the older teachers, gives Clement's teaching its distinctive character.

It had been Clement's aim to crown his writings on Christian education and Christian ethics, the *Paedagogus* and the *Stromateis*, with a systematic exposition of the deeper principles of the true Gnosis. This aim he never attained. His mind was too little disciplined and too weak in constructive ability to allow of his achieving a coherent doctrinal expression of the faith that was in him. Where Clement was weak his successor Origen was strong. Origen had studied systematically the Platonism which was the chief intellectual force of his age, and he had imbibed the genuine Greek spirit of philosophical inquiry. He is never the mere dogmatist. He follows reason whither it leads and

[1] See, e.g., *Quis Dives*, cxi *et passim*.

faces to the utmost the problems which thought aroused. The conditions of the time and the exegetical method of allegory which he inherited and used in all good faith, allowed him to follow out to its full extent the system of religious philosophy to which his bold mind carried him, without compromising his fidelity to the new, yet ancient, religion of the Christian Church in which he had been bred. Of Origen's whole-hearted allegiance to the Christian faith there could be no doubt. Leonides, his father, who had anxiously watched over his early education, fell a victim to the persecution of Severus, A.D. 202. Origen himself, then a boy of 17, coveted the same fate and was with difficulty restrained. At the early age of 18 he succeeded to the headship of the Catechetical school left vacant by Clement's forced departure, and from this post of influence he became known to a wide circle as an outstanding champion of the Christian faith. His lectures were attended and his advice was sought by Christian heretics, such as the wealthy and influential Ambrosius whom Origen brought over to the Church from Gnosticism, and by non-Christians as well as by full members of the Church. Unfortunately as time went on relations became strained between Origen and Demetrius, Bishop of Alexandria, who had appointed him in the first place to the headship of the school. Demetrius took umbrage at the conduct of Alexander, Bishop of Jerusalem, and Theoctistus, Bishop of Caesarea, who, when Origen had betaken himself to Palestine in consequence of disturbances in Alexandria, invited him, albeit a layman, to expound the Scriptures in the congregation. At a later date his friends the Palestinian bishops ordained him to the Presbyterate. This action made Origen's position in Alexandria untenable and he transferred his residence from Alexandria to Caesarea. Demetrius went so far as to secure the decision of a synod of Egyptian bishops that Origen should no longer teach in Alexandria. In the last ten or twelve years of his residence in Alexandria Origen had become an influential and prolific writer. To this period belong his great works on Christian Philosophy, the περὶ ἀρχῶν, and the earlier books of a great Commentary on St. John, perhaps also the beginnings of a monumental edition of the text of the Old Testament, the *Hexapla*, containing in six parallel columns the Hebrew, a transliteration of the Hebrew, the ancient Greek Version of the Seventy and the three later versions of Aquila, Symmachus, and Theodotion. After his settlement at Caesarea in A.D. 231, Origen laboured on unceasingly at his textual and exegetical work, at the same time instructing the whole body of the faithful and delivering homilies in the congregation. To this later period there belongs also his great work of Christian Apologetics, the *Contra Celsum*, in eight books, which has come down to us entire. Finally Origen died a martyr for the Christian faith. In the persecution of Decius he was thrown into prison, where he suffered terrible tortures. On the death of Decius in 251 he was released, but his sufferings had shattered his health and he died two years later at Tyre in the seventieth year of his age.

Thus the whole course of Origen's life shows him to have been whole-heartedly identified with the Christian Church. He was a philosophical thinker, but first and last he was a believing and confessing Christian. He begins the περὶ ἀρχῶν with a summary statement of the faith which all believers should and do accept. This rule of faith, with the Scriptures which substantiate the rule, has for him incontestable authority. And the theological principle is in harmony with his practical attitude. When the heathen Celsus chides the Christian teachers with being concerned exclusively with 'simpletons, low folk and fools, slaves, womenkind and children', Origen rebuts the charge, but only to insist that the Divine Word does indeed call such as these, though not these alone, 'since the Christ is the saviour of all men, and especially of such as believe, whether prudent or simple'.[1] This catholicity of temper distinguishes

[1] *Contra Celsum*, I. iii. 49.

Origen from the Gnostic teachers of the second century who, as we are to see, may be regarded as, in certain respects, his fore-runners. The Church for him is a true brotherhood of believers. Yet the mere faith of the simple believer, sound though it is, does not exhaust the wisdom of God or that knowledge of God which has been imparted to mankind in the books of Scripture.

'The holy Apostles', he writes,[1] 'when preaching the faith of Christ, took certain doctrines, those namely which they believed to be necessary ones, and delivered them in the plainest terms to all believers, even to such as appeared to be somewhat dull in the investigation of divine knowledge. The grounds of their statements they left to be investigated by such as should merit the higher gifts of the Spirit, and in particular by such as should afterwards receive through the Holy Spirit himself the graces of language, wisdom, and knowledge. There were other doctrines, however, about which the apostles simply said that things were so, keeping silence as to the "how" or "why"; their intention undoubtedly being to supply the more diligent of those who came after them, such as should prove to be lovers of wisdom, with an exercise on which to display the fruit of their ability.'

Among such 'lovers of wisdom' Origen was pre-eminent. Within the Scriptures of the Old Testament and the New he discovered and brought to light a comprehensive Gnosis of which most believers were ignorant. The Bible, Origen held, was, like mankind, threefold in its nature, consisting of body, soul, and spirit. The simple believer receives edification from the literal meaning of the Scripture, that is from its body. The believer who is making progress (προκόπτων) in divine knowledge penetrates further and is edified by the Scripture's soul. Lastly the spirit of the Scripture, 'the shadow of the good things to come' (Heb. x. 1), is apprehended by those who are 'perfect' in the faith.

What then was the doctrine concerning God, man, and the

---

[1] *First Principles*, Book I, preface, Engl. trans. by G. W. Butterworth (S.P.C.K. 1936).

world which Origen believed himself to have discovered beneath the text of Holy Scripture?

From Plato and the Platonists Origen had learnt that ultimate being is immaterial. The physical world in which we live our span of earthly life is not ultimate; it has had a beginning and at long last, when God 'shall be all in all', it will end. The invisible world of spirit is not thus temporally conditioned. It exists eternally in dependence upon the one true God, who is the Father. But the divine essence is not restricted to the Father (ὁ θεός), God supreme. Eternally God generates or creates His Word or Son, who, though not in the full sense God (ὁ θεός), is yet truly divine (θεός), a sharer in the divine οὐσία.[1] So also the Spirit, standing next in rank, is, like the Son, a being distinct from God Himself, yet also, like the Son again, truly divine. Through the action of His Word God is eternally the creative source of a limited number of free minds or spirits. These spirits do not stand in the same direct relation with God as the Son, yet they may be spoken of as θεοί 'gods'. The visible world is the consequence of a fall of certain of these dependent spirits who misused their freedom and fell away from fellowship with God, the author of their being. God created the world in order to provide a means whereby fallen spirits might through a long process of education and purification eventually be won back into the fellowship which they had forfeited. Even devils and the prince of the devils, who have fallen deeper than man, may one day share in the redemption. The agent in this process of redemptive education, as in creation, is the Divine Word. The supreme revelation of the Divine Word was through the Incarnation in Jesus Christ.

In his doctrine of the Incarnation, as in other respects, Origen was a pioneer and anticipated the guiding thoughts of later doctrinal development, though here, too, his positions were not taken over in their entirety. Origen guards carefully against

[1] See Origen, *In Evang. Joannis*, ii. 2, 3 (ed. A. E. Brooke, vol. i, pp. 58 ff.).

the crude idea that the Eternal Word could come into direct association with a human body. He insists that the Word required the mediation of a human soul in order to be incarnate in a human body, nor is the incarnation to be understood as though it imposed limitation upon the Word. Albeit uniquely associated with the human soul and body of Jesus, the Word remains in full possession of His divine character and functions. A main difference of Origen's view from what became the orthodox doctrine of Christ's person arises from his view that all human souls, including the human soul of Jesus, pre-existed. But whereas other human souls had in their pre-existent state fallen from God, the soul of Jesus Christ had remained in full union with God and the Word. This sinless human soul it was which came forth from God and assumed from Mary a human body, maintaining through all the sufferings and temptations which befell him upon earth unbroken unity with the Eternal Word.[1] By the resurrection and the ascension into heaven Christ's earthly body was, with his human soul, completely divinized, with the consequence that a way was thereby opened for all believers to share once more in the fellowship of God which had once been theirs.

Origen's system leaves no place for the older conceptions of a visible return of Christ to earth and of the establishment of the Kingdom from the New Jerusalem. These conceptions had been the prevailing belief in the second Christian century and they were long to continue to be the prevailing belief in the West; but for Origen the 'second coming' becomes another way of stating the transition from the temporal to the eternal. Even the Gospel of Jesus Christ as we know it is temporal, 'being preached in a world and an age that are destined to pass away', and it will yield place to the 'eternal Gospel'; as the Old Testament Law was but 'a shadow of the good things to come' in Christ,

[1] *De Principiis*, ii. cvi. 3 (Engl. trans., G. W. Butterworth, pp. 110 ff.); *In Evang. Joan.* xx. 19.

so even the first coming of Christ was a shadow to be fulfilled by the glory of 'the second coming'. Origen further entertained the speculation that the passion of Jesus Christ is destined to be repeated in other ages and in other worlds. This was one of the speculations which were to cause offence in after days. 'If there are "spiritual hosts of wickedness",' he wrote, 'in the heavenly places, consider whether, just as we are not ashamed to confess that he was crucified here in order to destroy those whom he destroyed through his suffering, so we should not fear to allow that a similar event also happens there and will happen in the ages to come until the end of the whole world.'[1]

Such were the leading features of the audacious and comprehensive scheme of doctrine which Origen discovered in the Scriptures. Not without cause did St. Jerome in his younger days speak of Origen as the greatest teacher of the Church since the Apostles.

It is no accident that this great role in Christian history fell to a native of Alexandria with a half-Egyptian name.[2] In the work of Origen religious forces which had been long at work in the Egyptian capital reached their widest extent and their maturest expression. To appreciate Origen's position we must look backward, first at the earlier history of Christianity in Alexandria and then, behind that, at Alexandrine Judaism.

It is a very remarkable circumstance that Egypt played so little part in the first expansion of Christianity. Antioch, not Alexandria, was the channel by which the new faith penetrated the Graeco-Roman world. In the Acts of the Apostles we hear of Egyptian Jews at Pentecost; we hear also in connexion with the controversy which resulted in the death of the first martyr Stephen (Acts vi) of a synagogue at Jerusalem which included Alexandrines. Otherwise there is but one reference to

[1] Fragment from the *De Principiis* preserved in Greek by Justinian, *Ep. ad Mennam.* See G. W. Butterworth, op. cit., p. 310.

[2] The first half of the name is that of the Egyptian god Horus.

Alexandria in the whole book and that is tantalizingly vague. From Acts xviii. 24 we learn that the Apollos who 'watered' what Paul had 'planted' in Corinth was an Alexandrian by birth. Was it in Alexandria that he had learned that imperfect version of the faith which Priscilla and Aquila taught him to amend? An editorial addition in the inferior 'Western' text of Acts states categorically that this was so. The text of the best manuscripts, however, has nothing to tell us on this point one way or the other. The only other reference to contemporary Egypt in the New Testament is the story at the beginning of St. Matthew's Gospel which records the flight of the Holy Family into Egypt. It is a story which appears merely to authenticate a prophecy and it is not represented as having historical consequences.

Later Church tradition, represented by Eusebius, recorded that the evangelist St. Mark was the founder of the Alexandrine Church, and this came to be generally accepted; but the tradition is unknown to Clement and to Origen, and so late as the second half of the third century Dionysius, Bishop of Alexandria, can record the history of John Mark without a hint that he had been concerned, or that he was believed to have been concerned, in the foundation of his see.[1] Now it is recorded of Mark by Papias and by other Church writers who followed him that he was the interpreter of Peter, and it may be that the tradition of Mark's connexion with Alexandria reflects the close association which existed in later times between the Church of Alexandria and the Church of Rome. Whatever value the tradition may have in other respects, it cannot be trusted as a guide to the origins of Alexandrine Christianity. What the real origins were is quite obscure.

Various early Christian writings have been ascribed to Alexandria or Egypt—the Epistle to the Hebrews, the Epistle of Barnabas, the so-called second Epistle of Clement of Rome, the

[1] Eus. *H.E.* vii. 25.

Didache. But, though an Egyptian origin for at least the Epistle of Barnabas seems very probable, in no case is the evidence at all decisive. Continuous and dependable history begins with Clement of Alexandria and Bishop Demetrius.

Yet something we do know concerning Christianity in Egypt in the first half of the second century, and our knowledge has recently been enlarged in a very interesting fashion. We actually possess a papyrus fragment of St. John's Gospel recovered from Egypt, which is assigned on palaeographical grounds to some date earlier than A.D. 150.[1] Thus we may feel certain that there were Christians in Egypt and that they read St. John's Gospel at a fairly early date in the century. This conclusion is confirmed by the even more interesting discovery of fragments, likewise early in date, of a Gospel writing hitherto quite unknown, which is almost certainly in part dependent on St. John. It is thought probable that the actual manuscript was copied about the middle of the second century, and the text itself has been tentatively ascribed to the first quarter of the second century.[2] These fragments include versions of other incidents—the healing of a leper, a question concerning payment of tribute—which though clearly related to narratives in the Synoptic Gospels are yet sufficiently different to leave it uncertain whether the unknown author depends upon the Canonical texts or, as is perhaps more probable, upon some parallel source. We know from other information that apocryphal Gospels were current in Egypt at an early period. Such were the Gospel according to the Egyptians referred to by Origen and on occasion quoted by Clement, and the Gospel according to Matthias. But there is no convincing reason for supposing that these new fragments come from any particular Gospel which is otherwise known to us.

[1] C. H. Roberts, *An unpublished Fragment of the Fourth Gospel*, Manchester University Press, 1935.

[2] H. I. Bell, *Recent Discoveries of Biblical Papyri*, Oxford, 1937, p. 20.

These scattered items of evidence—important though they are—scarcely do more than whet our curiosity. But we have other information about early Christianity in Egypt which serves to link it up with the most important currents of thought in second-century Christianity. The Gnostic teachers, Basilides and his greater successor Valentinus, both taught in Alexandria in the reign of Hadrian (117–38). Basilides, though he travelled outside Egypt, seems to have spent the greater part of his time in Alexandria and the Delta. Valentinus started his career as a teacher at Alexandria, but was later (*c.* A.D. 136) drawn to Rome, where indeed we are told that he entertained the hope of succeeding to the episcopal see.[1] These are the first definite names that we can link up with Egyptian Church History. How far they were representative of Egyptian Christianity and whether they secured ascendancy in the Church are questions which we cannot answer. It has been suggested that the meagreness of our information about early Christianity in Egypt is to be explained by the peculiar character of Alexandrine teaching; that Gnostic influences were so far dominant in the earlier part of the second century, that when later on the Canonical New Testament and the Church's rule of faith came to win acceptance, the earlier chapters in the Church's history were intentionally forgotten. Whether this was really so, or whether at Alexandria as elsewhere there was a nucleus of popular traditional faith which maintained itself alongside the Gnostic coteries we know too little to be able to say. In any case, there can be no doubt that both Basilides and Valentinus themselves, though they were affected by ideas which were widespread outside the Christian tradition with regard to the divine origin of the soul and the need for its redemption from the material

---

[1] Tert. *Adv. Valent.* 4. But the story is suspected. See E. Preusschen in Hauck-Hertzog, *R.E.* xx, pp. 396 f. According to Irenaeus, iii. 4. 3 (Greek text in Eus. *H.E.* iv. 11. 1) Valentinus came to Rome under Hyginus and lived on there till the episcopate of Anicetus, i.e. *c.* A.D. 136–165.

world, yet started from a Christian base and that from the beginning to the end they assigned a fundamental and central place to the person of Jesus Christ. They were heretics, but they were emphatically Christian heretics.

The writings of the early Church Fathers Irenaeus, Tertullian, Clement, Origen leave us in no doubt as to the widespread influence of the teaching of Valentinus and his disciples throughout the Church. His doctrine is known to us directly from a small number of fragmentary quotations and indirectly, but in a more complete form, from the full accounts of his ecclesiastical antagonists, especially Irenaeus. Briefly it may be said that Valentinus interpreted the world of ordinary human experience as the consequence of a Fall. *Sophia*, Wisdom, the youngest of the thirty Aeons who constitute the Pleroma or totality of spiritual existence, conceived a passion for direct knowledge of the Supreme Father—a knowledge reserved for *Noûs* Mind, *Noûs* being one of the pair of Aeons which issued directly from the primal pair. Though *Sophia* herself was induced by *Horos* (*"Opos*), 'Bound' or 'limitation', to abandon her design, that design itself when banished from her mind achieved a quasi-personal existence of its own and somehow imparted the principle of life to matter. Thus it came about that in man there resides a spiritual seed. To redeem this spiritual seed and to withdraw it from its material environment to its spiritual home, the Christ came down in a body of spirit to visit mankind. Now the Christ exercises a kind of redemptive function even within the Pleroma, for He is one of a final pair of Aeons who had come into being to prevent any further disorder in the Pleroma such as the initial passion of *Sophia* had originated. This same Christ visits the human race, which, as we have seen, has issued from *Sophia's* illicit thought, and recovers from out of it such as are capable of salvation.

The Gnostic systems, so difficult for us to appreciate, exercised an intense attractive power upon many minds, and they were in part responsible for important developments in the Christian Church. First and foremost they called forth a systematic appeal to apostolic tradition. The Gnostics themselves claimed to be the recipients of traditions going back to the Apostles. This was a claim which the body of the Church could not ignore. The answer of responsible Church teachers, such as Irenaeus of Lyons, was an appeal to apostolic tradition *publicly* attested by apostolic scriptures and guaranteed by the teaching continuously maintained by a succession of bishops in Apostolic Sees. Thus the Gnostic movement in general, and particularly the great Alexandrine Gnostics Basilides and Valentinus contributed, by the reaction which they provoked, to the development of the early Catholic Church.

But the influence of Gnosticism was not merely negative. Positively the Gnostic teachers pointed the way which the Church was afterwards to follow. Gnosticism produced the first Christian exegetes. The commentary of Basilides on the Gospel is the first work of its kind which is known to have existed. The commentary of the Valentinian Heracleon upon St. John's Gospel was well known to Origen, and if he more often expresses dissent than agreement in discussing Heracleon's exegesis, at least he treats it with respect. Furthermore, the Gnostics were the first to attempt a systematic exposition of the Christian teaching in terms of a religious philosophy derived in part at least from Greek sources.

Now Origen was essentially different from the Gnostic heresiarchs of the second century. He was, as we have seen, a Church theologian who accepted the rule of faith and the Scriptures not only of the New Testament but also—differing in this from the chief Gnostic teachers—of the Old Testament as well. Yet it is plain enough that Origen's system was no mere inference from the Scriptures; it embodied fundamental Biblical ideas, but it was derived from other sources as well as the Bible itself. It is not an accident that Origen worked out his theology in the land where Basilides and Valentinus had laboured two generations before. When Origen brought over his friend the Valentinian Ambrosius to the Church, Ambrosius will have unlearnt much and he will have adopted a new attitude towards the world-wide fellowship of Christians, but his mind will not have been wholly unprepared for the scheme of Origenistic doctrine with its pre-cosmic fall and its redemption.

It now remains to mention another antecedent of the Christian Platonism of Alexandria, even more important than the Christian Gnostics. Alexandria was the metropolis of Greek-speaking Judaism. It is probable that from the first foundation of the city Jews had formed an important element in the population. According to Josephus, Alexander the Great had himself assigned to the Jews one of the five city-quarters as their own possession.[1] At a later date the Jews held two quarters and overflowed into the other parts of the city as well.[2] It was in Alexandria that the great Greek Version of the Jewish Scriptures was made to meet the needs of Greek-speaking Jews. This epoch-making work was carried out in stages, the oldest part of the translation, that of the Law, dating back to the first half of the third century before Christ. The language is for the most part quite obviously translation Greek, but it varies considerably in literary quality, the Book of Job for instance reaching a higher standard than most of the rest. The work was carried out by and for men who used Greek for practical purposes and the language shows scarcely any tincture of philosophical culture. Philosophical terms, however, make their appearance in later books composed in the Greek language such as the Book of Wisdom and the Fourth Book of the Maccabees.

A large and influential Jewry speaking the Greek language and possessing an authoritative version of the Bible in its adopted tongue opened the way for further developments. Of the utmost importance for the later growth of Alexandrine Christian

---

[1] Josephus, *c. Apion*, II. c. iv.　　　[2] Philo, *In Flaccum*, 55.

Platonism was the work of the Jew Philo, an older contemporary of Jesus of Nazareth and of St. Paul. His voluminous works are for the most part exegetical tractates on the Pentateuch in which Greek Stoicism and Platonism are read into the sacred text by means of Allegorism. We know but little concerning the relations of this Alexandrine Jewry and the Church in the first two centuries. The influence of the Jewish community in Alexandria declined after the disastrous risings in Cyrene and Egypt in the reign of Trajan, and about the same time Judaism throughout the Empire was changing its character and yielding to the exclusive dominance of the Hebrew Scriptures and ortho- dox Rabbinism. It seems not unlikely that with the Septuagint Version of the Bible a not inconsiderable number of Hellenistic Jews may have drifted into the Church.

What is certain is the importance of Philo's writings and particularly of Philo's method for the development of Alex- andrine Theology. It is probable that Philo's works were not unknown to the author of the Epistle to the Hebrews—possibly also to the Fourth Evangelist. But in the New Testament direct dependence upon Philo is very rarely demonstrable. When we come on to the writings of the second-century Greek Apologists there are many parallels with Philo, but again there is probably little, if any, literary dependence. With Clement and Origen it is otherwise. From this time onwards Philo Judaeus, neglected and disowned by the adherents of his own faith, becomes a factor in the development of that Alexandrine theology which was the chief legacy of Greek-speaking Egypt to the Christian Church.

J. M. Creed

II. THE COPTIC CHURCH AND EGYPTIAN MONASTICISM

Monasticism in its various forms plays a leading part in the history of the Christian Church from the third century to the present time. The cloister was the home of culture in the darkest periods; from it proceeded many of the most diligent missionaries of the Christian faith, and amongst its inmates was developed that inner spiritual life of mysticism which has so profoundly influenced religious experience. The whole of this powerful movement, in all its diversified activities, traces back to one place, the Nile valley, as its cradle, and in giving birth to monasticism Egypt laid an indelible mark on the Christian Church whose traces can be discerned even in those professedly little in sympathy with monastic ideals.

The formation and development of monasticism did not take place in Alexandria, which was Greek-speaking and participated in Greek culture, but amongst the native Coptic-speaking Christians of Egypt, which strictly denotes the Delta, and Thebais or Upper Egypt, the whole area watered by the Nile between Aswân and the Mediterranean coast.

The formation of monasticism took place in two stages: first came the solitaries, some, but by no means all, of whom were hermits or 'desert men'; then came the formation of coenobia or monastic communities, at first simply groups of disciples gathered round some well-known and revered teacher. It was generally held that the first who went out into the desert to live the ascetic life in solitude was Paul of Thebes, and the first to form a coenobium by gathering a band of disciples round him was St. Antony. But Paul was not the first to live apart in the practice of asceticism, he simply was the first to retire to the solitude of the desert to do so. In many Egyptian villages where there were Christian congregations there were some devout persons who lived apart and devoted themselves to religious

exercises, usually in a hut or cave near by, and members of the
local congregation went out from time to time and supplied
them with food. Quite how this ascetic life began is obscure.
Some trace it to the *katoikoi* who lived in sanctuary in the
precincts of certain Egyptian temples, but these seem to have
been mostly fugitives from justice who went to the temple for
sanctuary. Eusebius takes a description of the *Therapeutae* from
Philo and seems to suppose that these were devout ascetes who
formed a link between the Old Testament 'Schools of the
Prophets' and Christian monasteries. But Philo seems to be
describing an imaginary Utopia which cannot seriously be
connected with Christian monasticism. One thing certainly
favoured this living apart: wherever there were ancient tombs,
in Egypt very numerous, there were lodgings provided for the
priests who offered sacrifice and recited liturgies for the souls
of the deceased, and many of these standing vacant offered a
convenient refuge for those who wished to dwell apart and
devote themselves to prayer.

In the days of Decius's persecution (A.D. 250) many fled to the
desert for safety, as is described by Dionysius, who was at the
time Bishop of Alexandria,[1] and when persecution was over
most of these returned home again, but some remained in the
'inner' or remoter desert, and of these was Paul.

St. Jerome wrote a life of Paul of Thebes, but it is legendary.
His life of St. Antony is altogether different and gives a biography
which must be taken seriously. Antony was an historical character who died in 356 and was known personally to St. Athanasius
and Serapion of Thmui. He recognized his call to the solitary
life when he heard Matt. xix. 21 read in church in Coptic,
for he knew no Greek, and in 270 left his home and became a
hermit, at first near his native village, then in the inner desert.
About 285 he crossed the Nile and settled in a deserted fort at
Pispir, where he stayed some twenty years. But his solitude was

[1] Cited Eusebius, *H.E.* vi. 42.

invaded by multitudes who desired him to be their spiritual guide and at length, in 305, he consented and formed a community at Pispir, himself retiring farther into the desert and occupying a cave in the face of a cliff. From time to time he visited his community and gave instructions, and has left a written rule containing precepts for their guidance. This rule, composed in Coptic, was translated into Greek by St. Athanasius. It seems to date from about 310. In 311, during Maximin's persecution, he went down to Alexandria to encourage those imprisoned for the faith, and as an aged man in 338 again visited Alexandria to support Athanasius in his controversy with the Arians. His cave is still shown. Near the base of the cliff is the monastery of Mar Antuni, which claims to be the oldest monastery in Egypt. But towards the end of the fifteenth century the Arab serfs who served the monastery and the neighbouring monastery of Abu Bolos (Father Paul) rose up and massacred the monks, and the monasteries lay desolate until they were re-colonized in comparatively modern times, so there has not been continuous occupation.

The coenobitic or community life of ascetes was inaugurated by St. Antony, but its full organization was the work of St. Pakhom (d. *c.* 349). He differed from St. Antony in making his monks an organized society under strict discipline, all engaged in the practice of various crafts whereby they earned their livelihood. At first Pakhom was a member of a community of ascetes directed by an aged hermit named Palaemon, but he left it in 305 and founded a separate community at Tabennesi, a ruined village near Akhmîm. At Palaemon's death most of his disciples joined the new community at Tabennesi. As numbers increased Pakhom removed to Pabau, a little to the north, and there founded a second house which became the head-quarters of what very much resembled a monastic order, a confederation of monasteries, all observing the same rule and under one central control. The organization was on semi-military lines—the

Roman Army was the one great model of efficient organization then in sight: the community was divided into various 'houses', each practising one trade and each under a prior, the whole assembling for Vespers and the Night Office. It was left to a monk's choice whether he shared in the communal meals or drew rations of bread and salt to eat in his own cell. Every August, at the Coptic New Year, the community assembled and elected officers for the ensuing year. When necessary the monks went out to work in the fields with the peasants of the neighbourhood and food was sent out to them from the monastery. Pakhom's rule had a wider influence than over the monasteries associated with what might be called his order, and many other monasteries adopted portions of his rule or imitated his system without following the whole of his discipline. St. Athanasius visited the monastery at Tabennesi and was warmly welcomed as a defender of the faith. Pakhom's influence lay chiefly in Upper Egypt, but branch houses existed as far away as the Delta.

Monastic history generally is a record of successive reforms and relaxations, very much as is the history of the Church at large. After Pakhom came a reformer in the person of Shenoute, who died probably about 451. Nephew of the abbot of Atripe near Akhmîm, he was trained in his uncle's monastery and succeeded him as abbot. In his day he enjoyed fame as a vigorous administrator and drastic reformer of the existing monasteries and convents. But his influence was confined to the Coptic community and his name was hardly known to the Greek-speaking clergy of Alexandria. Thus Shenoute's name never appears in Western calendars, though they mention Paul of Thebes, Antony, and Pakhom. Still he, as one of the leading Egyptian abbots, attended the Council of Ephesus in 431. His reforming activities were chiefly connected with the two great monasteries known as 'the White Monastery' (*Deir el-Abyaḍ*) on the rising ground west of Sohag, and the 'Red Monastery'

(*Deir-el-Aḥmar*) some three or four miles north-west. The former
of these has been occupied by villagers who find its fortress-like
structure a welcome security, though the presence of whole
families has led some hasty tourists to propagate absurd stories
of married monks. A more interesting thing about Shenoute is
that he was a great writer of letters and sermons, and fortunately
many of these survive, so that we can form a fair picture of monasticism in fifth-century Thebais. The monks under his rule
were native Egyptians, not Alexandrians, Egyptian fellahin like
those we see working in the fields to-day: sturdy, indefatigable
toilers who worked all the better for a stick laid about their backs,
a form of discipline to which they had been accustomed from
the days of the Pharaohs, and Shenoute did not spare the rod.
Simple-minded, rather child-like, they had a taste for practical
jokes and horse-play, a weakness which caused Shenoute much
annoyance. Shenoute must have been rather a trying superior,
as he seems to have had a hasty temper, and had no hesitation
in laying violent hands on a civil magistrate who came to inquire
about a monk who had unfortunately died from the effects of
disciplinary correction. No doubt it was difficult to keep the
monastery in order and to prevent noise, chiefly because of the
troops of children about, the *oblates*, foundlings or children of
poor parents who were sent to the abbot to be adopted into the
monastic community. Shenoute's many letters and discourses
were written in the Coptic dialect of Akhmîm and his fame as
a writer caused this to become the literary idiom of the Coptic
Church for many centuries: whatever dialect a man spoke, he
copied the speech and phrasing of Shenoute when he took pen
in hand.

No reliable account exists of the numbers of monks and hermits scattered over Thebais, but there must have been many
thousands, taking the evidence of the numerous remains of
monasteries over the country. Hardly a single ruin of an ancient
temple exists without remains of some Christian monastery built

into its edifice, and many of the larger tombs give similar proofs
of occupation. In certain districts there were whole colonies of
monasteries of men and women: such was the case about Armant,
Jeme near Thebes, the vicinity of Akhmîm, round about Siut,
and in the Faiyûm. Most of these are now deserted and ruinous,
but there are a few still in use, such as Deir Rîfa on the rising
ground some eight miles south-west of Asyût (Siut).

Meanwhile a separate monastic development had been taking
place in Lower Egypt, a development of the simpler Antonian
rather than the regimented Pakhomian. A pious man named
Amun went out to the edge of the Western Desert and settled
in Mount Pernuj close by the place where merchants came
periodically to get natron. Amun left his wife at her suggestion
as she urged him to join one of the colonies of ascetes settled
along the edge of the desert, so there were monks already settled
about there. Amun is said to have died before Antony, therefore before 356. But Mount Pernuj turned out to be not very
suitable because of the throngs of natron merchants who came
there, so Amun moved farther into the desert to Niri, Nimone,
or Kellia, 'the cells', where he built two domed cells and lived
twenty-two years. To this settlement came Macarius the Great,
possibly about 300, having already had experience as a village
recluse: at first he settled at Pernuj, then moved right into the
desert to a site afterwards known as Shiet or Scetis. The date
of this move is not given, but a community existed at Shiet in
340, and by 356 it was inconveniently crowded. Gradually
other monasteries were established near by. The whole district
was commonly known as Nitria, now Wâdi el-Natrûn 'the
Valley of Natron', where a group of monasteries, Deir Abu
Maqar 'the monastery of Father Macarius', and others still exist
and continue on the old lines. The teaching and spiritual tone
of these Nitrian monks can still be studied in the collected sayings of the fathers, the *Apophthegmata* written in the Saidic
dialect which Shenoute brought into fashion. Shiet stood well

away in the desert, but Pernuj was connected by road with Alexandria, so the Nitrian monks were in touch with Alexandria, where they went to sell the baskets they made, and St. Athanasius in the days of his trouble found a refuge amongst them and was still able to control Church affairs in Alexandria. In Nitria there were some Greeks of Alexandria who went out to adopt the monastic life, but they seem to have kept apart, not quite in accord with their Coptic neighbours.

Shiet and its vicinity, the modern Wâdi el-Naṭrûn, lay within the Western Desert and so was exposed to raids by the Berber tribesmen who repeatedly destroyed buildings and slew their inmates. Such raids took place in 407, 434, 444, 570, and 817. After each attack some scattered monks who had managed to escape came together and revived the monastic life. Gradually they learned that it was necessary to fortify the monasteries and provide a strong tower for refuge. Some of the monasteries have disappeared, but several survive and still continue on the old lines: the daily services duly recited, not in church, which is used only for the Eucharist, but the monks standing round in the open, no such luxuries as choir stalls, at most a crutch allowed for the use of the aged and infirm.

The monastic life of Egypt became famous throughout the whole Christian Church, and for a long time Egypt was regarded as the 'Holy Land' in preference to Palestine, because there could be seen the multitudes of saintly ascetes, and Christians came as pilgrims from all parts to see and hear them. Amongst these were St. Basil the Great, the founder of Greek monasticism, Hilarion, who introduced monasticism into Palestine, Rufinus and a Roman lady named Melania who spent six months in Egypt in 373. Then in 386 St. Jerome and a wealthy widow named Paula visited the monasteries of Egypt, and of this visit St. Jerome has left us an account (*Epistle* 108). Palladius, Bishop of Helenopolis, spent the years 388–99 and 406–12 amongst the monks of Egypt, the former period in

Thebais, the latter in Nitria: he would have joined their number, but found the discipline too severe for his health and age: he has left us an account of his visits and of the ascetes he met in the *Historia Lausiaca*, but seems to have kept to the monasteries where there were monks able to speak Greek, and so missed a meeting with Shenoute. St. John Cassian was in Egypt between 390 and 400, but he did not go so far as Thebais. On what he saw and heard he compiled two books, the *Institutes* and the *Collations*, published between 420 and 430. These became the classics of monasticism and held up before monks of every land the examples of the Egyptian ascetes as the model to be copied. All through the Middle Ages they were read aloud in Benedictine monasteries throughout western Europe, and still are so read. Thus there grew up a body of literature dealing with the monks of Egypt which exercised a great influence over all who adopted the monastic life. St. Benedict in his *Rule* reproaches the negligence and lack of fervour of those monks who recite less than the whole Psalter in the week, 'when we read that our holy Fathers courageously performed in one day what I would that we who are tepid may do in a week' (Benedict: *Regula*, 18): the reference is to Cassian's account of the desert fathers, not the Fathers of the Church. Reference to this passage appears in the prefatory matter prefixed to the Anglican *Book of Common Prayer*, where the 'ancient Fathers' who divided the Psalms into seven nocturns for weekly reading are held up as a model of devotion. The author is quoting John Cassian from memory, or via St. Benedict, but omits to specify that the 'ancient Fathers' he holds up for imitation were the early monks of Nitria.

In due course monasticism spread abroad and was copied in other lands; indeed one of the most striking features in its history is the rapidity with which it developed and then spread. As the movement passed westward along the Mediterranean various settlements were founded in some of the islands, the most secluded places available where there were no deserts. One of these was founded about 400 at Lerins (St. Honorat) and became a great centre of monastic activity, sending out missionaries and founding monastic colonies in other lands. There, it is said, the young Patrick was trained and, if this be so, it would help to explain the presence of several Egyptian details in the Celtic Church of Ireland, for the monastery of Lerins was organized and conducted on Egyptian models. Thus it came about that the Irish Church was monastic rather than diocesan. There were a few diocesan bishops, but the ruling dignitaries of the Celtic Church in Ireland were abbots who kept a bishop in their monastery ready for use at ordinations and consecrations, but otherwise living as an ordinary monk. The old Celtic monasteries of Ireland did not resemble the medieval abbeys of England: like the Egyptian coenobia they were simply villages where the huts of the ascetes were gathered round a modest oratory used for the week-end Eucharist. There were no deserts in Ireland, but it was the fashion to call the place where a monastery stood a desert, and so we find the term 'Disert' or 'Desert' in many Irish place-names, as Disertmartin, Disert in Westmeath, Killadysert in Clare, and many others. All this kind of thing was so utterly strange to the English invaders under Henry II that it received no toleration and the Celtic Church of the far west had to undergo a drastic reconstruction.

In spite of its remoteness the Celtic Church of Ireland retained direct contact with the monasteries of Egypt. In the Bibliothèque Nationale in Paris there is still preserved a guidebook for the use of Irish monks travelling to Egypt in order to visit the Fathers of the desert. As late as 1320 Simon FitzSimon and Hugh, Franciscans of Dublin, made the pilgrimage to Egypt and left us a record of their journey.

In some parts monasticism did not receive an enthusiastic welcome, and amongst these was Rome. The Romans were intensely conservative and resented innovation because it was innovation. St. Athanasius brought some Egyptian monks with him when he visited Rome, but they were regarded with strong dislike as specimens of oriental fanatics. The first Roman monastery was established by Sixtus III (432–40), who gave some monks care of the cemetery *ad Catacumbas* on the Appian Way; then his successor Leo (440–61) attached a monastery to the basilica of St. Peter, no doubt for the daily performance of the offices, presumably not to take over the pastoral duties for which the parochial clergy were already appointed.

The association of ascetes with great basilicas where they acted as a kind of cathedral choir was a departure from the older monasticism: the Spanish lady Silvia found it already established in Jerusalem when she visited that city in 385–8. According to the older Egyptian practice the monks recited some of the daily services privately, others in community, but only amongst themselves; there was no provision for a lay congregation. Every Saturday and Sunday they assembled in church for the celebration of the Eucharist, and of course a priest had to celebrate. If the priest were a member of the community, still, as a monk he held no specially favoured position: it was by no means a matter of course that the abbot or prior was a priest. The original coenobium was a lay institution which at most maintained a priest for occasional use. In a sense, therefore, the monastic movement was non-ecclesiastical, it stood apart from the official hierarchy; if a priest wanted to enter a monastery he had to do so like the humblest neophyte and had to go through his training step by step like any other: no special favour was shown him because he was a priest. Bearing this in mind, it is obvious that a group of ascetes attached to a great basilica was rather a departure from primitive monasticism. But these basilican monks gave to the Church: they introduced into the general life of the community the daily services of Matins, Vespers, Compline, &c., services purely monastic in origin and, because monastic, needing the presence of no priest. Such services, based on the regular recitation of the Psalter, which now figure so largely in Christian worship, were purely monastic in origin and trace back to the ascetes of the Egyptian deserts.

So far we have seen monasticism growing and prospering, but it also had to pass through its troubles. In the days of St. Athanasius the monks were the patriarch's loyal supporters against Arius. Perhaps in those and later disputes the Nitrian monks were rather inclined to violence and civic disturbance: certainly the civic authorities in Alexandria sometimes found them a trouble. When Theodosius ordered the closing of pagan temples but forbade their destruction, groups of monks in Lower Egypt led mobs to wreck the buildings and destroy the images in the temples, and many of the temples in Lower Egypt show traces of almost incredible force used in breaking into pieces immense monoliths of granite. Then came the great schism of the Church following the Council of Chalcedon in 451. The Byzantine Church and a majority of the Syrian Church accepted the decisions of that council, the Egyptian Church and a strong minority of the Syrian refused to do so, and thus arose a bitter strife between the State Church, armed with all the resources of the law, and the recalcitrant Egyptian Church. Egyptian patriarchs were removed and replaced by obedient Greek clergy, but these were rejected, sometimes murdered, by the Egyptians. This state of affairs lasted from 451 to 641, when the Muslim Arabs were welcomed as deliverers to set Christian Egypt free from Greek persecution. In 551 Byzantine oppression was very sorely felt and the Patriarch of Alexandria left his episcopal city and settled amongst the monks in the Wâdi el-Naṭrûn, which forthwith became the seat of government for the Egyptian Church. There the consecrations of bishops and the consecration of the Holy Chrism took place, and there the Coptic liturgy was shaped and took its final form.

As in all such cases imperial persecution was not always maintained with equal severity. The Emperor Justinian (527–65) was a defender of the Byzantine Church, as he had to be, but his wife Theodora was a supporter of the schismatic Church, perhaps an intentional arrangement, and under his protection the unreconciled Egyptians fared not so ill. Encouraged by her the Egyptian Church sent down missionaries to Ethiopia, and so the Ethiopian Church was founded as an offshoot of the Egyptian. Its head, the *Abuna*, is always a Coptic monk consecrated in Egypt and sent to rule in Ethiopia: some of these dignitaries have learned the Ethiopian language, others have not considered it at all necessary. We hear also of missions in Arabia and a flourishing Arabian Church: that has now totally disappeared, but Christian monks and clergy were well known in the Arabia of Muhammad and have laid their mark on the Qur'ân and early Arabic poetry. The Churches of Nubia and Sinai were not akin to the Coptic but purely Greek.

In 641 came the Muslim conquest, the enterprise of an ambitious chieftain 'Amr ibn al-'Âs, in the face of the khalif's opposition. The country fell to the invaders chiefly because the Byzantine government did not support its representatives and the Christian population generally regarded the Arabs as deliverers. After conquering the country the Arabs removed the seat of government from Alexandria to a camp-city called Fustât which they built at the apex of the Nile Delta, the strategical key to the land of Egypt. The secular government had moved to Fustât, the patriarch to the Wâdi el-Natrûn, and not long after the Muslim conquest the famous School of Alexandria, which had by then become exclusively a medical school, came to an end, so Alexandria was left entirely to the pursuit of commerce.

The Muslims allowed the Christians to follow their own religion on condition that they paid regular tribute; they were left to govern themselves and, as the Byzantine officials were withdrawn, the clergy were entrusted with the leadership. All police duty, repair of bridges and roads, and such-like things were left to the Copts to do or neglect as they would, at least in Christian villages, and the Christian population must have been well over 90 per cent.; indeed Egypt ranked as a Christian country for some centuries, although garrisoned by a Muslim army of occupation. Christians were forbidden to serve in the army, a prohibition that they liked very much for conscription was, and still is, their sorest grievance. Christian Copts remained in control of the civil service, all government offices were run by Christians who acted as tax collectors, accountants, &c., and still do so. They were disliked by the Muslim population because they were believed to feather their own nests. In fact they were capable business men, the Muslim Arabs were not. The Arab conquerors made one great mistake in supposing that Egypt was a land of almost unlimited wealth and so 'milked it like a cow'. The hardships and 'persecutions' endured by the Christians under Muslim rule were mostly due to financial exactions by their rulers.

Thus matters continued under the 'Umayyad khalifs of Damascus and their successors the 'Abbâsid khalifs of Bagdad. Egypt was simply a province ruled by governors and generally ill-governed. During that period the old Coptic language had been largely replaced by Arabic, and the native Christian litera-ture relating the martyrdoms of those who suffered under Diocletian and the lives of the famous hermits were mostly translated into Arabic. The Saidic language of Upper Egypt which Shenoute had brought into fashion seems to have become obsolete about the ninth century. Only in the Wâdi el-Naṭrûn, the monastic settlement around Shiet, did Coptic remain in general use, but there in the dialect known as Bohairic, the language of the shore, because it was spoken in the lowland near the coast. Thus arose a new Coptic literature, much of which shows obvious marks of having been retranslated from the Arabic translations, the proper names in Arabic form, not Coptic. There can be no doubt that with this was associated a nationalist movement amongst the Coptic Christians, which passed unchecked by the Arab rulers.

In 969 a great change took place. Egypt was conquered by the Fâṭimid anti-khalif of Kairawan and so cut off from the life of the main Muslim community under the khalif of Bagdad. For a while the change of rulers brought increased prosperity, and the Christian population suffered no harm: several of these Fâṭimid khalifs made their summer holidays in Christian monasteries, and some of them married Christian wives who were not required to change their religion. These rulers founded a new capital Kahira, our present Cairo, a suburb of Fusṭâṭ entirely devoted to government offices and officials. The old Fusṭâṭ, which lay on the south, fell very largely into the hands of the Copts and so there, in what we now know as 'Old Cairo', are a number of ancient Christian churches and monasteries.

But a great rivalry arose between the Coptic clergy of Cairo and the monastic dignitaries of the Wâdi el-Naṭrûn. At length a compromise was effected: the patriarch went down to the desert monastery for the Easter ceremonies and there each patriarch was consecrated, but part of his time he lived in Cairo, usually in high favour at the Fâṭimid court. Finally he was settled in Cairo altogether, but still retained the title 'Patriarch of Alexandria', though the patriarchs had ceased residence in Alexandria since 551.

Then in the days of the later Fâṭimids came the Crusades (1096–1291), the brunt of the attack falling on the Fâṭimids who ruled Palestine as well as Egypt. It was during this struggle that bitter party feelings arose between Muslims and Christians, exasperated when in 1171 the Turkish general Saladin conquered Egypt for his master the khalif of Bagdad. The Turks were fanatics in a way the Arabs never had been and the disasters suffered during the Crusades were not forgotten. The Christians of Egypt continued to be tolerated, but often suffered from outbreaks of popular disfavour, which explains why so many of the older churches in Old Cairo are fortified and have their doorways well concealed. Still, in spite of all, the Coptic Church still remains a living body, faithful to the religion of its fathers.

DE LACY O'LEARY

CHAPTER 13

EGYPT AND THE BYZANTINE EMPIRE

To speak of a legacy of Byzantine Egypt is perhaps to make, save in one respect, a *suggestio falsi*. The exception is in the sphere of religion. The catechetical school of Alexandria had indeed passed its zenith before the Byzantine Age, and though both the founder of the Arian heresy and its chief opponent claimed the city as their home, neither Arius nor Athanasius can be reckoned among the great formative influences of Christian thought. Cyril was statesman rather than thinker; and with Dioscorus and the monophysite schism the Egyptian Church fell out of the main stream of Christian development into an inglorious backwater. The great gift of Egypt to the Middle Ages was monasticism; and throughout the fourth century visitors flocked from the whole Mediterranean world, as formerly and in later days to see the remains of antiquity, so now to admire and converse with those 'athletes of God' whose austerities had caught the temper of the time. But religion, like art (of which, in this period, something might be said), lies outside the sphere of the present chapter. To law and administration such contributions of importance as Egypt had to render to the Roman world had been made before the empire fell to Diocletian, with whom, though Byzantium did not become the capital till the reign of Constantine, the Byzantine Age may be taken to begin. Politically and economically, whatever formative influences may have been germinating elsewhere, the history of Byzantine Egypt is in the main one of decline.

A legacy of a sort there is, however, even here; but it is a legacy rather to the historian than to the historic process. The papyri, of this as of earlier ages, are an unequalled source of information on social and economic conditions and illustrate one of the most momentous changes in the history of mankind.

In 284, when Diocletian became Emperor, we are still in a world Roman, pagan, and 'ancient'; in 642, when the Arabs of 'Amr marched wondering through the marble streets of Alexandria, we are in the Middle Ages, paganism is dead, and a frightened Christendom is facing the confident onset of Islam. The papyri which Egypt has bequeathed to us, fragmentary and incomplete as is their evidence in many important respects, enable us to follow, with a wealth of detail not elsewhere possible, the tremendous mutations of thought and feeling which the change implies; and this one country can, with caution and the necessary reserves, be made to exemplify a process which was taking place all over the Roman world.

It was to remedy existing evils that Diocletian undertook his reforms. The anarchy of the third century, when military chiefs disputed the empire between them, perhaps, too, a conviction that the provincial governors were over-burdened with a multiplicity of duties, suggested the creation of smaller units of government and the separation of civil and military authority. As a consequence of this reorganization Egypt, hitherto an administrative unity, was divided into three provinces, though complete separatism was avoided by giving to the governor of one of them, who bore the title *praefectus Aegypti*, an authority superior to that of the *praesides* who governed the others. All three, however, were purely civil officials; the whole military force of the country was placed under the Duke of Egypt. Successive changes were made later: the boundaries of the provinces were rearranged, their number was increased, and Egypt, made by Diocletian part of the diocese of the Orient, became, in conjunction with Libya, an independent diocese; but the separation of civil and military powers was maintained till the year 538, when Justinian, by his thirteenth edict, gave to all the governors military as well as civil powers and an equal and co-ordinate authority. The disastrous consequences were seen a century later, when the disunion of the provincial governors in face of the Arabs paralysed the defence and conduced to the success of the invaders.

Another administrative change was made not by Diocletian but by his successors. At some time shortly before A.D. 310 the immemorial division of Egypt into nomes, governed, during the Graeco-Roman period, by civil *strategi*, ceased, administratively, to exist, though they continued to figure in the general consciousness as geographical units. The nome, divided into numbered *pagi*, each under a *praepositus*, became simply the territory of the *metropolis*, which in this way at last received full municipal status and was financially responsible for the whole area.

In the period of the Antonines this change of status might have been received with enthusiasm, but the economic decline of Egypt had by this time proceeded so far that little gratification can have been given even to the municipal pride of the citizens by a measure which, in so far as it was more than formal, can only have increased their burdens. All through the third century it had grown steadily more difficult either to secure candidates for the municipal magistracies and liturgical posts or to cover the routine expenses of administration. A raising of rates which the papyri reveal for not a few taxes is perhaps more apparent than real, being designed to bring the payments into juster relation to the diminished value of money, and some taxes seem to have been discontinued. Thus the poll-tax, so important in the first and second centuries, though, strangely enough, it survived the *Constitutio Antoniniana*, played little part in this period, and there is no direct evidence for its collection after the middle of the century. It was, however, to an impost of a different kind, the *annona militaris*, that the government had recourse in its difficulties. Originally an exceptional charge, it now became a regular feature of the financial system, and its irregular incidence and varying amount made it so burdensome that it was probably among the chief causes of the peasant revolts which characterized this century.

In the year 297 Diocletian carried out a sweeping financial reform, simplifying and unifying the whole tax system and making the requisitions for the *annona*, hitherto arbitrary and irregular, a permanent institution. The new method was based on an assessment by fixed units of productivity, called for the land *iuga* (the *iugatio*) and for human beings and live-stock *capita* (the *capitatio*). Each year the estimated requirements were fixed by the annual *indictio*, and each province learned the amount of its quota from the *delegatio*, upon the receipt of which it was the duty of the provincial authorities to raise the required amount by an equitable apportionment among the taxable units. So far as the country districts were concerned (for, payment being at first chiefly in kind owing to the reduced value of money, it was upon the rural areas that Diocletian mainly relied), there was, in essence, but a single basis of taxation; and in fact the bewildering multiplicity of individual taxes so characteristic of the Roman period disappears from the papyri of the Byzantine Age.

Diocletian's intention was, by simplifying the system, to prevent fraud and secure a juster distribution of the burden; but the attempt proved a failure. The rich and powerful possessed opportunities denied to their poorer neighbours of evading part of their responsibilities. The higher officials were drawn from their ranks; the lower were too often accessible to bribery or intimidation. Thus, the better qualified was the taxpayer, by his wealth, to pay his full quota, the easier was it for him to avoid doing so; and under the system of collective responsibility, by which the burden rested ultimately on the community rather than on the individual, this meant that his deficit was made good by others. Faced with utter ruin, the small owner had but one resource: to invoke the protection of a patron, who in return for the surrender of his land undertook the responsibility for his taxes. In this way a free owner became the client, the *colonus adscripticius*, in effect the serf, of a great landlord, paying rent for the holding which had once been his property, and tied to the land he tilled, but at least safe from the exactions of the public tax-gatherers.

It was in vain that the government, all through the fourth century, struggled against the extension of the colonate; the steady pressure of economic forces, the great landowners eager to increase the area of their estates and the number of their clients, the peasants seeing in the new relationship their only means of escape from intolerable conditions, was too strong to be resisted by imperial constitutions. At last, in 415, the government yielded, and a constitution of that year recognized, in Egypt, the rights of patronage acquired before the year 397. Later acquisitions were pronounced illegal and the name of patron was to be abolished. Even this compromise solution was ineffective; the name of patron did not die, and the process of absorption by the larger estates continued. It involved more than the private land. The practice by which landowners were saddled with the duty of cultivating parcels of domain land for which no tenant could be found had become so fully established by the end of the third century that domain and private land were fused, and the former seems to have passed with the latter into the possession of the great landlords.

When, after the ill-documented fifth century, we reach the age of Justinian the change is obvious. Even so late as the early fourth century rural Egypt was still divided for the most part between the domain land of various categories and private land held mostly in small or medium-sized properties. In the sixth we find that the royal and public land has practically disappeared and the characteristic feature of the rural scene is formed by the estates of the great nobles, powerful enough, within certain limits, to defy the imperial authority. These estates were administered by a bureaucracy modelled on that of the empire and to some extent bearing the same titles. Their owners had their own postal services, their fleets of Nile boats, their private armies, their prisons, their banks and counting-houses, their baths, their hierarchy of secretaries and account-ants, stewards, tax-collectors, guards, and police, they founded monasteries and endowed churches. They possessed, too, the right (known as *autopragia*) of paying their taxes not through the local officials but direct to the provincial treasurers, some-times even, like the great Apion family of Oxyrhynchus, to the central authorities at Alexandria. To call these estates feudal is a misnomer, for the tenures were not military, the estates were not held in great self-contained fiefs but were scattered among lands of other ownership, and they never quite broke through the framework of the imperial bureaucratic system; but they can at least be termed semi-feudal, and it is not the least part of the debt we owe to the papyri from Egypt that they enable us to follow, in considerable detail, the process by which, under the pressure of similar forces but in very different conditions, there grew up in the East a state of society in some way resembling Western feudalism, in others diverging from it. In each case the environment determined the phenomenon; and as the feudal fief of the West, with its tenant-in-chief and its sub-tenants, each holding his lands on a military tenure and owing allegiance to his lord, was a replica in little of the feudal State to which it belonged, so the great estate of Byzantine Egypt reproduced in its smaller compass the bureaucratic despotism within which it existed.

The estates of churches and monasteries sometimes enjoyed the same right of *autopragia*; and it was further granted to certain villages of free landowners, perhaps in the unjustified hope of creating some counterpoise to the dangerous power of the nobility. The emperors and their wives also possessed ex-tensive properties, which, however, played a much smaller part in the rural economy of Byzantine Egypt than had the old domain lands in that of the Roman period. The remaining land was held as private property by smaller landowners subject to

the authority of the municipality in whose territory their holdings lay. So much of the nome area was now withdrawn from
municipal control that in the course of the fifth century the
division into numbered *pagi* under *praepositi* was abandoned
and all that was left of the municipal territory was placed under
the control of a single official known as a pagarch (the Greek
equivalent of the *praepositus pagi*). These pagarchs were drawn,
at least in the sixth century, from among the landed nobility.
Hence they were extremely jealous of the autopract villages, and
we hear of attempts by more than one pagarch to extend his
authority over a free community.

And what of the municipalities (the old nome-capitals) themselves? The evidence concerning them is much scantier in the
later Byzantine period than in the third and fourth centuries.
This is hardly an accident. All the indications point to a constant decline in their dignity and importance. The burden
placed upon them by their municipal status was too great for
the resources of an urban class already exhausted by the crisis
of the third century, and it was no doubt increased by the with-
drawal from their control of so much of the territory for which
they were responsible; for it is unlikely that the distribution of
the tax quotas between city and autopract estate was to the
advantage of the former. The land-owning nobles, who were
originally the richer members of the town council, lived, not
like their feudal counterparts of the West in castles on their
estates, but in palaces within the city itself, and as their power
grew the city tended more and more to fall under their control.
The history of the office of *defensor* is highly significant of the
evolution. Originally appointed to protect the interests of the
humbler against the more powerful members of the community, of the *humiliores* against the *potentiores*, the *defensor*
developed into the chief municipal magistrate; but about the
end of the sixth century we find a *defensor* of Cynopolis in a
private letter referring to an agent of the local landowner as

'our common master', and in another papyrus of A.D. 587 a mere tenant of the great Apion family describes himself as a deputy *defensor*.

The decay of civic life was helped and accompanied by other social changes. In the Roman period the *metropoleis*, though not possessing municipal status and containing a very mixed population, were by no means negligible centres of Hellenic culture. The education of the gymnasium, enjoyed by the privileged class, followed, at whatever interval, the old Hellenic ideal, with its twin pillars of athletics and 'music'. The ephebes practised the exercises of the palaestra; and the education of the mind, if the methods employed were by modern standards somewhat crude, was far from ineffective. Egypt, apart from Alexandria, was not, in the Roman period, very productive of literary talent, but finds of papyri show that there was a considerable and active reading public not only for such popular favourites as Euripides, Menander, and Callimachus but for authors as remote from the taste of the age as Aeschylus, Corinna, or the writers of the Old Comedy.

The basis of this urban culture was undermined by the economic decay of the third century, which impoverished the *bourgeoisie*; and it is likely that the grant of full municipal status carried with it new burdens, which still further weakened the middle class. It synchronized with the emergence of a new factor even more inimical to the Hellenic tradition. The ascetic tendency of fourth-century Christianity, with its distrust of the body, was not easily reconcilable with the gymnastic exercises of the palaestra, and absorption in theological controversy weakened the interest in Greek literature. In another way too the new faith threatened Hellenic ideals. It is one of the most striking features of oriental Christianity that it awoke the national feeling of classes and races hitherto drowned by the flood of Hellenism which swept over the East in the wake of Alexander's conquests. In Egypt the native culture, dormant and apparently moribund during the Roman period, awoke to new life. The Egyptian peasant found in Christianity a voice and a consciousness of his own worth which he had almost lost; and the religious fanaticism which in former days had led to rioting over the installation of an Apis bull or fierce feuds between villages of different cults now found expression in quarrels over nice questions of Christian theology or in the murder of a pagan philosopher like Hypatia. The adoption of the Greek script (with the addition of some characters taken from demotic) for the writing of the native language was quickly followed by the translation of the Scriptures into Coptic, the latest form of Egyptian, and soon a whole literature mainly translated from the Greek but containing also original compositions such as hymns, sermons, and lives of the Saints, provided for the Egyptian-speaking classes reading matter more congenial to their taste than the writers of Greek paganism. The true language of the Egyptian (as distinct from the Alexandrian) Church became in fact Coptic rather than Greek.

This nationalist trend was accentuated by theological differences. The almost complete absence from Egypt of Hellenistic city-foundations had given the bishops of Alexandria a preponderant position as against the bishops of the nome-capitals, which until comparatively late had lacked municipal status. The Melitian schism for a time threatened the authority of St. Athanasius, but with the decline of the Melitians, soon after the middle of the fourth century, into an insignificant sect the unity of Egypt was restored, and patriarchs like Cyril or Dioscorus could lead to the councils of the Church a solid phalanx of bishops devoted to their cause. At the Council of Chalcedon (A.D. 451) the monophysite dogma, which Dioscorus defended, was condemned and Dioscorus himself deposed; but the orthodox patriarch appointed in his place was murdered by the populace after a brief term of office, and under his successor

Timothy Aelurus the Egyptian Church as a whole went into permanent schism. It paid the penalty which so often attaches to sectarianism. Cut off from the main current of Christian development, it became provincial, its thought undistinguished, its energies wasted in sterile recriminations. Monophysitism was not indeed the only faith in Egypt; the government repeatedly endeavoured to recover the country for orthodoxy, and at Alexandria and among the official classes elsewhere Catholicism had its adherents, but the bulk of the people, and not only those of Egyptian blood, remained stubbornly loyal to their heretical belief. Inevitably Coptic influence was strengthened; for Greek was the language of government circles, and the monophysite cause found its chief bulwark among the Coptic-speaking monks. This heretical tendency was indeed the effect as well as the cause of the nationalist bias. Monophysitism has well been described as less a heresy than a schismatic intention. The differences between it and the Catholic position were in essentials not very great, and one attempt after another was made by the government to arrive at a compromise acceptable to Egyptian susceptibilities, but all its efforts proved unavailing. What Constantinople espoused the Patriarch of Alexandria, in this the mouthpiece of Egypt, must needs oppose; and if Constantinople condemned monophysitism the Egyptian Church, embodying as it did the perennial opposition of Egypt to Rome, became monophysite as a natural corollary.

Though Byzantine Egypt was predominantly a Christian country it must not be supposed that paganism died without a struggle. As late as the middle of the sixth century the town councillors of Omboi, complaining to the Duke of the Thebaid of a local notable, could accuse him of pagan practices. Ptolemais, the only Hellenistic foundation, save Alexandria, in the whole country, clung stubbornly to its Greek and pagan traditions; it is significant that, with one brief and doubtful exception, this important town, provided from its foundation with senate and assembly and all the paraphernalia of a city-state, seems never to have been the seat of a bishopric, though the nome-capitals, which did not win full municipal status till the very end of the Roman period, had their bishops long before the Council of Nicaea. In the University of Alexandria philosophy, much of it of a pagan character, was eagerly studied. The murder of Hypatia in 415 did not extinguish paganism there; so late as the latter part of the fifth century we meet with a group of pagan scholars, male and female, devoted to the study of philosophy.

These pagan circles, however, were by no means always Hellenic in their predilections. The old Greek deities had lost almost all vitality, and later paganism, even in its more Hellenic aspects, as exemplified by Julian the Apostate, was semi-Oriental in its theology. In Egypt the native religion still retained an appeal; and the group just referred to, whether in rivalry with contemporary Christianity or under the unconscious influence of the prevailing nationalism, cultivated Egyptian traditions with an enthusiasm not merely antiquarian. One of them, Horapollon, wrote a treatise on the hieroglyphic script.

The monasteries, which were the great centres of nationalist feeling in its most uncompromising form, were often situated on the desert fringes of the country, but they were found also in the towns, where their influence must have been potent. Hellenism was indeed doubly threatened. In the country districts the Egyptian elements, awakened to new self-consciousness by Christianity, were becoming predominant; in the towns, the decay of the institutions which had been the characteristic expression of Greek life and the influence of the Church were undermining the ancient culture. The great noble, in his town house, loyal to the emperor and professing Catholic orthodoxy (though as a matter of fact even the great Apion family was for certain periods monophysite), might cherish the Greek tongue and Greek culture, but the mass of the townsmen had probably neither the opportunity nor the inclination to follow the ancient ways.

It is, however, possible to exaggerate the extent of the change. If paganism was long a-dying the Hellenic tradition was even slower to pass away. It is to a fifth-century papyrus codex that we are most indebted for our knowledge of Menander's dramatic art. It was found among the papers of Dioscorus, a notary of Coptic origin but Greek education whose home was Aphrodito, once capital of the Aphroditopolite nome but then a village in the pagarchy of Antaeopolis. Menander was of course popular long into the Christian period; but with this manuscript was found a fragment of the *Demes* of Eupolis, a writer of the Old Comedy. If the taste for such reading existed in a village of the Thebaid we may be sure that Greek literature was still studied in the greater centres. And as a matter of fact papyrus discoveries prove what was *a priori* likely. True, as we advance into the Byzantine Age literary papyri become rarer, and the ratio of unknown works diminishes greatly; but authors represented in fragments of this period include, besides the ubiquitous Homer and the ever popular Menander, Hesiod, Sappho, Pindar, Aristophanes, Theocritus, and Callimachus. Moreover, Egypt, so comparatively poor in outstanding writers during the Roman period, produced, in the decline of Hellenism, several poets of note. The most prominent was Nonnus of Panopolis, but he was by no means a solitary figure. In the sixth century Dioscorus of Aphrodito exemplifies curiously the Greek culture of a small provincial centre. Sprung of a Coptic family, which was rising in social position, he was educated for the law, acquired a taste for Greek letters, studied classical literature and mythology, and was an assiduous writer of verse, execrable indeed in quality, not infrequently unmetrical, and full of words misunderstood or used with little sense of literary relevance, yet showing, with all its badness, the appeal which the world of Hellenic culture still retained, even for a man of

Egyptian race. And side by side with purely Christian allusions we find in his writing a whole galaxy of figures and motives culled from Greek mythology.

Sixth-century Egypt, as revealed to us in the papyri, bears indeed, in pre-eminent degree, all the marks of what is called an age of transition. A Christian country which retains a lively memory of its pagan past and in which the classics of Greek paganism still form the essential basis of a liberal education; an integral part of the bureaucratic empire of East Rome which has developed a social system exhibiting semi-feudal characteristics and inclining ever more towards something which might without great impropriety have been called feudalism; a society medieval in many of its aspects, with its monasteries and churches and hospitals, its serfs and autopract estates and private armies, yet steeped in the atmosphere of the ancient world—such is the picture that emerges: a system in equilibrium, uneasily balanced between the old and the new. And if the economic decay had already gone far, once populous villages become sand-covered ruins and fields reclaimed by the Ptolemies for agriculture relapsed into sterile desert, yet Egypt still made its contribution to the economy of the empire, and its corn was conveyed to the granaries, its gold to the treasuries of Constantinople. So far was it from having lost its importance that when Heraclius rose against Phocas in 609 his first act was to dispatch against it a force under Nicetas, just as, five centuries earlier, it was to Egypt that Vespasian turned as soon as he had resolved on revolt.

The equilibrium was, however, unstable and temporary, the balance tipping ever more decidedly in favour of the new order. The power of the landed nobility increased during the sixth century to a degree dangerous to the stability of the bureaucratic machine. The nobles tended to monopolize the office of pagarch, a single landowner sometimes holding the pagarchy of two or more nomes simultaneously. It is significant that the applications for agricultural implements and the like addressed by tenants to their landlords are couched in practically identical formulae whether the applicant came from a village of *coloni* in the domain of an autopract noble or one of free landholders subject to the authority of the pagarch. The only difference is that in the one case the village is described as 'belonging to your magnificence', in the other as 'under the pagarchy of your magnificence'. Indeed the lot of the *colonus*, to whom his magnificence was patron, may well have been better than that of the free landowner, who knew him but as a State official, collecting the imperial taxes. The papyrus evidence becomes scantier in the last half-century of Byzantine rule, but it is probably due to no accident of discovery that municipal activities play hardly any part in it. The municipalities seem to have been relapsing into the condition from which their development began, as little more than overgrown villages. The Greek language and culture were everywhere in decay; we find high Church dignitaries unable to write anything but Coptic, and finds of literary papyri from this period are rare. An unbridgeable gulf separated the Egyptian people from the government. The emperor might send orthodox patriarchs to Alexandria, just as he appointed the Augustal prefect to be the head of the civil administration, and a small wealthy and official class might profess the Catholic faith and loyalty to the Empire, but the mass of the people stood sullenly aloof, obstinately refusing any compromise of their monophysite faith, resolute to withhold co-operation with the imperial government.

Heraclius made an earnest effort at reconciliation, and compromised even to the extent of making terms with the monothelite heresy, a modification of monophysitism, but once more it was in vain; and his appointment of Cyrus to be at once patriarch and prefect proved disastrous. The fierce persecution of the monophysites on which Cyrus embarked yet further alienated the very people whom it was his mission to win over, and he proved an incompetent administrator and a weakling in the time of crisis. The impression given by all the evidence is that before ever the Arabs appeared in Egypt the country was already spiritually lost to the empire and rapidly relapsing into the Oriental world from which the conquests of Alexander the Great had in large measure separated it.

At the end of 639, after extorting a reluctant consent from the Caliph 'Omar, 'Amr led an Arab army against Pelusium. It numbered but four thousand men, far less than the Roman army of Egypt, but the latter was dispersed and of poor quality, and the division of authority within the country led to delay and want of co-operation in the defence. The local governors, appointed for their wealth rather than their administrative or military capacity, were quite unequal to the situation, and the mass of the people, though they hardly welcomed the invaders, showed little enthusiasm for the cause of a government which had impoverished and persecuted them. Nevertheless the Arabs, more than once reinforced, had to fight hard against some of the defending forces; but the incompetence of the Roman commanders and the poltroonery of Cyrus gave them victory in the end. In September, 642, the Roman army withdrew from Alexandria and the Arabs took possession of the city.

So ended the Graeco-Roman period of Egyptian history. Egypt, impoverished though she had become, was still a rich prize for the conquerors. Her corn helped to provide the allowances to the Muslims, her tribute in gold to fill the treasury of the Caliphs successively at Mecca, Damascus, and Bagdad, and her administrative organization provided the Arabs with valuable lessons for their new task of imperial government. Some things they modified. Taught by the success of their own invasion, they substituted for the subdivision of Byzantine Egypt an almost excessive centralization; they abolished *autopragia*, ended the power of the nobles, and swept away municipal government (though 'the city, the contributory villages and the notables' still appear, so late as A.D. 710, as the three divisions of a pagarchy); but for the rest the existing financial system and administrative machinery were taken over almost intact. How far Egypt can be held to have provided a model for the organization of the Caliphate as a whole it is difficult to say, since we know too little of local administration elsewhere, either just before or just after the Arab conquest, to be sure that the observable parallels were due to specifically Egyptian influence; but it is hard to believe that Islamic practice owed nothing to Egypt. In one respect we may be more positive. We know that workmen were recruited in Egypt for service outside the country and that Egyptian craftsmen were employed on the mosques of Jerusalem and Damascus. It can hardly be supposed that the great traditions of Egyptian craftsmanship did not contribute their quota to the formation of Islamic art. And if, later, the new capital Fustât under the Tûlûnid dynasty and the later capital Cairo under the Fâtimid Caliphs were the scenes of a busy artistic and literary life, may we not see in this yet one more instance of that burgeoning and blossoming of aesthetic productivity which the engrafting of an alien element has so often excited in the ever fertile stock of Egyptian culture?

H. I. BELL

CHAPTER 14

THE CONTRIBUTION TO ISLAM

§ 1

WEAKENED by internecine strife, a victim to bankrupt states-manship, Egypt was powerless to resist the surging tide of Arab expansion which quickly followed the death of Muḥammad and the establishment of the Caliphate. So rich a country, lying in such tempting proximity to the head-quarters of the Muslim State, and constituting a serious threat to its expanding communica-tions, could not long escape the attentions of an ambitious general. Late in the year 639, 'Amr ibn al-'Āṣ led his columns through Sinai. A month's siege reduced Pelusium, and the Arab invaders struck at the Byzantine armies under Cyrus and Theodorus, shutting Cyrus up in Babylon (near modern Cairo) until he agreed to humiliating terms and joined his colleague in Alexandria. The emperor Heraclius repudiated the terms and banished Cyrus: but after being invested for seven months, the fortress fell. The Muslim army then marched on Alexandria. The death of Heraclius in 641 was disastrous to the Byzantine cause, for his son and successor, Constans II, was immature in years and judgement, and consented to evacuate his army from Egypt in September, 642. A fruitless attempt was made in 645 to recapture Alexandria from the sea, but 'Amr, who had been hastily recalled to take charge of operations, quelled the hopes of the insurgent population of the city, and by 646 no other authority but that of the Arabs remained in the land. So Egypt, which had been for centuries the repository of Greek learning, and a battleground of Christian sects, passed over irrevocably into the hands of the Saracens, and has remained ever since a pre-eminently Muslim country.

For more than two centuries, Egypt was administered by governors, first for the Umayyad Caliphs, and then for their successors the 'Abbâsids. Wave after wave of migration converted the country into an Arab province, in the full sense of the term. For a long time Jews and Christians were employed as officials, but in the course of the centuries, as their technical knowledge became no longer indispensable to the administration, the whole conduct of affairs passed into the hands of Muslims. Christians and Jews lived as 'protected' minorities, subject to the disabilities and liable to the taxes imposed by their Muslim rulers.

In 868, Aḥmad ibn Ṭûlûn, a Turk by birth, being appointed governor of Egypt, declared his independence of the 'Abbâsid rulers, and set up a local dynasty (Ṭûlûnids) which lasted until 905. Thereafter for thirty years the central government was again supreme, but in 935 Muḥammad ibn Tughj, designated *ikhshîd* by the Caliph al-Raḍî, founded the short-lived Ikshîdid dynasty (935–69). The rise of the Fâṭimid Caliphate of the West led to the reabsorption of Egypt as a province of a Shî'ite empire (969–1171) of which Cairo was the capital, and two centuries passed before the country came under the independent rule of the Ayyûbid dynasty (1171–1250), of which the illustrious Ṣalâḥ al-Dîn (Saladin) was the chief glory. The Baḥrî (Turkish) Mamlûks, founded by Shajarat al-Durr, widow of the Ayyûbid al-Ṣâliḥ, were followed in 1390 by the Burjî (Circassian) Mamlûks, whose rule was terminated by the Ottoman occupation of Salîm in 1517. So Egypt once more sank to the status of a province. Napoleon's expedition of 1798 marks the beginning of the modern history of Egypt. Under the rule of the Khedivial house of Muḥammad 'Alî (d. 1849), the country still acknowledged the titular suzerainty of the Turkish Sulṭân, until its official termination in 1914 following the declaration of the British Protectorate. In 1922 Egypt's independence was proclaimed, subject to certain reservations, which were finally liquidated by the Anglo-Egyptian Treaty of 1936. The late King Fu'âd assumed the title of *malik* (king); and his son King Fârûq now rules, the constitutional head of a fully independent State.

§ 2

It is manifestly difficult, if not impossible, to determine, as with a rule and scalpel, what contribution Egypt, as an independent entity, has made to Islam. The political theory underlying the religion of Muḥammad lays it down as a principle that national frontiers are meaningless where the rule of Islam is concerned: the world is divided into two parts, the 'abode of peace', constituting the area of Muslim predominance, and the 'abode of war', regions where Islam may not be practised, against which it is the bounden duty of all Muslims to wage holy war (*jihâd*). Islam is an essentially international and interracial movement, and ideas germinating in one corner of the Muslim world spread with amazing rapidity throughout the whole extent of Muslim domination.

Egypt lies in the very centre of the Muslim world, and has therefore been peculiarly fitted to act as the receptacle and repository of all Islamic movements, as indeed she served during the Greek and Christian periods as the melting-pot of Eastern and Western ideas and cultures. It is further curious to remark that at the present day Egypt still fulfils that same world-role, interpreting the West to the Muslim East, and, to a lesser but still important degree, the Muslim East to the West. Such has been, and remains, the paramount function of Egypt, and in this function Egypt has played a far from negligible part in the destinies of Islam.

But Egypt has also, out of her own blood and soil, made important contributions to the history and achievements of the Muslim world.

In the early period of Islam, Egypt was naturally of little account. Arabs of pure birth were the protagonists of the first controversies, the founders of the first doctrinal schisms and schools of religious law. Until the advent of the Fâṭimids, the Mâlikî and Shâfi'î rites were predominant in Egypt. The

Fâṭimids, of course, introduced the Ismâ'îlî laws, but after their disappearance the Ḥanafî Code was established as the official code of the country, though the Mâlikî and Shâfi'î, and even the Ḥanbalî schools enjoyed patronage.

The foundation of the Azhar mosque by the Fâṭimid conqueror Jawhar in 972 was an event of profound import, not only for Egypt, but for Islam as a whole: liberally endowed by successive rulers, and in particular by the Fâṭimid al-'Azîz, it attained the status of the medieval university of Islam *par excellence*, especially after the sack of Bagdad by the Mongols in 1258, and to its courts students from all parts of the Muslim world came and still come for instruction in religion and law at the hands of its professors. At the present day its classes comprise Egyptians, Sudanese, Syrians, Palestinians, Moroccans, Algerians, Arabians, Indians, Javanese, and even Chinese, who return thence to administer and teach the ritual in their own towns and villages. Many distinguished names have been connected with the Azhar. To-day, its local fame has paled somewhat with the growth of the modern Egyptian University, and under its newest constitution it seems in danger of losing much of its former significance: but it remains for ever a portent, an example, still visible, of the patronage of learning which lent lustre to the martial glory of medieval Islam. Its Rector (*Shaykh al-Azhar*) has always played a leading religious, and therefore an important political, role in the affairs of Egypt.

To the mystical side of Islam, Egypt has made a full and worthy contribution—worthy of the land in which mysticism appears to be indigenous. It may be justly conjectured, though it cannot with certainty be proved, that the early Muslims were profoundly influenced by the example of the Christian monks and anchorites living in the deserts of Egypt and Sinai, and it is at least feasible that the rise of the ascetic movement in Islam during the seventh and eighth centuries may have been largely inspired by contact with such men. One of the earliest and greatest of Muslim mystics (Ṣûfîs) was an Egyptian, Dhu 'l-Nûn al-Miṣrî (d. 860), whose tombstone at Gîza has survived. Though much that is written of him and recorded of his sayings is doubtless apocryphal—and in particular the legend that he could read and understand the monuments of the Pharaohs— it is significant that to him is attributed the special credit of having first taught the doctrine of *ma'rifa*, the Arabic equivalent of γνῶσις. He is also mentioned as the author of works on alchemy, though his title in this respect may be no more secure than that of the Umayyad prince Khâlid b. Yazîd (d. 704): at all events, none of the alchemical treatises ascribed to him appears to be extant.

The various Ṣûfî brotherhoods (*ṭarîqa*) established themselves and flourished, and indeed still flourish, in Egypt. Relations between them and the official (Azharite) exponents of religion were in the earlier period cordial, or at least sympathetic: but for centuries now the two parties have been bitterly antagonistic, though it is with a smile rather of indulgence than of scorn that the modern theologian speaks of *taṣawwuf*.

Ibn al-Fâriḍ, the greatest mystical poet of Arabic literature, was born at Cairo in 1181, and died there in 1234: his tomb is beautifully preserved in the Muqaṭṭam hills, overlooking Cairo. His poetry is known by heart to modern Ṣûfîs, and has been studied by several European scholars, notably Von Hammer, Di Matteo, Nallino, and Nicholson. The following version by Nicholson of part of a well-known ode illustrates the mystical fire and beauty of his verse:

> With my Beloved, I alone have been
> When secrets tenderer than evening airs
> Passed, and the Vision blest
> Was granted to my prayers,
> That crowned me, else obscure, with endless fame,
> The while amazed between
> His beauty and His majesty

I stood in silent ecstasy,
Revealing that which o'er my spirit went and came.
Lo! in His face commingled
Is every charm and grace;
The whole of Beauty singled
Into a perfect face
Beholding Him would cry,
'There is no God but He, and He is the most High!'

The fame of another religious poet of Egypt, al-Bûṣîrî (b. 1213), is even more widespread, though resting on a far more slender foundation, a single poem of 165 verses: his 'Ode of the Mantle' (*Qaṣîdat al-Burda*), a panegyric of the Prophet, is generally acclaimed the most perfect example of its kind, and innumerable commentaries in various languages have been written upon it. The following version of its opening lines serves to indicate the curiously conservative nature of Arabic poetry, for they could have equally well introduced a typical ode of pre-Islamic days:

What fond remembered friendship
    At Dhû Salam thus sears
And flecks with blood thine eyeballs,
    And wets thy cheeks with tears?

Or blows the breeze at even
    From Kâẓima the blest,
Or flames the sudden lightning
    On Iḍam's darkened crest?

What ails thine eyes that, bidden
    To dam their flow, they pour?
What ails thy heart that, bidden
    To rest, it sorrows more?

Bethinks the ardent lover
    Love can be hidden so,
When eyes are bright with weeping,
    And heart with fire doth glow?

The famous ʿAṭāʾ Allâh al-Shâdhilî, founder of the Shâdhilî *tarîqa*, though born in Morocco, spent the greater part of his active life in Egypt, where he died in 1258. Another well-known Egyptian Ṣûfî poet is Ibn Wafâʾ, born at Cairo in 1357. Mention may also be made here of the celebrated Ṣûfî author al-Shaʿrânî (or al-Shaʿrawî), who was born at Fusṭâṭ (old Cairo) in 1492, and died at Cairo in 1565. Upwards of fifty of his works are extant, including some reputed autographs.

In the field of *belles lettres* Egypt has also produced many famous men. Court panegyrists in plenty there have been, many of whose *Dîwâns* (collected poems) are still admired: most famous among them perhaps, to English readers, is Bahâʾ al-Dîn Zuhayr of the Ayyûbids (d. 1258), a selection of whose poetry was published, with English verse-translations, by E. H. Palmer in 1876. In modern times the poetic tradition has been revived, though still the achievements in political verse (to us a strange and almost despised *genre*) appear to outshine the more purely subjective style of poetry. Bârûdî (d. 1905), a distinguished politician in his day, is much applauded for a touching elegy on the death of his wife, and for other poems. Ḥâfiẓ Ibrâhîm (d. 1932), called 'Poet of the Nile', was a mouthpiece of the Nationalist movement, and much literature has been written comparing his skill with that of the courtly Shawqî, 'Prince of Poets'. Shawqî (d. 1932) was without doubt one of the most original and fertile geniuses in the whole of Arabic literature; and if any of his titles to fame is more deserved than the others, it is his creation of the poetic drama in Arabic. Drama is a *genre* unrepresented in classical Arabic literature, though the popular farce or 'shadow-play' has its roots in the Middle Ages. Shawqî took familiar Arab legends—of the mad poet Qays and his beloved Layla, of ʿAntara the pre-Islamic bard—and celebrated chapters in Egyptian history—the conquest of Cambyses, the romance of Antony and Cleopatra, the career of the Mamlûk ʿAlî Bêg—and upon them constructed dramas which have

secured a more than ephemeral popularity. It will be of interest
here to illustrate the reactions of the modern poet to the refound
glory of ancient Egypt, as typified in the Pyramids. Ḥâfiẓ
Ibrâhîm writes:

> He mastered knowledge to his bent
> That he might raise a monument
> Above Nile's sloping banks, to be
> A sign, a deathless memory.
> What glowering frown wears yonder pile?
> Fond memory should ever smile.
> What skill sublime and wondrous brave
> Designed this broken tyrant's grave?
> Would art had had a worthier trust
> Than thus to sanctify the dust!
> For they had crafts beyond our ken,
> And sciences that lesser men
> Lack wit to grasp; with dexterous hand
> To rich invention wed, they planned
> Fair idols men might be forgiven
> For worshipping, in hope of heaven.
> These things they planned; their day is o'er:
> Time seals their secrets evermore.

The celebrated philologist Ibn al-Ḥâjib (d. 1248) studied in
Cairo and spent the greater part of his life in Egypt, dying at
Alexandria: his *al-Kâfiya*, an epitome of Arabic grammar, has
been used by centuries of Muslim schoolboys, and countless
commentaries and super-commentaries have been written upon
it. Ibn Hishâm (1308–60), at one time Professor of Qur'ânic
Exegesis in Cairo, was a noted grammarian, while al-Damâmînî
(1362–1424), a native of Alexandria, achieved fame in the field
of prosody. Al-Zabîdî (d. 1791), author of the great dictionary
Tâj al-'arûs, was a Cairene student and spent most of his days
in Egypt.

The greatest of all Muslim encyclopaedists and polymaths,
Jalâl al-Dîn al-Suyûṭî (1445–1505), was a native of Asyûṭ and

held various public appointments at Cairo, until he fell from grace and retired to the islet of Rauḍa. Hardly a branch of the Muslim 'sciences' is without some contribution from his facile pen, and Brockelmann's list of 333 treatises under his name is probably far from complete. It is doubtful whether any single author has so enriched the whole field of Arabic literature.

In a summary of this kind, only the most famous names can be mentioned. Al-Damîrî (1344–1405), author of the greatest zoological work in Arabic (*Hayât al-ḥayawân*), was a native of Cairo, as was also the celebrated alchemist al-Jildakî (d. 1342). Of Egyptian birth were al-Isrâ'îlî (d. 932) and Ibn Riḍwân (d. 1068), physicians; al-Mundhirî (d. 1258) and al-Munâwî (d. 1622), traditionists; al-Nawâjî (d. 1455), the anthologist; Ibn Sayyid al-Nâs (d. 1334), author of a well-known biography of Muḥammad; al-Jundî (d. 1365) the Mâlikî, Taqî al-Dîn al-Subkî (d. 1355) and his namesake Tâj al-Dîn (d. 1370), both Shâfi'î, and Ibn Nujaym (d. 1563) and al-Timirtâshî (d. 1595), Ḥanafî lawyers, as well as the Shâfi'ites al-Bulqînî (d. 1403), al-Aqfahsî (d. 1405), and Zakariyyâ al-Anṣârî (d. 1520); and al-Khafâjî (d. 1659), the philologist and poet.

Most noteworthy is the contribution made by Egyptian writers, mainly but not exclusively journalists, to the development of the 'new style' in Arabic, the vehicle of a vigorous modern prose. The subject is exhaustively treated in H. A. R. Gibb's *Studies in Contemporary Arabic Literature*, and here it will be sufficient to recall the names of Manfalûṭî, Mâzinî, Haykal, Ṭaha Ḥusayn, 'Aqqâd, Aḥmed Amîn and Fikrî Abâẓa, who have all assisted in adapting the archaic, stilted classical tongue to the requirements of the present day. It is necessary also to refer to the creation, by the late King Fu'âd, of the Royal Egyptian Academy, composed of distinguished European and oriental Arabic philologists, whose programme it is to purify the printed language of colloquialisms and neologisms, and to 'standardize' the Arabic of the future.

A branch of literature—though hardly recognized as such by the native Arabic scholar—in the history of which Egypt has played an important part, is the imaginative romance, of which the most celebrated example is the collection known as 'The Arabian Nights' (*Alf layla wa-layla*). Less known in Europe, but equally popular in Arab countries, are the romances of 'Antar, of Abû Zayd and the Banû Hilâl, of al-Ẓâhir Baybars the (Baḥrî) Mamlûk Sulṭân, and similar collections. The art of story-telling, at one time a familiar feature of Egyptian life, appears now to be dying out, at all events in the big towns, but perhaps it may one day be transmuted into a truly native literature of the Novel, in which tentative beginnings are already being made.

There remains to be mentioned what is perhaps Egypt's greatest and most characteristic contribution to Muslim literature, her historical writings.

On the no longer extant authorities upon which later accounts of the early history of Muslim Egypt are based, a detailed statement is prefixed to A. R. Guest's edition of al-Kindî's (d. 961) *Governors and Judges of Egypt* (*Kitâb al-Wulât wa-kitâb al-Quḍât*), an invaluable source for the period down to the author's own lifetime. An earlier writer whose history of the conquest of Egypt has survived is the Egyptian-born Ibn 'Abd al-Ḥakam (*Futûḥ Miṣr wa 'l-Maghrib*), who died at Fusṭâṭ in 871. Eutychius, Patriarch of Alexandria (d. 939), known to the Arabs as Saʿîd ibn al-Biṭrîq, wrote several historical works, of which the best known is his chronicle *Naẓm al-jawhar*: he also wrote on medicine. A native of Fusṭâṭ, al-Musabbiḥî (976–1029), was the author of a voluminous history of Egypt (*Akhbâr Miṣr wa-faḍâ'ilhâ*), of which only one part, the fortieth, has survived. A detailed account of the regulations of the State chanceries in the time of Saladin is contained in al-Mammâtî's (d. 1209) *Qawânîn al-dawâwîn*.

In al-Maqrîzî, born at Cairo in 1364, we have one of the

most celebrated of all Muslim historians. He is unfortunately not free from the charge of plagiarism—a sin committed by many Muslim authors—and his well-known topography and history of Egypt, *al-Mawâ'iz wa'l-i'tibâr fî dhikr al-khitat wa'l-âthâr*, has been proved to be based upon, and even in large part copied from, the work of a predecessor, al-Awhadî. Nevertheless, it is a primary source for our knowledge of Egyptian affairs, and has been edited and utilized by a number of scholars. Al-Maqrîzî also wrote a history of the Fâtimids (*Itti'âz al-Hunafâ'*), of which a unique autograph copy has been preserved, and another of the Ayyûbids and Mamlûks (*al-Sulûk li-ma'rifat al-mulûk*), now being edited by the Egyptian scholar Mustafâ Ziâda from an autograph copy. He planned an encyclopaedic biographical work in eighty volumes to contain notices of all famous Egyptians (*al-Muqaffâ*), but only completed sixteen volumes; another biographical work is his *Durar al-'uqûd*, on famous contemporaries, never completed, of which a small autograph fragment has survived. Several other works of al-Maqrîzî are also extant, including a tract on numismatics (*Shudhûr al-'uqûd*), and contributions to geography, dogmatics, and the science of Traditions (*hadîth*). He died at Cairo in 1442.

Almost equal in fame, and no less important as a primary source, is al-Maqrîzî's pupil, the historian Ibn Taghrîbirdî (1411–69), author of seven historical works, of which the most celebrated is the *al-Nujûm al-zâhira*, a history of Egypt from the Arab conquest to the year 1453. Another celebrated author is Ibn Duqmâq (1350–1406), whose history of Egypt (*Nuzhat al-anâm*), completed in 1382, has survived partly in autograph. Among other works of his are a history of the rulers of Egypt to the year 1402 (*al-Jawhar al-thamîn*), written at the instance of the Sultân Barqûq (d. 1398), and descriptions of the ten great cities of Islam (*al-Durrat al-mudî'a*), of which the volumes dealing with Cairo and Alexandria survive and have been published. Ibn al-Furât, born at Cairo in 1334, is the author of a chronicle of Islam (*Tarîkh al-duwal wa'l-mulûk*), planned to cover the whole period of Muslim history: the author commenced with the fourteenth century and worked backwards, but had only reached the tenth century when he died, in 1405. A Syrian scholar, C. K. Zurayk, is now editing the surviving nine volumes.

Of great importance for the history of Egypt is the detailed chronicle of Ibn Iyâs (1448–1524), the pupil of al-Suyûtî, called *Badâ'i' al-zuhûr*: the same author wrote also a Universal History (*Marj al-zuhûr*), and a cosmography with special reference to Egypt (*Nashq al-azhâr*). By al-Suyûtî himself three historical works were written, of which the most important is his local history, *Husn al-muhâḍara fî akhbâr Miṣr*, a valuable book of reference. Numerous other Egyptians of lesser fame but equal industry have compiled extant historical works.

In the nineteenth century wrote al-Sharqawî (d. 1812), bringing the story down to include the expedition of Napoleon; al-Jabartî, whose *'Ajâ'ib al-âthâr*, invaluable for the history of the eighteenth and early nineteenth centuries, and generally accounted the last great work of classical Arabic literature, is held by some to have been responsible for his being murdered on the Shubra road in 1822; and 'Alî Pâshâ Mubârak (1823–93), holder of various important official posts, whose principal work, *al-Khiṭaṭ al-jadîda*, intended as a continuation of al-Maqrîzî's *al-Mawâ'iz wa'l-i'tibâr*, was published, in twenty volumes, at Bûlâq in 1888.

Printing in the Arabic characters hardly began in the East before the end of the eighteenth century. When it did begin, however, Egypt at once took the lead, and remains to this day far in advance of other Islamic countries in both quantity and quality of output. The style of printing in use down to quite recent times was hardly attractive and quite ruinous to the eyesight: but since the Great War the art of typography has made great advances, and in particular the volumes produced by the press of the Royal Egyptian Library (*Dâr al-kutub al-Miṣriyya*) cannot be surpassed for elegance and legibility. Credit for raising the standard of printing must also be accorded to the French Institute, which has leavened the intellectual life of Egypt in many ways. To-day Egypt supplies the whole Muslim world with texts, classical and popular; and with the standard of literacy rising in every Islamic country, the importance of the work of distributing good literature, attractively produced and at astonishingly low prices, cannot be overestimated.

§ 3

So much for the intellectual side of Egypt's contribution to Islamic culture. It must be emphasized that mention has not been made, save in rare instances, of famous authors who, while not Egyptian-born, spent many or most of their productive years in Egypt, enjoying the patronage and security afforded by the successive dynasties which ruled the land. Egypt deserves some credit for their products also; but as this essay is primarily concerned with what has come out of the 'blood and soil' of the country, it is necessary that these limitations should be observed. In appraising Islam's debt to Egypt in respect of literature, it is not difficult to establish a criterion, since in almost every case it is possible to ascertain with certainty whether a given author is or is not Egyptian-born. Moreover, in literature the element of imitation, of following and developing a set style, is relatively unimportant, compared with the original contribution of the individual author. The remainder of this essay is concerned with the artistic output of Egypt during the Islamic period; and here the ground is far less sure. We shall write of buildings, handicrafts, the various branches of art, glorious examples of which are extant; but for the most part the identity of the architect, the artisan, the artist is unknown. It is known that many of the earliest specimens in particular are the work of non-Egyptians, and in any case the styles set by them, and in general most subsequent modifications or developments of these styles, likewise largely introduced by foreign artists, which have remained as models for succeeding generations of Egyptian craftsmen, are essentially non-Egyptian. Thus, it is certain that the architectural principles underlying the construction of the mosque were evolved in Iraq and Syria; that the art of calligraphy, and the related use of script in decorative ornament of stone, textile, or metal, spring from foreign origins; and that the designs of ceramics and other utensils have for the most part been introduced from Iraq, Persia, and even China. To isolate, then, the peculiarly Egyptian contribution to the sum of Islamic art is a task of the greatest complexity. The words of C. H. Becker, written some twenty-five years ago, that 'the really scientific study of Egyptian architecture and decorative art is still in its infancy, it has not even been satisfactorily explained what is peculiarly Egyptian in it'[1] do not stand in any great need of modification to-day.

Additional difficulties arise from the fact that, for a prolonged period of her Muslim history, Egypt was combined with Syria as an administrative province. Moreover, craftsmen were freely imported—if that is not too mild a term to cover what was at times forcible removal—from one part of the Muslim world to another, and non-Muslims were frequently employed by Muslim rulers. In Egypt especially, Coptic craftsmen were of immense utility to their Arab conquerors, and their noted skill, above all in ceramics and textiles, of which abundant evidence is provided by the material remains of the Coptic period, made a quite unique impression on the development of Muslim art.

For detailed information on the characteristics of each individual branch of art, reference must be made to the abundant specialist literature of each subject: here the treatment will perforce be cursory and superficial. It should also be remembered that the whole science bristles with controversy and partisanship,

[1] *E.I.* ii, p. 23.

and it is yet too early to evolve a detached and neutral stand-point. A perusal of Dr. A. J. Butler's admirable *Islamic Pottery* will serve to illustrate how fundamentally experts can differ in fields which they have made their own peculiar provinces.

In design, the characteristic arabesque, a complicated scroll based on simple geometrical patterns, already found in an elementary form at Samarra, the 'country residence' of the early Caliphs of Bagdad, developed extraordinarily in Egypt under the Fâṭimids. The earliest example of this feature in Egypt is found in the Ibn Ṭûlûn Mosque, to which reference will be made hereafter. It should be remembered that a prohibition has been placed since quite early days on the reproduction of the human figure in art, though the Qusair Amra frescoes prove that the prohibition was not very rigorously observed in private dwelling-places. The Shî'ites, who achieved ascendancy in Persia and parts of India, disregarded this vexatious restriction, and to their heterodoxy, or humanism, we owe the splendid art of miniature painting which is one of the chief glories of Islamic culture: miniature painting never flourished in Egypt. Bound by this restriction, the artistic urge had to find other outlets: and these outlets were provided by the development of geometrical design, in every imaginable kind of material. Book-binding, of which the earliest extant examples have their provenance in Egypt, gave full scope to this *motif*: experts find Coptic influence strongly at work in the most primitive examples, but later craftsmen were more catholic in their tastes. The use of gold tooling had its influence on the binders of Venice. Lacquered covers, gloriously designed with human and animal *motifs* by Persian artists, were never introduced into Egypt. Another manifestation of skill in design is provided by the art of calligraphy, one of the most highly esteemed of all Islamic arts. Princes and rulers were willing to pay fabulous sums to skilled artists to execute Qur'âns written on finely prepared

parchment in the beautiful *naskhî* Arabic script: a notable
collection of such volumes, written for the Mamlûk rulers, of
truly monumental size and beauty, is preserved in the Royal
Library at Cairo. Inscriptions also served to decorate the walls
of mosques and other public buildings, and of these many
examples are yet to be seen in Egypt. The peculiar Kûfic script,
extremely difficult to decipher, especially when it blossoms out
into a very riot of ornament, proved most suitable for execution
in stone. Later the *naskhî* script was also used for the same
purpose. A further example of the intricate use of design, very
characteristic of Egyptian Islamic art, is the *mashribiyya* or
lattice-work which formerly adorned private houses, as well as
certain public buildings: designed to secure privacy from outside passers-by, as well as to serve as a filter for strong sunlight,
these elaborately carved wooden shutters have now largely disappeared from the streets which until comparatively recent
times they so richly adorned. A parallel use of carved wood is
found in mosque doors—a notable example is the old door of
the Azhar mosque, now preserved in the Arab Museum at
Cairo—and furniture. Inlay work, already found in the Coptic
period, in which ivory, and later mother of pearl, is worked into
carved wood, has likewise exercised the skill of Egyptian carpenters. Bone and ivory also responded to similar treatment.
In stone, the truly amazing examples of delicate tracery, and
that most glorious of all Muslim masonry decorations, the
stalactite pendentive, still to be seen in abundance in the old
mosques of Cairo, bear witness to the consummate skill of craftsmen, as well as to the inspiration of artists. It may certainly
be said that intricacy of design and symmetry of pattern never
achieved greater perfection than in the carved work of the
medieval Muslim craftsmen. Egypt, and especially Cairo, is a
rich field for the investigator of this art, since monuments built
in the best period of Saracen art yet abound. Where for other
crafts, working in less durable materials, recourse has to be

made to private collections and to museums, architecture, with its allied art of design and carving, may be studied extensively *in situ*. The visitor to Egypt to-day, when he has made the tour of the ancient monuments and the museums, will be foolish if he does not capitulate to the importunity of his dragoman to show him the Muslim monuments.

The history of the primitive beginnings of Muslim architecture concerns other countries than Egypt—Arabia itself, where the first rude mosque was constructed, Syria, where Christian churches were converted to the worship of Allah, and Iraq, where the Caliphs, using Persian architects, built their own sacred shrines. Nothing was erected worthy of notice in Egypt during the first two centuries of Muslim domination. But the coming of the Ṭûlûnids was a signal for the advent of more spacious times. The Ibn Ṭûlûn mosque, still extant, was built at the command of Aḥmad ibn Ṭûlûn, founder of the dynasty: coming from Samarra, he had his building designed on Bagdad lines, decorated after the Samarra fashion. The present minaret was not constructed until 1296.

The Fâṭimid period was an age of great architectural activity. Reference has already been made to the foundation in 972 of the Azhar mosque: though much altered in later times, its original plan may still largely be traced; its transept is the earliest example of this feature in Egypt, though the Great Mosque at Damascus had already incorporated the device. The mosque of al-Ḥâkim, built between 990 and 1012, shows strong Iraqi and Syrian influences.

Under Saladin the military defences of Cairo were constructed, the greater part of the walls, and the Citadel which still overshadows the city. The same ruler introduced the *madrasa* into Egypt, to house the theological schools: later, a cruciform style was developed, convenient for accommodating professors of the four different persuasions, a plan first evolved in Egypt.

The Baḥrî Mamlûks are represented by the mosques of Baybars I (1269), al-Nâṣir Muḥammad (1318–35), and al-Mâridânî (1340): during this period the large wooden dome covering the sanctuary was evolved, replacing the little dome hitherto featured. The great *madrasa* of Sulṭân Ḥasan (1356–68) also stands to the credit of these rulers, of which K. A. Creswell writes:[1]

'When one stands at the entrance to the great sahn [courtyard], and observes its vast proportions, its rich yet restrained decoration, the grandeur and simplicity of its lines, the height and breadth of its great vaults, and the rich stalactite balconies of the minaret rising over the south corner, one feels bound to admit that this madrasa is one of the great things of the world.'

Many noteworthy additions to the architectural glory of Cairo were made under the succeeding dynasty of the Burjî Mamlûks, notably the Barqûq mosque situated in the Tombs of the Caliphs. Despite the economic difficulties which clouded the Turkish period—and the discovery of the Cape route to India is to be accounted an important contributory cause of this decline—there are yet evidences of the continuity of skill and craftsmanship, which did not receive the truly fatal blow until the advent of European influence at the end of the eighteenth century. Isolated buildings in the Saracen tradition have been constructed since that time, among which mention may be made of the Muḥammad 'Alî Mosque: but it is a melancholy fact that at the present day Western modes of architecture have completely superseded the true native art—serious mention need not be made of the rare attempts to rear bastard imitations of ancient Egyptian monuments—and almost all the buildings constructed during this century, public and private alike, might equally well have been erected in any modern European city. The future will show whether Muslim architectural tradition

[1] *The Art of Egypt*, p. 66.

can ever be adapted to the changed requirements of the twentieth and succeeding centuries, and still retain its individual character.

Our knowledge of the history of ceramics and textiles during the Muslim period has been immensely enriched by the excavation in recent years of the rubbish-heaps of the Old City of al-Fusṭāṭ. In both these crafts the immemorial skill of the native workman has contributed greatly to the story of Islamic art. In particular, the collections in the Victoria and Albert Museum, and the Metropolitan Museum of New York illustrate how Coptic elements survived into Arab times, to be fused into designs and fashions imported from other Muslim provinces. Special mention should be made of the lustre ware in pottery, for which A. J. Butler has shown Egyptian origins. Egyptian carpet-making, though never attaining the spectacular richness of Persian and Turkish products, nevertheless had a considerable reputation: the rigid geometrical designs, characteristic of other arts in Egypt, have survived to the present day in the pleasant brown Assiut rugs. A very fine example of Egyptian pile-carpet is preserved in the Austrian Imperial Collection at Vienna. But on the subject of these rugs the experts are again at variance, and geometrically patterned mats have been ascribed indifferently to Asia Minor, Damascus, and Morocco.

Under foreign influences, notably those of Mosul, the art of engraving in metal, and particularly of silver-inlay work, attained great perfection in Egypt during the Mamlûk period, the fourteenth century marking the peak of development. Human and animal figures, such as are found commonly on Persian pieces, were never featured in Egyptian work, which found ample scope in intricate design and lettering. Good work was still produced to within comparatively recent times: but since the art was debased to meet the demands of tourists, the markets are now flooded with monstrosities imitating the scenes of the Egypt of the Pharaohs.

Superficial as this sketch of the Muslim arts has of necessity been, it has sufficed to indicate the nature of Egypt's contribution. In architecture, ceramics, and textiles the native craftsmen have excelled, and the products of these arts have attained a more than local fame, and have indeed, in certain respects, influenced the development of the arts in other countries. The periods of greatest achievement were those of the Fâṭimids, when Cairo was the capital of a western empire, and the early Mamlûks, after the sack of Bagdad and the dispersal of the craftsmen of Iraq.

In the later decline of Islamic culture Egypt also shared. A new age dawned with the advent of European contact and the establishment of the house of Muḥammad 'Alî. This contact has been a misfortune, hitherto unmitigated, to the practice of the arts and crafts; but to literature, moribund at the end of the eighteenth century, it has proved a great stimulus. Theology, which has fought a defensive battle against the impact of modern 'scientific' thought, has by no means been routed, and scholars of the calibre of Muḥammad 'Abduh (d. 1905) have worked strenuously to preserve the traditions of the Muslim faith. Great indeed are the dangers of a cynically materialistic interpretation of the universe to a people but recently liberated from the shackles of the Muslim 'dark ages': but it is to be believed that the spiritual forces which have sustained Islam for over thirteen centuries, and in particular the mystical insight with which Egyptians have for all time been endowed, will triumph over the shocks from which religion the world over has, during these past decades, been suffering. At all events, it is to Egypt that the Muslim world turns for leadership in faith as in literature. Independent Egypt, her political destiny secured by the friendship of the British Commonwealth of Nations, looks forward to a future bright with possibilities, leading Islam in her religious and intellectual rebirth, and playing her part in laying the foundations of international understanding, co-operation, and peace.   A. J. ARBERRY

SELECT BIBLIOGRAPHY

Encyclopaedia of Islam (4 vols.+supplement), Leiden, 1908–38.

The Legacy of Islam (ed. Sir Thomas Arnold and A. Guillaume), Oxford, 1931.

SIR W. MUIR, *The Caliphate, its Rise, Decline and Fall* (revised edition by T. W. Weir), Edinburgh, 1924.

A. J. BUTLER, *The Arab Conquest of Egypt*, Oxford, 1902.

S. LANE-POOLE, *A History of Egypt in the Middle Ages*, London, 1901.

C. BROCKELMANN, *Geschichte der arabischen Litteratur*, 2 vols., Weimar, 1898, and Berlin, 1902, +Supplement, Leiden, 1937– .

R. A. NICHOLSON, *A Literary History of the Arabs* (2nd edition), Cambridge, 1930.

SIR E. D. ROSS (editor), *The Art of Egypt*, London, 1930.

M. S. DIMAND, *A Handbook of Mohammedan Decorative Arts*, New York, 1930.

A. J. BUTLER, *Islamic Pottery*, London, 1926.

CHAPTER 15

THE LEGACY TO MODERN EGYPT[1]

'EGYPT', says Lady Duff-Gordon, 'is a palimpsest in which the Bible is written over Herodotos and tne Koran over that.' Herodotus himself was written over the Pyramid Age which overlay the predynastic, and so on even perhaps to the Palaeolithic and beyond. It is still the custom to make prints of hands with blood on doors and on Saints' tombs. Red hand-prints are found in Europe in the Upper Palaeolithic.

The new is not always written over the old, but often beside it. Thus the ancient Egyptian water-lift was supplemented, not superseded by the water-wheel, and in Hellenistic times by the water-screw. The reason is that the earlier can sometimes work where the new cannot. The water-screw, for instance, is only suitable for small differences of level. Even the water-wheel has its limits, and when the Nile is low has to be eked out with the lift. As for the latest comer, the engine pump, it requires a capital which the smallholder never possesses, or he would not be a smallholder. It is no doubt partly for the same reason that the adze which we can see in use on the reliefs of Saqqâra can still be watched at work in streets traversed by the latest type of car. It is an all-round tool, armed with which a competent carpenter can achieve much with next to no capital.

New conceptions are continually arising which form the kernel of new systems of thought. Backed by the enthusiasm of newness, these attack and break up the older cultures, as a small keen army strikes at the heart of a large inert host, destroys

[1] If I have ventured at all on this study it is because I could count on Prof. H. Junker to place at my disposal both his vast knowledge of Egypt ancient and modern, and the excellent library of the German Archaeological Institute in Cairo. I have also been helped by the kindness of Prof. Sami Gabra, ʿAli Ahmed ʿIsa Effendi, Mahmud Gamal ed Din Hamdi Effendi, ʿAbdallah Hasan Effendi, and other friends.

the links between the units, and disperses them into scattered bands. So the new dispensation destroys the central ideas of the old, and leaves only fragments which are eradicated, assimilated, or left alone, according as they resist, surrender, or remain indifferent. Take Islam, the latest comer; it is a system of conduct with a limited range; a great part of human activities, such as mechanics, buying and selling, and others, lie outside its interests, and so have not been attacked, but carry on much as of old. The rest was often, as we shall see, revolutionized more on the surface than in the depths.

Egypt is now a highly centralized State, so centralized that it may be said that politically Cairo is Egypt. We know, however, from ancient records that it once consisted of two rival kingdoms, the Upper and the Lower. It is to the Ancients we owe the fusion; yet thousands of years of union have not completely concealed the join. Upper and Lower Egypt still form a contrast: a Delta man penetrating beyond the no-man's-land that lies between Cairo and Minya feels himself in a foreign country. The differences of custom and character are sufficient to keep the populations of north and south apart when they meet in Cairo, leading them in different paths, the Delta folk into the more individualistic occupations of domestic service and shops, the more gregarious Upper Egyptians into labour gangs on the railway, docks, and in quarries.

The manner in which these two realms have been welded into the solid mass we now see has been preserved to us. It was carried out in accordance with the ancient theory of kingship. The king represented the god of the land; to acquire new lands he had to become the god of those lands. He had to annex the god in order to annex the country. The king of Upper Egypt took the red crown, the abode of the goddess Buto, and added it to his own white crown in which resided the goddess Nekhbet, and so became the lawful ruler of the two lands. Since then the two lands cannot long remain apart.

The two kingdoms were themselves composed of what had once been principalities, nomes with their gods, temples, standards, and processions. Their crowns could be and were fused, fusing the deities. In time the all-embracing divinity of the king swallowed up the local gods, reducing a host of principalities to two kingdoms.

Thanks to the protracted labours of those early unifiers, whoever now takes possession of Egypt receives a ready-made centralization.

The king's divinity provided them with a theory for gathering all things into his hand. The land was tributary to him as to a god, and paid one-fifth of the produce. Like the gods he owned a considerable domain, so that the land was divided into royal domain, temple lands, and private tenures. This classification is still maintained by the Egyptian code. The proportions only have fluctuated. In the Pyramid Age it is estimated that the king owned the greater part of Northern Egypt. By about 1870 Ismail Pasha had built up once more this domain to include about one-fifth of the arable land; but his extravagance forced him to cede a great part to the State, thus introducing a new distinction between the public and the private domain. This latter has been built up again to a considerable size.

The temple lands are now represented by the religious *waqfs* or endowments. They have been estimated at one-twelfth of the cultivated land. The Minister of Waqfs represents the ancient 'scribe who establishes the endowments of all the gods'. The rest of the land, as land conquered from infidels, is considered to have been either distributed by the conqueror to Muslims as military fiefs subject to tithe or left to their owners on payment of tribute. Military fiefs were not an invention of the Arabs; they were well known to the ancient Egyptians.

As all divinity was concentrated in the king, so was all service, since godhead is there to be served, that is, to have such things done to it as will make it beneficiently efficacious to the people.

Already in the Old Kingdom this concentration had reached such a pitch that much of the energies of the people was dedicated to the service of the king.

Having done its work the divinity of kings has become superfluous and has so far evaporated that traces of it are now very hard to find. As has often happened in the history of civilizations, it has all been concentrated in one last holder, a prophet, who continues to reign in the spirit for ever and so has no successor.[1] In Islam even that prophet does not enjoy full divinity, but only the nearest that Islam allows to it, proximity to God. That belongs so pre-eminently to the Prophet that it can only be enjoyed in a minor degree by anyone else. Much that was royal has thus passed to the Prophet. If Pharaoh's name was mentioned it was followed by some such prayer as 'May he live, be hale and healthy'. Now it is the Prophet who enjoys the addition, 'God bless him and preserve him'.

The gap between the god and the king had already begun to widen in very early times. Already in the Fifth Dynasty the king from being Horus and Great God had been lowered to Son of Rē' and Good God. Successive ages have widened it into that proximity which, as we shall see, is so characteristic of Islam.

This lowering of the king's status in relation to the deity has not always had such a disturbing effect on custom as might be expected. Thus the ancient Egyptians used to build temples in connexion with the tombs of their kings, mortuary temples, as they are called. The modern Egyptians build domed tombs for their rulers and attach to them a mosque. These tombs form cities not unlike those of the Pyramid Age. The externals have changed: domes, rare in the Sixth Dynasty, are now inevitable; the Qur'ân provides the decoration instead of bas-reliefs forbidden by the religion; if the ceiling is still adorned with stars

[1] Hocart, *Kingship* (Clarendon Press, 1927), 120 ff.; *Kings and Councillors* (Luzac & Co., 1936), 168 ff.

it is as an artistic motif, and no longer to make the temple a world in miniature; finally this city of the dead need no longer be in the West. In spite of all these changes the main idea remains. It may not appear at first sight, because the tomb-mosque is not dedicated to the king but to the one and only God; but then the old mortuary temple was not really dedicated to the king either in the New Kingdom, but to Amūn, the real recipient of the cult, and the priests were priests of Amūn. It was the dead king's temple only in so far as he embodied the god, and when he died he returned to the gods, to the Sun, to Rē', to Amūn. It is not then a change from the worship of man to worship of God, but in both cases the worship of the god is linked with a deceased sovereign. The difference lies in the exact nature of the link. Pharaoh was an impersonation of the god, and when he died 'the limb of the god returned to its creator'. The rigour of Islam forbids any such identity; the most that it allows is nearness to God.

Here we have the hard kernel of Islam to which all ancient customs must fit themselves or break. In this case the custom has fitted itself with ease. As of old, continuous worship goes on in the tombs of kings, and, as of old, endowments are made to pay for this worship; only it is no longer addressed to the deceased identified with the god, but on his behalf to Allah; there are no special texts to promote this identity with the deity, but the texts come from the one and only book that is read alike in mosque, tomb, house, or street, the Qur'ân, and it is read to ensure the nearness of God. The reciters are not priests specially affected to the cult of the dead, but generalized scholars selected and paid to do what every scholar does any-where, to read the revelation. There has been a complete level-ling out of all worship. Islam means standardization, and stan-dardization becomes inevitable when everything is concentrated at the head.

Thus, after the king's divinity has been reduced to nothing

the habits it has engendered remain. Centuries of vice-royalty
have not weakened them. Everything still revolves round the
king; he is still the master without whose consent nothing can
be done. He can still defeat popular leaders, especially if he
plays his ancient part of religious leader. To deserve the title
of 'the pious king' is to win over the masses, and to enjoy a
reverence that is not adoration but readily suggests it. 'The
universal demonstrations of loyalty', writes an Egyptian, 'prove
beyond the least shadow of a doubt that King Fârûq is almost
adored by his subjects. . . . In this connexion it should be borne
in mind that Ancient Egyptians actually worshipped their kings
who were looked upon as symbols of Egypt's greatness and
glory.' It remains the official doctrine that the monarchy is
purified by God, and it is preached on Fridays that he who
disobeys the king disobeys Allah.

As constantly happens in the history of man, a reasoned
system has left behind a deposit of unreasoned (not necessarily
unreasonable) behaviour.

One element in the glamour and power of kingship is the faith
that distant greatness is ever more ready to help the oppressed
than nearer and smaller greatness. The modern proletarian is
just as convinced as his distant forebears that if he could only
reach Pharaoh he would get redress, but the petty powers stand
in the way.

These petty powers were in the nineteenth century recast on
European lines; but Ancient Egypt had fully worked out the
essential features of a bureaucracy. By the Eighteenth Dynasty
it had completed an evolution which has been repeated elsewhere. Like the kings of modern France the Pharaohs had
drawn their vassals into their orbit as mere satellites. The great
lords became officials. There has been no solution of continuity.
The nome lords went on under Christianity. 'The Arab conquest merely substituted Moslem sheikhs or emirs for pagan and

Christian nobles.' There have been fluctuations between feudal independence and bureaucratic dependence; there may yet be. 'In the last century the beys divided Egypt among themselves almost in the same manner as the chiefs of the mercenaries in the VIIIth century B.C.'[1]

A highly centralized system requires a host of clerks, men who can write letters and keep documents. In Ancient Egypt to administer and to make a record are synonymous: the official is a scribe. Then, as now, government employment enjoyed the greatest prestige and appeared to offer the most desirable career, because it seemed an easy life compared with other occupations and ensured a steady livelihood from the government, or, as the ancients expressed it, 'from the king's house'.

Since the end of the New Empire at least the governmental machinery could scarcely be said to function as it was intended to do. Centuries of mismanagement have schooled the village to withdraw into itself and to run its own affairs, not by a cadre of officials, but by public opinion. It has its code of loyalty and secrecy. Between it and the administration stands the mayor, half official, half squire, ready, if the central power should weaken, to become a feudal lord, as has happened in the past. As official he has to represent the government; as chief to keep the secrets of the village.

Behind this invisible rampart of exclusiveness more effective than walls of stone, the Egyptian village runs itself along grooves traced in ancient times, by habit rather than by system. There is no social theory, and so no crystalline pattern such as we find in countries to the south and to the east, but a somewhat amorphous, yet highly cohesive, crowd. Comparative evidence, however, aided by fragments from Ancient Egypt, convince us that this absence of system is the residue of a system as

[1] G. Maspero, 'Un manuel d'hiérarchie égyptienne' (*Journ. Asiatique*, no. 4, 1888).

definite as the caste system of India and farther east, and akin to it.[1]

That system once gravitated round the king and the gods. The service of the court and temples required priests, sculptors, linen-workers, washermen, cobblers, butchers, bakers, carpenters, fly-whisk bearers, a whole panoply of occupations. We can see the divine counterpart of that organization officiating round the god in the bas-reliefs; for 'the divine court is organized on the model of the terrestrial', or rather the two are one, since the king of Egypt is king of the gods. There is Ptah, the artificer; Khnum, the potter; Thoth, the scribe; Hathor, the nurse; Heket, the midwife; Anubis, the embalmer, each playing his part in the royal ritual.

With the breakdown of the old religion these courts dispersed, the craftsmen were set adrift. They no longer revolve round king, feudal lord, or temple. Having lost its old meaning, the old organization has also lost its fullness: in a community struggling for bare existence there is no room for painters, sculptors, superintendents of stables, and such luxuries; the occupations have been pared down to the minimum requirements of the village. It is no longer a monarchic theory that prescribes the occupations, but the necessities of existence and of a simplified democratic religion.

The barber, for instance, is a village dignitary, but his status is not defined, as it is in India, by a theory of society. He is hereditary in practice, but not by rule; he is neither appointed nor paid by a lord or by the community jointly, but establishes himself where there is work and is paid by individuals a fee fixed by custom. However much his status may have changed, his purpose has changed but little: he is there because the modern peasant, like the ancient, has to have his head shaved and be circumcised. As for the reason why, it has got lost long

[1] Hocart, *Kings and Councillors*, chap. ix and *Les Castes*, Musée Guimet, Paris, in the press.

ago; but the Egyptian barber still carries on the habits without the reason.

Even more attenuated is the washerman of the dead. He appears to be the last vestige of the embalmer. Mummification has been swept away by new systems of thought, but the washing of the corpse goes on. The original priestly character of this craftsman still survives in the prayers he has to speak, and the elaborate rules that complicate a simple operation.

It is commonly asserted that there are no priests in Islam. That is purely a matter of definition. What interests us here is not the definition of the man but his function. Now there is in Egypt a body of men who perform much the same functions as do priests elsewhere. If we will not call them priests because they are laymen as well, landowners perhaps or village shop-keepers, then Ancient Egypt had no priests either, for under the Old Kingdom 'nearly every person of rank assumed besides their worldly profession one or more priesthoods'.[1] Priesthoods were in fact often identical with State appointments.

The hereditary character of the priests is gone. Even in Roman times when it was most strict it was not absolute. Ability to read a hieratic book was then accepted as a substitute for descent. Now proficiency in the sacred books is the only basis. To be a sheikh it is necessary to know the Scriptures and the law. The seminaries of El Azhar scatter over Egypt these clerics who, as preachers, teachers, registrars, bind the country together more effectively than the administration. A peasant speaks of 'us Muslims', not of 'us Egyptians'. Even so, of old they were primarily worshippers of Rēʿ and Amūn with all the common customs that implies, and their wars were the wars of Amūn. The Arabs introduced no new principle when they warred in the name of Allah.

These clerics continue in the simplified and standardized form so characteristic of Islam the functions of the ancient

[1] A. Erman, *Aegypten und aegyptisches Leben*, new ed. (Tübingen, 1923), 331.

priests. They read the Qur'ân as the ancient *kherheb* used to read the holy books of paganism; they are authorities in law like the priests of Ma'at, the goddess of justice; they teach reading and writing for sacred rather than for everyday purposes.

There is the *imâm* who is the authority on all those social relationships that come within the orbit of Islam.

The schoolmaster carries on the work of those who dictated the Instructions of Amenemhēt I, the Teaching of Duauf, the Story of Sinuhe, and all those texts that were copied by generations of schoolboys in antiquity. Only, he does not range so widely; he is confined to the Qur'ân.

This narrowing of scope is characteristic of Modern as contrasted with Ancient Egypt. There are those who complain that it is impoverishment; but sometimes, at least, it means a welcome simplification. Thus the writing which the schoolmaster now teaches is a great improvement on the old one. The hieroglyphs were a combination of several principles that had succeeded without superseding one another. The Arabic writing contains no new principle, but employs only one out of the several ancient ones. It should be noted, however, that some simplification had already been undertaken by the later ancients under Greek influence, producing demotic.

There were priestesses in Ancient Egypt. Islam will not have women in office; but, cast out of the official system, they have found a refuge in the popular religion, which, in Egypt as elsewhere, subsists in the basement of the intelligentsia's edifice of thought. They live on in reduced circumstances as the self-appointed vehicles of the spirits of the dead.

Besides clerics the village has craftsmen: potters, blacksmiths, wheelwrights, mat-makers, shearers, farriers, and others. They settle where there is work, and the father hands on his occupation to his son. This was noted by Herodotus as characteristic of Egypt, and he is confirmed by numerous inscriptions: we know of one headship of the painters of Amūn which was inherited by seven generations. There is no rule about it, as usual in Egypt. Unlike the Hindu jurists, the teachers of Islam are not interested in popular organization; they leave that to the people themselves, and the people do not think, but simply carry on. So used are the people to the heredity of occupations that if a man does not succeed to his father's work he nevertheless retains the title and is known as the Carpenter, the Engineer even though he may be a clerk in government employ.

The village functionaries are paid not in cash but in kind. The barbers and the ferryman will turn up at the harvest to get their annual fee of maize or wheat. Even so, the Pharaohs paid their workers in fish, beans, corn, and firewood. A peasant will now engage a learned man to recite the Qur'ân weekly so that the Lord may have compassion on a deceased kinsman and be with him in the grave; at every harvest he will pay him his due in wheat or maize. Even so, an ancient Egyptian would make arrangements for paying in produce from his lands those who made periodic offerings of bread and beer at his tomb.

It was foreigners who brought coinage to Egypt, and coinage never has become acclimatized. In the big towns the economy is largely foreign; the village retains the primeval barter. Even the landowners who know and use coinage at the town end of their transactions still follow the ancient way at the village end. The tenant pays his rent by surrendering $\frac{1}{4}$, or $\frac{1}{2}$, or $\frac{10}{14}$ of his crop according to the degree of assistance he receives. There are estates where the labourer rarely handles money, save for the few piasters he makes on selling chickens and eggs. We have indeed the remarkable spectacle of a modern international bank owning an estate where the tenant-in-chief pays both labour and landlord with the beans he grows. I have seen an even later institution, the ice-cream vendor, come into contact with that primeval economy, surrender to it, and accept eggs in payment.

It may seem unaccountable that a people that has so often

led the world, and was tutor to the Greeks, should have been so slow to profit by one of the greatest inventions of mankind. It is not that money is strange or unwelcome: everyone understands it and grasps at it; yet the same peasant who uses money in the town goes back to barter when on the land. Perhaps the best reason I have heard is that 'they are accustomed to do so from ancient times'. The real problem is not why customs persist, but why they ever change. Inertia has preserved barter, but not stupid inertia.

We are apt to ascribe to customs and institutions an absolute value. We believe money to be a boon everywhere under all conditions, and conclude that a people that cannot see those advantages must be dense indeed. The Egyptian peasant, however, has been trained for millennia in the hard school of experience and not of abstract economics. He prefers barter because it eliminates the middle man. An excellent reason for being paid in maize is that maize is food; but if food is to be had directly from the neighbour's field, why go a roundabout way to get it through a shop?

From the landowner's point of view it is submitted that to pay in money means keeping a reserve at the bank to be drawn on weekly or monthly, whereas under the sharing system settlement takes place twice a year as the crops come in. The Egyptians have never taken kindly to finance. Greeks and Syrians were welcomed in antiquity because they supplied a missing sense. They still continue as grocers to fill a gap which the Egyptian is disinclined by temperament to fill.

The configuration of Egypt has never favoured the growth of such an ability in the country-side. Commercial genius finds most opportunity in long-distance trading. It is only through a narrow opening to the north that Egypt can export and import on a large scale. Internally each bit is so like every other that there cannot be much exchange of commodities. Overseas trade has therefore been undertaken mainly by maritime neighbours such as the Greeks, the Phoenicians, and the British. Now, as of old, Alexandria is essentially a foreign town.

Nature has allowed Egypt to become a land of large economy in one dimension only, north and south. Hence not only the exchange system of the country-side, but its transport also remains much as it ever was. The donkey has continued to be the chief conveyance since before the Pyramid Age, because he is so well fitted to the conditions. The only change is that he is now ridden as well as driven, and that the camel has come in to share his task.

The distances east and west are small, the land thickly populated, the towns numerous, the holdings small. Imagine the dream of an enthusiastic modernist come true, and every peasant owning a car. To make all the little holdings, down to one acre and less, accessible to cars would sterilize so much land as would seriously affect the food supply, nor would the capital invested in carriage be proportionate to the loads carried. What produce is not consumed locally, perhaps within earshot of the field, has at most a few miles to go to the river or the nearest collecting centre. Within easy reach of most villages flows a great waterway which is blessed with a wind that blows one way and a current in the opposite direction. It is the great artery fed by innumerable capillaries, the banks of the canals and drains, and nothing has yet been found more suitable to run along these banks than the Egyptian donkey.

The slow and cheap transport is still provided by sailing barges. They have changed their shape and enlarged their capacity, but still convey the same kind of grain and the same kinds of pots, and load the same stone from the same quarries. The nineteenth century has added cotton, maize, coal, and other goods; it has supplemented sail with steam, and has duplicated the river with a railway for fast transport; but once more the new does not displace the old, but merely ekes it out.

The local circulation centres in the local market, which, like
so much else, retains a great deal of its ancient character simplified. It has not quite the same range as on the reliefs at Saqqâra.
That is an inevitable consequence of extreme centralization
which impoverishes country life, as we can see happening in
Europe. In ancient reliefs the men dominate the market. Now
in Lower Egypt it has passed almost entirely into the hands of
the women, but south of Minya the men still retain it, because
they disapprove of their women selling in public.

Where the sphere of trade is restricted the sphere of marriage
tends to be restricted also. The peasant, and still more his wife,
do not like their daughters to pass out of easy range. A girl who
marries at what is for us a short distance is cut off from her
family. In Upper Egypt it is even more a matter of kin than
of distance: it is a shame to marry one who is not kin, even if
he lives in the village. The proper marriage everywhere is that
of agnatic first cousins. This is only a little less exclusive than
the ancient custom. Kings used to marry their sisters. The
wives of the common people are often described as sisters; but
we do not know how far the term we so translate has the same
meaning as our own word, or how far it does not include, besides
sisters, other female agnates of the same generation. Many, if
not all, the 'sister marriages' recorded among the common
people may be unions with cousins. In that case no change has
occurred beyond condemning the closer union which was certainly encouraged in high circles, if not in lower ones.[1]

Islam has, unlike Christianity, absorbed very little of the

[1] In technical parlance it all turns on the question whether the ancient
kinship system of Egypt was classificatory or genealogical. There can be no
doubt that it was derived from a classificatory system, if not itself classificatory.
Kinship terms are still used at the present day in the same manner as in
classificatory systems; e.g. paternal uncles may be addressed as fathers, at least
among the peasantry. See Hocart, *The Progress of Man* (London, 1933), chap.
xxi, and 'Kinship Systems', *Anthropos*, xxxii (1937), 545.

marriage ceremony. The procession, the mock fights, the feasts, and all those wedding episodes which are common in some form or other all the world over are completely ignored. They are customary, not part of Islamic law. The one episode which Islam has annexed is the marriage contract. Curiously enough it is the very one about which the ancients have left us very detailed information. It has been taken over almost unchanged. In antiquity, as now, the husband paid a dowry and promised to pay a further amount on divorcing his wife. The proportion that now prevails in the Western Delta between the immediate and the deferred payments is 2 : 1, but 1 : 1 occurs as in ancient times. Note that this is now one of the few money transactions: payment is never in kind. The ancients had no coinage, but they paid the dowry in weights of precious metal, not in corn. Coins later took the place of weights, but the principle remained the same: it was not, and still is not, a commercial transaction like barter. Then, as now, the bride brought various materials with her, then mainly garments, now furniture; but the ring which the bride presents to the bridegroom has not changed. Then, as now, all that she brought with her was hers, to be taken away at divorce. In the ancient contracts it was stated that the children inherited the property. The claim of the children to inherit seems to have been in the process of solidifying as law. The process is now complete, and so it is no longer necessary to specify their right in the marriage contract, since it follows marriage automatically.

Plurality of wives was not of course instituted, but only sanctioned by Islam, for it is world-wide. Cases of two wives occur from the Middle Kingdom on. Polygamy was undoubtedly royal in origin, a duty of kings rather than a privilege. It is this aristocratic character that has caused its spread, rather than any advantage, for not every man is capable of managing several wives. Polygamy is often a sacrifice of peace to prestige. Yet such is the force of snobbery that polygamy has spread right down to the peasantry. At the same time it is disappearing at the top. Europe is now the arbiter of *bon ton*, and Europe has decreed that polygamy is barbarous. Thus we are assisting at a complete reversal of the ancient institution: from being first royal, then aristocratic, polygamy is becoming plebeian, because the peasant is the last to be reached by the changes of fashion; besides, his wives and children work, and so are an asset instead of a burden, as they are in higher spheres.

Concubines, as distinct from wives, were an important part of Pharaoh's state. They were kept in a seclusion as strict as that which still prevails and has become associated with Islam. The Pharaoh's harem was known as the 'House of the Isolated', and a foreign princess who entered it was lost to the world.

We have by now acquired some experience of the way in which a new dispensation establishes itself on the ruins of its forerunners. Of the pre-existing structure parts lie completely outside the new plan, and so remain untouched, for instance marriage observances. Others, like the marriage contract, fit in so well that they are incorporated with scarcely a change. Yet others had to be remodelled to harmonize with the new theology. We have seen how kingship had to be reconciled with the new conception of God. So had all beliefs and customs which were associated with the old theology: they had to shed their paganism.

Thus the pig was so unclean to the Ancient Egyptians that it never figures in texts or pictures of the Old Kingdom, and in the days of Herodotus swineherds were not allowed to inter-marry with the rest of the people. It was alleged that Set had taken the form of a black pig in order to attack Horus. The myth thus links the pig's uncleanness with a cosmological system in which it was the vehicle of the Adversary. When that Adversary became the Devil his vehicle perforce became evil. When the old gods became obnoxious this uncleanness was not abolished, for it was strongly held among the Semites, but its last tenuous links with its theoretical basis were cut, and it was set adrift as an isolated, inexplicable, but all the more tenacious observance.

The principle of ablutions before worship was known to the Egyptians as it was to many other nations. Pharaoh was purified by having water poured over him. This, and not bathing as in India, is still the prescribed technique. The people were also accustomed to wash before reading the holy books and before entering the temple. All that was necessary was to detach the observance from the temple and attach it to the mosque.

The attitudes of prayer too were not very different from what they are now. The two sets are merely variants. No great change of form was therefore needed. The main change was in the intention. Islam reserves them strictly for God. In the bas-reliefs they *appear* to be accorded to men, but it must be remembered that the king was a god, not a man. The true points of difference are whether there is one god or many, and whether a man can be identified with the god or not.

Some Arab customs came in the wake of the new system of ideas, not as an integral part of it. They could thus settle down in peace beside similar indigenous fragments. Thus the new shape of tomb was not obligatory. It acquired considerable popularity, for some reason or other, and is by far the commonest now; but it did not oust completely the old, stepped, *mastaba* form which is now known to be at least as old as the First Dynasty. Having come down to the masses it is naturally much reduced in size. So far from being antagonistic the two types can actually blend, as is usual in tombs of the Khedivial family: the simple Arabic tomb is superposed on two or three high plinths. The result is a *mastaba* with the high proportions of the Arab type.

There are cases, however, where compromise is impossible,

because the old is irreconcilable with the new. The only course left is for the new to exterminate the old. But that is not easy when the mass of the people are attached to the old. The old custom can only be eradicated by eradicating the people, and it is obviously impossible to wipe out several million people. Persecution is ineffective, for it merely drives the old practices into concealment.

Men are very tenacious of their hopes of salvation and health. Possession by the spirits of the dead promises relief from the ills of body and mind, and the sufferers will therefore defy bell, book, and candle in pursuit of this relief. Hence the unimpaired vitality of possession.

In antiquity many diseases were ascribed to it. It still holds its ground as a theory of hysterical disorders, a theory clear-cut and easy to grasp: the soul controls the body; let another soul get possession of the body, and the patient will become to all intents and purposes a new person. The theory does seem to work, as many wrong theories do. It appears to act as a mental cathartic, and while that is so the negative fulminations of the learned are in vain. Only a positive policy of better scientific treatment can hope to drive out this crude, but popular method.

It is the women who are the stronghold of possession. It is they who generally hold out longest against new notions, the more so in Egypt as Islam addresses itself especially to the males. So long as the men almost monopolize the mosques women feel its influence less. Thus they persist in wailing for the dead according to the ancient custom, although this is forbidden by the Islamic Tradition. Worse still, they daub their faces with blue, the ancient colour of mourning. Among the men are some better acquainted with the law and they disapprove. Sometimes they are resolute enough to prevail, and Islam wrests another conquest from the ancient culture even now in the twentieth century; but the women can be very obstinate, and forestall opposition by hastily painting their faces and presenting their male folk with a *fait accompli*.

We speak of culture and ideas conflicting, but that is only a figure of speech. In fact, of course, it is the bearers of one set of ideas conflicting with the bearers of others. It may be men *versus* women, but the more important conflicts follow the lines, not of sex, but of social and intellectual status. The intelligentsia has one point of view and it is fond of imposing it upon the lower classes. They are much addicted to systems and apt to dislike anything that does not fit into the system, merely because it does not fit. The masses, on the contrary, often prefer the meaningless because it is meaningless.

When a practice becomes detached from the ideas that inspired it it becomes meaningless, like our fear of being thirteen at table. Ancient Egyptian medical treatises abound in formulae and recipes which had evidently lost their meaning at the time they were written down in the form in which we possess them. The systems to which they belonged had already decayed then and must belong to a much earlier stratum. In some cases the very words are a mere jumble of nonsense syllables.

Such charms being meaningless are apt to be unstable, since meaning helps to keep customs true to type. It is a thankless task therefore to try to identify ancient examples with modern ones. Nevertheless the industry of scholars has unearthed definite evidence that ancient Egyptian medicine survived into modern times. A treatise by Abu Saḥl ʿIsa ibn Yaḥya contains prescriptions which can be termed translations of some of those found in the Ebers Papyrus, and the author constantly appeals to a work by Thoth, the old god of science. Another proof of continuity is that in modern, as in ancient magic formulae, the patient is referred to as the son of his mother, not of his father as in everyday usage; Ahmed the son of Fatma, not of Mahmud. Erman has even produced an old Egyptian charm against any kind of witchcraft closely resembling a modern remedy for haemorrhoids. In both cases a beetle is cooked in oil, the wings and head separately in fatty matter. It is the same remedy become more specialized in its application. This narrowing down of the purpose is also to be observed in tattooing. This world-wide custom is in origin part of a generalized rite for promoting life; in Modern Egypt it is used for specific diseases.[1]

Modern opinion is not as favourable to ancient charms as Abu Saḥl, and a continuous attack is being made on them, but they show considerable tenacity. Even more tenacious is the belief in the evil eye. It seems once to have belonged to a cosmological system in which the sun and moon were the eyes of the world. Special virtue was attributed to the eye of Horus, by which the moon was generally meant. Models of it were therefore used as amulets. The good eye abounds in our museums of antiquities; but of the evil eye we hear little beyond the mention of 'a chapter on warding off the evil eye'. Now-a-days fear and jealousy, sentiments which seem to be the aftermath of great civilizations, have given exclusive prominence to the evil eye, while the good one has disappeared. What remains has of course been attuned to Islam by the masses, who are usually equally loyal to the new and to the old. It is Allah who is now invoked against the evil eye which is supposed to be inspired by the devil. They assimilate it to temptation which can be set aside with the aid of God. That is another characteristic of the change that has come over Egyptian culture: its tone is strongly moral. The old religion was a quest of prosperity; it has yielded its place to a rule of good conduct.

Light blue was much favoured by the ancients as a lucky colour, probably because it is the colour of the clear sky. Beads of that colour are still to be seen on the radiators of the latest

---

[1] Hocart, 'Tattooing and Healing', *Man*, 1937, 196; H. Kees, *Kulturgeschichte des alten Orients*, i, *Aegypten* (München, 1933), 89; K. Sethe, *Dramatische Texte zu altaegyptischen Mysterienspielen* (Leipzig, 1928), 9, 1. 9.

in cars as a protection against the evil eye. The cosmic connexion, however, is gone.

The conflict between intelligentsia and the masses goes on over the fairs which are annually held in honour of the saints. These remain too obviously pagan to be left in peace by the purists of Islam. Whether any particular festival is the lineal descendant of an old heathen one is not of great importance; it is sufficient that the genus continues the ancient way with its processions, its visits to the shrines, and so on. Only, having lost the support of the great, these fairs are much simplified and amorphous. The celebrations have not the elaborate structure of the ancient rituals; the variety of episodes is gone with the variety of the pantheon, though the ship is still carried in procession at the mosque of Abu'l Haggag in Luxor. There is now only one God to glorify, and the ways of doing so are reduced to one or two. All the rest which cannot be reconciled with the severe simplicity of Islam is relegated to the secular. Juggling, games, dramatic performances which are incompatible with the austerity and single-mindedness of Islam are despised, and even persecuted, by the purists. If they cannot be abolished altogether they are segregated from the religious exercises. Thus a wedge has been driven between the religious and the profane which did not exist before. The profane is merely the religious that has been cut out by a new system, and left to sink into pure amusement, even fooling.

The low estimation in which these fairs are held reflects the diminished state of all the minor powers before the rise of one supreme God. Whether any of the modern saints are old local gods in disguise is doubtful; some are definitely known to be real men who lived in Arab times, perhaps all are; but that is as immaterial as the antiquity of their fairs. As a class they continue the functions of the ancient gods and of the ancient dead (the two run into one another in virtue of the fundamental principles of the religion). This is shown by such concrete cases as that of Imam Shafa'i, a famous jurist, to whom letters are still written for advice, just as they used in antiquity to be addressed to the dead. It is the continuity of idea that interests us, not of persons.

The saints are able to continue the ancient tradition, though on a lower plane, because they fill a void which monotheism has left between the humble peasant and the Lord of the World. They are interested in individuals, not in the universe, and they specialize in different ailments. Already in antiquity the great gods seemed too remote to concern themselves with the wishes and troubles of the simple folk, and so in private magic recourse was had to the lesser gods.

These saints are no longer gods, but only near to God. Theoretically they have no power in themselves, but only as intercessors. The change of theory, however, makes little difference to the procedure among the common folk. Vows are made just as if the saint's power were his own. Tombs are visited, physical contact is sought by stroking or kissing. The devotees pass their hands over the rails which enclose the tomb, then stroke themselves and their children as if they were collecting and dispensing an emanation from the saint himself. In the same way the ancients are to be seen in the bas-reliefs transmitting with their hands the vital principle represented by the '*ankh* symbol. Only their descendants do not transmit anything as concrete. They act as if *baraka*, blessing, streamed from their hands, but if asked to explain their action they say that *baraka* consists in having good children, money, much luck; there is no hint of any supernatural property that can be communicated like a fluid. The whole theory of the act has vanished leaving behind it only the act and its effects.

The act, however, is so concrete in its suggestion that it is only too easy to put back into it the concrete intention, to interpret it as what it seems to be, the gathering and dispensing of life as a kind of fluid. One feels it is only the vigilance of the

teachers of religion that keeps the thought from being pulled
by the action in the direction of frank heathendom.

The same suspicion attaches in some quarters to sacrifices.
These still take place on occasions such as funerals and the
Great Feast. The interpretation, of course, has been revised:
the ancient identity of god and victim and worshipper is gone.
The sacrifice is only allowed to draw the worshipper nearer to
God; hence it is called *qurban*, from *qirib*, to draw near. Yet
even this concession does not reconcile the more extreme purists.

The process of narrowing down all worship and all life to the
service of one God was completed, but not begun, by Islam.
The seed of monotheism was inherent in the old religion. The
gods had not such distinct individualities as we are accustomed
to expect of gods. Two can be combined into one, like Amūn
and Rē'. The king, the magician, or the dead man can be several
deities at once. The process of fusion can be carried out systematically till one god absorbs all the others and becomes all in all.
By the time of the Eighteenth Dynasty Amūn, fused with Rē',
had outdistanced all the other gods. The heretic king Akhenaten
made too sudden a jump towards monotheism, and there was
a reaction; but at the end of the Nineteenth Dynasty the gods
were being neglected; and by Roman times Egypt was prepared
to take an active part in the spread of monotheistic religion.
Muḥammad carried the process still further by rejecting all
compromise and focusing all thought on one indivisible god.
He thus reduced all worship to a simple and uniform expression.
As the god is a god of right conduct which has prosperity as a
consequence, and no longer of prosperity which is to be obtained
by right conduct, the ritual has been simplified in the extreme.
A technique of prosperity is no longer needed, but only the
observance of rules.

That indeed sums up the evolution of Egypt since antiquity:
simplification and levelling, with a consequent loss of structure,

and a strong moral tone. The process began before Islam. It would probably have continued without the aid of Islam, since it has affected those departments of life which lie quite outside the interests of Islam, such as the village organization.

The ancient, more complex structure seems to have served its purpose by fixing the relations of man to man; then it dissolved away. We might compare Ancient Egypt to a live coral full of animalcules building up with admirable activity. As the building is completed they die, leaving a solid mass to be battered by successive storms and corroded by events till the clear and geometric outlines are obliterated.

Every now and then there is renewed activity. We are now witnessing such a revival. Modernism is the new leaven that has succeeded to Islam. Its core is so different from that of Islam that the two seem in no danger of conflicting. A mechanical gospel seems too remote from one centred on the unity of God ever to cross its path. But you cannot drop mechanism into the waters of life without its sending out eddies that expand and expand till they must collide with the older eddies of Islam.

The outcome we cannot foretell, but we must note that the new movement tends more and more to seek its inspiration from ancient rather than medieval Egypt, in accordance with a general rule that the more 'advanced' a movement is the farther back it goes to find its golden age. It is significant that the statue of the awakening of Egypt in Cairo reverts to ancient motives. Even more so does the mausoleum of Sa'ad Zaghlul, the apostle of Egyptian independence. The Ophthalmological Congress was honoured with a stamp bearing the Horus eye. When the Khedivial Mail line registered in Egypt it did so under the more ancient style of Pharaonic Mail Line.

No revivalist movement has ever brought back the past, nor will this one; but it can take and adapt old ideas from the past. That is not, however, the chief benefit that can be expected of a renewed interest in Ancient Egypt. It may not contribute a single artistic motif, or mechanical device, or scientific concept, but it must inevitably break down much narrowness, enlarge the sympathies, and fire ambitions by bringing into contact with greatness that is not less great for not being modern.

A. M. HOCART

INDEX

E e

PRINTED IN GREAT BRITAIN AT THE UNIVERSITY PRESS, OXFORD
BY CHARLES BATEY, PRINTER TO THE UNIVERSITY